Appraising Residential Properties

Readers of this text may be interested in:

Appraising Residential
Properties

Third Edition

APPRAISAL INSTITUTE® 875 N. Michigan Ave., Suite 2400
Chicago, IL 60611-1980

Vice President, Educational Programs and Publications:	Sean Hutchinson
Director, Content Development and Quality Assurance:	Margo Wright
Manager, Book Development:	Stephanie Shea-Joyce
Manager, Design/Production:	Julie B. Beich
Technical Writer:	Michael McKinley
Production Specialist/Book Design:	Michael Landis
Cover Design:	Amy Reichard

For Educational Purposes Only

Nondiscrimination Policy

Library of Congress Cataloging-in-Publication data

Appraising residential properties.—3rd ed.

     p. cm.

Includes bibliographical references and index

ISBN 0-922154-57-0

1. Real property—Valuation—United States. I. Appraisal Institute (U.S.)

HD1387 .A685 1999

333.33'82—dc21

99-044576

TABLE OF CONTENTS

Foreword

Residential real estate has undergone many changes since the last edition of *Appraising Residential Properties* was published. Most significantly, more information than ever before is now available to many of the participants in housing transactions. Although appraisers can no longer claim to be the sole purveyors and analysts of market data, they retain a competitive advantage that can be leveraged in this changing field. They have the sophisticated tools and methods needed to analyze residential real estate markets competently and the experience to communicate meaningful conclusions to clients.

Since the first edition of the text was published in 1988, *Appraising Residential Properties* has been essential preparation for a career in the field of home appraisal. The third edition has been redesigned to be more useful to both students new to the subject and established practitioners. Revisions to the text focus on topics specific to residential appraisal and emphasize practical applications. The sources of essential property and market data have been fully explored, and changes to the regulatory environment affecting appraisers are outlined. In addition, important terms and concepts are highlighted graphically throughout the text, and a design scheme using more illustrations and tables makes the text more readable than ever.

The third edition of *Appraising Residential Properties* represents the contributions of a team of experts in the field, who reviewed the text and guided the revision. The successful completion of this project required the significant efforts of Sherryl V. Andrus, SRA, Margaret A. Hambleton, SRA, Frank E. Harrison, MAI, SRA, and Sheila Crowell. The Appraisal Institute would also like to recognize Michael S. MaRous, MAI, SRA, Chair of the Educational Publications Committee, and David C. Lennhoff, MAI, SRA, Chair of the Educational Programs and Publications Committee, for their support of this project and their contributions to the review process.

Bert L. Thornton, MAI
1999 President
Appraisal Institute

1 INTRODUCTION TO RESIDENTIAL APPRAISAL

Owning a home has always been an essential ingredient of the American Dream—part of the basic trio of "food, clothing, and shelter." Buying a home is the single largest investment most people will ever make, both financially and emotionally, and the residential real estate appraiser plays an important, but often publicly unacknowledged, role in the transaction.

Home buyers have many reasons for making that investment, which may be as diverse as the people making the purchases. Some people buy homes so that they can establish and raise a family. Others may seek homes near to where they work, shop, and entertain. Practically all purchasers have an interest in the financial benefits of owning a residence. Sometimes these benefits take the form of rental income, but more commonly they include the availability of home equity loans and the anticipation of realizing a higher resale value when the property is sold.

Individual home owners are not the only people to benefit from the purchase and ownership of residential property. The community as a whole and the national economy are also enriched. Many home owners invest labor and capital to maintain and improve their properties. Property ownership often gives people a greater sense of community responsibility and civic attachment. In many areas citizens form groups to influence zoning boards and other political bodies for the protection and maintenance of their neighborhoods. Moreover, the purchase of a new home supports the construction industry and adds to the tax base of the local government. Because home ownership has such far-reaching consequences, government organizations often try to improve conditions in the housing market to stimulate the general economy.

If society is to have any stability, the rights to own and use real estate must be safeguarded. The successful management of this limited resource is an essential activity. Appraisers of real property evaluate the utility and desirability of property and estimate its value for various purposes: purchases and sales, financing, taxation, investment, and insurance. Residential appraisers consider the utility and value of residential properties, thereby helping to ensure that decisions made by buyers, sellers, government officials, insurers, investors, and others

For many people, buying a home is the largest investment decision they will ever make.

are based on well-informed, carefully reasoned judgments. In this way, residential appraisers help promote the stable and orderly development of a fundamental societal resource.

WHAT IS AN APPRAISAL?

Appraisal is the act or process of estimating value.[1] An appraisal provides an answer to a client's specific question about the value of a real property interest. It is important to keep in mind that the appraiser's answer is an *opinion*; it does not establish the value of the real estate.

Appraisers base their opinions on research in the appropriate market, the assemblage of pertinent data, and the application of appropriate analytical techniques. When these activities are combined with the appraiser's knowledge, experience, and professional

> **TERMS**
>
> **appraisal:** the art or process of developing an opinion of value.
>
> **value:** the monetary worth of a property, good, or service to buyers and sellers at a given time or the present worth of the future benefits that accrue to real property ownership.

---

1.   In the 1999 edition of the *Uniform Standards of Professional Appraisal Practice*, the definition of *appraisal* was changed from an *estimate of value* to an *opinion of value*. In this edition of *Appraising Residential Properties*, *opinion* has been used where the term specifically describes the results of the valuation process. *Estimate* has been used for intermediate value conclusions within the valuation process and for more generic references.

judgment, they result in a solution to the client's problem. Because the opinion offered by a professional real estate appraiser is substantiated by relevant data and sound reasoning, it carries considerable weight.

The purpose of an appraisal is to estimate the defined value of a real property interest in real estate. (See Chapter 2 for definitions of *real property* and *real estate.*) *Value* may be loosely defined as the monetary worth of property, goods, or services. Many people are involved in real estate activities—buyers, sellers, tax assessors, investors, and insurers—and each may have specific concerns about a parcel of real estate. Therefore, the monetary worth of real estate can be considered in several different ways.

Typically an appraiser is asked to estimate the price at which a property would most likely sell in the market under certain specified conditions. The appraiser's opinion of market value reflects the probable price that knowledgeable parties would agree upon when acting freely, without duress. It is an estimate of the most likely value that a competitive market would set. (The concept of market value is discussed more fully in the next chapter.) Most residential appraisal work is devoted to estimating the most likely selling price of residential real estate. This book will focus on the background, data, and techniques needed to research and form sound judgments of the market value of residential properties.

CONCEPT

Professional real estate appraisers base their value opinions on market data obtained through careful research. These data are analyzed by applying judgment, and the results are communicated to clients in appraisal reports.

TERM

consulting service: the act or process of providing information, analysis of real estate data, and recommendations or conclusions on diversified problems in real estate other than estimating value.

APPRAISAL AND CONSULTING

There are two broad types of assignments that appraisers may be asked to perform. An appraisal is the act or process of estimating value. This may be market value or some other properly defined value of an identified interest or interests in a specific parcel or parcels of real estate as of a given date. If the problem to be solved is not a question about a defined value, the assignment is considered a consulting service rather than an appraisal. Consulting services include

- Land utilization studies
- Supply and demand studies
- Economic feasibility studies

- Highest and best use analyses
- Marketability or investment studies for a proposed or existing development

An appraiser retained to act as a disinterested third party in rendering an unbiased analysis cannot be compensated in a manner that is contingent on the results of the analysis. However, an appraiser may be retained to perform a legitimate business activity such as providing brokerage, mortgage banking, or tax counseling advice for a fee that is contingent on the results achieved, but only when the role being performed by the appraiser is clearly disclosed. In accepting a consulting assignment, an appraiser must carefully consider and determine whether the service to be performed is—or would be perceived by third parties or the public to be—a service that carries with it an implied impartiality on the appraiser's part. If impartiality is implied, the assignment can only be accepted for a fee that is not contingent on the result of the consulting service.

Appraisal Assignments

In the Uniform Standards of Professional Appraisal Practice (USPAP), The Appraisal Foundation distinguishes between complete appraisals and limited appraisals. Most often, the appraiser conducts a complete appraisal. An example of a limited appraisal might include an appraisal of residential real estate using only one of the three approaches to value.[2]

The Appraisal Report

Whether the purpose of an assignment is to estimate a defined value of an interest in real property or to provide a consulting service, the conclusions and methodology employed in the assignment are conveyed to the client in an appraisal report. This report may be long or

---

2. The Departure Rule of USPAP states that an appraiser may enter into an agreement to perform an assignment in which the scope of the work is less than, or different from, the work that would otherwise be required by the specific requirements, provided that prior to entering into such an agreement:

    1. the appraiser has determined that the appraisal or consulting process to be performed is not so limited that the results of the assignment are no longer credible;
    2. the appraiser has advised the client that the assignment calls for something less than, or different from, the work required by the specific requirements and that the report will clearly identify and explain the departure(s); and
    3. the client has agreed that performance of a limited appraisal or consulting service would be appropriate, given the intended use.

short, and it can be presented as a self-contained, summary, or restricted use report. (Descriptions of the various types of appraisal reports are provided in Chapter 20.) The type of report prepared depends on the needs of the client, the type of property being appraised, the nature of the appraisal assignment, and regulatory requirements.

Purpose and Intended Use of an Appraisal

The purpose of an appraisal is the stated reason for an appraisal assignment—e.g., to estimate a defined value of a real property interest. The purpose of the appraisal reflects an agreement between the client and the appraiser about the appraisal problem to be solved. The information sought by the client directs the appraiser's work, but any specific conclusion the client hopes to reach must not.

The client's intended use of the appraisal and its purpose are distinct. The intended use of an appraisal is determined by the client's needs. A client may want to know the market value of a residence to avoid paying too much for its purchase or accepting too little for its sale. A lender may need to know whether the market value opinion is high enough to justify the loan requested. Another client may prefer a low value opinion because the estimate is to serve as the basis for the collection of inheritance taxes. The appraiser's role, however, is to provide an objective value opinion regardless of the use of the appraisal. The appraiser is an independent third party with a responsibility to provide competent and unbiased service.

APPLICATIONS OF RESIDENTIAL APPRAISALS

The refined, intuitive skills that consumers and dealers bring to the market for most goods and

TERMS

Uniform Standards of Professional Appraisal Practice (USPAP): current standards of the appraisal profession, developed for appraisers and users of appraisal services by the Appraisal Standards Board of The Appraisal Foundation. The Uniform Standards set the procedures to be followed in developing an appraisal, analysis, or opinion and the manner in which an appraisal, analysis, or opinion is communicated.

complete appraisal: an opinion of value or the act or process of developing an opinion of value performed without invoking the Departure Rule of the Uniform Standards of Professional Appraisal Practice.

limited appraisal: an opinion of value or the act or process of developing an opinion of value performed under and resulting from invoking the Departure Rule of the Uniform Standards of Professional Appraisal Practice.

appraisal report: the written or oral communication of an appraisal; the document transmitted to the client upon completion of an appraisal assignment.

CONCEPT

The purpose of an appraisal is to estimate a defined value of a real property interest, while the intended use of an appraisal is determined by the client's needs.

services are the products of years of experience comparing the prices and quality of various commodities. Unlike knowledgeable stock investors or seasoned comparison shoppers, buyers and sellers of homes usually have little experience in the real estate market. Consequently, most do not have the judgment needed to consider the utility of the real estate and estimate its value wisely.

Each year buyers, sellers, lenders, builders, insurers, brokers, and government officials make real estate decisions involving billions of dollars, and these decisions depend on real estate appraisals. Informed investment or loan decisions based on competent real estate appraisals help prevent business failures. In many ways, appraisals encourage the appropriate use of our nation's land—a limited and valuable resource.

It is extremely important that appraisers exercise objectivity. In many real estate decisions, one or both parties have a strong, vested interest in a particular conclusion, such as a high or a low value opinion. As an objective investigator, an appraiser must provide an unbiased opinion that can be relied upon and even used in court testimony, if necessary.

The services of a professional real estate appraiser may be required in a variety of circumstances, including

- Decisions concerning market transactions
- Tax questions
- Legal claims
- Investment planning and counseling
- Other real estate-related matters

Market Transactions

To prepare for a market transaction in which property ownership is transferred, different parties may request separate appraisals to answer specific questions. For most sales of residential properties, the financial institution from which the buyer requests a loan needs certain information. Because the amount of the loan is usually based on a set loan-to-value ratio, the institution requires a market value opinion. Most commonly in sales of residential property, the appraiser delivers an appraisal of market value to the lender even though the borrower (in this case, the home buyer who is seeking a mortgage) pays for the appraisal.

Financial institutions may also be interested in long-term forecasts of neighborhood stability and conditions in the real estate market because the property will be pledged to them as security for a fairly long period of time. Potential insurers and underwriters of mortgage loans are interested in similar information.

Both the seller and the potential buyer are typically interested in the real estate's market value. The buyer needs to know the property's market value to decide on an acceptable offering price, while the seller, or sales agent, may use the market value opinion to select a price at which to sell or list the property. The buyer and the seller, separately or together, may also want to investigate suitable forms of financing to ensure that the sale goes through.

Tax Questions

Tax assessors need estimates of real estate values to calculate ad valorem taxes, which are based on property value. Property owners who wish to challenge their tax estimates may hire appraisers. To calculate gift and inheritance taxes on real estate, value estimates of the bequeathed property are required. Various income tax provisions require appraisals as supporting evidence. For example, estimates of historical values may be needed to establish capital gains taxes.

Legal Claims

> **TERM**
>
> **ad valorem taxes:** a real estate tax based on the assessed value of the property, which is not necessarily equivalent to its market value. *Ad valorem* is Latin for *according to value.*

When the government exercises the right of eminent domain and takes possession of private property for a public use, an appraisal is frequently required to estimate the amount of just compensation to be paid to the owner. Just compensation is sometimes set at the market value of the property taken, but additional compensation may also be required by the law. When only a portion of the real estate is taken, market value estimates may be needed for the property as a whole before the taking and for the property that remains after the taking. Many state courts require a valuation of the part taken and an estimate of the severance damage or special benefits to the remainder. Appraisals may also be required for arbitration between adversaries, such as lawsuits over damage to real estate or court division of property after a divorce.

Investment Planning and Counseling

An appraiser's expert opinion on real estate matters is often sought by investors, builders, and government officials. Investors in residential apartment buildings may seek advice from appraisers on investment goals, alternatives, resources, constraints, and timing. Individuals who invest in capital markets may need appraisal advice to decide whether to purchase real estate mortgages, bonds, or other types of securities.

Home owners who are considering renovation work may be interested in an analysis of the costs and benefits involved. Home builders may consult appraisers on the feasibility of a project, its market value, or the marketability of specific design features in the local area. Zoning boards, courts, and planners often need to consult appraisers about the probable effects of their proposed actions.

Other Applications of Appraisals

There are many other situations in which residential appraisals may be required. Financial institutions that are considering whether or not to foreclose on a property may be interested in the price the real estate might bring in a forced sale or auction. Appraisals can facilitate corporate or company purchases of the homes of transferred employees.

Questions about insurance often necessitate an appraisal. A home owner may want to know how much insurance to carry and which parts of the property are covered under the provisions of an insurance policy. The insurer may be interested in the value of the insured parts to decide how much to charge for the policy. Value estimates may be needed by the policyholder to support casualty loss claims, or an insurance adjuster may hire an appraiser to examine and evaluate the property damage and provide a basis for a negotiated settlement.

These examples do not represent all of the circumstances in which an appraisal may be requested, but they do suggest the broad scope of a professional appraiser's activities.

CHARACTERISTICS OF A RESIDENTIAL APPRAISER

Given the public's reliance on the opinions of appraisers and the scope of appraisal activities, appraisers must possess personal integrity, diligence, and professionalism. Other specific skills, experience, and qualifications are also required of residential appraisers.

Licensing, Certification, and Designation

Until the late 1980s, most states did not require that individuals who perform appraisals meet specific qualifications. Now, however, every state has an appraiser regulatory law, which requires that value estimates be prepared by knowledgeable, unbiased individuals who have been licensed or certified.

The Appraisal Institute encourages professionalism by awarding membership designations to appraisers who meet its requirements for experience, education, and ethical practice. By enforcing The Appraisal Foundation's Uniform Standards of Professional Appraisal Practice and its own Code of Professional Ethics and by sponsoring educational programs, the Appraisal Institute has worked to advance the status of professional real estate appraisers throughout the United States and to make the public aware of the quality work performed by designated appraisers.

Continuing education is the cornerstone of professional development; by pursuing continuing education appraisers demonstrate their commitment to maintain their skills at a level far above the bare minimum required to satisfy state licensing requirements. Individuals who complete a rigorous educational program and earn recognized professional designations find that their employment and business prospects are considerably enhanced. A commitment to professionalism helps regulate the industry and ensures quality appraisal work.

Skills

An appraiser must possess strong communication, investigative, and analytical skills. Good communication skills are needed because appraisers must regularly seek essential information from diverse individuals. Furthermore, appraisers must sometimes obtain that information from reluctant sources. Moreover, it is essential that appraisers be able to communicate their findings in an orderly, logical, and grammatically correct manner. Clear communication is a sign of clear thinking and sound, considered judgment. Written reports to clients must be clear and persuasive. Ambiguity and inconsistency are unacceptable.

Good appraisers are like good detectives. They are naturally inquisitive and enjoy knowing where and how to obtain information. An appraiser must be sensitive to new trends and developments in the community and be aware of the countless ways in which data can be misinterpreted. Appraisers must also be open-minded. Market value, which the appraiser seeks to estimate, is shaped by the needs, desires, and motivations of the marketplace; it may not conform to the appraiser's personal preferences or opinions.

Analytical skills are also important. Appraisers must know how to analyze the data they collect and draw logical conclusions. They should understand the reasoning behind the three approaches to value—the cost, sales comparison, and income capitalization approaches—and recognize that one approach may be more or less reliable than the others in a particular situation. With good analytical skills, an appraiser can divide an assignment into a series of distinct tasks and provide efficient appraisal service.

Two final attributes are essential in appraisal practice: reasonableness and common sense. These characteristics, which are refined through experience, help the appraiser gather and analyze data and draw sound, supportable conclusions.

Experience

Knowledge of techniques and skills is important, but an appraiser's ability is developed on the job. Experience is essential in appraisal and it is generally reflected in the salaries and fees an appraiser can earn. Learning the art of real estate appraisal takes time but time alone is not enough. Appraisers will benefit from experience only if they constantly work at self-improvement through independent study and formal education offerings sponsored by the Appraisal Institute and other professional organizations.

EMPLOYMENT AS A RESIDENTIAL APPRAISER

To dedicated, qualified professionals, the field of residential appraisal can present stimulating challenges and rewarding opportunities. Each property presents unique problems and each assignment challenges the appraiser to find creative, efficient solutions. The many appraisers who work in public and private institutions receive salaries commensurate with their experience, ability, and education. Those with effective business skills may choose to enter private practice, where they can enjoy the greater flexibility and remuneration that independent practice can often supply.

In addition to challenging work and monetary rewards, professional appraisers derive satisfaction from knowing that their services are important to the community. The public relies on real estate appraisers' opinions to make decisions concerning investment, land use and development, and critical legal matters. As a result, the integrity, responsibility, and sound judgment of professional appraisers earn them the respect of the community in which they practice.

USING THIS BOOK

This book provides an introduction to residential appraisal for those entering the field and can be used as a review and reference text by more advanced students and practicing residential appraisers. Other individuals involved in the field of real estate who may find this book useful include

- Brokers and sales associates
- Representatives of lending institutions (underwriters)
- Housing contractors, developers, and builders

- Court and government officials
- Individuals considering the purchase, sale, rental, leasing, or renovation of residential property

All the essential steps in the valuation process, the procedure that appraisers follow to reach appraisal conclusions, are presented and explained in detail. Many practical examples and illustrations are provided to enhance the reader's understanding.

Chapters 1 through 4 introduce fundamental real estate appraisal terms and concepts and provide an overview of the valuation process. Chapter 5 describes the types of data and analysis that are needed in the first phases of the valuation process. Chapters 6 through 8 discuss the information needed to complete the property description section of an appraisal report. Chapter 9 covers market analysis and Chapter 10 discusses highest and best use, both fundamental components of all appraisals. Chapters 11 through 18 cover the analytical techniques appraisers apply to the data collected to reach a value conclusion. Chapter 19 addresses the final reconciliation of value indications, and Chapter 20 describes how appraisal results are communicated to the client.

2 REAL PROPERTY OWNERSHIP AND VALUE

What is valued in an appraisal? Although appraisers investigate and analyze land and structures, these physical entities do not, strictly speaking, possess value or utility. Rather, it is the right to use property that has value. The various rights to use real estate are conveyed in a deed and corroborated by a title or contract. When the ownership of a parcel of real estate is transferred, these rights change hands. To highlight this distinction, property is divided into two legal categories: real estate and real property.

REAL ESTATE

Real estate is the physical land and appurtenances attached to the land—i.e., structures. Real estate is the physical entity, which includes everything that is fixed and immobile. It encompasses all the natural attributes of the land as well as everything affixed to the land in a relatively permanent way by people.

The concept of real estate incorporates three important elements:

1. Land is the earth's surface, both land and water, and all its components. Land includes all natural resources in their original state—e.g., mineral deposits, timber, water, coal deposits, and soil.

2. Improvements are buildings or other relatively permanent structures or developments that are located on, or attached to, land. This category includes both improvements *to* the land such as access and utilities, which prepare the land for a subsequent use, and improvements *on* the land such as buildings and landscaping.

CONCEPT

Real estate and real property are distinct concepts. *Real estate* refers to physical land and the improvements to and on the land. *Real property* refers to the benefits, interests, and rights inherent in the ownership of real estate.

TERMS

land: the earth's surface, both land and water, and anything that is attached to it whether by course of nature or human hands.

improvements: buildings or other relatively permanent structures or developments located on, or attached to, land.

3. A fixture is an item that was once personal property—i.e., a movable possession that is not part of the real estate—but has since been installed or attached to the land or the building in a rather permanent manner.

It is not always apparent whether an item is truly a fixture, and thus part of the real property, or whether it should be considered personal property, and therefore not included in the real estate value opinion. An appraiser may need guidance to appreciate these legal distinctions, which are usually set forth in state law and may vary according to statute. Most courts use the following criteria to judge the status of an item:

1. The manner in which the item is affixed. Generally an item is considered personal property if it can be removed without causing serious injury to the real estate or to itself. (Note: There are exceptions to this rule.)
2. The character of the item and its adaptation to the real estate. Items that are specifically constructed for use in a particular building or installed to fulfill the purpose for which the building was erected are generally considered permanent parts of the building.
3. The intention of the party who attached the item. Frequently the terms of a lease reveal whether the item was meant to be permanent or whether it was to be removed at some time.[1] For example, an apartment or house lease may specify that items such as bookshelves and mini-blinds may be installed by the tenant and removed as personal property at the termination of the lease.

To ascertain the full extent of the physical entity being appraised, the various components of the property must be distinguished in an appraisal. The appraiser must determine the exact boundaries of the site, the nature of any improvements to and on the site, and the status of any improvements, including fixtures. Obviously, the inclusion or exclusion of an item from the appraiser's analysis can increase or decrease the total value opinion. If an appraiser is asked to include the value of certain items of personalty in the final value opinion, the effect of these inclusions must be precisely stated in the appraisal report.

---

1.   Raymond J. Werner and Robert Kratovil, *Real Estate Law*, 10th ed. (Englewood Cliffs, N.J.: Prentice-Hall, Inc., 1993), 11–16.

REAL PROPERTY

Real property refers to all interests, benefits, and rights inherent in the ownership of physical real estate. The concept of real property is useful because the ownership of real estate consists of various interests, benefits, and rights that can be separated without dividing the physical real estate. Real property has been compared to a bundle of sticks in which each stick represents a separate, transferable right. The individual rights to real estate include the rights to occupy the real estate, to sell it, to lease it, to enter it, to give it away, to borrow against it, or to exercise more than one or none of these rights. This aspect of real property divisibility is reflected in the bundle of rights theory.

Because real property rights are divisible, larger or smaller bundles of rights can be created by selling or leasing all or part of the property. These partial bundles of rights are contained in estates. An *estate* is the degree, nature, or extent of interest that a person has in property. Various possible estates are discussed below; each represents a different degree of real property ownership.

> **CONCEPT**
>
> A fee simple title implies full ownership of the complete bundle of rights. Leased fee estates, leasehold estates, estates encumbered by mortgages, and estates subject to easements are all less-than-complete forms of property ownership.

Fee Simple Estates

Most residential properties are held in fee simple. A fee simple estate is an absolute ownership unencumbered by any other interest or estate. The owner of a fee simple title possesses all the rights and benefits of the real estate subject only to the powers of government, which include taxation, eminent domain, escheat, and police power. The owner of a fee simple title possesses a complete bundle of rights.

Leased Fee Estates

When an owner enters into a lease agreement with a tenant, two less-than-complete estates are created: a leased fee estate and a leasehold estate. A leased fee estate is an ownership interest held by a landlord with the right of use and occupancy conveyed by lease to others; the rights of the lessor (the leased fee owner) and the leased fee are specified by contract terms contained within the lease. Specific lease terms vary, but a leased fee

> **TERMS**
>
> **estate:** a right or interest in property.
>
> **fee simple estate:** absolute ownership unencumbered by any other interest or estate, subject only to the limitations imposed by the governmental powers of taxation, eminent domain, police power, and escheat.

TERMS

leased fee estate: an ownership interest held by a landlord with the rights of use and occupancy conveyed by lease to others. The rights of the lessor (the leased fee owner) and the leased fee are specified by contract terms contained within the lease.

leasehold estate: the interest held by the lessee (the tenant or renter) through a lease conveying the rights of use and occupancy for a stated term under certain conditions.

equity: the value of the owner's interest minus the debt or mortgage.

easement: an interest in real property that conveys use, but not ownership, of a portion of an owner's property. Access or right-of-way easements may be acquired by private parties or public utilities. Governments dedicate conservation, open space, and preservation easements.

generally provides for rent to be paid by the lessee (the tenant) to the lessor (the landlord) under stipulated terms. The lessor has the right of repossession at the termination of the lease, default provisions, and the rights to sell, mortgage, or bequeath the property during the lease period. When a lease is legally delivered, the lessor must surrender possession of the property to the lessee for the lease period and abide by the lease provisions.

Leasehold Estates

A leasehold estate is the right to use and occupy real estate for a stated term under certain conditions as conveyed by the lease. Under a lease, the tenant usually acquires the rights to possess the property for the lease period, to sublease the property, and to improve the property under restrictions specified in the lease. In return the tenant must pay rent, surrender possession of the property at the termination of the lease, and abide by the lease provisions established with the lessor.

Estates Encumbered by Mortgages

Property owners can limit or restrict their real property interest in exchange for a mortgage loan. The owner is obligated to repay the loan according to a certain schedule and to pledge the real estate as security. The value of an owner's interest minus the debt, or mortgage, is called *equity*. The lender's interest consists of the right to repayment plus the right to foreclose on the loan if the owner defaults; the lender can legally force a sale of the property to recover all or part of the money owed.

Estates Subject to Easement

Granting or selling an easement can also create a less-than-complete estate. An easement is an interest that conveys use, but not ownership, of a portion of a real property. In other words, someone is allowed to perform a specific action on another person's property; for example, a city diverts a road through privately owned land. A right-of-way allows the owner of the dominant estate (the easement holder) access rights across the servient estate (the property subject to the easement), and the owner of the servient estate (the property owner) is not permitted to restrict access.

Often easements are attached to the land and continue to burden the servient estate even when the property is sold; these easements are called *appurtenant easements.* A utility easement that permits power lines to run along one side of a property is an appurtenant easement. Information on the burdens and benefits of easements can be found in title reports.

Identifying Property Rights

Fee simple estates, leased fee and leasehold estates, mortgages, and easements represent only a few of the many ways in which property rights may be divided. Just as various components of the physical real estate must be separated for appraisal purposes, an appraiser must precisely identify which property rights are being included in a valuation. The value conclusions reached in appraising the same parcel of real estate will differ depending on whether the fee simple estate or some other estate is being valued.

> **TERM**
>
> **property rights:** an enforceable, legal claim to title of or interest in real property.

LIMITATIONS ON PROPERTY USE

Individuals who own estates in real property are limited in their use of the property by the legal property rights they possess, by the physical

---

Figure 2.1   Components of Real Property Rights

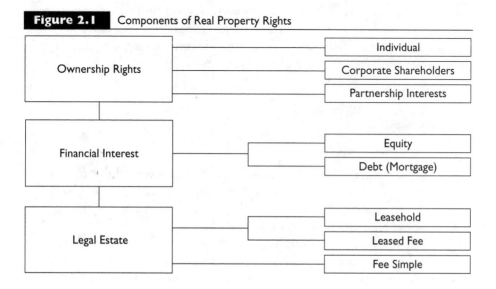

characteristics of the real estate, and by economic feasibility. This fact has considerable significance in real estate appraisal because value is created by the expectation of benefits that can accrue from ownership rights. Because various factors limit the potential uses and benefits that an estate can provide, the estate's value is limited as well. Thus an appraiser must carefully study the legal limitations, physical limitations, and economic limitations to which a parcel of real estate is subject. If any of these limitations change, the highest and best use and the value of the parcel may change as a result.

Legal Limitations

Legal limitations effectively restrict the ways in which property can be used. In the United States, public laws governing the use and development of land give the property owner the greatest possible freedom consistent with the rights accorded to others. However, the government reserves certain powers over property use, which take precedence over the rights of individuals who hold title to property. Subject to constitutional and statutory requirements, the government can, at any time, exercise four powers for the public benefit. All property ownership is limited by these four powers of government:

1. Taxation
2. Eminent domain
3. Escheat
4. Police power

Taxation is the right of government to raise revenue through assessments on valuable goods, products, and rights. Under eminent domain, the government can take private property for public use upon the payment of just compensation to the owner. Escheat gives the state titular ownership of a property when its owner dies without a will or any ascertainable heirs. Police power is the right of government under which property is regulated to protect public safety, health, morals, and general welfare.

Under the power of taxation, state and local governments can tax the owners of real property at any level so long as the taxes are imposed fairly.[2] Property taxes in different jurisdictions vary, and high taxes can limit or discourage many kinds of land use development.

The power of eminent domain can be exercised by agencies acting under government authority such as housing departments and public utilities. Under this power, the agency can take private property and use it for public purposes upon payment of just compensation to the owner. The private use of property can also be restricted by eminent domain. For example, a utility can acquire an easement in a property for an underground electrical line or a sewer and water line.

The government's police power is the most direct, comprehensive, and frequently invoked legal limitation on property use. Through its police power, the government has the right to enforce zoning ordinances, sanitary regulations, rent controls, historic preservation acts, utility requirements, and building, housing, plumbing, electrical, and other codes and regulations. These controls can affect almost every detail of property use, from permitted land uses to the size of windows and doors; even the type of finish can be regulated. Often the codes also specify what action is to be taken if a building does not conform to the ordinance requirements. It is essential that appraisers be familiar with all zoning ordinances and other regulations in effect in the area.

In addition to government restrictions on property, private voluntary and involuntary legal limitations exist. Private voluntary limitations include deed restrictions, lease agreements, CC&Rs (conditions, covenants, and restrictions), mortgage notes with provisions that limit property use, and party wall agreements, which grant owners of adjoining properties the common right to use a wall erected on the boundary line between them. Private involuntary limitations include easements, rights-of-way, and encroachments.

Private legal limitations can restrict the use or manner of development and even the way in which ownership can be conveyed. The

> **TERMS**
>
> **just compensation:** in condemnation, the amount of loss for which property owners are compensated when their property is taken; should put a property owner in as good a position pecuniarily as the owner would have been if the property had not been taken; generally held to be market value, but courts have refused to rule that it is always equivalent to market value.
>
> **conditions, covenants, and restrictions (CC&Rs):** a list of expressed assurances and limitations on land use; often found in contracts between a land subdivider and a lot purchaser.

---

2. Under the U.S. Constitution, the federal government is prohibited from taxing real property directly.

The physical characteristics of land limit the uses of real estate in certain areas, though the risk of natural disasters such as flooding and hurricanes in coastal areas can be offset by certain lifestyle amenities such a locale affords.

purchaser of an encumbered property may be obligated to use the property subject to restrictions. Thus, there are many legal restrictions created by private agreement or imposed by government that affect the potential uses of real estate.

Physical Limitations

The land's physical characteristics and the laws of nature dictate that many conceivable uses of real estate are difficult or impossible to achieve. Obviously a 120-ft.-by-150-ft. mansion cannot be built on a 100-ft.-by-120-ft. tract of land. Furthermore, it is not practical to build houses, raise crops, or construct office buildings in many places on the surface of the earth.

Land with irregular topography, earthquake fault areas, wetlands, floodplains, areas with the potential for landslides, and excessively cold or hot areas have limited utility for residential users, although some people may be willing to endure a certain amount of discomfort or risk. In fact, in recent years the largest population growth in the United States has occurred in coastal areas, which are most at risk from natural disasters such as flooding and hurricanes; people often migrate to these areas because of the amenities associated with a mild climate and proximity to a body of water. Physical factors affect the engineering and design of

CONCEPT

Physical limitations on the use of property result from the natural condition of land and the environment in any given location. However, these conditions may change or be overcome through technological advances.

structures as well. Due to climatic conditions, construction in an area may be limited to a narrow range of building types.

The physical characteristics of real estate and the environment are influenced not only by natural conditions but also by man-made conditions. Proximity to roads and highways and access to shopping centers, workplaces, and recreational facilities can affect how a given parcel of real estate is used.

The laws of nature do not change, but the effects of natural conditions on specific locations can be mitigated. The limits of physical possibility are constantly being pushed back by technological advances. For this reason, appraisers must keep abreast of both changing physical conditions in the area and developments in science and technology, particularly construction techniques and building design. These factors can affect the range of possible uses to which real estate may be put.

Economic Limitations

Although a use may be legally permissible and physically possible, it may not be economically practical. The market strongly discourages uses that are not economically feasible. Conversely, uses that are economically productive or beneficial are encouraged by the market so long as they are legally permissible. (Chapter 3 examines economic conditions that affect property use decisions.)

Changing economic forces and constraints can alter the balance of legal and physical limitations on property use. If economic pressures are strong enough, existing physical and legal limitations can be overcome or modified. For example, zoning ordinances can be changed if a large constituency will benefit from their revision. Similarly, significant physical limitations can be overcome if enough money is available to correct them. Often these funds *will* be spent if there is a likelihood that greater benefits or income can be secured from the projected use of the real estate.

> **CONCEPT**
>
> Economic limitations seriously influence land use decisions. Uses that are too expensive or do not produce sufficient benefits are generally avoided.

Limitations Combined

Together legal, physical, and economic limitations shape the ways in which real estate can be used. Legal restrictions limit the rights of individuals to use property in specific ways. Physical limitations can make certain uses impossible or difficult. The economic limitations created by market forces also have a strong impact on property use. To study how real estate can be used productively, real estate appraisers and analysts examine these limitations and their effect on the benefits the real property is expected to produce.

THE CONCEPT OF VALUE

As mentioned previously, *value* can be broadly defined as the monetary worth of goods or services to people. This definition is not sufficiently precise for appraisal purposes, though, because *monetary worth* may have different meanings to various people involved in real estate activities. The concept of value may have one meaning to a buyer or seller and another to a lender, owner, investor, insurance adjustor, or tax collector. These different interpretations can be attributed to the fact that different individuals tend to focus on distinct aspects of real estate—i.e., different benefits, interests, or possible uses. Consider the following examples:

- Buyers and sellers consider the monetary worth (market value) of a residential property in terms of the prices of other, nearby properties that are similar in quality and utility.
- Lenders may consider the price a property would bring in a forced sale (liquidation value), rather than the prices obtained for comparable properties under typical market conditions.
- Investors with unusual investment criteria may find that a particular property is ideally suited to their needs. For these investors, the monetary worth (investment value) of the real estate may be higher or lower than the value of a similar property to other buyers and sellers.

A property may provide its owner with certain valuable benefits and income that could not be realized by another owner. The monetary worth of the real estate to that owner might then be different than its worth to typical buyers and sellers of similar property. If the property were sold on the open market, the price obtained could be different from its investment value or use value.

Opinions of value may vary depending on the investor's perspective. In defining the appraisal problem, therefore, the appraiser *must* specify the precise type of value to be estimated—e.g., market value, use value, assessed value, or some other type of specified value. The value concept selected must be precisely defined at the beginning of the valuation process and in the appraisal report.

> **CONCEPT**
>
> Because the term *value* has many meanings, a specific value definition must be selected and stated at the beginning of an appraisal assignment.

MARKET VALUE

The concept of market value is of paramount importance to the business and real estate communities. Vast sums of debt and equity capital are committed each year to real estate investments and mortgage loans based on estimates of market value. Individuals involved in real estate taxation, litigation, and legislation also have an ongoing, active concern with market value issues. In virtually every aspect of the real estate industry and its regulation at local, state, and federal levels, market value considerations are of vital importance.

For these reasons, the definition of market value used by appraisers and their clients must be clearly understood and communicated. The various definitions of market value used reveal the different beliefs and assumptions about the marketplace and the nature of value among practitioners. Although market value is basically a simple concept—i.e., an objective value created by the collective behavior patterns of the market—the definition of market value is controversial and debate on the subject continues, sometimes producing rather fine distinctions.

Despite differing schools of thought, it is generally agreed that market value results from collective value judgments, not isolated opinions. A market value opinion must be based on objective observation of the collective actions of the marketplace. The standard of measurement must be cash, so increases or decreases in market value caused by financing and other terms are measured against an all-cash value.

A good market value definition incorporates the concepts that are most widely agreed upon—e.g., willing, able, and knowledgeable buyers and sellers who act prudently—and gives the appraiser a choice among

1. All cash
2. Terms equivalent to cash
3. Other precisely revealed terms

Increments or diminutions from the all-cash market value must still be quantified in terms of cash.

TERM

market value: the most probable price, as of a specified date, in cash, or in terms equivalent to cash, or in other precisely revealed terms, for which the specified property rights should sell after reasonable exposure in a competitive market under all conditions requisite to a fair sale, with the buyer and seller each acting prudently, knowledgeably, and for self-interest, and assuming that neither is under undue duress. (*The Appraisal of Real Estate,* 11th edition)

CONCEPT

Market value is the most widely recognized value concept, and it is the type of value most commonly estimated in appraisals. Definitions of market value vary, but the one selected for use in the appraisal must be precisely understood and communicated.

If the value being estimated is market value, the Uniform Standards of Professional Appraisal Practice require that the appraiser clearly indicate whether the opinion is the most probable price

(i) in terms of cash; or

(ii) in terms of financial arrangements equivalent to cash; or

(iii) in such other terms as may be precisely defined; if an opinion of value is based on submarket financing or financing with unusual conditions or incentives, the terms of such financing must be clearly set forth, their contributions to or negative influence on value must be described and estimated, and the market data supporting the valuation opinion must be described and explained.

Although these requirements include financing terms that are not cash equivalent within the scope of the market value of the appraised property rights, these rights are valued in relation to cash. Increases or decreases in market value that are attributable to financing terms are measured against an all-cash standard, and the dollar amount of variance between the financed value and the cash standard must be reported.

The following definition of market value is used by government agencies such as the Federal National Mortgage Association (Fannie Mae), the Federal Home Loan Mortgage Corporation (Freddie Mac), the Department of Veterans Affairs (VA), and many other federal financial institutions:

> The most probable price which a property should bring in a competitive and open market under all conditions requisite to a fair sale, the buyer and seller each acting prudently and knowledgeably, and assuming that price is not affected by undue stimulus. Implicit in this definition is the consummation of a sale as of a specified date and the passing of title from seller to buyer under conditions whereby:
>
> 1. Buyer and seller are both typically motivated;
> 2. Both parties are well informed or well advised, and acting in what they consider their own best interests;
> 3. A reasonable time is allowed for exposure in the open market;
> 4. Payment is made in terms of cash in United States dollars or in terms of financial arrangements comparable thereto; and
> 5. The price represents the normal consideration for the property sold unaffected by special or creative financing or sales concessions granted by anyone associated with the sale.[3]

---

3. *Federal Register,* vol. 55, no. 163, August 22, 1990, pages 34228 and 34229; also quoted on the Uniform Residential Appraisal Report (URAR) form (Freddie Mac Form 70/Fannie Mae Form 1004) and in the introduction to the Uniform Standards of Professional Appraisal Practice of The Appraisal Foundation.

In litigation matters, appraisers must use the precise definition of market value that is applied in the jurisdiction in which the services are being performed. Because government and regulatory agencies define or interpret market value from time to time, individuals performing appraisal services for these agencies or for institutions subject to their control should use the applicable market value definition.

OTHER VALUES

Along with an increased emphasis on market value, the realities of today's real estate market frequently require that other kinds of value be considered. These other values include use value and assessed value. Anticipated sale price is a related value concept.

Use Value

Use value is the value of a specific property for a specific use. This value concept is based on the productivity of an economic good. Use value refers to the value that the real estate contributes to the enterprise of which it is a part, without regard to highest and best use or the monetary amount that might be realized upon its sale. Use value may vary with the management of the property and external conditions such as changes in the business environment. For many real properties, use value and market value will differ.

> **TERMS**
>
> **use value:** the value a specific property has for a specific use, which may not be the highest and best use.
>
> **special-purpose property:** a limited-market property with a unique physical design, special construction materials, or a layout that restricts its utility to the use for which it was built.

When the property being appraised is of a type that is not commonly sold or rented, it may be difficult to determine whether an opinion of market value or use value is appropriate. Limited-market properties can present special problems for appraisers.

Many limited-market properties are improved with structures that have unique physical designs, special construction materials, or layouts that severely restrict the property's utility. Generally they are only suitable for the use for which they were built. Consequently, such properties are often called *special-purpose* or *special-design properties*. Homes that have been adapted to other uses or homes designed for the physically disabled are examples of special-purpose or special-design properties. In some locales, places of worship and schools may be limited-market properties.

In certain circumstances, limited-market properties may be appraised at their use value based on their current use. In other circumstances, they are appraised at market value based on the most likely alternative use. Because there is a relatively small market for these properties and lengthy market exposure is often required to find a buyer, evidence to support a market value estimate may be sparse. Nonetheless, if a market exists, the appraiser must search diligently for all available evidence of market value. If a property's current use is so specialized that there is no demonstrable market for the property but the use is viable and likely to continue, the appraiser may render an opinion of use value.

A use value opinion should not be confused with a market value opinion. If no market can be found or if data are not available, the appraiser cannot conclude a market value and should say so in the report. However, for legal purposes it is sometimes necessary to estimate market value even though no market can be found. In these cases, the appraiser must comply with the legal requirement but will have to reach an opinion of market value by other means, relying on judgment rather than direct market evidence.

Assessed Value

Assessed value is applied in ad valorem taxation and is established by the municipal authority legally charged with this responsibility. Assessment schedules may not conform to market value, but they usually relate to a market value base.

Anticipated Sales Price

Anticipated sales price is defined by the Employee Relocation Council as

> The price at which a property is anticipated to sell in a competitive and open market, assuming an arm's length transaction whereby:
>
> 1. The analysis reflects the property "as is."
> 2. Both parties are well-informed or well-advised and acting in what they consider their best interests.
> 3. Payment is made in cash or its equivalent. Financing, if any, is on terms generally available in the community and typical for the property type in its locale. (When the client has specifically requested consideration of special financing or an assumable loan, its effect on the sales price should be addressed.)
> 4. A reasonable marketing period, not to exceed 120 days and commencing on the date of appraisal (inspection), is allowed for exposure in the

open market. The analysis assumes an adequate effort to market the subject property.

5. Forecasting is applied in making an opinion of a future happening or condition, based on an analysis of trends in the recent past, tempered with analytical judgment concerning the probable extent to which these trends will continue into the future, and reflecting an estimated impact, if any, upon the sales price.[4]

---

4. Residential Appraisal Report Form, Employee Relocation Council, 1994.

3 | PRINCIPLES OF REAL ESTATE ECONOMICS

Every residential appraiser should be familiar with the fundamental principles of real estate economics. These concepts originate in basic economic theory and have been refined and made practical by real estate appraisers. Although economic principles provide a conceptual base, real estate appraisal is concerned with more than just theoretical

> **CONCEPT**
>
> The fundamental concepts and principles of real estate economics provide the theoretical basis for residential property appraisal.

matters. Every objective, professional appraisal must be supported by a solid understanding of the economic principles that govern how value is created and how it changes in the real estate market. To conduct professional appraisals, practitioners must recognize how economic principles operate in particular valuation situations. These fundamental ideas are referred to throughout this book.

PRINCIPLES OF REAL ESTATE ECONOMICS

The principles of real estate economics may be organized into three broad categories:

1. General economic principles, which can be observed in a wide variety of markets
2. Characteristics unique to real estate markets
3. Principles relating to the agents of production, which create real estate and the benefits that accrue from its use

General Economic Theory

The general principles of economic theory are the laws and concepts that characterize the actions of buyers and sellers who exchange various types of goods and services. These fundamental ideas apply to real estate markets and to related markets that directly or indirectly influence property values. Four key concerns applicable to real estate are

1. The principle of supply and demand
2. The concept of competition

3. The principle of substitution
4. The definition of a market

Supply and Demand

The law of supply and demand is the most fundamental of all economic principles. As applied to real property, this law states that the price of real property varies directly, but not necessarily proportionately, with demand and inversely, but not necessarily proportionately, with supply. This principle applies to the prices of all goods and services that are bought and sold in competitive markets. It affirms that, all else being equal, less money will usually be obtainable for an item when it is available for sale in greater quantity, and more money will generally be obtained for the item when less of it is available. Similarly, when the number of items that purchasers demand increases, the prices paid for these items can be expected to rise provided the supply remains constant; if demand decreases, prices can be expected to fall.

In residential markets, increases in supply may result from new construction, conversion from other uses, or the actions of many owners who decide to sell at a given time. Decreases in supply usually result from demolition, conversion to other uses, abandonment, slow or limited construction of new residences, and the actions of owners who decide to abstain from selling their property. Changes in demand typically occur more rapidly than changes in supply, so demand is the more critical price determinant. (Analysis of supply and demand is a basic component of the market analysis process, which is presented in detail in Chapter 9.)

Figures 3.1 and 3.2 illustrate the operation of supply and demand in real estate markets. Supply is represented by various amounts of a type of real estate available for sale or lease at various prices. As the upward-sloping supply curve in Figure 3.1 suggests, suppliers are usually more willing to increase production when prices are higher. Similarly, demand is reflected in the amounts of a type of real estate demanded at various prices for purchase or rent. The demand curve in the figure slopes downward because more is demanded at lower prices. The point where these curves intersect is the price at which a given property will most probably be sold.

Figure 3.1   Operation of Supply and Demand

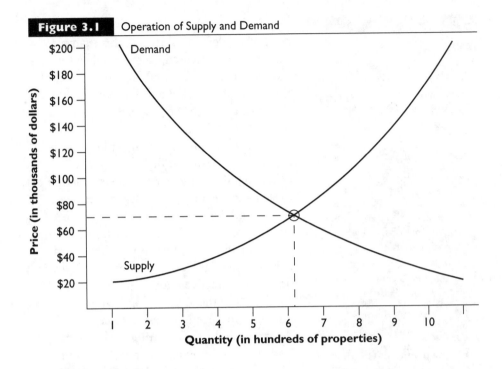

Figure 3.2   Operation of Supply and Demand (Demand Shifts)

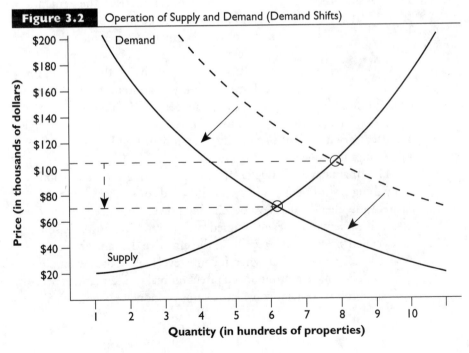

Figure 3.2 shows how real estate markets react when demand shifts. In this example demand has decreased, so the whole curve moves to the left. If supply remains constant, the curves intersect at a different point and the price at which the property will most probably be sold drops.

Four economic factors must be present to create value: desire, utility, scarcity, and effective purchasing power. The interaction of these factors is reflected in the principle of supply and demand.

Desire is a purchaser's wish for an item to satisfy an actual need or an individual want beyond essential life-support needs. Desire is limited by effective purchasing power.

Utility is the ability of an item to satisfy a human want, need, or desire. It varies with the wants and needs of different individuals. Sometimes improving the usefulness and quality of an item can increase the demand for it. However, changes in utility can only go so far toward augmenting demand.

Scarcity is the present or anticipated supply of an item relative to the demand for it. The availability of an item must be somewhat limited for needs or wants to be perceived. If an item is abundant, its existence will be taken for granted. Air is the classic example of a necessary item that is typically so abundant that it has no definable economic value.

The final factor of value is effective purchasing power, the ability and willingness of people to pay for the goods or services that they desire. Individuals must have purchasing power to translate their desires into demand. Desire coupled with purchasing power is sometimes called *effective demand*. Often the effective demand for an expensive item diminishes when income levels fall. Changes in purchasing power have a pronounced effect on real estate markets because real estate transactions involve large sums of money.

Competition

Supply and demand exert pressure on prices through competition. An auction is a familiar example of competition among buyers. Most markets are not like auctions, however, because sellers must also compete. When demand is weak compared with supply, competition between sellers can become especially intense. The quality and utility of the item may be improved and special incentives may be offered to attract the limited number of buyers. In many cases, prices must also be reduced.

Competing sellers hope to make a profit by obtaining prices that are somewhat greater than their expenses for acquiring or producing the item. When strong demand for an item emerges, the first sellers frequently do make sizable profits. Soon, however, other sellers join the competition, which drives prices down. Sometimes so many suppliers join the market that competition is very intense and prices fall below the cost of production, which undermines profits for everyone. In this situation, some sellers go bankrupt and others refrain from any further production or acquisition until all the oversupplied items have been absorbed and demand can resume at higher prices.

In the long run, balance is restored in the market, at least in theory. When demand is not strong enough to raise prices nor weak enough to lower prices, prices stabilize and the forces of supply and demand are in equilibrium. At the point of equilibrium, prices are generally fairly close to the costs required to produce the item and compensate developers with an acceptable margin of profit, called *entrepreurial incentive* or *profit*.

> **TERMS**
>
> **competition:** between purchasers, the interactive efforts of two or more potential purchasers or tenants to make a sale; between sellers, the interactive efforts of two or more potential sellers to complete a sale; among competitive properties, the level of productivity and amenities or benefits characteristic of each property considering the advantageous or disadvantageous position of the property relative to its competitors.
>
> **substitution:** the appraisal principle that states that when several similar or commensurate commodities, goods, or services are available, the one with the lowest price will attract the greatest demand and widest distribution. This is the primary principle upon which the cost and sales comparison approaches are based.

Substitution

Substitution is another principle that has broad significance in all economic activities. The principle of substitution affirms that when several similar or commensurate commodities, goods, or services are available, the one with the lowest price will attract the greatest demand and the widest distribution. Because competition underlies this principle, the prices at which similar items are sold in a market tend to grow increasingly uniform. Sellers who face a shrinking demand for their products are soon forced to lower their prices to prevailing levels if they are to sell at all. Sellers who experience the most intense demand for their products due to their lower prices may raise prices to established levels to reap greater profits.

When the items that different sellers are offering are physically similar, like oranges at a fruit market, it is easy to see how the principle of substitution operates. But substitution works equally well when the characteristics of items of similar utility are more abstract. For ex-

ample, investors may perceive bond issues, mortgage loans, and other long-term capital instruments to be more or less interchangeable for their purposes. These investments all involve similar levels of risk, tie up money for approximately the same amount of time,

The prices of similar items tend to grow increasingly uniform, according to the principle of substitution, a basic tenet of the three approaches to value.

and produce similar yields. As a result, these investments directly compete with one another for investors' funds.

Because investments compete for investment capital, conditions in the mortgage market closely follow conditions in financial markets, and the mortgage market is sensitive to developments that affect investment in other financial markets. Appraisers must perceive these market relationships to understand changes in price levels in the residential market. The amount and terms of mortgage money available at any given moment strongly affect the demand for housing.

The principle of substitution is also basic to the three approaches to value in the valuation process.[1] In the cost approach, a value indica-

---

1.   The valuation process is covered more fully in Chapter 4, and the individual approaches to value are discussed in Chapters 12 through 18.

tion is produced by adding the cost of producing a substitute residence to the value of the land. The reasoning behind this approach is that no one will spend more money for a property than it would cost to buy similar land and erect a similar structure on it without undue delay. In the sales comparison approach, the market value of a residence is estimated by examining the prices at which comparable residences have recently been sold. In the income capitalization approach, market value is based on the economic benefits that a property offers, which are indicated by market-derived rates of return.

Markets

Competition, substitution, and supply and demand are all demonstrated in the operation of markets. A market is a set of arrangements in which buyers and sellers are brought together through the price mechanism. A stock exchange, for example, is a market established in a convenient location where buyers come to obtain the goods or services offered by sellers. However, the product does not always have to be brought to market, as the real estate industry demonstrates. Real estate markets qualify as markets because buyers and sellers interact, compete, and cause identifiable changes in real estate prices.

Each market has its own unique characteristics, which depend on the arrangements
that buyers and sellers have developed and the
patterns of activity that have evolved. Perhaps
the most important feature that identifies a
specific market is the degree of direct competition among the different items sold in it.

> **TERM**
>
> **market:** a set of arrangements in which buyers and sellers are brought together through the price mechanism.

When the competition is direct, the activities are considered to be taking place in the same market. The distance between individual properties is not as significant as their substitutability.

Real estate markets have many characteristics that set them apart from other markets. Five different real estate markets can be identified in terms of typical users and property types:

- Residential markets
- Commercial markets
- Industrial markets
- Agricultural markets
- Special-purpose markets

Each of these markets can be further divided into various submarkets, in which buyers seek and sellers offer properties with specific features,

TERM

market segmentation: the process by which submarkets within a larger market are identified and analyzed.

locations, and prices. When the characteristics of the properties are very similar, the result is direct competition among the buyers who represent demand and the sellers who represent supply. Increased similarity makes price relationships closer and the market more focused. Identifying and analyzing smaller markets within a larger market is called *market segmentation*.

Neighborhoods, Districts, and Market Areas

A neighborhood is defined by certain characteristics that differentiate it from other neighborhoods and adjacent areas. Often neighborhood residents have common social characteristics such as age, income, and lifestyle. Many neighborhoods are identified by landmarks and defined boundaries; properties may have similar architectural styles or a particular blend of styles. A neighborhood can also be characterized by the mix of amenities and services that appeal to the people who choose to live there.

These defining features are not constant or uniform in all neighborhoods. They usually change over time and in different ways in each particular case. The character of a neighborhood is continually evolving in response to changing social, economic, governmental, and environmental (physical and geographical) conditions. The life of a neighborhood frequently follows a cyclical pattern and is affected by many factors, including its age, its position within the larger community, and the appeal of competitive neighborhoods.

The idea of a neighborhood is familiar to most people, but appraisers use the term in a specific sense. For appraisal purposes, a *neighborhood* is an area of complementary land uses. One essential aspect of this definition is the concept that the various land uses function as a unit. Most residential neighborhoods contain a variety of land uses. Different areas are improved with detached single-family dwellings, apartment buildings, and amenities and services such as parks, churches, cinemas, schools, and businesses. All of these elements tend to function together in a neighborhood, and the state of each element can often strongly affect the state of the whole neighborhood. As the principle of balance suggests, failing businesses, poorly maintained residential blocks, an inappropriate mix of land uses, and other detrimental conditions that affect segments of a neighborhood can directly reduce the appeal of the other neighborhood properties. These conditions often signal a pattern of change in a neighborhood, which may affect the value of all properties within its boundaries.

A *district* is a type of neighborhood that is characterized by homogeneous land use. Districts are commonly composed of apartments or of commercial, industrial, or agricultural properties. In large cities, an apartment district usually covers an extensive area; in smaller cities, an apartment district may be limited in size. The apartment buildings in a district may be multistory or single-story, high-rise or row, garden or townhouse. Individual units may be rented or privately owned as cooperatives or condominiums.

> **CONCEPT**
>
> Distinctions can be made between neighborhoods, districts, and market areas. A neighborhood is an area of complementary land uses, while a district is a type of neighborhood characterized by homogeneous land use. A market area can extend beyond the boundaries of a single neighborhood or district to encompass competitive properties in other areas.

The concepts of neighborhood and district overlap, but a necessary distinction must be made. The term *neighborhood* suggests a variety or balance of complementary land uses, while the term *district* refers to an area where one type of use predominates. Sometimes a neighborhood is composed of various districts. Often a commercial district marks the edge of a residential neighborhood.

The *market area* is the area in which properties effectively compete with the subject property in the minds of probable, potential purchasers and users.[2] The residential market area usually includes much of the subject neighborhood. Occasionally, however, only a segment of the neighborhood may be in the market area. The market area can also extend beyond the neighborhood when other neighborhoods compete with the subject neighborhood in the minds of potential purchasers. Often these other neighborhoods are near the subject neighborhood or located a similar distance away from a major employment center. The market area for rural properties is far more extensive than the market areas for urban or suburban properties. A market area is defined by the type of property, the type of transaction (e.g., rental or sale), and the geographic area in which competition exists.

Characteristics of Real Estate Markets

Real estate markets share some general characteristics with markets of all kinds, but other features make them unique. These features can best be illustrated by comparing real estate markets with a perfect, hypothetical market in which supply and demand operate smoothly, freely, and efficiently. As Table 3.1 clearly shows, real estate markets

---

2.   Note that the term *neighborhood* was changed to *market area* in Rule 1-3(a) of the Uniform Standards of Professional Appraisal Practice.

Table 3.1	Comparison of Efficient Markets and Real Estate Markets

Efficient Markets	**Real Estate Markets**
Goods and services are essentially homogeneous items that are readily substituted.	No two parcels of real estate have identical characteristics, so the price of one parcel cannot be directly inferred from the price of another.
Because the quality of goods and services tends to be fairly uniform, prices are relatively low and stable.	Prices are not low. Most transactions involve a mortgage loan, so financing considerations affect prices. Purchasing power is also very sensitive to demographics, wage levels, employment rates, etc.
A large number of market participants creates a competitive, free market, and none of these participants has a large enough share of the market to have a direct and measurable influence on price.	There are usually only a few buyers and sellers interested in a particular type of property at one time, in one price range, and in one location. An individual buyer or seller *can* influence price by exerting control on supply and/or demand.
Self-regulating markets require few government restrictions.	Federal, state, county, and local regulations govern the ownership and transfer of real estate. The demand for specific uses of real estate is often legally limited through zoning. The Federal Reserve System manipulates the market by controlling the supply of credit.
Supply and demand are never far out of balance. The market returns to equilibrium quickly through the effects of competition.	Supply and demand tend toward equilibrium, but this point is seldom achieved. The supply of real estate for a specific use does not adjust to market demand quickly, and demand can change while new supply is being developed.
Buyers and sellers are knowledgeable and fully informed about market conditions, the behavior of other market participants, past market activity, product quality, and product substitutability.	Market participants are not always well informed and are seldom experienced in the market.
Market information is readily available.	Information is not readily available.
Buyers and sellers are brought together through an organized market mechanism. Sellers can easily enter the market in response to demand.	Buyers and sellers are not brought together formally.
Goods are easily transported from place to place.	Real estate is immovable. Demand in one place cannot be met by supply in another.
External economic conditions can have an effect on price.	Externalities have a very significant effect on value.

are not efficient. In fact, many economists believe that real estate markets are among the least efficient markets in existence.

Four Forces

Appraisers must understand the forces that influence value. As discussed in Chapter 2, legal, physical, and economic restrictions limit the use of real property. They can also increase, sustain, or diminish property values by affecting the supply of or demand for properties of a specific type in a particular area at any given time. Appraisers consider four broad, dynamic forces that influence value:

• Social trends and standards
• Economic conditions
• Government rules and regulations
• Environmental conditions

The interaction of these forces affects the value of every parcel of real estate available in the market; all four forces are studied in a full analysis of the market for any real property. (See Chapter 9.)

Social Forces

A change in demographics, such as an influx of population into or a migration out of an area, directly alters the number of properties demanded in that area. Changes in birth and death rates, marriage and divorce rates, population age, and household formation can also influence the characteristics of real estate in demand. Different types of consumers have different neighborhood and building preferences, and their favor or disfavor is reflected in the prices they will pay for property.

Economic Forces

A population's purchasing power limits the quantity and quality of affordable real estate and directly influences demand. Purchasing power is determined by economic conditions such as employment and wage levels, the contraction or expansion of industry, the community's economic base, price levels, and the cost and availability of credit. On the supply side, influential economic conditions include the stock of available vacant and improved properties, new properties under construction or in the planning stage, occupancy rates, the rent and price patterns of existing properties, and construction costs.

Government Forces

The legal climate at a particular time in a specific place can impede the normal operation of supply and demand. The government's readiness or reluctance to provide necessary facilities and services helps shape land-use patterns and, hence, affects property values in certain locations. Significant government activity may include

- Public services such as fire and police protection, utilities, refuse collection, and transportation networks
- Local zoning, building, and health codes, which may support or obstruct specific land uses
- National, state, and local fiscal policies
- Special legislation that influences general property values—e.g., rent control laws, statutory redemption laws, restrictions on forms of ownership such as condominiums and timeshare arrangements, homestead exemption laws, environmental legislation regulating new development, and laws that affect types of loans, loan terms, and the investment powers of mortgage lending institutions

Environmental Forces

Natural barriers to future development include rivers, mountains, lakes, and oceans. Man-made features such as federal and state highways, railroads, airports, and navigable waterways also influence the potential use and value of real estate. Climatic conditions such as snowfall, rainfall, temperature, humidity, topography, and soil conditions are other important environmental influences. The natural character and desirability of a property's surrounding area or neighborhood are environmental factors that can exert a substantial influence on property values.

Access to public transportation, schools, stores, service establishments, parks, recreational areas, cultural facilities, places of worship, sources of employment, and product markets all have a very strong effect on a property's marketability in the eyes of potential buyers. The use of land can be changed if it is economical to do so, but the location of land is fixed. Property location is therefore a critical consideration.

The four forces that affect property value are not mutually exclusive; often they are interrelated. For example, political forces such as the actions of the federal government stimulate the housing market, so they must also be considered economic forces. Classifying these forces is useful in considering the variety of value influences that exist and how they interact to affect supply and demand in real estate markets.

Four Forces in the Local Residential Market

An appraiser is typically most interested in the market area for the subject property. Within this geographic area or political jurisdiction, similar properties effectively compete with the subject property in the minds of probable potential purchasers and users. Outside this area, zoning regulations may differ, locations may not appeal to the same buyers, builders may not incur the same costs, and other value influences may have different effects. Thus the market area is the geographic area where value-influencing forces have similar effects and the principle of substitution has the greatest applicability.

Because the location of real estate is fixed, the area in which buyers and sellers compete directly is often small and can be delineated geographically. People with a certain level of income and demographic characteristics—e.g., age, number of young children—often shop for residences in particular neighborhoods. These buyers compete most directly with other buyers who have the same income level and preferences. Similarly, home sellers usually face the most direct competition from neighbors who have similar properties for sale. Less direct competition may come from sellers of comparable properties in competitive neighborhoods some distance away.

In another context, many of the costs of residential development in an area are determined by competition in local construction and financial markets and by municipal development policy and regulations. Early in the valuation process, the appraiser must specify the submarket to which the subject property most likely appeals by identifying the area in which the four forces affect value in a similar manner. Recent sales considered comparable and other indications of value drawn from within the market area generally have the greatest reliability for valuation purposes.

CHANGES, TRENDS, AND CYCLES

Most of the changes that affect supply and demand in real estate markets are not random. An appraiser must understand why the market is changing because this knowledge may affect the outcome of the appraisal assignment. Changes that are pervasive or relate to many other changes that are occurring are called *trends*. A trend is a series of related changes brought about by a chain of causes and effects. Trends reflect the momentum of the market and develop in recognizable patterns. An appraiser can analyze these patterns to make forecasts.

For example, the increase in energy costs in the 1970s produced a major trend that affected the general economy and had a pronounced impact on real estate. Some of the consequences of this trend were recessions in regions of the country economically reliant on cheap, plentiful sources of energy (such as Texas and the aging centers of heavy industry in the Midwest and Northeast), high inflation and interest rates throughout the nation, and increased demand for smaller, energy-efficient housing.

Many important trends that affect real estate prices occur in cycles. Frequently real estate values follow the larger business cycle, and fluctuations in value are related to the rise and fall of the gross domestic product. Another influential cycle is the typical neighborhood life cycle described below, which is usually much longer than the business cycle.

Seasonal cycles also affect real estate values. In many areas of the country, for example, construction slows down during the winter, thus decreasing supply. In some areas, people prefer to sell their homes when the landscaping is most attractive, usually in late spring or summer. Market activity generally increases during these periods. Many leases turn over on an annual basis. Neighborhoods near large universities may have rent cycles tied to segments of the school year.

Neighborhood Life Cycles

Most neighborhoods go through a natural cycle of changes, which affects their character, their desirability, and the value of real estate located there. Neighborhoods usually go through periods of growth, stability, decline, and revitalization.

Growth

A neighborhood begins its life when buildings are constructed on vacant, newly cleared land or when properties are converted from a different use. This development may create a new community or it may expand an existing community to accommodate new demand for real estate. Neighborhoods often begin their growth during periods of local economic expansion. When employment prospects are good and interest rates are relatively low, developers are motivated to construct new units.

A neighborhood's growth period may be short-lived or it may last several years. Growth may continue as long as the neighborhood is perceived as a good value. Growth may stop when the demand for new housing diminishes as a result of shifts in buyer preferences or when the supply of housing is restrained by high construction or financing costs. If the neighborhood is successfully developed, new construction will attract new residents. As the neighborhood gains public recognition and favor, demand is sustained. As long as vacant land is plentiful, land prices will usually remain low in comparison to improved property prices. In a successful development, prices for both vacant land and improved properties usually increase as growth continues.

Because neighborhood growth frequently coincides with expansion in the local and regional economy, funding for public works to support the development often increases. Public works are usually not profitable on a small scale. For example, a sewer trunk line, which may open thousands of acres for development, is generally not extended in small sections. Public restrictions on development often accompany public funding. In many cases further development must conform to detailed land-use plans drawn up by local government and municipal agencies.

During the growth of a neighborhood, activity is generally vigorous. As a result, the buildings constructed during this period tend to be relatively similar in appearance, reflecting the building practices and market preferences of a particular time. The economic history of a city can often be discerned by studying the dominant architectural styles of its neighborhoods.

Stability

Neighborhood growth ends when it is no longer profitable to build or when other neighborhoods become better values. The neighborhood then enters a relatively stable period. A period of stability can also occur after a period of revitalization, when it is no longer profitable to convert properties from one use to another or to renovate them. In the stable phase, changes do not usually stop completely but they proceed at a slower pace. New construction may continue on a limited basis once demand increases or financing terms improve.

Neighborhood stability is characterized by the absence of marked growth or decline. The neighborhood settles into a comfortable pattern of activity. The demand for both new and existing units is generally balanced with the supply. Many residents remain, so property turnovers are relatively low. Real estate values stabilize and may even appreciate depending on the neighborhood's popularity and the strength of demand. Zoning codes are enforced and there is strong economic and social pressure for dwellings to conform to neighborhood and legal standards. The boundaries of the neighborhood are usually clearly demarcated.

This period of stability may last for some time. Buildings are aging but residents have enough income to meet their maintenance costs, so deterioration is not substantial. Neighborhoods have no established life expectancy, so decline is not imminent in all older neighborhoods.

Decline

A period of decline begins when a neighborhood can no longer compete with comparable neighborhoods. Maintenance costs may become too high due to the age of the dwellings or, more likely, because the location, style, and utility of residences have lost their appeal.

During this period, prices may fall to attract buyers.[3] "For sale" signs appear more frequently and turnovers increase. Neither new nor older residents have enough money to maintain the buildings adequately. Because residents cannot support the community businesses and services that were formerly in demand, building maintenance declines, vacancies increase, and businesses change hands. During a period of decline, building codes and zoning regulations may not be enforced. The boundaries of the neighborhood become less distinct and the number of rental units often increases in comparison with owner-occupied units.

Revitalization

Neighborhood decline ends when the dominant land use changes or a period of renewal begins. The decline in values ceases and a new balance is struck. Deteriorated buildings are torn down, other buildings are converted to more intensive uses, and the neighborhood is ready to begin its cycle of change once more.

When revitalization occurs, it is usually the result of changing preferences and community patterns. For example, economic growth in the larger community may increase the demand for housing in the neighborhood. Organized community efforts such as redevelopment programs and historic renovation may contribute significantly to revitalization; revitalization can also begin spontaneously, without planning or formal municipal assistance.

In a process that has become known as *gentrification*, middle- and upper-income people purchase properties in urban neighborhoods to

---

3. At one time lenders were accused of contributing to discrimination against minorities by unfairly penalizing neighborhoods because of the low incomes and racial backgrounds of their residents; this practice is known as *redlining*. The integration of neighborhoods was mistakenly thought to signal the beginning of a decline in their life cycles. Some banks refused to make mortgage loans in certain inner-city areas due to their high default rates, rather than basing their discussions on individual investment risks. This practice was held to be unlawful by the courts and by federal agencies that have regulatory authority over lending institutions.

For more information, see William B. Rayburn and Dennis S. Tosh, *Fair Lending and the Appraiser* (Chicago: Appraisal Institute and Philadelphia: Robert Morris Associates, Inc., 1996).

renovate or rehabilitate them, thereby revital-
izing the neighborhood. These properties may
have been of marginal quality and reflected
residential or other uses. Often apartment
buildings are upgraded, converted to condominiums or cooperatives, and removed from
the rental stock. Sometimes obsolete office
buildings and former industrial sites are
converted into residential uses. This type of
activity can change the orientation of the entire neighborhood.

> **TERM**
>
> **gentrification:** a neighbor-
> hood phenomenon in which
> middle- and upper-income
> persons purchase neighbor-
> hood properties and renovate
> or rehabilitate them.

Gentrification appears to stem from the preponderance of single
people and small families in metropolitan areas who want to live in
proximity to urban activities. As a consequence of gentrification,
poorer residents are displaced due to high rents and rising prices.
These lower-income groups may have moved into older city neighborhoods when others found them unappealing and unattractive. The
scarcity of federal funds for low-income housing has compounded the
plight of those groups.

A period of revitalization, like a period of decline, is often marked
by increased change and greater disparity between values in different
parts of the neighborhood. Revitalization usually proceeds block by
block. Once the effort gathers momentum, more remodeling is
undertaken by residents who foresee a substantial increase in property
values. Neighborhood revitalization usually fosters an atmosphere of
hope as large numbers of property owners work to repair or remodel
neighborhood properties.

Analyzing Change in Neighborhoods

The four stages described reflect how neighborhoods and districts
usually evolve, but they should not be taken as rigid guides to market
trends. Changes do not necessarily occur in sequence. Decline may
proceed at a barely perceptible rate. At any time, major changes can
occur to interrupt the order of the neighborhood life cycle. An external influence such as a new highway that changes traffic patterns can
bring about decline or revitalization. A neighborhood that is in a stage
of growth may decline suddenly rather than stabilize. An area that is
developing as a residential neighborhood may, due to a sudden external change, begin to grow as a commercial district. Appraisers can only
reach conclusions about the stage of a neighborhood and the likely
trend in its property values after they have conducted careful market
observation and research. Discussions with local residents, merchants,

brokers, bankers, appraisers, municipal planners, zoning officials, and other knowledgeable persons can contribute greatly to an appraiser's understanding of neighborhood development.

Siting Factors and Economic Base Analysis

The forces that affect property values can often be best understood by studying how a specific community has evolved in shape and character. How do the various neighborhoods in a city affect one another? Does the subject neighborhood lie in the path of an expanding, wealthier community or are residents moving to locations that offer access to workplaces by less congested routes? An appraiser notes the community's siting factor—i.e., the reason the site was originally chosen for settlement—as well as the reasons for subsequent growth, patterns of change, and factors likely to encourage, direct, or restrict future development. This information can help the appraiser complete the analysis of market conditions in the city and region and begin to focus on market conditions in the specific neighborhood—i.e., the formal process of market analysis.

Historically, people have settled in locations because of their particular advantages:

- Defensible terrain
- Access to water
- Location on trade routes or at intersections where goods could be profitably traded
- Availability of economic resources such as arable or mineral-rich land
- Proximity to political centers

Many of these considerations influenced the sites selected for early American communities and they continue to affect community development today.

In addition to the historical factors, an appraiser is interested in what makes an area a desirable or undesirable place to live now. The economic health and stability of the region or community is particularly important. The economic soundness of an area is formally studied in an economic base analysis. An economic base analysis examines which local businesses and industries draw purchasing power into the area and which serve the local population. Such an analysis also assesses the diversity of the economy in the area and its ability to weather cyclical fluctuations in economic activity.

If an area's economic base is concentrated on a single industry, the area may be susceptible to resource depletion, competition from products produced elsewhere, or technological developments that supplant the need for its products. Similarly, areas that cannot weather cyclical economic fluctuations will present greater risks to lenders, who will be forced to raise rates, which in turn will discourage growth and demand in the area. In contrast, areas that have a diversity of basic industries and occupations tend to fare better over the long term.

Sometimes an appraiser must consult specialists with expert information on the region's economic base, particularly if a long-term study of supply and demand or a marketability study is needed. For most residential appraisals, however, a detailed, formal analysis of the area's economic base is not required. Nonetheless, appraisers should be sensitive to changes in the economic climate of a region, especially changes that may not have been anticipated by market participants. The sudden arrival or departure of a major employer, for example, can have a substantial effect on the demand for housing in an area.

Important technological, economic, and political developments also influence the shape and character of American communities. With an understanding of these factors, an appraiser can develop a useful perspective on ongoing trends that affect many cities and regions in the United States.

> **TERMS**
>
> **siting factor:** the origin of settlement in a city, which generally influences subsequent land use and growth patterns.
>
> **economic base analysis:** a survey of the industries and businesses that generate employment and income in a community as well as the rate of population growth and levels of income, both of which are functions of employment. Economic base analysis is used to forecast the level and composition of future economic activity.

4 | THE VALUATION PROCESS

The valuation process is a systematic procedure developed to produce well-researched,
well-supported opinions of real property
value. The process consists of a series of steps,
beginning with the definition of the valuation
problem. The process proceeds through the
collection of data pertinent to the problem's
solution, the selection and application of
appropriate analytical approaches, the reconciliation of value indications, and the final opinion of value. It concludes when the value
conclusion is reported to the client. The steps in the process and the
methods of analysis can be adapted to address many appraisal situations. Although the valuation process is designed primarily for market
value appraisals, it provides a general framework within which most
valuation assignments are conducted.

> **TERM**
>
> **valuation process:** a
> systematic procedure employed
> to provide the answer to a
> client's question about the value
> of real property.

The valuation process consists of seven basic steps, which are
illustrated in Figure 4.1. Each phase of the process will be briefly
discussed in this chapter, and more detailed discussion of specific steps
will be presented in subsequent chapters.

DEFINITION OF THE PROBLEM

The first step in the valuation process is to define the problem accurately. An exact definition eliminates ambiguity about what the client
requires and alerts the appraiser to the amount and nature of the data
that will be needed to solve the problem. The definition of the appraisal problem has seven specific components:

1. Identification of the real estate
2. Identification of the property rights to be valued
3. Intended use of the appraisal
4. Definition of value
5. Effective date of the value opinion
6. Description of the scope of the appraisal

Figure 4.1   The Valuation Process

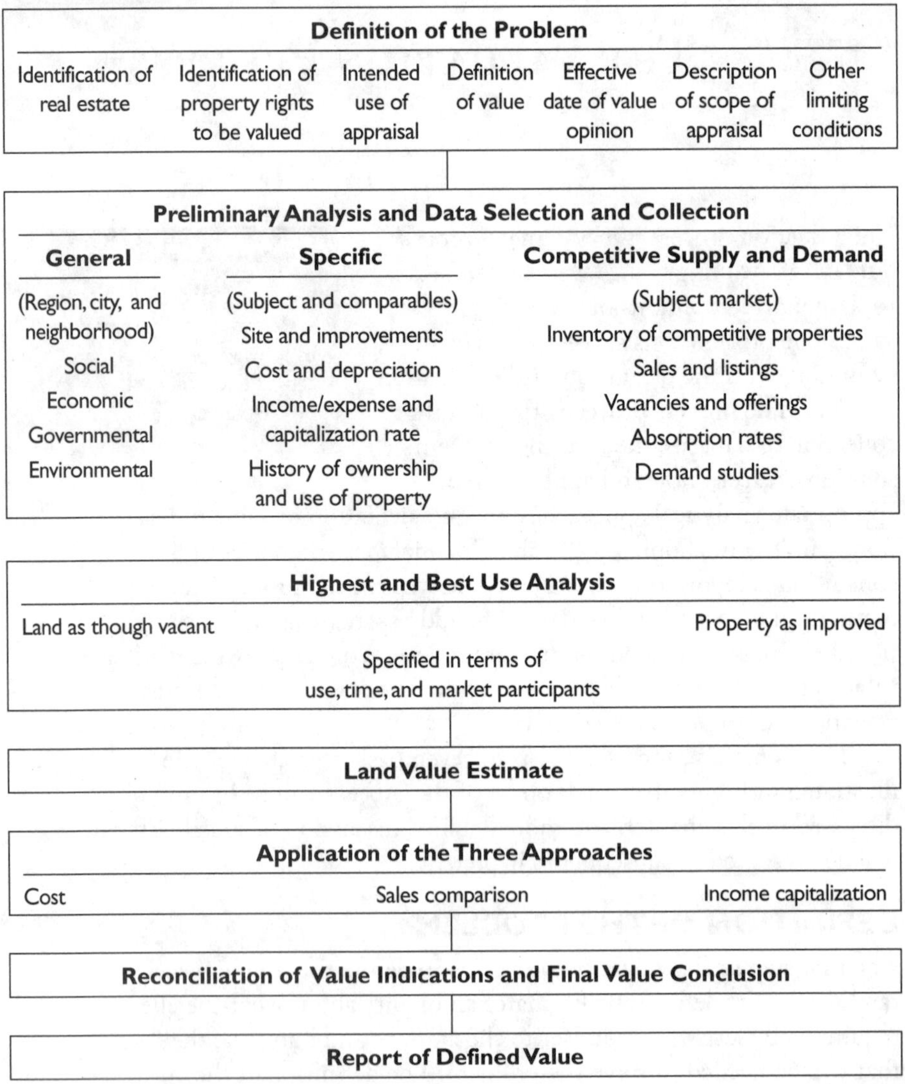

Definition of the Problem						
Identification of real estate	Identification of property rights to be valued	Intended use of appraisal	Definition of value	Effective date of value opinion	Description of scope of appraisal	Other limiting conditions

Preliminary Analysis and Data Selection and Collection		
General	**Specific**	**Competitive Supply and Demand**
(Region, city, and neighborhood)	(Subject and comparables)	(Subject market)
Social	Site and improvements	Inventory of competitive properties
Economic	Cost and depreciation	Sales and listings
Governmental	Income/expense and capitalization rate	Vacancies and offerings
Environmental	History of ownership and use of property	Absorption rates
		Demand studies

Highest and Best Use Analysis	
Land as though vacant	Property as improved
Specified in terms of use, time, and market participants	

Land Value Estimate

Application of the Three Approaches		
Cost	Sales comparison	Income capitalization

Reconciliation of Value Indications and Final Value Conclusion

Report of Defined Value

7. Limiting conditions and assumptions

Identification of the Real Estate

The property to be valued must be precisely identified. A street address is often acceptable, but a complete legal description is preferred. Legal descriptions are derived from land surveys and maintained in public records under state and local law. They may be found in deeds, abstracts of title, mortgages, and other public documents.

Land may be described using various systems of identification:

1. The metes and bounds system
2. The rectangular or government survey system
3. The lot and block system

Appraisers should be familiar with the types of legal description that are most prevalent in the local area. (The three systems of land description are discussed in detail in Chapter 5.)

A detailed description and analysis of the improvements are presented later in the appraisal, but some appraisers mention the property type within the definition of the problem. This is a matter of choice and custom. The identification of the real estate should leave no doubt as to the location and identity of the property being appraised.

Identification of the Property Rights To Be Valued

After the real estate is identified, the ownership rights must be precisely defined. Most residential appraisal assignments are performed to estimate the value of the rights of absolute ownership—i.e., the fee simple estate. Occasionally appraisals to estimate the value of other rights are requested. Fractional rights such as easements, encroachments, and subsurface mineral rights may have to be valued separately. Appraisers may also be asked to estimate the value of partial interests created by the severance or division of ownership rights. Liens and other limitations on ownership should be identified in the definition of the appraisal problem. Because real property value is the value of the rights of ownership, it is important to specify the particular rights to be valued in an appraisal.

Intended Use of the Appraisal

Appraisals may be used in many various ways by different clients:

- Lenders may want to know how much money to lend to a home buyer.
- Buyers and sellers may want a value estimate to analyze offers to buy or sell.

- Courts may use value estimates as a basis for just compensation in eminent domain proceedings.

An appraiser can often avoid misdirected effort and other problems by agreeing with the client in advance on the intended use of the appraisal and the form of the appraisal report.

Definition of Value

Many types of value may be estimated in appraisals—e.g., market value, use value, and assessed value. Each of these values has a separate definition, and special techniques may be required to estimate the value sought. Therefore, it is essential to specify the value being reported. If this value is market value, the clients or the courts may request that the appraiser use the specific legal or economic definition that is appropriate to the assignment. The Uniform Standards of Professional Appraisal Practice require an appraiser to define the value being estimated.

Once the value to be estimated has been identified, the appraiser can select the most appropriate valuation techniques and determine the data to be collected. Including the definition of value in the report also communicates the objective of the appraisal to the reader.

Effective Date of the Value Opinion

A specific date of value is essential because the factors that influence value change constantly. Abrupt changes in business and real estate markets affect property values. Even without dramatic market shifts, values are subject to gradual change. Therefore, a value opinion must be reported as of a particular date, although that date is not necessarily the same as the date of the appraisal report. Using a specific date allows an appraiser to isolate and quantify all the factors that influence value at this time.

Most appraisals require current estimates of value, and the client and the appraiser usually agree on the exact date in advance. The date of inspection is often used as the effective date of the value opinion if no other date is specified. However, retrospective and prospective appraisals are not uncommon.[1] An appraisal for inheritance tax purposes usually requires a value opinion as of the date of the testator's death. To make insurance adjustments, insurers may require a value opinion as of the date of casualty. Appraisals used in lawsuits frequently require a value

---

1. Appraisers are advised to check with their clients as to the specific date of value required. For lending purposes, Fannie Mae will not accept appraisals of prospective value that are based on adjustments for anticipated market conditions.

opinion as of a date set by the court. In eminent domain proceedings, for example, value is estimated as of the date when the petition to condemn was filed, or as of some other date stipulated by statute or the court. Similarly, appraisals for divorce litigation require value opinions as of a specified date, e.g., the date of filing or dissolution. Some appraisals prepared for mortgage financing require value opinions as of a prospective or future date, e.g., when a house is being appraised from blueprints and specifications.

Description of the Scope of the Appraisal

The scope of the appraisal refers to the extent of the process in which data are collected, confirmed, and reported. The scope is described to protect third parties whose reliance on an appraisal report may be affected by this information. An appraiser determines the extent of the work and of the report relative to the significance of the appraisal problem. The appraiser is responsible for describing the scope of the appraisal in the report.

Limiting Conditions and Assumptions

To complete the definition of the valuation problem, all limitations and assumptions inherent in the appraisal report must be identified. Limiting conditions might specify that no court testimony or attendance in court will be required unless separate arrangements are made, that no engineering survey has been made by the appraiser, or that data on the size and area of the property have been obtained from sources believed to be reliable.

The Uniform Residential Appraisal Report (URAR) form, which is used in assignments for federal agencies and most financial institutions, contains an expanded limiting condition clarifying that the appraiser is not an expert in the field of environmental hazards and the appraisal report is not to be considered an environmental assessment of the property. This limiting condition acknowledges that the appraiser is responsible for noting in the appraisal report any adverse conditions (including, but not limited to, hazardous wastes and toxic substances) that were observed during the inspection of the property or that became apparent during the normal research involved in performing the appraisal.

> **TERMS**
>
> **scope of the appraisal:** extent of the process in which data are collected, confirmed, and reported.
>
> **Uniform Residential Appraisal Report (URAR):** a standardized appraisal form developed jointly by Fannie Mae, Freddie Mac, the Federal Housing Administration, the Veterans Administration, and the Farmers' Home Administration and used to communicate valuations of one- to four-family residential properties.

PRELIMINARY ANALYSIS AND DATA SELECTION AND COLLECTION

The second phase of the valuation process consists of a preliminary analysis of the problem and selection and collection of pertinent data.

Preliminary Analysis

Planning the steps required to complete the assignment is useful in the preliminary analysis because it allows the appraiser to create a schedule for data collection. Each task is allocated a certain amount of time and a place in the sequence. Then a person is selected to complete each task—i.e., the appraiser, someone on the appraiser's staff, or an outside specialist. Detailed work plans are especially essential in long, complex assignments. They can help prevent errors and omissions and may make data collection more productive. A work plan can also be useful when the client and appraiser negotiate the appraiser's fee.

To perform a preliminary analysis, an appraiser investigates the subject neighborhood, itemizes the data that will be needed, and creates a work schedule.

> **CONCEPT**
>
> Once the problem is defined, the appraiser makes a preliminary investigation of the subject property and the area, itemizes the kinds of data that will be needed, and prepares a work schedule.

Neighborhood Investigation

Driving around the subject neighborhood can help familiarize the appraiser with the task ahead. Any special conditions that may require additional research can be noted. A neighborhood investigation may not be necessary if the appraiser has had considerable experience with the area and the property type.

Data Needed

A useful work plan includes a list of all the general and specific data needed. Information on value influences in the area and the neighborhood should be listed along with data on the subject and comparable properties. If information from soil experts, engineers, legal specialists, or other professionals will be required, this should be noted as well.

Work Schedule

The main procedures to be performed and the types of data needed should be identified in a flowchart, and the responsibility for completing each task should be properly delegated.

Data Selection and Collection

After the preliminary analysis, the appraiser is ready to begin collecting pertinent data. The amount and type of data required will vary with the type of property being appraised, the value being estimated, the presentation of the report, and the intended use of the value conclusion.

Most appraisal assignments require information on market transactions of similar vacant and improved real estate, cost and depreciation estimates, and income, expense, and gross rent multiplier data. Data fall into three categories:

1. *General data* about conditions in the nation, region, city, and neighborhood that affect value
2. *Specific data* about the site, the improvements, and comparable properties
3. *Competitive supply and demand data* that relate to the competitive position of the property in its future market

The accuracy of all data obtained should be verified by cross-checking different sources and inspecting the subject property.

General Data

The collection of general data usually involves all or many of the following steps:

1. Compile information on how social, economic, governmental, and environmental forces interact and affect real estate values on national, regional, and local levels. Appraisers need this information to develop an understanding of how these four forces influence the value and use of the subject property.
2. Inspect and observe the neighborhood, identifying its boundaries and major characteristics. Neighborhood inspection is usually performed during the preliminary survey. Because many of the forces that influence value affect most properties in a neighborhood in the same way, identifying neighborhood boundaries is an important step toward selecting relevant market data.

3. Identify the stage in the life cycle of the neighborhood. Neighborhoods typically go through a cycle of changes—i.e., growth, stability, decline, and revitalization—which affect property values. Understanding the reasons behind these changes can help an appraiser identify the highest and best use of a property.

4. Conduct additional research into the local market. Although some changes that affect values in a neighborhood are immediately discernible, others may require time-consuming study. In particular, appraisers should focus on factors that pertain to the long-term prospects of the area. Neighborhood zoning ordinances, municipal development projects, locally available financing terms, and plans for transportation networks can provide useful indications of how neighborhood values have been evolving. This information may enable an appraiser to forecast future trends.

5. Rate the quality of the neighborhood. Appraisers must try to identify and understand the amenities and shortcomings that make a neighborhood more or less attractive to market participants. This critical step in data collection will allow the appraiser to determine the locational advantages or disadvantages of the subject and comparable properties.

Specific Data

Specific data are collected for the subject property and each proposed comparable; they form the basis for property productivity analysis, the final step of the market analysis process. (This process is described in the next section.) First the appraiser inspects the subject property's site and improvements. Site data include information on the size, shape, and location of the lot, the orientation of the building(s), the topography, available utilities and site improvements, and the property's compatibility with surrounding land uses. The improvements are described in terms of their style, design, and layout as well as their structural and mechanical components. The appraiser rates each component for its quality, condition, functional utility, energy efficiency, and market appeal. Comparable properties are usually analyzed in less detail than the subject, but all factors that affect their values must be analyzed fully and accurately.

Specific data also include information on financial arrangements that could affect the selling prices of the comparables. The history of ownership and use of the subject property should be investigated to establish whether toxic wastes or hazardous materials may be present on the property.

If sales comparison is the primary approach applied, the data collected must be sufficient to allow the appraiser to recognize and adjust for differences between the subject and similar properties. When the cost approach is emphasized, the subject property description must be detailed enough to support a valid estimate of the costs of reproducing or replacing the improvements with a comparable structure and to indicate an accurate measure of depreciation. If the real estate produces income, the appraiser may need to investigate comparable properties to estimate rents and expenses and to derive income multipliers and overall capitalization rates. The appraiser must determine the degree of comparability between the subject and comparable properties to ensure that their sources of income are similar.

Competitive Supply and Demand Data

Competitive supply and demand data relate to the competitive position of the property in its present and future market. Supply data include inventories of existing and proposed competitive properties as well as vacancy and absorption rates. Demand data include population, income, employment, and survey data pertaining to potential property users. From these data an estimate of future demand for the present use or for prospective uses of the property is developed in the market analysis process. The neighborhood analysis section of the URAR form calls for a description of market conditions in the subject neighborhood.

MARKET AND NEIGHBORHOOD ANALYSIS

In the Uniform Standards of Professional Appraisal Practice, *market analysis* is defined as the study of real estate market conditions for a specific type of property. A description of prevalent market conditions helps the reader of an appraisal report understand the motivations of participants in the market for the subject property. An economically depressed region exhibits a certain pattern of real estate transactions, while a region with a growing population and an expanding economic base exhibits another. Broad market conditions provide the background for local and neighborhood market influences that have direct bearing on the value of the subject property.

Even the simplest valuation assignments must be based on a solid understanding of prevalent market conditions. Market analysis serves two important functions. First, it provides a background against which local developments are considered. For example,

> **TERM**
>
> **market analysis:** a study of real estate market conditions for a specific type of property. (USPAP, 1999 edition)

property values may rise because an area is becoming more economically attractive than the areas that surround it. To develop an understanding of the conditions in the subject area and surrounding areas, an appraiser interviews market participants and relates their perceptions to statistical data. Second, a knowledge of the broad changes that affect supply and demand gives an appraiser a sense of how values change over time. Changes in residential real estate values do not relate only to the subject property's neighborhood. The supply of and demand for housing are affected by broader trends and cycles as well. Recognizing that these broader changes cause values to shift over time, appraisers carefully scrutinize long-term regional price trends.

The data and conclusions generated in market analysis are essential in other parts of the valuation process. Market analysis identifies the most probable alternative uses for a particular site, suggests which alternatives will be financially feasible, and provides support for assessing the risk and probability of the highest and best use selected for the subject property within its local market.

CONCEPT

Analyses of market conditions and highest and best use are crucial to the valuation process.

In addition, market analysis yields information needed in each of the three traditional approaches to value. In the cost approach, market analysis provides the basis for making an adjustment to reflect the depreciation affecting the subject property, i.e., measuring physical deterioration and functional and external obsolescence. In the income capitalization approach, all the necessary data—the net operating income (*NOI*), capitalization rate, and forecasted rent, expenses, and occupancy levels—used in discounted cash flow analysis are determined by analyzing the market forces of supply and demand. In the sales comparison approach, the conclusions of market analysis are used to delineate the market and thereby identify comparable properties, to identify potential buyers and their criteria for purchases, and to determine a market conditions adjustment.

The extent of market and neighborhood analysis and the level of detail appropriate for a particular assignment depend on the valuation problem. For standard residential appraisal assignments, the neighborhood analysis process is often a straightforward description of the state of the local market at a particular time. Appraisers valuing property in a generally stable market on a daily basis should have ready access to all the necessary demographic and economic information to document market conditions. When the assignment is complex—e.g., an analysis of the feasibility of a subdivision development—a more detailed market analysis will be required. In every appraisal assignment, the logic of the market analysis must be communicated to the reader in the appraisal report.

HIGHEST AND BEST USE ANALYSIS

Highest and best use analysis is essential to the valuation process. The highest and best use of both the site as though vacant and the property as improved must meet four criteria. The highest and best use must be

1. Legally permissible
2. Physically possible
3. Financially feasible
4. Maximally productive

These criteria are usually considered sequentially. For example, a use may be financially feasible, but this is irrelevant if it is legally prohibited or physically impossible.

Highest and best use analysis is performed in two steps. First the site is analyzed as though vacant and available for development. This process serves two important functions: identification of comparables and estimation of site value. The highest and best use as though vacant of all comparable property sites should be similar to that of the subject property. Analyzing the highest and best use of the site as though vacant also helps the appraiser develop an estimate of site value.

In this first analysis, the potential uses of the vacant land are analyzed with respect to the four criteria. Each use is tested to determine whether it is legally permissible, physically possible, and financially feasible. Uses that do not pass these tests are eliminated from further consideration. The uses that remain are analyzed and the one that is maximally productive is selected as the highest and best use of the site as though vacant.

The highest and best use of a site may be to remain vacant or it may be to develop the site. If development is contemplated, the appraiser identifies what type of building or other improvement should be constructed and when. The highest and best use conclusion for a site should be as specific as the marketplace indicates.

In the second step of the analysis, the highest and best use of the property as improved is examined. This process also serves two functions. The appraiser can confirm that each comparable improved property has a highest and best use similar to that of the subject property. The analysis also helps the appraiser determine whether the improvements should be demolished, renovated, or maintained in their present condition. Identification of the existing property's most productive use is crucial.

In this second analysis, the same four criteria are applied to the existing improvements. Of the legal uses that are physically possible and financially feasible, the one that is maximally productive is the highest and best use of the property as improved. In analyzing the highest and best use of owner-occupied properties, appraisers must consider any rehabilitation or modernization that is consistent with market preferences. For example, the highest and best use of a residence should reflect all rehabilitation required to provide the amenities that are standard in the market.

In residential appraisal, analysis of the highest and best use of a property is often a simple matter that is implicit in the selection of a particular report form. Nevertheless, the conclusions reached in the market analysis process have a significant effect on subsequent analyses. They influence depreciation analysis in the cost approach, the selection and adjustment of improved property sales in the sales comparison approach, and the selection of rents and multipliers in the income capitalization approach.

SITE VALUE ESTIMATE

In most market value appraisal assignments, a separate estimate of the value of the site is required. Some appraisals are performed to estimate site value only. Ad valorem tax assessments in some areas require separate estimates of site value, and a site value estimate is also essential to highest and best use analysis.

The most reliable method for estimating site value is the sales comparison approach. Sales of similar vacant parcels are researched, analyzed, compared, and adjusted to provide a value indication for the land being appraised. When sufficient data are not available for sales comparison, however, several other allocation or extraction procedures can be used to value land (land valuation is described in chapter 11).

APPLICATION OF THE THREE APPROACHES

Once pertinent data have been collected, the appraiser is ready to apply one or more of the three approaches to value. Each approach will result in at least one indication of value. The appropriateness of a given approach depends on the nature of the valuation problem and the amount of reliable data available. For example, the sales comparison approach is most applicable when sufficient data can be collected on recent sales of comparable properties. If a property has many special features or no comparable properties have been sold recently, the sales comparison approach may not be very reliable. In such a case, the appraiser might place greater emphasis on the cost approach. If the property being appraised appeals to an active rental market, the income capitalization approach may be given serious consideration. All applicable approaches should be used whenever possible.

All three approaches rely on market data and on the principle of substitution, which holds that the price or rent that a property is likely to command will closely reflect the prices or rents obtainable for similar properties in the same market. The cost of constructing a similar structure, minus depreciation, can be added to site value to produce one value indication, while sales of comparable properties can be analyzed to produce another. Studying the value of properties that have similar gross incomes provides a third method for deriving a value indication. Because all three approaches are based on an understanding of how buyers and sellers interact, they should yield similar value conclusions.

Cost Approach

The cost approach is based on the premise that property value is indicated by the current cost to construct a new improvement minus depreciation plus the value of the site. The cost approach is applied in eight steps:

1. Estimate the value of the site as though vacant and available to be developed to its highest and best use.
2. Estimate the direct (hard) and indirect (soft) costs of the improvements as of the effective appraisal date.
3. Estimate an appropriate entrepreneurial incentive or profit from analysis of the market.
4. Add estimated direct costs, indirect costs, and an entrepreneurial incentive or profit to arrive at the total cost of the improvements.
5. Estimate the amount of depreciation in the structure and, if necessary, allocate it among the three major categories: physical deterioration, functional obsolescence, and external obsolescence.
6. Deduct the estimated depreciation from the total costs of the improvements to

TERM

cost approach: a set of procedures through which a value indication is derived for the fee simple interest in a property by estimating the current cost to construct a reproduction of, or replacement for, the existing structure; deducting depreciation from the reproduction or replacement cost; and adding the estimated land value plus an entrepreneurial profit or incentive. Adjustments can then be made to the indicated fee simple value of the subject property to reflect the value of the property interest being appraised.

derive an estimate of their depreciated cost.

7. Estimate the contributory value of any site improvements that have not already been considered. (Site improvements are often appraised at their contributory value, i.e., directly on a depreciated cost basis.)

8. Add the site value to the total depreciated cost of all improvements to arrive at the indicated value of the property.

The cost approach is most reliable when the property improvements are new or nearly new and reflect the highest and best use of the site. If the utility and condition of the property are close to ideal, depreciation will be minimal. Because depreciation can be difficult to estimate, the cost approach is less reliable and less convincing when it is used to value older properties. When an improvement has special construction features or sales considered comparable are unavailable, the cost approach is especially useful.

Sales Comparison Approach

The sales comparison approach is used to value most residential properties because it is direct and easy to understand. When properly applied, this approach is usually the most reliable and the most persuasive. To apply the sales comparison approach, the appraiser considers the prices of similar properties that have recently been sold. These prices can indicate the value of the subject property once they are adjusted to reflect any differences between the subject and the comparables. The procedural steps are:

1. Identify and research comparable properties that have been sold recently, and ascertain the price, property rights conveyed, financing terms, conditions of sale (buyer and seller motivations), and market conditions (time) involved in each transaction. Verify the accuracy of this information.

2. Examine each sale considered comparable to determine how it differs from the subject property and how these differences affect its value. The elements of comparison include

- Expenditures made immediately after purchase
- Real property rights conveyed
- Financing terms
- Conditions of sale
- Market conditions
- Location
- Physical characteristics (size, construction quality, condition of improvements)
- Use (zoning)
- Non-realty components of value

3. Adjust the sale or unit price of each comparable for observed differences between the subject and the comparables. In other words, compare the comparable to the subject. If the comparable is inferior to the subject, adjust the price of the comparable upward; if the comparable is superior to the subject, a downward adjustment is made to the price of the comparable.

4. Reconcile the results of these comparisons into a single value indication or a range of values.

Income Capitalization Approach

In the income capitalization approach, property value is measured in relation to the anticipated future benefits that can be derived from property ownership. When the property being appraised competes in an active rental market, an appraiser can derive an indication of value by capitalizing the anticipated future benefits into a present value. The capitaliza-

CONCEPT

To apply the sales comparison approach, the appraiser collects sales data on comparable properties, analyzes differences between the subject and each comparable, makes appropriate adjustments to the prices of the comparables, and reconciles the resulting value indications.

TERMS

elements of comparison: the characteristics or attributes of properties and transactions that cause the prices of real estate to vary; include expenditures made immediately after purchase, real property rights conveyed, financing terms, conditions of sale, market conditions, location, physical characteristics, and other characteristics such as use and non-realty components of value.

income capitalization approach: a set of procedures through which an appraiser derives a value indication for an income-producing property by converting its anticipated benefits (cash flows and reversion) into property value. This conversion can be accomplished in two ways. One year's income expectancy can be capitalized at a market-derived capitalization rate or at a capitalization rate that reflects a specified income pattern, return on investment, and change in the value of the investment. Alternatively, the annual cash flows for the holding period and the reversion can be discounted at a specified yield rate.

tion technique applied depends on the income
characteristics of the subject property and the
data available for analysis.

The income capitalization approach is not
commonly used to estimate the value of single-
family residential properties. However, some
residential properties are bought on the basis of
their gross rents. To value these properties, a
gross rent multiplier (*GRM*) can be applied to
an estimate of market rent. The steps are

1. Identify and research competitive rental
   properties that have been sold recently.
   Divide the sale price of each by its gross
   monthly rent at the time of sale to obtain
   its *GRM*.

2. Estimate the monthly market rent that
   the subject property should command in
   light of present and anticipated rent levels
   and the property's market appeal.

3. Multiply the subject property's monthly
   market rent by a *GRM* selected from the
   GRMs of competing properties to obtain
   an indication of the value of the subject
   property.

To derive reliable *GRMs*, the appraiser
must analyze truly comparable properties that
have very similar ratios of operating expenses
to gross rent.

RECONCILIATION OF VALUE INDICATIONS

The last step in the valuation process is the reconciliation of the
various value indications into a final value conclusion. Obviously the
application of more than one approach will result in more than one
value indication. Even if only one approach is applied, a range of
values may be derived and this range must be refined into a single
figure.

To perform reconciliation, an appraiser reviews each stage of the
valuation process and tests the reasonableness of each conclusion
reached. The appraiser asks the following questions:

- Which data seem to be the most reliable?
- Which approach should be given the greatest weight in light of the purpose of the assignment and the information available?
- Finally, and perhaps most importantly, do the results make sense?

These questions must be asked and answered throughout the valuation process, but final reconciliation is the appraiser's last opportunity to perform such a review.

Each valuation approach serves as a check on the other approaches used. A wide variation among the value estimates derived often suggests that one approach is not as applicable as the others or that valuation procedures have not been properly applied. Unrealistic conclusions must be scrutinized. Once the appraiser is satisfied that the general range of value estimates is justified, each estimate is weighted according to its appropriateness and reliability. Finally, the appraiser selects a single value opinion or a range of value opinions based on the market data and on his or her informed judgment.

REPORT OF DEFINED VALUE

An appraisal is not complete until the conclusion and the reasoning behind it have been communicated to the client, usually in a written report. In addition to the final opinion of value, a written report should include all the pertinent data considered and all the methods of analysis used in the appraisal.

The appraisal report is a tangible expression of the appraiser's service, so its organization, presentation, and overall appearance are important. By signing a report, the appraiser accepts responsibility for its contents. Appraisal reports prepared by members of the Appraisal Institute must meet certain requirements.[2]

Appraisals may be communicated orally or in writing. Examples of written reports include self-contained reports, summary reports, and restricted use reports. Form reports, which are often used in appraising residential properties, may be restricted use reports, though most individuals involved in residential

> **CONCEPTS**
>
> The data and analysis on which the value opinion is based are communicated to the client in an appraisal report, which may be an oral report or a written report.
>
> All appraisal reports must meet the requirements of the Uniform Standards of Professional Appraisal Practice.

---

2. See the Standards Rules relating to Standard 2 of the Uniform Standards of Professional Appraisal Practice for the specific requirements that apply to reports of value opinions (appraisals) performed by Appraisal Institute members.

self-contained report: a report that, in compliance with Standards Rule 2-2(a), fully describes the data and analyses used in the assignment. All appropriate information is contained within the report and not referenced to the appraiser's files.

summary report: a report that, in compliance with Standards Rule 2-2(b), summarizes the data and analyses used in the assignment.

restricted use report: a report that, in compliance with Standards Rule 2-2(c), simply states the conclusions of the appraisal.

form report: a summary or restricted use appraisal report presented on a standard form such as those required by financial institutions, insurance companies, and government agencies. The reporting requirements for form reports, which are the same as for other types of reports, are set forth in the Standards Rules relating to Standards 2 and 5 of USPAP and the Appraisal Institute's Guide Note 3.

real estate recognize them as summary reports.

Form reports are preprinted documents that appraisers complete as they proceed through the valuation process. These standardized forms allow users of appraisal reports to compare and consider many appraisals quickly, to discern immediately whether all the required information has been supplied, and to analyze the reported data with computers. Form reports are commonly used by lending institutions, government agencies, and employee transfer companies, which must process large numbers of appraisals.

A self-contained report is the most comprehensive way to communicate the results of an appraisal to a client. This type of report is used when complete, detailed documentation is needed. A self-contained appraisal report presents the pertinent evidence and the logic employed to reach the final value opinion in a manner that is simple and convincing. Self-contained reports are usually organized to follow the steps in the valuation process.

Sometimes a client requests that a summary report be prepared. A summary report must meet extensive reporting requirements, but the level of detail presented is substantially reduced.

Restricted use reports include many of the items in the definition of the problem in abbreviated form, a brief statement of how the appraisal was conducted, and the value conclusion. A restricted use report must contain a prominent use restriction statement to ensure that the client understands the limited utility of such a report.

5 BEGINNING THE APPRAISAL

An assignment to estimate property value usually begins when a client contacts an appraiser and they reach an agreement on the character and scope of the appraisal. The client may be a representative of a financial institution, an employee of a relocation company, a property owner, a prospective buyer, or another party. The appraiser must first determine why the client wants the appraisal—e.g., to make a loan to a home buyer, to purchase a home, or to facilitate the transfer of a company employee. Sometimes the client does not know exactly what is needed and the discussion takes the form of a consultation. Once the nature of the appraisal assignment is established, the valuation process can begin.

Appraisal practices vary considerably, so the order in which data are collected and the nature of the information sought can differ. The elements discussed below are common to most appraisals.

The appraiser notes the property owner's name and phone number, the property address, and any legal identification of the property the client can provide. Together the client and the appraiser determine the appropriate device for communicating the appraisal conclusion. The appraiser's conclusions are generally provided in a written form or narrative report, although they may sometimes be presented orally (e.g., when the appraiser acts as an expert witness).

The purpose of the appraisal is discussed next. If it is a valuation assignment, the appraiser and the client decide which kind of value is appropriate to the problem. In most assignments, market value opinions are sought.

The appraiser asks what property rights are to be considered in the appraisal. The client may be seeking the value of the fee simple estate or the value of a fractional interest created by the legal or financial division of property rights in a lease or mortgage. The appraiser also elicits any pertinent information the client may have

CONCEPT

A residential appraiser and the client arrive at a mutual understanding as to the purpose, intended use, and effective date of the appraisal.

about the property—its type, condition, most recent sale price, and existing financing. Any items of personal property that will be included in the valuation should be specified.

The appraiser also asks the client whether there are any special conditions or assumptions that must be considered in performing the appraisal. In some cases, for example, the value opinion may be contingent upon painting the exterior of the property or completing some other repair. If the value opinion is contingent on an extraordinary condition, that condition must be clearly and accurately disclosed in the report.

Based on the client's description, an appraiser carefully considers whether he or she has the knowledge and experience needed to complete the appraisal competently. Most residential assignments are not beyond the abilities of a professionally trained, experienced appraiser. In some cases, however, special expertise may be required. In these instances the Uniform Standards require that the appraiser immediately disclose the lack of knowledge or experience to the client and take all steps necessary or appropriate to complete the appraisal competently.[1]

> **CONCEPT**
>
> To define the appraisal problem, the real estate must be precisely identified, usually with a legal description. The property rights to be appraised, the scope of the appraisal, and all limiting conditions and assumptions are specified at the start of the appraisal.

Next the appraiser ascertains when the client will need the appraisal report. Mortgage lenders and relocation companies, which commission many residential appraisal reports, frequently need reports in 3 to 10 days. Once the appraiser estimates how long the valuation process and the report writing should take and fits that process into a work schedule, the client and the appraiser can choose a date for the property inspection. Then the appraiser quotes a fee and a financial agreement is reached. The assignment is entered in the appraiser's logbook or computer. The oral contract may be followed up with a written contract or letter of engagement. If the

---

1. The Competency Rule of the Uniform Standards of Professional Appraisal Practice states:

    Prior to accepting an assignment or entering into an agreement to perform any assignment, an appraiser must properly identify the problem to be addressed and have the knowledge and experience to complete the assignment competently; or alternatively:

    1. disclose the lack of knowledge and/or experience to the client before accepting the assignment; and

    2. take all steps necessary or appropriate to complete the assignment competently; and

    3. describe the lack of knowledge and/or experience and the steps taken to complete the assignment competently in the report.

assignment is being performed for a large client such as a bank or government agency, the appraiser may complete the appropriate section of a master contract.

This hypothetical scenario describes how many residential appraisals begin. Although the appraiser and the client have entered into a contract, the definition of the problem is not complete. Seven separate elements are essential to define the appraisal problem:

1. Identification of the real estate
2. Identification of the property rights to be valued
3. Intended use of the appraisal (i.e., why the client needs the appraisal)
4. Definition of value
5. Effective date of the value opinion
6. Description of the scope of the appraisal
7. All limiting conditions and assumptions

Of these seven items, only three or four are likely to be well established when the appraiser agrees to begin the assignment: the intended use of the appraisal, the definition of value, the effective date of the value opinion, and perhaps the identification of the property rights to be valued. Limiting conditions and assumptions are often not revealed until after the property inspection. Two other elements—the identifica-

tion of the real estate and the property rights conveyed—should be directly investigated. At this stage the appraiser may have only a street address to identify the property, not a legal description. Similarly, the property rights may have been named by the client—e.g., fee simple, leased fee estate, fee subject to a mortgage—but the specific character of these rights and any limitations imposed by private restrictions and the four powers of government have not yet been established. The scope of the appraisal refers to the collection, confirmation, and reporting of data, which will vary depending on the requirements of the appraisal problem.

All seven elements define the appraisal problem and usually must be known before the appraiser can proceed. This detailed information, which is normally collected at the start of the valuation process, is the focus of this chapter.

PRELIMINARY STRATEGY

Specific information about the subject property obtained from the owner or broker can usually provide the appraiser with a preliminary description of the subject. This information may be detailed enough to enable the appraiser to select potentially comparable properties from research data collected before the field inspection. These comparable properties may be improved properties, vacant land, or competitive rental properties, depending on the type of property being appraised. From these properties the appraiser can derive the data applied in the cost, sales comparison, and income capitalization approaches. Data that characterize the subject property and potential comparable properties are often compiled initially from the appraiser's data files or from public records. The list of potentially comparable properties is narrowed down to actual comparables after the subject property has been inspected. If the comparable data initially identified are not adequate, other sales may need to be considered.

CONCEPT

The appraiser inspects the subject property and comparable properties to collect descriptive data and determine their comparability.

By applying this strategy, an appraiser can study the neighborhood, the subject property, and potentially comparable properties all in a single field inspection. Many appraisers use this method for routine residential appraisals, but some precautions are necessary. To use this strategy the appraiser must have a good sense of the kinds of data that will be needed and why they are relevant. Specific data describing the subject and potentially comparable properties can only be collected once the appraiser has identified the value influences operating in the neighborhood and the region at the time of the appraisal. Perhaps more importantly, the appraiser must also fully understand the concept of comparability, which is central to real estate valuation. Appraisers must be able to recognize when the sale price of one parcel of real estate can provide a useful indication of the value of another parcel and when it cannot. They must know when and how to make adjustments to the price of a comparable. (Some basic requirements for property comparability are discussed in this chapter; sales comparison and adjustment techniques are more fully developed in Chapters 15 and 17.)

The appraisal strategy described in this chapter is just that—a strategy. It is not a specific procedure to be applied in every circumstance but a description of the steps followed to collect data in many residential appraisals. Appraisers are contractually bound to fulfill the services agreed upon with their clients. They also have a duty to the public, to third parties using the appraisal report, to the appraisal profession, and to themselves to perform appraisal services in accordance with high ethical and professional standards. Within these parameters, however, appraisers have considerable leeway. Appraisal clients have different needs, and different real estate arrangements, political entities, and legal practices are found in different areas of the country. In various markets different types of information will be more or less reliable. Moreover, all appraisers have developed their own methods for researching and compiling data. With these differences in mind, the data collection steps presented below are those usually undertaken at the beginning of the valuation process.

OBTAINING DATA FROM INDIVIDUALS

The appraiser needs to collect reliable data on the subject property from informed sources within a brief period of time. The most knowledgeable source is usually the property owner, who may also be the occupant, or the property manager in the case of rental property. Sales agents and brokers often have detailed information on property characteristics. A representative of the financial institution that holds the property mortgage may also be a good source. Often an appraiser with good communication skills can secure the cooperation of these important individuals.

Several kinds of information can be obtained from the property owner or agent by asking questions like the following about the sales history of the subject property:

- When was the property last sold?
- If the sale occurred within the past year or two, what was the reason for the sale?
- What was the sale price and what type of financing was involved?
- Is there a current listing, option, or agreement of sale?
- If so, what is the price and what are the terms?

Knowing the subject property's sales history can be vital. The statements and actions of actual buyers and sellers of the property may be more indicative of the property's value than the patterns revealed by the sales of other properties, even the most comparable ones. Indeed, the Uniform Standards require that the property's sales history be considered if it is available. Information on current listings, offers, or agreements of sale can suggest a probable range of value within which the appraiser's final value conclusion may fall. Usually a sale is concluded at a price that is lower than the seller's offering price but higher than the buyer's initial bid.

The appraiser asks a second set of questions to obtain a preliminary description of the subject:

- What type of house is it?
- How many stories does it have and how many bedrooms and bathrooms?
- How old is it and are there any additions to the original structure?
- What is the size of the lot?
- Does the owner or agent have a legal description or a recent survey of the property?
- Are there any additional improvements to the site such as a pool, guest house, or barn?

The answers provided by the owner or agent help the appraiser form a general picture of the property to be appraised. This preliminary description will help the appraiser select comparable properties for analysis.

The appraiser will also want to determine if non-realty items of property should be considered. Are items of personal property to be included in the sale? If the appraiser has agreed to consider these items as part of the opinion of value, they must be identified. The question of personal property is relevant if the appraisal has been requested for a sale transaction. The appraiser may also ask the owner about non-realty items during the property inspection. The inclusion of personal property will affect the value conclusion and therefore must be specified in the appraisal report. In appraisals needed for lending purposes, appraisers are often specifically requested to omit personal property. However, if personal property is to be included, its treatment should conform to the requirements of the Uniform Standards.

After the sales history and preliminary description have been established, the appraiser makes an appointment to inspect the property. Appraisers should be very courteous to home owners and maintain good relations with brokers and agents because these individuals can be important sources of vital data in the present and in the future. The information obtained from these interested parties must be verified by checking with other sources and inspecting the property. An examination of public records and an onsite inspection of the subject property provide data that are essential to property analysis.

SCHEDULING AND DELEGATING APPRAISAL TASKS

Once the appraiser has a general definition of the appraisal problem and a preliminary description of the property to be appraised, a schedule for data collection can be developed. Experienced appraisers who are familiar with the type of property being appraised can review the necessary steps mentally, but appraisers with less experience and those performing complex assignments should list the kinds of data needed and draw up a schedule for the collection effort. Written schedules are particularly helpful if the services of additional staff or outside professionals will be needed; tasks such as performing property inspections and collecting market data must be carried out competently because they influence the final value opinion.

Appraisers who delegate tasks that are part of the valuation process should recognize that they are personally responsible for any work conducted in their name. To ensure that clients, the public, and third parties are not misled, the Uniform Standards require that an appraiser certify in the report that no one provided significant professional assistance to the person signing the report. If there are exceptions, the name of each individual who provided significant professional assistance must be stated.

IDENTIFYING COMPARABLES

Selecting properties that are *truly* comparable to the subject property is essential to all three valuation approaches. (Chapter 15 provides a detailed description of the requirements a comparable must satisfy.) For a property to be considered comparable, it should include features similar to the subject property and be competitive with it. In other words, the comparable property should appeal to many of the same people who would consider purchasing the subject property. It should be located within the subject property's market area and must have been sold recently.

Comparable properties are identified to provide data that can be applied in each of the three approaches to value. To gather data for the sales comparison approach, the appraiser identifies improved properties that have been sold recently and are comparable to the subject property. To apply the cost approach, the appraiser needs data on unimproved property, or vacant sites, that have been sold recently and are comparable to the subject site. Site sales may indicate site value, to which depreciated improvement costs are added to provide an indication of the value of the total property. The income capitalization approach usually requires data on comparable or competitive rental properties. These properties must be identified to determine market rents and sale prices and to derive gross rent multipliers. Market rent, the rent that the subject rental property should command in the open market, is multiplied by an appropriate gross rent multiplier to yield a value indication. Thus, the appraiser must identify comparable improved, vacant, and rental properties.

Data Sources for Comparables

Experienced appraisers need skill and judgment to locate potential comparables. They should be familiar with all sources of information on a particular type of property in a given area. An appraiser wants to collect all the information required and make sure that the information ultimately used is reliable. Data can be verified by consulting and cross-checking several sources. Some of the many data sources that can be used to identify comparables are explained below.

Multiple Listing Services

Multiple listing services (MLS) are extremely useful to real estate appraisers. These services are usually sponsored by local boards of Realtors® or individual brokers. Information on listings received by participating brokers and completed sales transactions is collected in the MLS and made available by subscription, often to members only. Current listings and sales information are available by computer and can be accessed using a modem. Subscribers to the MLS can enter the description of a property and specified parameters and receive a printout of similar properties. Listings and sales data are also published in a book that includes an index of recently sold properties. MLS books published quarterly or annually summarize all sales activity and indicate which listings have expired or have been withdrawn from the market during that period.

Property descriptions in the MLS may specify house size and type, the number and type of rooms, the year built, and the lot size. Information on zoning, taxes, the school district, and utilities may also be cited. Room sizes are often cited, but gross living area is generally not. The sale price of each property is indicated and sometimes the financing is specified. The broker's name is listed and often a photograph of the house is included. Much of this information is collected from property owners and the information is only as reliable as its source. Often property owners do not know the precise area of the plot in square feet or the exact date of construction. In general, however, an MLS can be extremely useful as an initial source of information.

Title Insurance Companies

Title insurance protects property owners from the possibility that their title will be contested. To do this, title insurance companies obtain copies of many public records relating to the real estate, including assessment records and a detailed history of past sales of the property. Title companies issue title reports, which summarize their findings. Many title companies will research sales in an area for an appraiser. Generally a fee is charged, but if the research is limited their services may be free. Title companies can be an extremely valuable source of information for identifying comparables.

Transfer Records

Most jurisdictions have a public office or depository for deeds where transactions are documented and made public. This process, known as *constructive notice,* ensures that interested individuals can research and, when necessary, contest deed transfers. Most county recorder's offices keep index books to deeds and mortgages so that the book and page on which the deed is recorded can be located. Some county offices, usually those in large metropolitan areas, have developed searchable computer databases that allow electronic access to public records.

> **TERMS**
>
> **title report:** a summary of the results of a study of liens, encumbrances, easements, and other conditions that affect the quality of the ownership title; prepared by title insurance companies.
>
> **constructive notice:** the accessibility of public records; notice is assumed by the existence of the records. The law presumes that an individual has the same knowledge of all instruments properly recorded as if he or she were actually acquainted with them.
>
> **cash consideration:** the actual price at which a property was transferred.

Deeds contain important information on potentially comparable properties, including a legal description of the real estate and the date the deed was recorded. A deed also lists the names and addresses of people who can be contacted to verify the transaction. The names of the buyer, the seller, and the title company; mailing addresses for the buyer, the buyer's attorney, and the broker; a lender loan number; and the buyer's new tax billing address may all be found in a deed.

Some deeds indicate the cash consideration, the actual price at which the property was transferred. Others have a stamp that indicates the transfer tax paid, from which the cash consideration can be calculated. However, these figures do not always reflect the actual sale price. Some purchasers deduct the estimated value of personal property from the true consideration to reduce the amount of transfer tax paid. If these personal property values are inflated, the recorded consideration for the real property may be less than the true consideration. In other circumstances, the recorded consideration may be overstated to obtain a higher loan or understated to justify a low property tax assessment. Some states require that the true and actual consideration be reported on the deed, but other states will accept a minimal recording such as "$1.00 and other valuable consideration." The appraiser should verify that the recorded consideration corresponds to the actual price paid for the property. If there is a discrepancy, the circumstances that account for the recorded consideration should be determined.

Tax Records

Another important public record is the tax assessment roll, which is usually kept with other tax records at the municipal or county assessor's office. All privately owned property in the county or district is listed on the assessment roll, which indicates the taxpayer's mailing address, the assessed value of the property, and often the date of the most recent transfer of ownership (see Figure 5.1). Other records kept by the local tax assessor may include property cards with land and building sketches, area measurements, and sale prices. Some of the information on property cards may be dated and unreliable. In many states, tax information is now computerized, and some assessor's offices can provide online access to public property tax records. Tax assessment data can be quite useful for the preliminary identification of comparables.

Published News

Most city newspapers feature real estate news. Although some of this news may be incomplete or inaccurate, an appraiser may be able to confirm the details of transactions by contacting the negotiating brokers and the parties involved, who are usually listed.

Realtors®, Appraisers, Managers, and Bankers

Real estate and financial professionals often have information about real estate transactions and can provide valuable leads. These sources may be definitive, but if the information obtained is third-party data, the appraiser should try to verify it independently.

Figure 5.1	Sample Assessment Roll

Source: Kane County Assessment Office, Geneva, Illinois.

Electronic Data Interchange (EDI)

In 1994 a coalition of real estate organizations, including the Mortgage Bankers Association, Fannie Mae, Freddie Mac, and the Appraisal Institute, formulated standards for electronic data interchange, which has greatly influenced appraisal practice.[2] EDI automates the transmission of data stored electronically, thereby improving accuracy, reducing input time at each data entry point, decreasing labor costs, and eliminating lost data and the uncertainties of work product

> **TERM**
>
> **electronic data interchange (EDI):** the electronic exchange of information between entities using standard, machine-processable, structured data formats.

2. In July 1995 The Appraisal Foundation adopted the Statement on Appraisal Standards No. 8, which deals with the electronic transmission of appraisal reports. According to the statement, "an electronically transmitted report is a written report and must meet the USPAP reporting requirements." For further discussion of the implications on appraisal reporting practices, see Sherwood Darington, "Transmitting Reports Electronically," *The Appraisal Journal* (October 1995): 436-439.

delivery.[3] Data from EDI-formatted appraisals prepared on the Uniform Residential Appraisal Report (URAR) form can be entered into a standardized database on appraisal properties, which in turn can be accessed electronically using translation software.

As initiatives such as the Appraisal Institute's National Residential Database, Freddie Mac's Home Value Estimator, and various automated valuation models (AVMs) created by software companies are implemented and gain acceptance, the existence of centralized repositories of data on residential property transactions could fundamentally alter the traditional services provided by residential appraisers. With precise, reliable data readily available, appraisers could spend less time on data collection and more time on analysis.

Some appraisers see the increasing use of AVMs and other computer models for calculating value as a threat to established practices, whereas others see the development of new valuation tools as a challenge to appraisers to learn more sophisticated techniques.[4] Unlike fax transmissions and e-mail correspondence, which remain person-to-person communications, EDI eliminates the human error implicit in data entry. Although fax and e-mail transmissions provide some efficiencies, that data cannot be directly processed by a computer, one of the primary benefits of EDI technology.

The lending community has actively pursued the establishment of data standards for all mortgage market functions involving interaction among sellers, servicers, and investors in mortgages. Federal agencies, including secondary mortgage market agencies such as Fannie Mae and Freddie Mac, have also implemented electronic commerce and data standardization measures.

Internet Sources

The growth of the Internet and the World Wide Web in the mid-1990s as a repository of information and a medium of commerce has made a wealth of information available to appraisers, although finding useful information remains a challenge. Most national residential real estate brokerage firms have online listing services designed for home buyers and sellers, and appraisers can find useful information at these sites as well. The federal government has facilitated the dissemination

---

3.   W. Lee Minnerly, *Electronic Data Interchange (EDI) and the Appraisal Office* (Chicago: Appraisal Institute, 1996), 2.

4.   For further discussion of the issue, see William B. Rayburn and Dennis S. Tosh, "Artificial Intelligence: The Future of Appraising," *The Appraisal Journal* (October 1995): 429-435 and the handbook on automated valuation models scheduled for publication by the Appraisal Institute in early 2000.

of census and economic data via the Internet. In addition, state and local governments have begun to make many sorts of public records available online, increasing access to these data and lowering the cost and amount of time appraisers spend on research.

Internet search engines are useful tools for finding local sources for the information that an appraiser needs; e-mail is useful for communicating with these sources. Figure 5.2 lists several Web sites that are useful starting points in the data collection process. Just like other forms of third-party data, information from the Internet must be cross-checked and verified with independent sources. An appraiser should question the reliability of much of the information disseminated via the Internet because of the wide access and relative anonymity the medium affords to proponents of marginal or controversial viewpoints.

The Appraiser's Files

Whenever possible, appraisers should accumulate information on properties offered for sale. They can request that their names be added to the mailing lists of banks, brokers, and other individuals who sell property. Classified ads can provide information on asking prices, which may indicate the strength or weakness of the local market for a particular type of property and the trend of activity in the area. Offers to purchase are also useful and may be obtained from brokers or managers. Generally, listings are higher than eventual transaction prices and offers are somewhat lower.

ESSENTIAL PROPERTY INFORMATION

Certain critical information must be collected for the subject property and for each proposed comparable:

- A legal description of the real estate
- The property rights conveyed and any public or private use restrictions
- The tax status of the property, including tax rates, tax burdens, and assessed values

Legal Descriptions of Real Estate

A legal description of real estate describes a parcel of land, which may be called a *lot, plot,* or *tract,* in such a way that it cannot be confused with any other parcel. Legal descriptions of real estate are based on precise surveys and are maintained as public records in accordance with local and state laws. They may be found in the deed filed in the public recorder's office or in the copy held by the owner. Because legal

Figure 5.2 Internet Resources for Residential Appraisers

Government Sites	Mortgage and Loan Information
www.bea.doc.gov	www.allregs.com
www.bls.gov	www.bankrate.com
www.census.gov	www.loanlocator.com
www.fedstats.gov	**Professional Associations**
www.hud.gov	www.appraisalfoundation.org
Residential Real Estate Industry Information	www.appraisalinstitute.org
	ww.appraisers.org
www.amrex.com	www.boma.org
Cost Service Information	www.ccim.com
www.marshallswift.com	www.irem.org
Demographic and Economic Information	www.mbaa.org
	www.nahb.com
www.econ-line.com	www.nmhc.org
www.ExtendTheReach.com/allocate	www.realtor.com
	www.uli.org

descriptions of real estate are the most accurate, they are the form of identification required in most appraisals.

There are three principal systems for the legal description of land:

1. The metes and bounds system
2. The rectangular or government survey system
3. The lot and block system

Each system is used in a different part of the country, and combinations of these systems are used in some areas.

Metes and Bounds System

The metes and bounds system is the oldest form of real estate identification currently in use, dating back centuries to when a buyer and seller would pace around the property, note boundary markers, and make property measurements. In the metes and bounds system, a point of beginning (POB) is established and related to a survey benchmark. Then the boundaries of the tract are described by proceeding from the POB in certain distances and along certain courses until the boundary line is "closed" by returning to the exact POB.

While the metes and bounds system can be quite accurate, particularly for irregularly shaped parcels, the resulting description can be extremely long and cumbersome to employ, with increased chances of typographical errors. Most states still use this system, often as a supplement to other systems of legal description.

Figure 5.3 is an example of a metes and bounds description of a parcel of land.

Figure 5.3   Metes and Bounds System

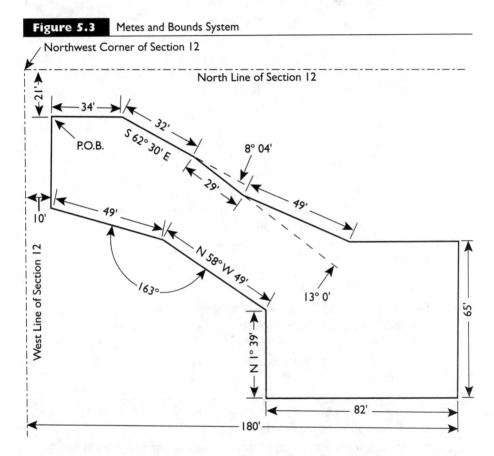

Description of Tract: Commencing at the Northwest corner of Section 12 thence South along the section line 21 feet; thence East 10 feet for a place of beginning, thence continuing East 34 feet; thence South 62 degrees, 30 minutes East 32 feet; thence Southeasterly along a line forming an angle of 8 degrees, 04 minutes to the right with a prolongation of the last described course 29 feet; thence South 13 degrees, 0 minutes to the left with a prolongation of the last described line a distance of 49 feet; thence East to a parallel with the West line of said Section and 180 feet distant therefrom; thence South on the last described line a distance of 65 feet; thence due West a distance of 82 feet; thence North 1 degree West 39 feet; thence North 58 degrees West a distance of 49 feet; thence Northwesterly along a line forming an angle of 163 degrees as measured from right to left with the last described line a distance of 49 feet; thence North to the place of beginning.

Rectangular or Government Survey System

In 1785 the federal government passed a land ordinance establishing the rectangular survey system, also known as the *government survey system,* which would become the principal method of legal description used for most land west of the Ohio and Mississippi Rivers, as well as in Alabama, Florida, and Mississippi. The system was established to facilitate the rapid sale of land the government had acquired through purchases and treaties.

In the rectangular survey system, a tract of land is identified by the portion of a map grid to which it corresponds. East-west baselines and north-south meridians intersect at initial reference points established by the Commissioner of the U.S. General Land Office. Range lines and township lines are drawn parallel to meridians and baselines respectively at six-mile intervals, forming a grid of six-mile squares which identify individual townships. These lines are adjusted for the curvature of the earth every 24 miles. Townships are further divided into 36 one-square-mile sections, with sections numbered in a back-and-forth or serpentine manner, as shown in Figure 5.4. Sections, in turn, can be divided into increasingly smaller fractions as shown in Figures 5.5.

Lot and Block System

The lot and block system identifies small parcels through subdivision maps submitted by real estate developers. Lot and block lines are recorded on a map with each lot and block labeled with a letter or number. When that map becomes public record, each lot in the development can be precisely identified by its lot and block number.

The short and easily understood lot and block descriptions are used for many routine transactions, and lot and block maps identified by subdivision name or number can be found by searching map records in the public recorder's office. A complete legal description states the lot number, block number, subdivision name or number, and either the location of the subdivision within the survey system or the volume and page number of the map record. Figure 5.6 is an example of a lot and block land description.

Some government authorities use a variation of the lot and block system to identify property for taxation purposes. Parcels are grouped together in blocks. Although a tax parcel cannot be used as a legal description for property conveyance in most jurisdictions, some appraisal report forms provide space for recording the tax parcel number of the subject property.

Figure 5.4 Government Survey System

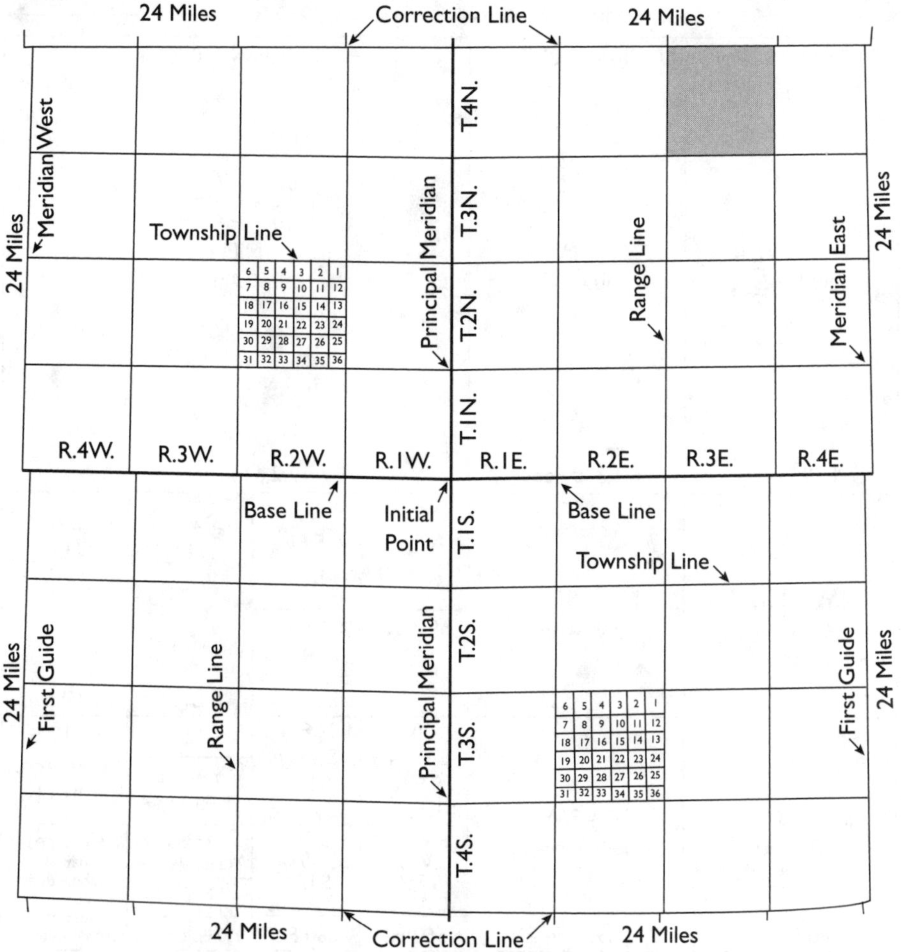

Description of the shaded township: Township 4 North. Range 3 East (T.4N., R.3E.). The township is four township rows north of the baseline and three range lines east of the principal meridian. (The township is located in northern California, so the baseline and principal meridian may be further identified as Mt. Diablo Base and Meridian.)

Source: John S. Hoag, *Fundamentals of Land Measurement* (Chicago: Chicago Title and Insurance Company, 1976), 8. Reprinted through the courtesy of Chicago Title Insurance Company.

Figure 5.5 Division of a Section of Land

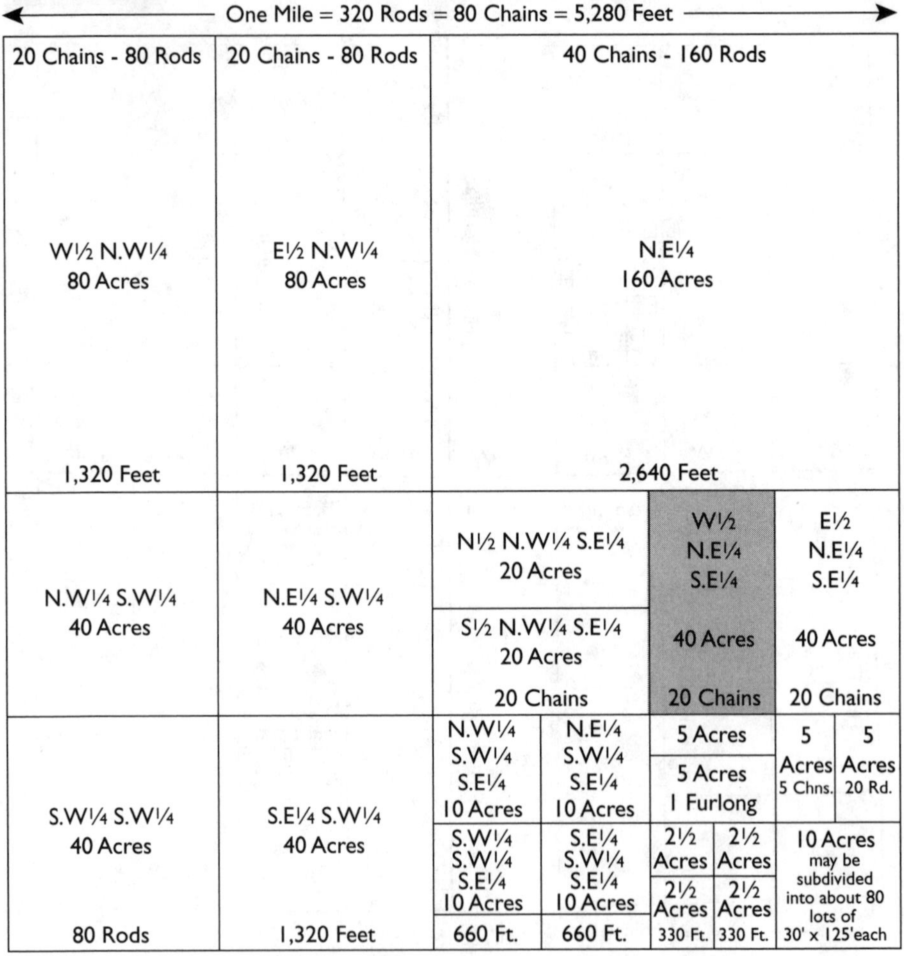

One Mile = 320 Rods = 80 Chains = 5,280 Feet

20 Chains - 80 Rods	20 Chains - 80 Rods	40 Chains - 160 Rods			
W½ N.W¼ 80 Acres	E½ N.W¼ 80 Acres	N.E¼ 160 Acres			
1,320 Feet	1,320 Feet	2,640 Feet			
N.W¼ S.W¼ 40 Acres	N.E¼ S.W¼ 40 Acres	N½ N.W¼ S.E¼ 20 Acres		W½ N.E¼ S.E¼	E½ N.E¼ S.E¼
		S½ N.W¼ S.E¼ 20 Acres		40 Acres	40 Acres
		20 Chains		20 Chains	20 Chains
S.W¼ S.W¼ 40 Acres	S.E¼ S.W¼ 40 Acres	N.W¼ S.W¼ S.E¼ 10 Acres	N.E¼ S.W¼ S.E¼ 10 Acres	5 Acres 5 Acres 1 Furlong	5 Acres 5 Chns. 2½ Acres	5 Acres 20 Rd. 2½ Acres
		S.W¼ S.W¼ S.E¼ 10 Acres	S.E¼ S.W¼ S.E¼ 10 Acres	2½ Acres 2½ Acres	2½ Acres 2½ Acres	10 Acres may be subdivided into about 80 lots of
80 Rods	1,320 Feet	660 Ft.	660 Ft.	330 Ft.	330 Ft.	30' x 125'each

Figure 5.6 Lot and Block System

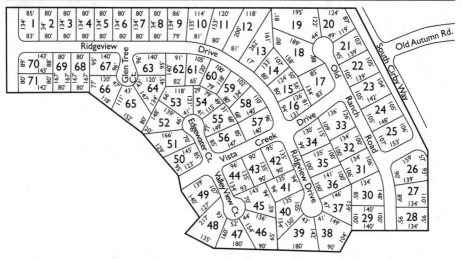

Woodridge Unit #1. Owner: Sunrise Properties, Sacramento, Calif.; engineer: Morton & Pitalo, Sacramento, Calif.

Property Rights Conveyed

Identification of the property rights to be appraised begins with specification of the legal estate to be valued—i.e., the fee simple interest or a partial interest created by the legal or financial division of interests in a lease or mortgage. The Uniform Standards require that the real property rights appraised be clearly identified.

Public Limitations

Zoning ordinances and a variety of building, plumbing, fire, and electrical codes are among the many public limitations that restrict property rights. These restrictions are imposed under police power, which gives the government the right to regulate land use and development for the public's benefit. Zoning laws may originate at the city or county level, but they are often subject to regional, state, and federal control.

Generally land is zoned to allow a specific type of use—e.g., residential, agricultural, commercial, industrial, or special-purpose. Along with the type of use, a maximum intensity of use may also be indicated. Special zoning ordinances are imposed in zones subject to floods, earthquakes, and other natural disasters. Zoning laws also restrict new construction in coastal areas and historic preservation districts.

TERM

zoning: the public regulation of the character and extent of real estate use through police power; accomplished by establishing districts or areas with uniform restrictions relating to improvements; structural height, area, and bulk; density of population; and other aspects of the use and development of private property.

Zoning ordinances and building, plumbing, and electrical codes may specify building height, front, side, and rear yard requirements; density of use; building setback; construction materials; and the architectural detailing of improvements. These regulations may also influence room sizes; floor plans; heating, plumbing, sanitary, and electrical systems; and many other details. In short, zoning ordinances and other legal codes derived from police power can regulate almost any aspect of property use.

Zoning regulations frequently specify the action to be taken if a property does not conform to a particular ordinance. This information is significant in appraisals because a property that does not conform to legal requirements usually may not be replaced if it suffers major damage. Often a property owner wants to retain a nonconforming use when the existing property is worth more than the ideal improvement allowed by the zoning regulations, but many zoning codes allow a nonconforming use to continue only if the property suffers less than a certain percentage of damage. Thus in some cases a nonconforming property may incur a value penalty in comparison with conforming properties. (Chapter 10 will examine the subject of nonconforming use in more detail.)

Where to Find: Data on Public Limitiations

Property rights are identified in property deeds and abstracts of title. A copy of a deed can be found in the public records office or obtained from the property owner. Information on the police power limitations applicable in an area can be requested from local zoning offices and county or municipal planning offices. Maps are used to show areas where specific requirements apply and books describe the corresponding laws in detail. Many appraisers acquire copies of the maps and regulations in effect in the areas where they work for office use.

Zoning laws are not static. They can and do change in response to strong community and economic pressures. Consequently, an appraiser should be aware not only of the ordinances that are currently in effect but also of the possibility that these regulations will change. The market for the subject property will take the probability of zoning changes into account and may hold different ideas about the highest and best use and value of the property than the existing zoning would suggest. However, an appraiser who relies on the likelihood of such a change in a valuation must usually collect documentary evidence to support this belief. Information on the probability of zoning changes can normally be obtained from local zoning or planning boards.

Private Agreements and Restrictions

Private agreements can also limit the rights to use property. In certain parts of the country—e.g., the city of Houston, Texas, and much of Alaska—private deed restrictions are preferred to zoning laws as a means of regulating property use. In addition to private agreements, restrictions arising from eminent domain proceedings limit property use. Some examples of private agreements and restrictions follow.

Easements and Rights-of-Way

Easements and rights-of-way are rights extended to nonowners of property usually for specific purposes. For example, easements or rights-of-way may be granted to neighbors. They may also be acquired by the government upon payment of just compensation. Through eminent domain proceedings, governmental agencies can acquire the right to install electrical transmission lines, underground sewers, and tunnels or to allow for flowage, aviation routes, roads, walkways, and open space. These restrictions generally run with the land and continue to encumber the property even if it is sold. Similarly, an easement or right-of-way across a neighboring property that benefits the subject property constitutes an enhancement of the property rights of the subject.

> **TERM**
>
> **right-of-way:** a privilege to pass over the land of another in some particular path; usually an easement over the land of another; a strip of land used in this way for railroad and highway purposes, for pipelines or pole lines, and for private or public passage.

Other Deed Restrictions

Other restrictions on use may be described in property deeds. Developers frequently impose such restrictions as part of the initial sales agreement to protect the value of all the properties in the development. For example, a sales agreement may include a clause that prohibits the outside storage of boats or recreational vehicles on a site. In general, conditions, covenants, and restrictions (commonly known as CC&Rs) are written into deeds or leases to specify permissible uses in a neighborhood and thereby stabilize property values. Property characteristics that can be controlled through CC&Rs include

- Lot size
- Setback
- Placement of buildings
- Number and size of improvements

- Architecture
- Cost of improvements

Party Wall Agreements

A party wall agreement may be needed when improvements are erected so that a common wall is used by owners of abutting properties. Because many party wall agreements are not recorded in writing, party walls must be examined during field inspections.

Riparian and Littoral Rights

Riparian and littoral rights are concerned with the use of water or a shore by an owner whose land borders a stream, river, lake, ocean, or other body of water. Riparian rights may include the right to construct piers, boathouses, and other improvements over the water or to use the water for fishing and recreational purposes. Littoral rights pertain to the use and enjoyment of the shoreline, and they safeguard the owner against artificial interference that might change the position of the shoreline.

Where to Find: Data on Private Agreements and Restrictions

Title reports and abstracts of title may contain some information about restrictions on property rights, but they do not always go into detail. A copy of the property deed or other conveyance should be obtained from the county recorder so that all limitations imposed on the property can be thoroughly identified.

Tax Status

Like public and private restrictions, taxes constitute a legal limitation on property rights. The burden of taxation can also influence the highest and best use of property and its market value. In certain school districts, for example, taxes may be disproportionately high. High taxes may discourage buyers who have no school-age children from purchasing a home there. Because taxes can affect property values, comparing the tax burdens of the subject property and each proposed comparable property can reveal important clues about their differences. If taxes are found to influence the values of comparable properties differently, the appraiser can allow for the difference in the adjustment process.

TERM

tax burden: amount of tax charged to a property owner based on the assessed value of the property, the tax rate applied in the particular jurisdiction, and local and state multipliers.

The tax burden of a property is calculated from three variables:

1. The assessed value of the property
2. The tax rate applied in the particular jurisdiction
3. Local (e.g., township or county) and state multipliers

The property's assessed value may be of interest to mortgage lenders.

A property's assessed value, or assessment, is the value of the property according to the tax rolls. Taxes are assessed in relation to this value, hence the term *ad valorem* (according to value) *taxation.* Tax rolls often show the assessed value of the property as a whole as well as an allocation of value between the land and the improvements. In some areas different tax rates are applied to the assessed values of these two property components.

Assessed value usually bears some relation to market value, but the assessed value of a property often differs from its market value for several reasons. First, assessed value may be based on a percentage of market value—e.g., 80% rather than 100% of market value. This percentage is called an *assessment ratio.* Second, and more important, properties are assessed in many communities at infrequent intervals by understaffed tax assessment offices. Consequently, unless a property has been revalued recently, its assessed value may not reflect a realistic relationship to market value. Appraisers do sometimes use assessment data such as land-to-improvement value ratios to derive market value conclusions, but only when there is little other evidence available and then only with extreme caution.

The tax rate is the ratio between the taxes levied and the assessed value. Tax rates may be expressed in dollars owed per $1,000 of value, called a *mill rate* (one mill = 0.1% = 0.001), or in dollars owed per $100 of value (1% = 0.01). Thus the tax burden of a property can be calculated by multiplying the tax rate by the property's assessed value. Consider the following examples:

Assessed value	$50,000
Mill rate	25 (0.025 × $50,000)
Taxes	$1,250
Assessed value	$100,000
Mill rate	40 (0.04 × $100,000)
Taxes	$4,000

This system is sometimes confusing and makes it difficult to compare the taxes in one community with the taxes in another. Very different assessment ratios and mill rates can produce the same tax burden, depending on their combined influence. Appraisers must recognize this to compare the tax status of different properties correctly.

Special Assessments

Special assessments may be levied by a district taxing authority for a finite period of time to pay for public improvements such as sewers, street paving, and sidewalks. Usually the tax assessment is based on the benefits that the property will derive from the improvement, not the cost of providing the improvement to a specific property. Thus, if two lots are assumed to derive a similar value enhancement from the installation of a sewer line, they will probably be subject to the same special assessment even if the installation costs for one property are higher than the costs for the other. Special assessments cannot be deducted from the property owners' income tax.

Special service areas are contiguous areas within counties or municipalities that are provided with special public improvements. These improvements are paid for by levying a tax on all properties within the area for a designated period. Generally this special tax levy is added to regular property taxes for a specified period of time and can be deducted from the property owners' income tax. Appraisers must identify special service areas and analyze how special tax levies affect property values. If the tax bill on a particular property seems abnormally high compared with the taxes on competitive properties, the appraiser should investigate the cause.

Where to Find: Data on Tax Status

Just as an appraiser may be interested in future zoning laws, future trends in property taxes must be investigated along with current assessments. A short history of tax assessments and tax rates can help an appraiser form a conclusion about the probable trend in property taxation. Discussions with tax officials can give the appraiser a sense of the probability of revaluation, the likely direction of future assessments, and the possible imposition of a cap or limit on real estate taxation.

INFORMATION ON THE SUBJECT PROPERTY AND COMPARABLES

The subject site and improvements must be inspected to determine the highest and best use of the property, collect data on the property's physical characteristics, and establish criteria for the selection of comparables. (The procedures followed in the onsite inspection of the subject property and the descriptive data that an appraiser obtains in this inspection are discussed in depth in Chapters 6, 7, and 8.)

After the potential comparables have been narrowed down, the appraiser will want to verify the sales data on the remaining comparable properties. Later, adjustments will be made to the sale price of each comparable to reflect how it differs from the subject property. The information needed to verify sales data for property considered comparable and to make adjustments is normally collected at the outset of the appraisal.

Data Verification

Sale prices and financing terms are often listed by multiple listing services. The transfer tax stamped on a deed may also indicate the sale price, but this information must be used with caution. Title companies also supply this type of data. In all cases, however, it is best to verify information with the parties involved in the transaction—i.e., the buyer, the seller, the sales agent or broker, the attorney for either party, or the mortgage lender. Not only are these sources often more reliable, but these individuals can answer important questions about the conditions of the sale like the following:

- What were the specific financing terms?
- Was the sale affected by duress?
- Was any personal property included in the transaction?
- How long was the property on the market and did it receive enough exposure?
- Were the buyer and seller related or unusually motivated?
- Was the sale atypical for any other reasons?

> **CONCEPT**
>
> The appraiser can often obtain information on the physical characteristics of the subject property and its recent sales history from the owner or the owner's representative. Data on comparable properties are collected from MLS books or computer services, title insurance companies, in-house files, and interviews with brokers. All data should be verified by cross-checking sources.

The conditions of the sale can affect the property price and therefore its reliability as an indication of market value. In most cases, only an individual involved in the sale can supply this type of information. The names and addresses of the parties involved in a transaction can be found in the MLS, title records and abstracts, and public records—particularly the property deed.

Descriptive Data

Finally an appraiser collects descriptive information on the characteristics of each comparable property.

- What are the size and shape of the lot?
- Does the property have a favorable or an unfavorable location in the neighborhood?
- What is the composition of the soil?
- What is the topography in the area?
- How old are the structures and of what type?
- Does the property have any special feature such as a remodeled basement, a desirable view, or built-in kitchen appliances?
- Are there any problems with the property?

Appraisers rarely have the opportunity to inspect the interiors of comparable properties. Generally appraisers will only be familiar with the interiors of comparables if they have already appraised them. Much of the appraiser's information must be obtained from parties to the transactions or from real estate agents and other appraisers who work in the same market area. It is wise to collect as much data as possible and then contact knowledgeable parties for further information or clarification. Additional data can be found in plat books, topographical maps, soil maps, floodplain maps, street and highway maps, and utility maps. (These maps are discussed in more detail in Chapter 6.)

6 | SITE DESCRIPTION

An important distinction exists between the terms *site* and *land*. Land, or raw land, refers to the condition of a plot in its natural state. A site is land that has been improved so that it is ready to be used for a specific purpose. Both onsite and offsite improvements are usually needed to make a plot ready for its intended use or development. Grading, drainage, sewers, utility lines, and access to roads are all improvements that convert land into a site.

Site value often differs from the value of a parcel of raw land. Site value is often higher because the presence of improvements means that less work must be done to develop the property. If, however, the improvements are faulty, inadequate, or otherwise inappropriate to the property's highest and best use, then site value may be lower than land value. A lower value may also result if a valuable surface resource has been stripped away in clearing the land.

To avoid misunderstandings appraisers should use terms consistently when researching land or site value. If sales of sites rather than raw land are used to derive a value indication, the appraiser should recognize that site value, not land value, is obtained. In ordinary usage, the terms *land* and *site* are often treated synonymously. This is acceptable so long as it does not lead to inappropriate or inconsistent reasoning. If necessary, the appraiser should describe the steps used to convert the indication of land value into an indication of site value.

> **TERMS**
>
> **site:** land that is improved so that it is ready to be used for a specific purpose.
>
> **land:** the earth's surface, both land and water, and anything that is attached to it whether by course of nature or human hands.

> **CONCEPT**
>
> The value of the raw land can be different from the value of the site.

SITE IMPROVEMENTS

The description and analysis of the site begin with an inspection of the site and all site improvements. Generally improvements included in site value (commonly called improvements *to* the site) are treated in the site description, while all others (known as improvements *on* the site) are described with the building improvements. Appraisers should follow the practices common in the market area to avoid misleading the client or other readers of the appraisal report. The final value opinion of the property as a whole should not be affected by how various improvements are classified in the analysis. In calculating depreciation for income tax purposes, however, improvements that are part of the site are usually not considered depreciable. Various examples of improvements to and on a site are listed in Figure 6.1. Improvements to the site are included in the site value estimate; improvements on the site are usually included in the building value estimate.

Figure 6.1 Site Improvements	
Included in the Site Value Estimate	Clearing, grading, drainage, public utility installation, site access routes, curbs
Included in the Building Value Estimate	Sidewalks, landscaping, septic systems, wells, driveways, parking areas, courtyards, swimming pools, fences, walls, lights, poles

PURPOSES OF SITE DESCRIPTION AND ANALYSIS

An appraiser describes and analyzes the site for several reasons. A detailed description of the site being appraised is required in the appraisal report along with descriptive data on site dimensions, area, zoning, location, topography, utilities, site improvements, present use, and highest and best use. The appraiser considers the conformity of the site size and whether the site improvements meet zoning and building setback requirements. The site description also helps the client and third parties form an opinion as to how the highest and best use of the site was determined.

The appraiser uses the site description to establish criteria for the selection of comparable properties. Comparable properties should be similar in size and other physical characteristics. In most cases the sites of comparable properties will have the same or a similar highest and best use as the site of the subject property. Transitional properties may pose special problems.

Site description and analysis provide much of the data needed to form a separate estimate of land or site value. This separate estimate is needed for the cost approach and provides the basis for any site adjustment required in the sales comparison approach. A separate land or site value estimate may also be required when the appraisal is being prepared for casualty loss estimates, local tax assessments, or eminent domain proceedings. (Site valuation techniques are described in detail in Chapter 11.)

Site analysis gives the appraiser an understanding of how the property is currently being used. The desirability of the property as a whole is affected by the general relationship between the building and the site and by the pattern of zones into which the improved site is divided. Maintenance and landscaping can also affect property value. Site analysis combined with building analysis indicates how the property as a whole can be used most productively in its improved state and what effect its present condition has on the total property value.

A final purpose of site analysis is to form a basis for determining the highest and best use of the land as though vacant. Having studied the neighborhood and the local market, the appraiser is in a position to understand how the physical and legal characteristics of the site interact with its surroundings to shape its maximum economic potential—i.e., highest and best use, which is the key to estimating the market value of the property.

Typical land-to-building ratios indicate economic utility and should be considered in measuring property productivity. Surplus land, in regard to an improved site, is additional land not needed to serve or support the existing improvements, though surplus land may be used for expansion of the existing improvements. In relation to a vacant site or a site considered as though vacant, excess land is the land not

CONCEPT

Site description and analysis are performed to collect data for a site description, establish criteria for the selection of comparables, provide data for a separate estimate of land value, understand if the site and improvements are combined in a complementary, maximally productive way, and identify the highest and best use of the land as though vacant.

TERMS

surplus land: additional land that allows for future expansion of the existing improvement(s); cannot be developed separately and does not have a separate highest and best use.

excess land: in regard to an improved site, the land not needed to serve or support the existing improvement; in regard to a vacant site or a site considered as though vacant, the land not needed to accommodate the site's primary highest and best use. Such land may be separated from the larger site and have its own highest and best use, or it may allow for future expansion of the existing or anticipated improvement.

needed to accommodate the site's primary highest and best use. Such land has its own highest and best use. (The differences between excess and surplus land are examined in more detail in Chapters 10 and 11.)

If the lot being appraised is unimproved, vacant land, the detailed data on various characteristics may have to be collected as part of site analysis. Often developers want highest and best use or feasibility studies performed before they prepare land for a particular use. Among other factors, these studies examine the quality of the soil and the cost of bringing utilities to the site. When the property is already improved and the highest and best use is not for redevelopment of the site, the appraiser may assume that the soil is suitable and the site is physically usable, but these assumptions and their effects must be clearly stated in the appraisal report.

STEPS IN SITE DESCRIPTION AND ANALYSIS

Site description and analysis involve several steps, which may be grouped into two general tasks:

1. The appraiser prepares for the field inspection by gathering the necessary tools and equipment and reviewing legal, tax, and assessment information on the property. Using this information, the appraiser notes the legal description of the property and all public and private restrictions that limit property use.
2. The appraiser then makes a field inspection of the site. In describing the site, the appraiser observes how site characteristics combine to shape the highest and best use of the site and notes any problems or special advantages that may affect site value. The site description includes a plot plan of the site.

PRE-INSPECTION PREPARATION
Assembling Essential Tools and Equipment

Before making the actual field inspection, the appraiser gathers all the tools and equipment necessary for this phase of the assignment. The appraiser will probably want to collect information on the subject site, the subject improvement, and potential comparables all in one trip, so careful planning is needed. Useful tools for data collection and subsequent steps in the analysis include

*   Measuring equipment
*   Photographic equipment
*   Maps and plats

- Calculators
- Dictation equipment
- Carrying equipment
- Miscellaneous office supplies

Most appraisal offices have these items on hand.

Measuring Equipment

To measure the building and site improvements, the appraiser may want to have a 50- to 100-ft., wind-up tape measure and a 12- to 20-ft. tape measure that can be worn on a belt. A carpenter's folding rule and a bevel can also come in handy, the latter for measuring angles. The appraiser should take measurements consistently, using the units of measure and techniques that are standard in the market.

To transfer measurements to scale drawings, the appraiser may use a straight edge, an architect's scale, an engineer's scale, and graph paper. A template and protractor can be used to draw curved lines and measure angles on sketches.

Photographic Equipment

A Polaroid camera can be used to take instant photographs. These reference shots can be used while photos taken with more professional equipment are being processed. A camera that develops the photos instantly can also be used to document particular problems or record noteworthy features during the inspection.

Many appraisers use 35mm cameras, which are easy to use and produce clear pictures. Because various kinds of photographs are required, the appraiser may need a regular lens, a wide-angle lens, and a telephoto lens as well as a flash attachment for interior photographs. Many cameras have a feature that records the date the photograph was taken on the printed photo.

With recent advances in digital photography and the decreasing price of electronics, many appraisers have started to use digital cameras. This technology allows appraisers to download images directly to a personal computer and import those files into documents using word processing and desktop publishing software.

Maps and Plats

Maps and plats can serve as useful references for the field inspection. Copies of these maps may be included as supplements to the appraisal report. Many appraisers have maps of the areas where they regularly appraise in their office files.

These maps may include

- Street and highway maps
- Address maps
- Municipal maps
- Plat books
- Census maps
- Soil maps
- Topographical maps
- Floodplain maps
- Zoning maps
- Traffic count maps
- Survey plats
- Subdivision maps

Calculators

An inexpensive pocket calculator is convenient for simple calculations. A portable financial calculator may be needed for more complex computations.

Dictation Equipment

The appraiser can use dictation equipment to record a running description of the property during the inspection and have the tape transcribed later. A variety of equipment is available commercially. Appraisers should select equipment that is compact, portable, and compatible with the transcription equipment in their offices.

Carrying Equipment

Briefcases are functional and present a professional appearance. Portfolios, catalogue cases, and file folders are also used frequently. Clipboards are very convenient for taking notes during an inspection. The appraiser may want to bring along a toolbox to carry additional equipment such as

- A screwdriver
- A pocket knife
- A flashlight
- A level to check surfaces

Miscellaneous Equipment

It is wise to have a change of clothing and extra supplies available in the office. With hiking boots, waterproof boots, and work clothes available, an appraiser is prepared to inspect rough terrain.

Figure 6.2	An Appraiser's Tools
Measuring equipment	50- to 100-ft., wind-up tape measure
	12- to 20-ft. tape measure that can be worn on a belt
	Carpenter's folding rule
	Bevel
	Straight edge
	Architect's scale
	Engineer's scale
	Graph paper
	Template
	Protractor
Photographic equipment	Polaroid camera
	35mm camera with regular, wide-angle, and telephoto lenses
	Digital camera
Maps and plats	Street and highway maps
	Address maps
	Municipal maps
	Plat books
	Census maps
	Soil maps
	Topographical maps
	Floodplain maps
	Zoning maps
	Traffic count maps
	Survey plats
	Subdivision maps
Calculators	Pocket calculator
	Financial calculator
Dictation equipment	Tape recorder that is portable, compact, and compatible with transcription equipment in the office
Carrying equipment	Briefcase
	Portfolio
	Catalog case
	File folders
	Clipboard
	Toolbox with screwdriver, pocket knife, flashlight, and level
Miscellaneous office supplies	Hiking boots
	Waterproof boots
	Work clothes
	Inspection forms

Any forms the appraiser is likely to need should be kept on hand; these include inspection forms as well as appraisal forms.

Reviewing Legal, Tax, and Assessment Information

One reason to review legal information on the property is to identify the precise area to be valued in the appraisal. Often the appraisal assignment will be to value the fee simple interest in a detached, single-family dwelling with access from a public street. The site is the area identified in the legal description of the real estate. The appraiser should verify that the legal description corresponds to the property being appraised. Sometimes other areas must be investigated as well. For example, if a right-of-way across an adjoining property runs with the title, this property should be examined to verify the ease of access.

The appraiser should review the deed or abstract of title to the property, which specifies the property rights conveyed and any limitations on these rights. The records of the county tax assessor or tax collector should be examined for information on the property's assessed value, annual tax burden, and any special assessments.

CONCEPT

The appraiser should review the legal description of the real estate, a deed or title abstract specifying the property rights conveyed, and any limitations, and tax assessment information before the field inspection.

TERM

field inspection: inspection of the physical characteristics of a site to describe its principal features and gather data that could be used in later analyses.

FIELD INSPECTION

An appraiser inspects the physical characteristics of the site to describe its principal features and any advantages or disadvantages the market is likely to consider. The appraiser then determines how the site can best be used, given its legal and physical limitations and its relationship to its surroundings. Assuming the site is put to its highest and best use, the appraiser considers how the physical characteristics of the site and the present condition of the existing site improvements add to or detract from property value. Value influences are examined in light of neighborhood and local market preferences.

Many physical characteristics of a site are considered in the site description, including

- Size and shape
- Topography, soil, and drainage
- Location, access, and environmental influences
- Onsite and offsite utilities

Size and Shape

To describe the size and shape of a site, an appraiser notes the site dimensions, including frontage, width, and depth. The appraiser plots the site's shape to calculate its area. Dimensions are usually expressed in feet and tenths of feet for easy calculation. Area is usually expressed in square feet or sometimes in acres. The appraiser also considers whether plottage (i.e., the combination of two or more sites) is desirable and whether excess or surplus land is present.

Dimensions

The site's width is the distance between the side lines of the lot. When the shape of a lot is irregular, the average width is often used. Many communities prescribe a minimum width for detached, single-family residential lots. Another important measurement is the width at the building line. Many zoning regulations specify a minimum width at this line so the site can be used to construct a particular type of improvement.

Frontage refers to the length of a site where it abuts a thoroughfare or accessway. Minimum frontage is often specified by zoning requirements. In the valuation of residential lots, front footage is sometimes used as a unit of comparison, most often in the case of waterfront properties, but the importance of frontage varies from one location to another. Consequently, care must be exercised in using this unit of comparison for residential lots. Frontage in excess of the standard amount considered acceptable in the neighborhood may not add proportionate value to the value of the lot.

Most residential neighborhoods have a standard lot depth. Lots that have less depth generally sell for less and lots with excess depth for more, but the premium or penalty is rarely proportionate to the dimensions involved. In many communities, a zoning ordinance specifies the minimum depth for detached, single-family residential lots. The minimum depth for attached, single-family residential lots varies, but these lots usually need not be as deep as detached, single-family residential lots.

The size and shape of a site affect the uses to which it can be put and therefore its value. For instance, an odd-shaped parcel may be

> **TERMS**
>
> **average width:** average measured distance between the side lines of a lot; used when the shape of a lot is irregular.
>
> **width at the building line:** distance between the side lines of a plot measured at the building line, i.e., the line established by ordinance or statute that delimits an area up to the street line where no structure is permitted.
>
> **front footage:** the distance between the side lines of a plot measured along the property line that abuts a road, waterway, railroad, or other facility.

appropriate for a dwelling but inappropriate for commercial or industrial use. Zoning, neighborhood standards, and community development goals all have an impact on how sites of various sizes and shapes may be used. Given a particular use, the appraiser can determine how the size and shape of a site affect its value by analyzing sales data on parcels of various sizes and shapes. If the subject property has a characteristic that is unusual for the neighborhood, this should be noted.

An appraiser considers not only the overall dimensions of the site but also how different parts of the site can be developed. A regularly shaped parcel may have a swamp, stream, or cliff within its borders that limits its utility. All such features should be described and their effects on value carefully considered.

Size

The size or area of a parcel is determined by its linear dimensions and by its shape. An appraiser can consider both of these variables by drawing a scale figure of the site, dividing the drawing into standard geometric figures, and calculating the area of each figure.

Specialized computers and software programs can readily compute the areas of both the site and the improvements. A geographic information system (GIS) can automate the process of computing areas. Although computer assistance is available, appraisers should be familiar with the geometric formulas for calculating areas, which are used to compute site size and to measure improvement characteristics. Some basic formulas are described and illustrated in Figure 6.3.

TERMS

geographic information system (GIS): a communications technology that combines spatial information from a national database compiled by the Bureau of the Census with computer mapping and modeling capabilities.

plottage: the increment of value created when two or more sites are combined to produce greater utility.

Plottage and Excess Land

In analyzing how site size affects site value, the appraiser must also consider plottage and excess land. Plottage is an increment of value that results when two or more sites can be assembled or combined to produce greater utility and value. A parcel has plottage value when its highest and best use is realized by combining it with one or more other parcels under a single ownership or control. When the parcels have a greater unit value together than they did separately, plottage value results. Analysis of neighboring land uses and values will indicate whether the property being appraised has plottage value.

Figure 6.3	Basic Formulas for Calculating Area

A **square** is a four-sided figure with sides of equal length that meet at right angles—i.e., angles of 90 degrees. The area of a square is the length of one side squared.

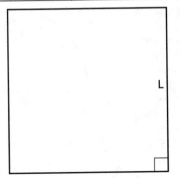

$$A = L \times L$$

Area = Length × Length

The **rectangle** is a four-sided figure with sides that meet to form right angles. Parallel sides of a rectangle are of equal length. The area of a rectangle is its length times its width.

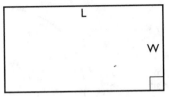

$$A = L \times W$$

Area = Length × Width

A **triangle** is a three-sided figure. The height of a triangle is measured by drawing a line from one of its corners to the side facing it, called the *base*, to intersect the base at a right angle. The area of a triangle is its height times its base divided by two.

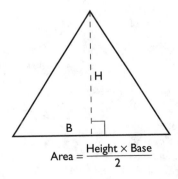

$$A = \frac{H \times B}{2}$$

$$\text{Area} = \frac{\text{Height} \times \text{Base}}{2}$$

A **trapezoid** is a four-sided figure with two parallel sides and two sides that are not parallel. The angles that join the sides in a trapezoid are not usually right angles. The area of a trapezoid is the sum of the lengths of its parallel sides, multiplied by the height, and divided by two.

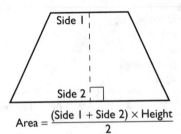

$$A = \frac{(S1 + S2) \times H}{2}$$

$$\text{Area} = \frac{(\text{Side 1} + \text{Side 2}) \times \text{Height}}{2}$$

Figure 6.3   Basic Formulas for Calculating Area *(continued)*

A **circle** is a curving figure in which all points along the curve are of an equal distance from one central point. This distance is called the circle's *radius*. A *diameter* is a line that passes through the center of the circle and divides it in half; it is always twice as long as the radius. The area of a circle is 3.1416 (π) times the radius squared.

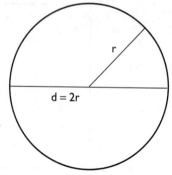

Area = 3.1416 (π) × Radius²

A **slice of a circle** is a pie-shaped area bounded by two radius lines and an arc of the circle. As the angle between the radius lines grows larger, a broader arc and larger area of the circle are sliced out. A circle has 360 degrees, so to calculate the area of a slice, divide the angle by 360 and multiply by the area of the circle.

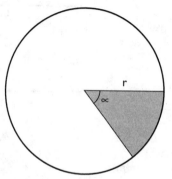

$$\text{Area} = \frac{\text{Angle subtended}}{360°} \times \text{Area of the circle}$$

To measure the area of a **fragment of a circle,** compute the larger area of the slice that corresponds to its arc and then subtract the excess triangular area. The area of the slice is calculated as described above. The area of the triangle can be found by measuring the base and height and applying the standard triangle formula, i.e., base × height/2.

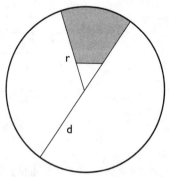

Area = Area of corresponding slice − Area of triangular shape

Excess land, defined earlier as an unused portion of a site that can have a different highest and best use than the existing improvements, differs from plottage in that excess land need not be combined with another parcel to add value. In any given market, the land and improvements that form an economic unit reflect a typical ratio. If an improved property has excess land, this land may not add a proportionate amount of value to the value of the property. Depending on its size, configuration, and location, the excess land may be considered separately from the land that supports the improvements. If the excess land is marketable or has value for a future use, its market value as vacant land constitutes an addition to the estimated value of the property.

Topography, Drainage, and Soil

To evaluate the topography of a site, an appraiser examines

TERM
topography: the relief features or surface configurations of an area, e.g., hills, valleys, slopes, lakes, rivers.

- Land contours and grades
- Natural drainage and drainage systems
- Soil conditions

Land Contours

All variations in elevation should be described. Sites with extreme topographical features tend to have lower values because of the increased cost of building improvements. Steep slopes are more susceptible to landslides and may increase construction costs or preclude construction altogether. In some cases, however, the disadvantages of a high elevation may be offset by an excellent view.

An ideal residential lot has a slope that rises slightly from the street to the improvement and then gently falls off. What is desirable in one neighborhood, however, is not necessarily desirable in another. A lot that is higher or lower than the level of the abutting street may create additional costs for owners due to poor drainage, erosion, or diminished accessibility. If the site is unimproved, these features can limit the usefulness of the site for development.

Drainage

Drainage depends on natural topography and the ability of the soil to absorb water. Natural drainage may be a problem if the site is downstream from properties that have a right to direct excess flows onto it. Some system must be provided to drain the site of surface water and groundwater. Storm sewers should be present in the water disposal

TERM

drainage: a system of drains (e.g., tiles, pipes, conduits) designed to remove surface or subsurface water or waste water and sewage.

area. In some cases, a simple swale, or shallow depression in the land, may efficiently channel the water from the surface of the lot to the street or into natural drainage, or a system of tiles can be used to remove surface and subsurface water from some sites. When the site is located in a designated flood hazard area, the appraiser must consider whether any of the topographical features of the site increase or decrease its susceptibility to flooding in comparison with other neighborhood properties.

The appraiser should be particularly concerned with how the site's drainage characteristics may affect the improvements. A house with a basement must have drains to carry the water out from under the basement and prevent leaks from developing. If a house is built on a slope, special precautions must be taken to keep the runoff water away from the sides of the house.

Soil Conditions

The character of the subsoil can have a substantial effect on the usefulness of a site and the cost of preparing it for building. Subsoil quality can also affect where improvements can be constructed on the site and influence building design. If bedrock must be blasted or the soil is unstable, the cost of improving the site will increase. Similarly, extra expenses may be incurred for building foundation walls or sinking piles if a site must be filled in. Percolation, permeability, and the absorption capacity of the soil must be considered to assess the site's suitability for septic and storm water systems.

In many areas the fertility of the surface soil of a site can affect the lawn and landscaping surrounding the property, which are important to the site's marketability. The appraiser notes whether the soil appears to be suitable for cultivation and typical of the surrounding neighborhood. When appraising a new subdivision, an appraiser determines whether or not the natural surface soil, the topsoil, will need to be replaced after construction with better soil. If the topsoil is naturally sandy or rocky, it may need to be replaced.

Frequently subsoil conditions are known to local builders and developers. An appraiser may ask that an engineer trained in soil mechanics be retained to test the quality of the soil for construction, but an expensive soil study is not usually part of the appraisal. If the soil-bearing capacity is in doubt, however, the appraiser should inform the client of the need for a soil study. If soil tests are not made, the appraiser must describe the assumptions made concerning soil characteristics in the limiting conditions and assumptions section of the report.

Location, Access, and Environmental Influences

The study of location includes analysis of

- The relationship between the site and transportation routes and neighborhood facilities
- The type and orientation of the lot within the existing street pattern
- Access to the site
- Street improvements
- Environmental nuisances and hazards
- Climate and view

Transportation

The highest and best use of the site and therefore its value are strongly affected by the site's location in relation to transportation routes. Lots that are far away from major transportation routes or accessible only from narrow streets are less appealing to commercial and industrial users. Lots with easy access to schools, workplaces, and recreational facilities often have greater appeal to residential users. Both vehicular and pedestrian access should be considered.

The quality of highways and the density of traffic during rush hours are also important considerations in the study of transportation. The availability, proximity, and quality of public transportation systems are also significant, particularly if many neighborhood residents commute. An appraiser is especially interested in any aspects of the site that make it different from other neighborhood sites and from comparable properties.

Lot Type and Orientation

Some common types of lots are

- Interior
- Corner
- Cul-de-sac
- Flag

Interior lots have frontage on only one street. The main access to the lot is usually from that street, although a rear alley may also provide access. Interior lots are often the most regular in shape, particularly if the neighborhood is designed in a grid format. When inspecting interior and cul-de-sac lots, the appraiser should note the distance and direction to the nearest intersection(s).

Corner lots have frontage on two or more streets—often a main street and a side street. These lots often appeal to commercial users because of their increased visibility, greater frontage, and more convenient access from the rear.

If the highest and best use of the site is for residential use, a corner location may pose both advantages and disadvantages. A corner site can have an automobile entrance on the side street, thus reducing driveway areas. This can be especially advantageous in areas where interior lots have little frontage. Corner lots may also allow greater flexibility in the building layout and provide more light and air than interior lots.

However, corner lots may also have disadvantages such as less privacy, less security, and greater susceptibility to traffic hazards and nuisances. Corner lots may have two building setback lines, one from each street, which reduces the area on which improvements can be built. For this reason, corner lots are generally larger than interior lots. Corner sites may also be subject to higher special assessments because they have more sidewalk area and street frontage. Because corner sites have both advantages and disadvantages in the market, an appraiser must assess the impact of such a location, called *corner influence*, by studying market data.

Cul-de-sac lots are located at the end of dead-end streets where circular turn-around areas are common. These lots are generally tapered, have very little frontage, and are somewhat irregular in shape. Parking may be more difficult on cul-de-sac lots, but there can be compensatory advantages. Cul-de-sac lots may have bigger backyards and less street traffic, so they may be particularly desirable to families with children.

A flag lot is a rear lot with a long narrow accessway. The lot and access route resemble the shape of a flag on a pole. Flag lots have greater privacy, but a residence built on such a lot may be difficult to find and have poor access.

Access to the Site

Access to the site is closely related to lot type. Access may be provided by a public street or alley, a private road or driveway, or a right-of-way across an abutting property. When access depends on a private road, the appraiser should find out who maintains the road and

Figure 6.4	Types of Lots

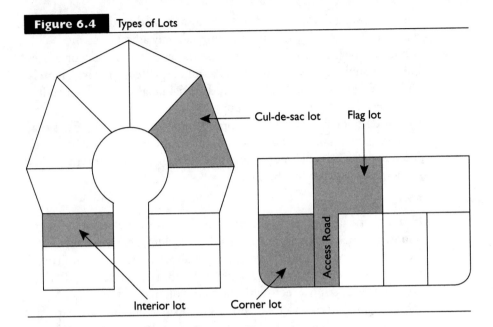

whether the lending institutions serving the neighborhood write mortgages for houses without a public street address.

The ease of entry to the lot by car is also noted. The grade of the driveway should provide reasonably convenient access. Lots with driveways that slope up to the street are often less desirable than lots with driveways that are level or slope down. It is dangerous to back into traffic or enter traffic when oncoming cars cannot be seen well. The market often penalizes a site for access problems.

Street Improvements

The quality and condition of abutting streets and street improvements also affect the value of a site. A description of street improvements includes information on the width of the street or alley, the type of paving, and the condition. The direction of traffic and the number of lanes are also important, as are the quality and condition of gutters and storm sewers, curbs, streetlights, sidewalks, trees and plantings, and bicycle lanes. In some areas lenders may require additional information if the property frontage is on a private road.

Nuisances

Convenient service facilities contribute to the value of a site, but they can detract from site value if they are too close. Hospitals, firehouses, gas stations, public schools, stores, restaurants, and medical offices are desirable if they are nearby but not immediately adjacent to the property. The presence of industrial plants, large commercial or office buildings, noisy highways, utility poles and high-tension wires, motels and hotels, and vacant houses in a residential neighborhood generally has a negative effect on nearby property values. Uses that do not mix well or do not conform to neighborhood standards and properties that are poorly maintained or produce odors, noises, and pests can decrease the value of residential properties and may suggest an alternative highest and best use for the site.

Hazards

Heavy traffic is the most common hazard in residential neighborhoods. The market often recognizes this problem, and properties located on heavily traveled streets are penalized for their proximity to noise, fumes, congestion, and accidents. Within the same neighborhood, lots bordering streets with different volumes of traffic can have substantially different values. Families with small children are particularly concerned about traffic hazards. Speed controls, speed bumps, and well-maintained sidewalks to schools and play areas can reduce traffic hazards.

The potential for floods, landslides, and earthquakes must be considered as well as the hazards presented by ravines, bodies of water, subsurface mines, gasoline storage tanks, toxic wastes, and railroads. If possible hazards are observed in the neighborhood, the appraiser should investigate what measures have been taken to protect the subject property from danger.

In some areas radon gas, which can cause lung cancer, percolates up through the soil and infiltrates homes. Even when high concentrations of radon are found in the soil surrounding a residence, experts do not yet know whether the interior of the house will have a high level of radon as well.

Flood hazards are especially important in appraisals because in many parts of the country lenders cannot issue a mortgage in a flood hazard area unless the mortgagor purchases flood insurance. If an appraiser learns that the site being appraised is in an identified flood hazard area, the appraiser should investigate the availability and cost of flood insurance. The potential for flooding on the subject property and comparable sites must be discussed in the appraisal report.

Local government offices often maintain flood maps and officials will know whether or not a site is in a flood zone. It is wise to obtain copies of local flood maps for regular office use. Figure 6.5 is an example of a county flood map. These maps identify different kinds of flood zones such as areas of 100-year flooding or areas of 100- to 500-year shallow flooding. Maps are also available from the Federal Emergency Management Agency (FEMA). Most clients require that the appraiser cite the FEMA panel number in the appraisal report.

> **TERM**
>
> **Federal Emergency Management Agency (FEMA):** a federal agency established by the Flood Disaster Protection Act to provide directives on where to build and where not to build in coastal and floodplain areas.

Climate

Most climatic conditions affect the subject property and comparable properties in the same way, so general climatic conditions are usually described with community and neighborhood characteristics. However, a particular site may benefit or suffer from a special climatic characteristic such as high winds. If so, this must be noted in the site description. Climatic conditions may suggest the best orientation for building improvements. If the position of the site relative to the street precludes a building orientation that suits climatic conditions, a value penalty may result.

The significance of climate and its effect on property value may differ depending on the highest and best use of the site. The appraiser must consider how climatic considerations and other environmental influences affect the highest and best use of the site.

View

The view from a property can substantially affect its value. Lots in the same neighborhood that are similar in all respects except their locations and orientation often have different values attributable to the difference in view. Views of water, mountains, or valleys are most popular. A commanding view of the surrounding landscape can sometimes compensate for adverse topographic or climatic characteristics. Conversely, a poor view can produce a value penalty. An appraiser should also consider the likelihood of the property's view being obstructed in the near future.

Onsite and Offsite Utilities

An appraiser inspects the utilities present on the site and those that are available nearby. Essential utilities in most residential markets include

- Water
- Electricity

Figure 6.5   Flood Map

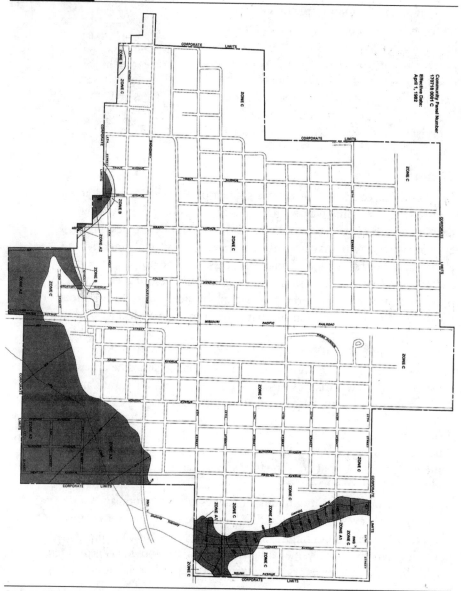

Courtesy of Digital Media Services, Perrineville, New Jersey

- Natural or propane gas
- Telephone and data lines for Internet connections
- Sewerage
- Trash collection
- Cable television

If the utilities on the site are inadequate, the availability and cost of obtaining utility service must be considered. Both highest and best use and site value may be strongly affected by the availability of utilities.

Water

A residential site must have an adequate supply of acceptable water. Water may be obtained from a municipal or private company or from a well. FHA minimum property standards require that a public water supply be used if one is available. Some residents obtain water directly from rivers, streams, or lakes or from rainwater collected and stored in tanks on the roof. These houses are not considered satisfactory by FHA standards because they do not have a consistent, adequate supply of safe water.

When water is supplied by a public utility or a publicly regulated company, the appraiser usually checks its availability on the site and determines if the water pressure is sufficient. When water is supplied by an unregulated company, the appraiser must report this fact and investigate the dependability of the water supply. Shallow or artesian wells should be capable of sustaining a flow of five gallons per minute. The water should meet the bacterial and chemical purification requirements set by local health authorities.

When appraising vacant land that is not linked to a public water supply, an appraiser may try to determine the likelihood of finding an adequate water supply for the site by checking the wells dug on surrounding properties.

Sewage Disposal

Connection to a municipal sewage system is usually desirable, but many areas have no sewer system. If no public sewers exist, a percolation test may be required to determine whether the soil on the site can absorb the runoff from a septic system, or if some other private sewage disposal system is required. If a percolation test is not made, this fact should be reported in the appraisal report.

TERM

percolation test: a test conducted by hydraulic engineers and others to determine the percolation rate of soil; used by health departments to determine the amount of land area needed for the operation of a septic system.

Garbage Collection

Some sites are not served by garbage collection services because they are located on private roads or in rural areas. If these services must be purchased separately, a value penalty may result depending on the expectations of market participants in the area. In the absence of public disposal systems, owners may resort to using private dump sites, which create many problems.

CONCEPT

The appraiser should prepare a plot plan drawn to scale, showing lot boundaries and dimensions, topographical features, the location of improvements, and any legal limitations on property rights.

DRAWING A PLOT PLAN

To complete the site description, the appraiser draws a plot plan that shows the boundaries of the lot and the location of all improvements. The plot plan can also be created with the proper measurements using appropriate computer software. A good plot plan is drawn to scale, with lot dimensions indicated on the boundary lines. In addition to the house and the garage or carport, the plot plan may show sidewalks, driveways, patios, and pools. Any rights-of-way, easements, or encroachments should also be indicated on the plan. A typical plot plan is depicted in Figure 6.6.

Figure 6.6 Plot Plan Drawing

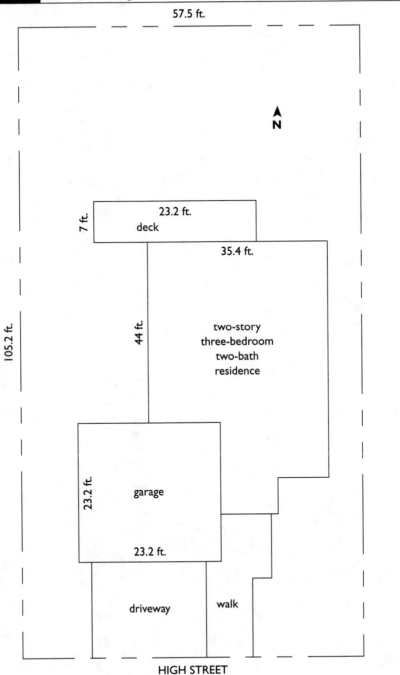

Courtesy of Johnson Appraisal Services, Breckenridge, Colorado

CHAPTER 7

BUILDING DESCRIPTION

Once the site has been examined, the appraiser is ready to begin inspecting the improvements. An appraiser describes improvements by noting the size, style, design, and layout of all buildings; examining the construction quality and maintenance condition of each building; and describing the structural components, materials, and mechanical systems as well as the quality and condition of each component. Any special problems are noted. The appraiser considers how the building elements observed combine with the site's characteristics to shape the highest and best use of the property as improved. Any problems or deficiencies in the present condition of the improvements that might prevent the property from realizing its highest and best use must be described.

> **CONCEPT**
>
> In the building description, the appraiser notes the size, style, design, layout, construction quality, and maintenance of the improvement(s).

To complete the building description step properly, an appraiser must be familiar with building design and construction. The purpose of the building description, the background data and materials needed, and the steps normally taken to complete this stage in the valuation process are discussed in this chapter, along with architectural style, building design and layout, and the house zones and rooms found in residential properties. Chapter 8 rounds out this discussion with information on building construction and the mechanical systems used in residential properties. In that chapter, specific structural components, equipment, and attachments are covered in depth.

PURPOSES OF BUILDING DESCRIPTION

A building description can help an appraiser select suitable comparable properties from a preliminary list of potential comparables. In the sales comparison approach, the appraiser uses the complete building description of the subject property to make adjustments for differences between the subject and each of the comparable properties. The building description also provides the data needed to estimate reproduction or replacement cost and depreciation in the cost approach and operating and maintenance expenses in the income capitalization approach. Thus, the quality of the building inspection and description directly affects the reliability of all three approaches to value.

Background Data and Building Inspection Materials

Much of the background data and building inspection equipment used in the site inspection is needed again for the building inspection. The following items are especially important:

- Information on zoning and building codes
- Blueprints or plans
- An appraisal form or checklist

Zoning and Building Codes

The appraiser should be thoroughly familiar with all zoning regulations, building codes, and private restrictions that are applicable to the subject property. This information is needed to determine whether existing or potential property uses conform to local codes. The design and construction of buildings are regulated by building, plumbing, electrical, and mechanical codes and may be limited by deed restrictions as well.

During the building inspection the appraiser should look for current uses that do not conform to legal requirements and consider how these uses might affect the property's value. If, for example, a garage has been remodeled without a building permit, it may now require upgrading to meet building code standards. A building that does not comply with local codes probably has less value than a similar building that does. Making a building conform to the standards set forth in the code may produce additional expenses for its owners and limit the future use of the building.

Blueprints or Plans

When building blueprints or plans are available, they can help an appraiser identify the structural and mechanical details of an improvement. Plans and blueprints may also be used to verify the dimensions of a building, but an appraiser cannot rely on plans for size calculations. The appraiser must measure the improvements during the building inspection because the plans may not have been followed accurately or, more likely, alterations and additions may have been made after the plans were prepared.

Appraisal Form or Checklist

The appraiser may want to bring a checklist to the building inspection to ensure that no important items are overlooked.

DESCRIBING AND RATING THE IMPROVEMENTS

With the data requirements in mind and the necessary equipment and materials at hand, the appraiser is ready to begin inspecting the improvements. In each step of the inspection, the appraiser performs two tasks: he or she describes and classifies the building element being studied, and then rates the element. Each physical component must be rated for quality and condition to determine the building's effective age (the age indicated by the condition and utility of the structure) as opposed to its actual age (the number of years that have elapsed since building construction was completed). Effective age is determined by the appraiser's judgment; it is not market-derived. The rating process is called a *quality and condition survey*. Layouts and designs are also considered in terms of their functional utility. The appraiser determines how the functional utility of the building relates to its construction quality and maintenance.

In the context of a building description, *quality* refers to the character of construction and the materials used in the original work. The physical deterioration of the improvements is not considered in rating their quality. When well-chosen materials are applied in a suitable manner with sound construction techniques and good workmanship, quality is produced. Published cost-estimating guides provide four quality ratings—low, average, good, and very good to excellent—and indicate separate costs for each category.

A structure may have a functional layout and attractive design but be constructed with inferior materials and

> **TERMS**
>
> **quality and condition survey:** an analysis of the quality and condition of building components that distinguishes among deferred maintenance items (those in need of immediate repair), short-lived items (those that must be repaired or replaced in the future), and items that are expected to last for the remaining economic life of the building.
>
> **functional utility:** the ability of a property or building to be useful and to perform the function for which it is intended according to current market tastes and standards; the efficiency of a building's use in terms of architectural style, design and layout, traffic patterns, and the size and type of rooms.

poor workmanship. These deficiencies increase maintenance and utility costs and affect the marketability of a property adversely. On the other hand, a building can be too well constructed—i.e., its cost is not justified by its utility. Most purchasers will not want to pay excess costs even though they may be recaptured through reduced maintenance expenses.

An excess in the capacity or quality of a structural component, as determined by market standards, is called a *superadequacy*. For example, a single-family house with an antique wrought-iron fence would have a superadequacy if the houses in the market generally had chain link fences. Superadequacies should be considered in the quality survey, as should the related concept of overimprovement. An overimprovement is an improvement that does not represent the maximally productive use of the site on which it is placed because it is too large or costly and cannot develop the highest possible land value. For example, a house with a below-ground pool in the backyard would be an overimprovement in a transitional neighborhood, where the value of that property is constrained by the declining values of the surrounding properties.

Conversely, a deficiency is an inadequacy in a structural component, as determined by market standards. For example, a single-family house with a laundry area not wide enough to comfortably accommodate a modern washer and dryer suffers from a deficiency. An improvement that is inadequate to develop the highest and best use of its site is an underimprovement. Underimprovements are usually structures of lesser cost, quality, and size than typical properties in the neighborhood. For example, a three-bedroom house with a one-car garage in a neighborhood where garages generally accommodate two cars would be an underimprovement.

The *condition* of an improvement refers to the extent of physical deterioration or structural damage. Overall wear and tear and the level of maintenance dictate a building's condition. An appraiser generally

TERMS

superadequacy: an excess in the capacity or quality of a structure or structural component; determined by market standards.

overimprovement: an improvement that does not represent the most profitable use for the site on which it is placed because it is too large or costly and cannot develop the highest possible land value; may be temporary or permanent.

deficiency: an inadequacy in a structure or one of its components; determined by market standards.

underimprovement: an improvement that is inadequate to develop the highest and best use of its site; usually a structure that is of lesser cost, quality, and size than typical neighborhood properties.

distinguishes between items that must be repaired immediately and those that may be repaired or replaced later.

Functional utility is the ability of a property or building to be useful and to perform the function for which it is intended, according to current market preferences and standards. The term also refers to the efficiency of a building's use in terms of architectural style, design and layout, traffic patterns, size and type of rooms, and energy efficiency. A building may have functional utility but an undistinguished architectural style, while another building may have an admired style but little utility. Form and function should work together to create successful architecture. An appraiser considers the functional utility of a building in relation to its construction quality and condition.

STEPS IN THE BUILDING DESCRIPTION

There is no set sequence of steps in the building description that can be used for all appraisals. Different types of properties and varying appraisal styles dictate that different procedures be used to inspect improvements. The following steps are presented in a sequence common to many appraisals.

The appraiser begins by observing the general placement of the improvements on the subject site and considering the effects of their location. The exterior of the residence is examined in detail, starting with the foundation, framing, exterior covering, and roof.

> **TERM**
>
> **compatibility:** the concept that a building is in harmony with its use(s) and its environment.

(These structural components are discussed in the next chapter.) The building features and the materials used are noted, and each feature is rated for quality of construction, condition, and market appeal. The appraiser measures the exterior dimensions of the main improvement and draws a scale diagram of the improvement on a sheet of graph paper. Photographs of the improvements are taken, the architectural style of the main improvement is identified, and the compatibility of the residence with its use and environment is considered.

The interior of the residence is inspected next. The appraiser notes the number and type of rooms and considers the functional utility of the layout. The quality of workmanship and the materials used in the interior finish are examined. Potential problems are carefully studied, and their cause and cost of repair are evaluated. Photographs of the interior of the improvement are often taken.

During the interior inspection the appraiser also checks the mechanical systems—heating, cooling, electrical, plumbing, hot water, and waste disposal. (Mechanical systems and equipment are described in the next chapter.) Air-conditioning, insulation, and energy efficiency are investigated and any built-in equipment is inspected.

Building additions such as porches, patios, decks, and balconies are examined, and wall attachments, stairs, roof attachments, special rooms, basements, and attic areas are inspected. Finally the appraiser returns outside and examines the garage and any outbuildings. These structures are rated for construction quality, condition, and market appeal.

Orientation and Placement of Improvements on the Site

As mentioned previously, an appraiser observes the location and orientation of the improvements on the site at the outset of the building inspection. In examining the improvements, the appraiser notes how the residence is situated in relation to the sun and how it is adapted to the benefits or constraints of the site location.

During the summer, the sun rises in the northeast, travels in a high arc, and sets in the northwest. During the winter, it rises in the southeast, travels in a low arc, and sets in the southwest. A well-designed house takes advantage of the movement of the sun with a southward orientation and small or few windows to prevent air leakage. A large roof overhang shades the house in the summer months when the sun is high. In the winter when the sun is low, the warmth of the sun can enter the windows of the house. Outbuildings, trees, and vegetation that are appropriately placed can shelter the main improvement from the sun, wind, and noise.

Size Measurements, Diagrams, and Photographs

Measuring Size

Determining the size of a building is sometimes a formidable task. Methods and techniques for calculating building size vary regionally and according to property type; local practices may reflect biases that significantly affect value opinions. Appraisers must be familiar with the measurement techniques used in their areas as well as those used elsewhere in the market. An appraiser must also be consistent in the use, interpretation, and reporting of building measurements within each assignment. Failure to do so can adversely affect the quality of the appraisal report.

The most common building measurement, gross living area, is always calculated. The dimensions of a building can be ascertained from plans, but these dimensions should be checked against the actual building measurements. The area of attached porches, detached garages, and minor improvements is calculated separately.

Standards for measuring residential properties have been developed by several federal agencies, including the FHA, VA, Fannie Mae, and Freddie Mac.[1] Because these agencies are major players in the mortgage market, their standards are used in millions of appraisals. Gross living area is the standard measure applied to single-family residences. *Gross living area* is defined as the total area of finished, above-grade residential space. It is calculated by measuring the area within the outside perimeter of a house and includes finished and habitable, above-grade living area only. Finished basement or attic areas are not included in total gross living area.

The gross living area of a rectangular house is measured by attaching the end of the tape measure to one exterior corner of the residence, measuring the distance to the next corner, and then repeating this process until all exterior walls have been covered. After noting the measurements on a rough diagram of the house, the appraiser checks to see whether the measurements of parallel sides of the structure are equivalent. This procedure is known as squaring the house. The total front building measurements should equal the total rear measurements, and the total left-side measurements should equal the total right-side measurements. Minor discrepancies may suggest that the corners of the structure are not perfect right angles, while greater discrepancies may be attributable to errors in measuring or to rounding inconsistencies.

If the house has attachments or an irregular shape, the appraiser sketches the shape of

CONCEPT

Most houses are measured in terms of gross living area—the total area of finished, above-grade residential space. Even if building plans are available, actual measurements must be taken by the appraiser.

Gross living area, as defined by Fannie Mae, is calculated for all residential properties (except condominiums and cooperatives) using the exterior building dimensions of each floor. Garages and basements are excluded. Fannie Mae considers a level to be below grade if any portion of it is below grade, regardless of the quality of its finish or the window area of any room. Therefore, a walk-out basement with finished rooms would not be included in gross living area.

The agency does recognize that below-grade rooms not included in gross living area may contribute substantially to the value of a property, particularly when the quality of the finish is high. In completing the URAR form, the appraiser reports such areas on the line provided for "basement and finished areas below grade," which appears in the sales comparison analysis adjustment grid, according to Fannie Mae, *Property and Appraisal Analysis: Reviewing the Appraisal Report* (Washington, D.C.: U.S. Government Printing Office, June 30, 1990), section 404.06, 757-758. For further discussion of problems encountered in measuring gross living area, see Cliff L. Cryer, MAI, "How Big Is This House?" *The Real Estate Appraiser* (April 1992): 21-26.

---

1. The American National Standards Institute has created standards for the measurement of residential properties. These standards have been adopted by the National Association of Homebuilders (NAHB), but certain aspects of the standards remain controversial. In 1996, the NAHB Research Center Inc. published *Method for Calculating Square Footage of Single-Family Residential Buildings* (ANSI Z765-1996) to allow organizations that use different terminologies to calculate quantities on a common basis.

the house and measures each side. Once all the measurements have been verified, the appraiser divides the figure drawn into smaller geometric units, calculates the area of each, and adds the areas together. (Formulas for calculating the area of various geometric shapes were presented in Chapter 6.) Areas not normally considered part of the gross living area such as attached garages and entryways must be excluded from the calculations. Computer programs are available for calculating areas, but the appraiser must still "square the house" to obtain the measurements.

An appraiser should never accept a statement as to the size of the subject residence without verification. However, the sizes of comparable properties can often be obtained from tax records, real estate brokers, and other appraisers.

The method applied to calculate property size must also be determined. If an unverified statement of property size is used in a value analysis, the resulting opinion could be erroneous. Different description practices in local and regional markets further complicate the situation. For example, a comparison of condominiums based on square footage may produce inaccurate results if the size of the subject property is expressed in terms of net living area, which is measured along interior walls, while the comparable data are expressed in terms of gross salable area.

Sketch of the House

A sketch or floor plan of the residence and its garage or carport showing the location of doors, windows, and interior walls is sometimes included as part of an appraisal report. Many appraisers take pride in their ability to draw professional diagrams, but detailed drawings are not required for most residential appraisals. Simple, neat sketches drawn to approximate scale are usually requested by lenders. These sketches should indicate the placement of interior walls and show the same dimensions used to calculate the gross living area.

Photography

Photographs are an important part of an appraisal report. Photographs that are out of focus or badly developed are not acceptable. Instant photographs are acceptable in some circumstances, but more professional photographs taken with a 35mm camera are often preferred. Color photographs have become a standard part of appraisal reports in many parts of the country. Color photographs taken with a digital camera and output on a high-quality color printer are increasingly common and affordable.

There is no general rule as to what property features should be photographed. At a minimum, appraisal reports should include

- Photographs of the front and rear of the house, showing the sides as well
- Photographs of any major site improvements
- A street scene

If the assignment warrants the additional expense, photographs of construction details and the interior of the house should also be included.

ARCHITECTURAL STYLES

In the building description, the appraiser identifies the architectural style of the main improvement and considers its effect on property value. Architectural style is the character of a building's form and ornamentation. A wide variety of architectural styles may be identified. An appraiser uses the system of description or identification prevalent in the specific market area so that the client and other users of the appraisal report will understand the style identified.

> **TERM**
>
> **architectural style:** the character of a building's form and ornamentation.

Architectural Compatibility

One important factor affecting the desirability of a particular architectural style is its conformity or compatibility with the standards of the market. Compatibility indicates that a building is in harmony with its use or uses and its environment. This harmony applies to the form, materials, and scale of the structure. Styles of different periods frequently clash. A cubistic dwelling would not harmonize with eighteenth-century colonial buildings. A monumental or ostentatious building is out of place in a modest setting. Market value is frequently diminished by incompatibility of design.

There are several types of incompatibility. The various elements of a structure can be incompatible with one another. Alternatively,

> **CONCEPT**
>
> An appraiser identifies the building's architectural style and considers whether the building is compatible and in harmony with its uses and environment.

a structure can be incompatible with its site or location in the neighborhood. Compatibility is influenced by a variety of factors, including

- Zoning
- Construction and maintenance costs
- Land value
- The physical features of the site
- Architectural trends
- Technology

Sometimes these influences impose conformity.

The materials used in a structure should be in harmony with one another and with the building's architectural style. A building designed to be built of a particular material will not necessarily be effective if it is constructed of another material. An architectural design should not combine distracting features or building materials that vary excessively.

Architectural design and building materials should be well integrated and in harmony with the site. A frame building in a wooded, hilly area will probably harmonize with its setting more than a brick building. A frame residence located in a neighborhood of brick homes usually suffers a value penalty.

Perhaps most important, the architectural style of a building should be in harmony with the styles of neighborhood structures and with market standards. Often the predominant uses and building styles in an area can be readily observed; however, the trend of development may be more difficult to discern. An architectural style that appears atypical may actually indicate a future trend.

The impact of a nonconforming building design should be carefully considered. A somewhat unusual design that is attractive and generally in harmony with other buildings in the area may command a higher price than its more typical neighbors. A house with an incongruous design, however, will probably sell at a price below the general market level. If it does not, it may have special features that compensate for its lack of conformity.

Evaluating the value effect of a nonconforming design may require appraisal judgment. There may be sufficient demand for a detached dwelling in a neighborhood of row houses to mitigate any value penalty resulting from incompatibility. Sometimes functional utility may override design as a primary market requirement. If the general proportions and scale of an atypical building are in harmony with its surroundings and the structure has functional utility, the unusual design may not impose a value penalty. In any case, the positive and negative effects of a building's nonconformity should be carefully considered.

Trends in Architectural Styles

Neighborhood properties that conform to the standards of the local market generally have the highest value in relation to construction costs. Although there is room in a free market economy for individual expression, commonly shared tastes characterize most of the real estate market. These preferences form the standards of the market, but market standards do change over time.

Market tastes and standards are influenced by both the desire to preserve tradition and the desire for change, variety, and efficiency. Architectural trends respond to the desire to preserve tradition by incorporating elements of past architectural styles, while new elements of architectural design are developed in response to the desire for change.

When an architectural style becomes extreme, tastes may shift back to past styles. Extreme ornateness is often replaced with simple forms. A reactive shift provides contrast to the dominant architectural style that precedes it. Changing tastes produce avant garde or experimental building styles, which are ultimately tested in the market. An experimental style eventually is abandoned or becomes accepted. Design elements discarded in a reactive swing are not lost forever, however. Old forms may disappear for a time and later reappear in a modified form. Figure 7.1 illustrates some common architectural styles.

Changes in architectural style often correspond to the economic life cycles of buildings. Major revisions in architectural styles typically occur at the end of a building life cycle, about every 30 to 50 years.

Newly constructed buildings, which may or may not be designed by professional architects, tend to have broad market appeal. When a building is no longer new, however, it will be compared with other buildings in terms of the quality and functionality of its architectural style. Form and structure are the most basic components of architectural style. They define the possible uses and modifications of a building, and their influence on value increases as time goes by.

Various architectural styles are found in different parts of the country. These style differences can largely be attributed to the availability of natural materials such as wood, stone, and clay and to differences in climate. Changes in building technology have made

Figure 7.1 Common Architectural Styles

Cape Cod

Garrison Colonial

Dutch Colonial

Southern Colonial

California Ranch

Georgian

Tudor

Queen Anne—Victorian

Contemporary

Spanish Villa

Eastern Brick Row Houses

Bungalow

styles more uniform in recent years and have changed the way buildings are designed and constructed.

The development of the Franklin stove, for example, modified the layout of rooms in residences because fireplaces were no longer needed to provide heat. The introduction of household appliances in the early twentieth century eliminated the need for root cellars, pantries, and large laundry rooms, reducing the number of rooms in homes and changing room arrangements.

The prevalent use of central heating and air-conditioning in the mid-twentieth century has resulted in the standardization of architectural styles throughout the country. Regional building styles that were developed to use local building materials and meet the demands of climate have been almost obliterated. The thick, mud masonry walls and small windows of Southwestern architecture were well-suited to the hot, dry weather of the region. Overhanging roofs were used on homes in the rainy Northwest so that windows could be opened for ventilation without admitting the rain. The saltbox houses of New England were windowless and steep-roofed on one side to provide protection against the harsh north wind.

Although central heating and air-conditioning made many regional style differences unnecessary, energy considerations have become important, and builders have once again begun to incorporate structural defenses against climate into new construction. Thus, an energy-conscious market has prompted climate-compatible designs to resurface. Energy-saving features must be considered in estimating market value because consumers have become increasingly interested in energy conservation.

Types of Houses

To describe the architectural style of a residence and evaluate its conformity or compatibility with market tastes and standards, appraisers should be familiar with the advantages and disadvantages of various types of houses. Common house designs include one-story, one and one-half story, two-story, bi-level, and split-level houses. These types of houses and others are discussed below.

One-Story House

A one-story house may be a ranch, a rambler, or a bungalow. The entire living area in this type of house is on ground level. One-story houses have proven to be acceptable in the resale market. They generally have a simple design that can be adapted to any type of topo-

Figure 7.2 One-Story House

graphy. Because most of the exterior is accessible, a one-story house is easier to maintain and attachments can be made at ground level. The absence of stairs is appealing to many purchasers.

A one-story house has disadvantages too. All the living area is on one level, so noise spreads throughout the house. In some communities, a single-story design is associated with tract developments, which may have limited appeal. A one-story house generally requires a wider lot than other house designs and houses of this type have the highest ratio of foundation and roof area to living area, which results in higher construction costs per square foot. Furthermore, without sufficient screening or proper site placement, a one-story house may lack privacy.

One and One-Half Story House

A one and one-half story house, which is called a *Cape Cod* in some areas, usually has its main rooms and one bedroom and bathroom on the ground floor. Other bedrooms and bathrooms may be located on

Figure 7.3   One and One-Half Story House

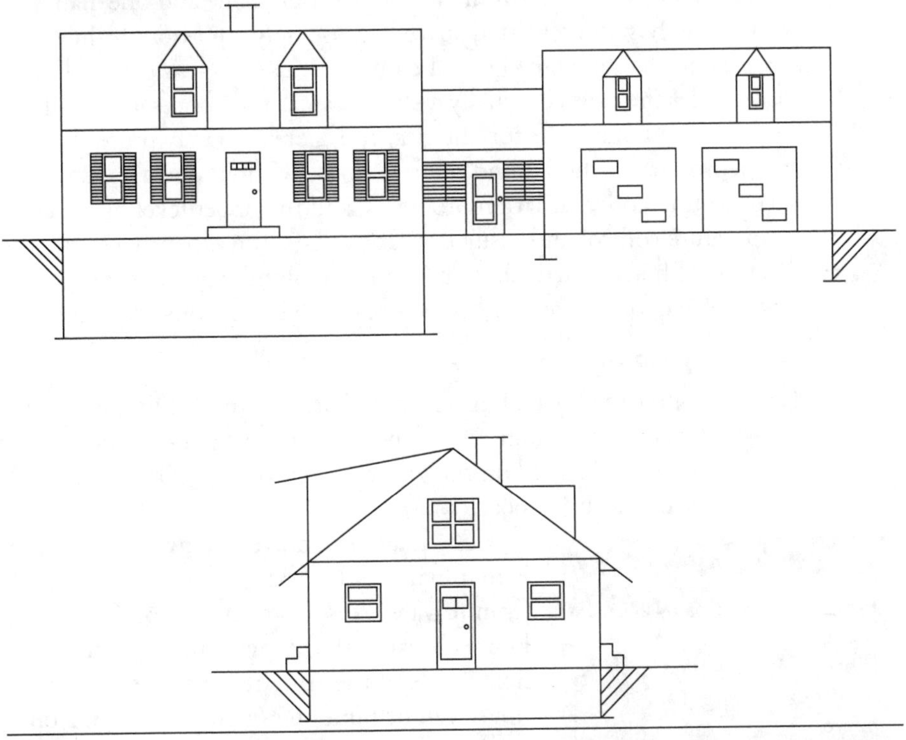

the second floor, or the entire second floor may be unfinished and used for storage.

One advantage of a one and one-half story house is its compactness. This type of house is less expensive to heat than a one-story residence with the same square foot area. A one and one-half story house also has visual appeal. Houses with dormers can be especially attractive. During the 1950s and 1960s, many of these homes were built and sold with only the first floor finished. The second floor was often completed later to provide extra living space for an expanding family. These houses provide a practical advantage to growing families with limited means.

In certain markets the one and one-half story house design is regarded as old-fashioned. The design has other disadvantages. The stairway to the second floor in such a house is often narrow and steep.

TERM

one and one-half story house: a dwelling based on the design of a single-story cottage with additional bedrooms and bathrooms or unfinished storage space on a second floor; called a Cape Cod in some areas.

These stairs take up little room on the ground floor, but they make it very difficult to move furniture upstairs. Often a one and one-half story house has much wasted space because only a portion of the second floor has enough ceiling height to be used as living area. The space under the eaves is usually a storage area. The rooms are small in many one and one-half story homes, and there are rarely more than two bedrooms on the ground floor. A house without dormers may have lighting and ventilation problems, and the upper level may lack temperature control and insulation. It can be quite expensive to finish this type of house, particularly if electricity, plumbing, and other services have to be extended to the upper level after construction.

Two-Story House

Two-story houses may be built in several architectural styles. In most two-story homes, the main rooms and sometimes a guest bedroom and bathroom are located on the ground floor; other bedrooms and bathrooms are on the upper floor.

> **TERM**
>
> **two-story house:** a dwelling with two levels in which the lower level is at ground level, differentiating it from a bi-level house.

The main advantage of a two-story house is that living and working areas are separated from private areas. Many buyers prefer these houses because they suggest the gracious living style of the American past. A two-story house can be built on a smaller lot than a one-story house with the same amount of living area. Foundation and roof costs are lower for the same total floor area.

The stairway that connects the ground level to the private areas of a two-story house can pose problems. Closets and storage areas can make good use of the space under the stairway, but rooms on the second level have no direct access to the exterior. This can be hazardous in the event of a fire or emergency. Furthermore, a two-story design is not easily adapted for expansion upward or outward.

Bi-Level House

A bi-level may also be known as a *raised ranch* or *split-foyer* house.[2] The living area in a bi-level house is all on the upper level. The lower level may serve as an extra family room, recreation room, or spare bedroom. A bi-level house usually rests on a concrete slab with foundation walls that rise four feet or less above ground level. The remaining one and one-half stories are built over the foundation walls.

---

2. In some parts of the country, *bi-level* may also denote a two-story dwelling or a split-level (tri-level) dwelling.

Figure 7.4 Two-Story House

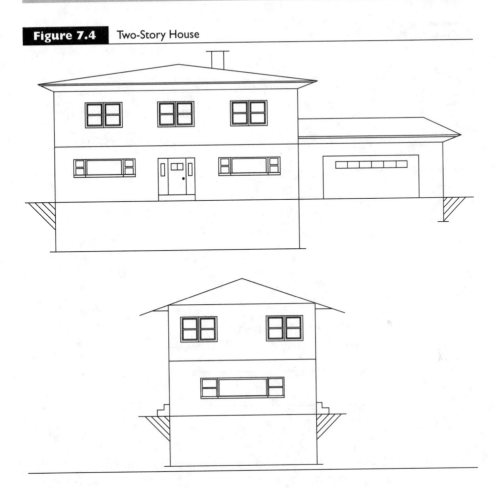

This type of house provides additional living area at the lowest cost. In most markets, the lower level is not regarded as a basement but as part of the gross living area. Both levels lend themselves to a variety of attachments. Part of the lower level can be converted into a garage or finished after the upper level is completed. The lower level may have windows to provide light and ventilation and doors to allow for exterior access and more convenient traffic patterns.

The main disadvantage of a bi-level design is that the lower level is sometimes cold and damp and may require special heating and insulation. Heat rises from the

> **TERM**
>
> **bi-level house:** a house built on two levels, with the lower level partially below ground level. In different parts of the country, bi-level may denote a two-story dwelling, a raised ranch, or a split-foyer dwelling.

Figure 7.5 ○ Bi-Level House

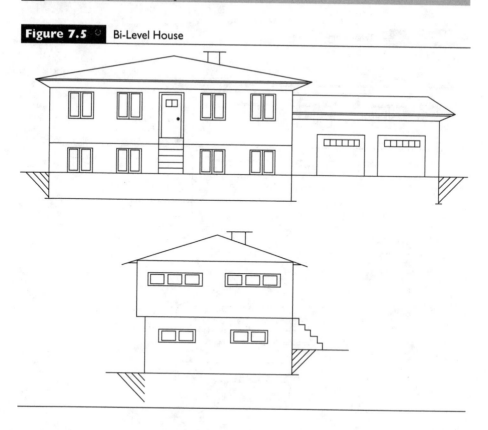

lower level through the split entryway and warms the upper level. Heating costs can be high if the house is poorly designed.

The ductwork in a bi-level house is hard to install because the foundation level is a functional living area, not a basement or crawl space. All traffic between the two levels must go by way of the interior stairs, which are usually located in the center of the house.

Because of its design limitations, the bi-level house poses challenges for architects. In a poorly designed bi-level house, the division of interior zones may be clumsy or the exterior may be visually unappealing.

Split-Level House

Split-level houses include tri-levels and quad-levels with basements. This type of house allows its residents to live on several levels. Two levels are normally finished prior to occupancy. A split-level house consists of a two-story portion, which is constructed like a bi-level, and a one-story portion. The two-story portion is built over a slab and a partial basement; the one-story portion sits on a slab or above a

Figure 7.6 Split-Level House

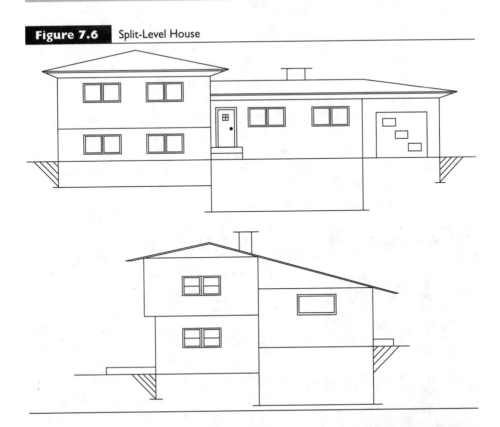

basement or crawl space. The design of the structure can be described as side-to-side, front-to-back, or back-to-front, referring to the relative placement of the one-story and two-story sections.

The upper level of a split-level house, which is separated from the middle level by a half flight of stairs, is reserved for bedrooms and bathrooms. The middle level, which is separated from the upper and lower levels by half flights of stairs, contains a living room, a dining area, a kitchen, and a laundry area. The lower level has additional living areas such as a family room, a recreation room, a den, or extra bedrooms. The lower level usually provides access to the garage.

A split-level home provides additional living area at a very low cost. In most parts of the country, the lower level is considered part of the gross living area, not a basement. The design lends itself to irregular topography, and both the middle and lower levels can accommodate exterior attachments. All the zones within the residence are well set off from one another, yet easily accessible. The traffic pattern is efficient. The lower level provides convenient access to the garage and can be finished after the middle and upper levels are complete. The design can accommodate an overhanging upper level, if desired.

A split-level house may have the same heating and insulation problems as bi-level houses. Because heat rises, the upper levels tend to be warmer than the lower level. The architectural limitations of the bi-level are also found in the split-level design, although split-levels have more versatility. Split-level houses may have less visual appeal if the topography of the site is flat.

CONCEPT

As part of the interior inspection, the appraiser notes how the house is divided into zones: the private-sleeping zone, the living-social zone, and the working-service zone.

TERMS

house zones: portions of a residence's interior layout differentiated by function.

private-sleeping zone: area of a home containing bedrooms, bathrooms, and dressing rooms.

living-social zone: area of a home containing the living room, dining room, family or recreation rooms, den, and any enclosed porches.

working-service zone: area of a home containing the kitchen, pantry, laundry, and other work areas.

HOUSE ZONES

As part of the building inspection, an appraiser examines the interior layout of the house. A house can be divided into three zones and various circulation areas. The private-sleeping zone contains the bedrooms; the family, master, and private bathrooms; and the dressing rooms. The living-social zone consists of the living room, the dining room, the family or recreation room, the den, and any enclosed porches. The working-service zone consists of the kitchen, the laundry, the pantry, and other work areas. Corridors, stairways, and entrances are considered circulation areas. Figure 7.7 shows the zone divisions in a well-designed house.

The three zones within a home should be separated from one another so that activities in one zone do not interfere with those in another. The private-sleeping zone should be insulated from the noise of the other two zones. Occupants should be able to move from bedrooms to bathrooms in the private zone without being seen from the other areas of the house.

The working-service zone is the nerve center of the house where most household chores are performed. Someone working in the kitchen should be able to monitor the guest and family entrances as well as activities in the private zone, the porch, the patio, and the backyard.

Figure 7.7   House Zones

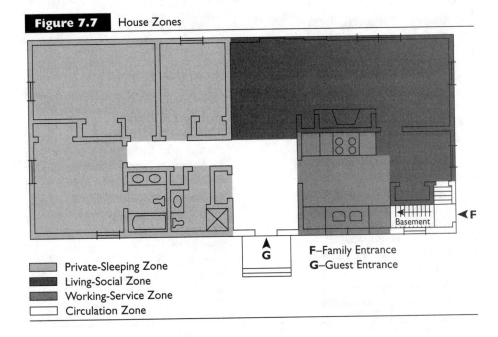

Private-Sleeping Zone
Living-Social Zone
Working-Service Zone
Circulation Zone

F—Family Entrance
G—Guest Entrance

Basement   ◀**F**

▲
G

The guest entrance should lead into the center of the house. This entrance should be near a guest closet and the guest lavatory. Ideally the entrance will lead directly to the living-social zone and be separated from the private-sleeping area by a noise and visibility barrier. Hard flooring is needed in the guest entrance to withstand mud and dirt tracked in from the outside.

The family entrance should lead into the kitchen from the garage, carport, or breezeway or from a circulation area such as a porch or deck. Traffic coming in this entrance should not have to pass through the work area in the kitchen. Residents should also be able to move from the family entrance through the service zone to the private-sleeping zone without going through the living-social zone.

A house with a basement may have a separate, outside entrance to the basement. The basement entrance should lead to stairs and hallways that have direct access to the private-sleeping zone, the living-social zone, and both the guest and family entrances. Circulation areas such as the main hallway, a bedroom hallway, stairways, and a rear or service hallway should provide access to the different house zones without passing through individual rooms. Circulation areas should be well-lit and wide with closets and storage spaces in strategic locations.

Residential Design Problems

In a national survey of home owners, the following design problems were noted by many respondents:

- Front door opens directly into living room.
- No closet in front hall.
- No direct access from the front door to the kitchen, bathroom, or bedroom without passing through other rooms.
- Rear door does not lead directly into the kitchen and does not provide convenient access to the street, driveway, and garage.
- No comfortable eating area in or near the kitchen.
- No convenient access from the kitchen to the separate dining area.

- Stairways are located off a room, not off a hallway or foyer.
- Bedrooms or bathrooms are visible from the living room or foyer.
- Recreation or family room is poorly located and not visible from the kitchen.
- No access to the basement from outside.
- Walls between bedrooms are not soundproof.
- Outdoor living areas such as decks and patios are not accessible from the kitchen.

Floor plans depend on the size and value of the individual residence and vary from region to region.

ROOMS IN RESIDENTIAL PROPERTIES

In performing the interior inspection, an appraiser studies the specific dimensions and characteristics of the individual rooms in the structure and notes any problems with the building's design.

Living Rooms

Until the middle of this century, the living room was considered the center of a house. More recently, the status of the living room has undergone change. Many home owners socialize, relax, and entertain in their family rooms, patios, and kitchens, rather than in living rooms. These other areas have expanded, and the size and importance of the living room has diminished.

The living room may be located in the front of the house or, if the view or access to outdoor areas is better, at the back or side of the house. Often the dining room is located at one end of the living room, usually adjacent to the kitchen. Ideally the living room should be located away from the traffic patterns to other rooms but easily accessible from the guest entrance.

In a three-bedroom house, the living room should be at least 11 feet by 16 feet, or approximately 170 square feet in area. A maximum width of 14 feet is desirable, but if traffic crosses the living room area, the width should be at least 15 to 16 feet. If a dining area is located at one end of the living room, the minimum dimensions are 16 feet by 26 feet. Regardless of its size, the living room should be able to accommodate a conversation circle that is 10 feet in diameter.

Living rooms can be square, rectangular, or L-shaped. Square living rooms make furniture arrangement difficult and are the least desirable. Rectangular living rooms should be neither too narrow nor too wide. Living rooms combined with dining areas are usually L-shaped. A living room should have at least one wall with windows for a view and ventilation and another wall long enough for a couch and other furniture. Many home owners complain that too many breaks in the walls of rooms for doorways, windows, and fireplaces make it difficult to arrange furniture comfortably. Sufficient outlets should be available for lamps and appliances. Traffic should not have to pass through the conversation circle in the living room.

Kitchens

The kitchen is the most important room in the house. It serves more functions than any other room, and at least 10% of the total cost of the house is normally spent on the kitchen. More than 120 miles are walked each year in the average kitchen during the preparation of just two meals a day; a well-designed kitchen can eliminate 40 miles from this route.

The best location for the kitchen depends on many factors, including the lifestyle of the household and the size of the family. The kitchen should have access to the dining area and to the front or rear entrance. If outdoor areas are used for meals, the kitchen should also have access to them. If the house has a family room, the kitchen should be visible from this room and allow convenient access to it. The kitchen is ordinarily close to but separated from the dining area.

The size of the kitchen depends on the space available in the house and the desired equipment or appliances. A kitchen should be at least 8 feet by 10 feet; approximately 10 feet by 10 feet is average. A spacious kitchen is 12 feet by 14 feet or larger. A large kitchen is usually combined with a dining area.

Kitchens should be well ventilated and well lit. The window area should be no less than 10% of the floor area and a window over the sink is ideal. In addition to the work areas, cabinets, storage space, appliances, and built-in equipment are needed. A kitchen may also accommodate a family activity center, a dining area, a laundry area, a trash storage area, or a pantry.

All kitchens with more than one counter have a work triangle as an essential design feature. Most kitchen layouts are based on the three points of the work triangle:

1. The sink/food preparation area
2. The refrigerator
3. The cooking area

In a well-designed kitchen, the cumulative length of the legs of the triangle does not exceed 23 feet.

The sink area is the place where food is prepared, dishes are washed, and garbage is disposed of. This accounts for 40% to 45% of kitchen activity. Appliances in the sink area may include a dishwasher, a trash compactor, and a garbage disposal. Single-basin sinks are generally adequate and are common in new construction when dishwashers are installed. Double-basin sinks are better suited to washing dishes by hand. Counters at least 18 inches deep are required on either side of the sink. The space beneath the sink is used to store cleaning products and utensils.

The sink area should be lit by a window above the sink and overhead lighting. Wall cabinets are useful nearby and the dishwasher should be no more than 12 feet away. The sink should be approximately 4 to 6 feet from the cooking area and 4 to 7 feet from the refrigerator.

Usually perishable foods are stored in a combination refrigerator and freezer. The refrigerator is ideally located at the end of a counter adjacent to 36 to 42 inches of uninterrupted counter space. The refrigerator should be near the food preparation area and close to a spigot that supplies water if it has an icemaker. It should also be convenient for unloading groceries. For energy efficiency, the refrigerator should be located away from the cooking area.

The cooking area in a kitchen combines a range/cookstove with a conventional oven. Many homes now have microwave ovens as well. Counters at least 15 inches deep are useful on each side of the stove and they should be made of a heatproof material. Cooking appliances should be powered by gas or electricity. The cooking area should never be near a window. Curtains can catch fire, reaching across a range to get to the window is dangerous, and cleaning above the range can be difficult. All cabinets should be at least 30 inches above the range. A ventilator or fan over the range is desirable to remove smoke and cooking fumes. Many fire-related injuries and accidents occur in the cooking area, so a fire extinguisher should be close at hand.

Cooking practices are changing, so kitchen layouts and appliances are changing too. Today many people cook on barbecues and outdoor grills or with microwaves, woks, and other appliances, which are personalty rather than realty. Although this style of cooking may only be a passing phase, the conventional oven has become the least used appliance in the kitchen.

Kitchens may be U-shaped or L-shaped with one counter or two. Larger kitchens may have an island in the center. Figure 7.8 illustrates several common kitchen layouts.

In a U-shaped kitchen, cabinets and counters are located along three walls. This design requires the most space, but it is considered to be the most efficient. The work triangle is compact so it is easily separated from traffic patterns through the kitchen. The sink is at the base of the U and the refrigerator and cooking area face each other on the arms of the U. The counter space is continuous and storage space is ample.

Some U-shaped kitchens have certain disadvantages. Too compact a triangle cramps the work area, while too open a triangle necessitates too much walking.

The L-shaped kitchen has counters and work areas arranged in two perpendicular, adjacent lines. The sink is usually centered on the long side of the L, with the refrigerator at the end of this counter; the cooking area is on the other side of the L. This design is best for small kitchens. It also works well for large kitchens because the work triangle is separated from traffic and the rest of the kitchen can be used for other purposes. This configuration is popular because it can accommodate various arrangements. Its major disadvantages are the placement of appliances, the potential for wasted space, and the distance between the work centers at the ends of the L.

A two-counter kitchen, which is also known as a *corridor* or *Pullman kitchen*, has cabinets and work areas on two opposite walls. The work triangle also serves as a passageway for traffic through the kitchen. The sink and cooking area are on one side across from the refrigerator. There should be at least 4 feet between the two counters so that cabinets and appliances can be opened.

A one-counter kitchen, which is also known as a *strip kitchen*, has all the work areas along one wall. This design does not create a work triangle, but it suits scaled-down appliances and works well when kitchen space is limited to less than 12 feet along the wall. The sink

Figure 7.8 Typical Kitchen Designs

U-shaped

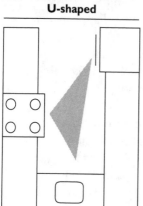

Corridor

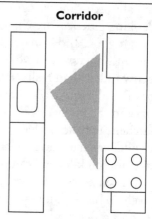

L-shaped

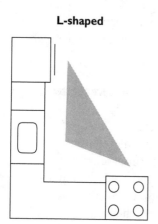

One Counter

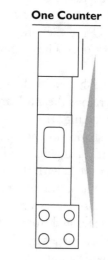

L-shaped with Island

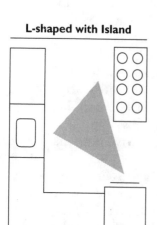

U-shaped with Island

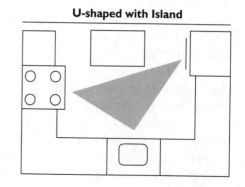

should be centrally located, with the refrigerator and the range at opposite ends of the wall. One-counter kitchens are most often found in apartments and small condominiums.

Island kitchens may be U-shaped or L-shaped. One-counter kitchens may have an island in the center—usually for the sink or the cooking area. Because the island reduces the area of the work triangle, islands are usually used in larger kitchens. In large kitchens the island may also set off an informal eating area.

Some kitchens have additional areas located outside the work triangle. A separate food preparation area, for example, may require counter space, extra electrical outlets, and storage for cooking utensils. A work desk or personal computer area may be included in a kitchen if space permits. This area may include a desk and chair, a personal computer, and a telephone.

Kitchen Design Problems

- Insufficient base cabinet storage
- Insufficient wall cabinet storage
- Insufficient counter space
- No counter beside the refrigerator
- Not enough window area
- Poorly placed doors that waste wall space
- Traffic through the work triangle

- Too little counter space on either side of the sink
- No counter beside the range
- Insufficient space in front of cabinets
- Too great a distance between the sink, range, and refrigerator
- A range located under a window

Some kitchens have special work surfaces for baking and extra storage for baking supplies and utensils. Home owners who entertain frequently may have kitchens with wet bars and storage areas for bottles and glasses. A serving or buffet counter in a pass-through area between the kitchen and dining room can facilitate informal meals. A barbecue inside the kitchen may be handy for special types of cooking, but this equipment must be located near an exhaust fan or hood. Unusual kitchen features may constitute overimprovements, depending on the standards of the market.

Dining Areas

Most houses built before the middle of this century had separate dining rooms. Many newer houses have dining areas that are part of another room. Eat-in kitchens, breakfast nooks, and living room-dining room combinations are common. Most home buyers prefer a

Dining Area Design Problems	
• Stairs that open into the dining area • Inadequate outlets, switches, lighting, and ventilation	• No partition between the kitchen and dining areas • Traffic passing through the dining area • Insufficient space for arranging furniture

house with a family room and an eat-in kitchen to one with a formal dining room and no family room.

The dining room is part of the living-social zone of a house. It should be directly accessible to the kitchen but separate from it. The dining room should be at least 9 feet by 11 feet, and ideally no less than 10 feet by 12 feet. More area may be required if traffic passes through the room. Three and one-half feet of space is needed behind each chair, and the area should accommodate a table that seats six persons. Extra room is needed to store dishes, silver, and glassware, and artificial light is usually provided by a chandelier.

Bedrooms

The number of bedrooms in a house is an important design consideration. The standard may be indicated by neighborhood analysis. Two- and three-bedroom houses have wide acceptance in the market. Houses with four or more bedrooms may represent an overimprovement in many areas. They usually appeal only to large families. Of course, luxury homes may have five bedrooms or more.

Privacy is important, so bedrooms should be located in the most secluded parts of the house. They should be accessible from a central hallway, which connects to the other zones of the house, but should be insulated from the noise produced in other parts of the house and the street outside. Placing closets along bedroom walls can minimize the transmission of sound from adjacent rooms.

The largest bedroom is usually the master bedroom, which often has access to a master bathroom. Other bedrooms may be used for children and guests. Extra bedrooms may be converted into dens, studies, or family rooms.

A bedroom with a single bed must measure at least 8 feet by 10 feet. This size will only be satisfactory if the layout is efficient. The minimum size for a bedroom with a double bed is 10 feet by 11½ feet. In some markets, bedrooms are expected to exceed the minimum size, but in others buyers will not pay extra for larger bedrooms. Each bedroom should have at least one closet that is 2 feet deep, 3 feet wide,

Bedroom Design Problems	
• Insufficient room to arrange furniture	• Not adequately separated from other house zones
• Not located near a hallway or bathroom	• No soundproofing
• Serves as a passageway to basement, attic, or another room	• Insufficient closet space
	• Lack of lighting in bedroom or closet

and high enough to accommodate 5 feet of hanging space. Every closet should have interior lighting, a pole for hangers, and a shelf not more than 74 inches above the floor with at least 8 inches of storage space above the shelf.

Some bedrooms have additional space for clothes storage and dressing areas. Because cross ventilation is important, corner bedrooms are preferred. Bedrooms should have adequate natural and artificial light. For safety, each bedroom should have a window that provides exterior access and be equipped with or near to smoke and fire detectors.

Bathrooms

Bathrooms are the smallest rooms in the house and they often seem to be the least adequate. Each residence should have at least one full-size bathroom. In many markets houses with only one bathroom are obsolete. Neighborhood analysis will indicate the standard for the area. With the exception of low-priced and resort residences, the minimum standard for housing is one and one-half baths. Two bathrooms are standard for two-story residences in many areas. A bathroom may be identified as the family bathroom, a powder room, or a master bath.

The terminology used to describe bathrooms and lavatories varies in different parts of the country. In most areas a full-size bathroom consists of a room with a toilet or water closet, a washbasin or sink, and a tub. A three-quarter bathroom has a toilet, a wash basin, and a stall shower. A half-bath or two-thirds bath, which is also known as a *lavatory, lavette,* or *powder room,* has a toilet and a washbasin. The number of fixtures present and the sufficiency of the plumbing should be noted.

There should be at least one bathroom on each floor of a multi-level residence. The best location for bathrooms is determined by the plumbing and the room layout. The family bathroom and the master bath are part of the sleeping-private zone. The powder room is usually part of the living-social zone. Entry to the bathroom should be private, and walls shared by bathrooms and other rooms should be soundproofed.

A full-size bathroom must be at least 5 feet by 7 feet. The minimum size for a powder room is 4 feet by 5 feet. The ideal size for a full-size bathroom is 6 feet by 8 feet or larger. There should be enough space for doors to open.

Bathrooms require the most heat and the best ventilation of any rooms in the house. A window may not be necessary. Interior bathrooms without windows are cheaper and generally acceptable in the market. Ventilation can be provided by a vent to the outside or a fan that starts automatically when the light is turned on.

Family or Recreation Rooms

The concept of a family room evolved in America after World War II. A family room is the area set aside for recreation and relaxation away from the more formal living room. The first family rooms were finished basements or attics. Later, enclosed porches and extra bedrooms were converted into family rooms. Today a family room may be used as a den, a study, a guest room, a nursery, a library, a TV room, or a game room.

Ideally a family room is near the kitchen, but it may be located wherever space is available. If possible, it should be toward the rear of the house to provide access to the outside. A family room should have a minimum width of $10^{1}/_{2}$ feet. The typical size is 12 feet by 18 feet, but the room can be much longer. There is no standard layout for a family room.

A badly designed family room may have poor access to the kitchen and the outside, insufficient heat, too few electrical outlets, or too many walls and doors that do not allow for suitable furniture arrangement. The condition of the floor covering, which may be carpet or vinyl, should be checked.

Laundry Areas

The laundry area and kitchen make up the working-service zone of the house. The location of the laundry room is a matter of convenience. Several locations are acceptable in the market. The laundry area can be on the same level as the living area or on another level. Ideally the laundry area should be a separate room that is accessible to the kitchen and the exterior of the house. Laundry facilities may be located in a closet or pantry, an enclosed porch, a mudroom, a breezeway, an attached garage, a detached garage connected to the house by a breezeway, a bedroom/bathroom area, or a basement. The main consideration is the location of the plumbing fixtures needed for the washing machine. There should also be ventilation for the dryer and room to fold clothes. Laundry rooms are not usually included in the room count.

Figure 7.9	Standard Room Sizes
Living rooms	11 feet by 16 feet (170 sq. ft.)
	Minimum width: 14 feet (15 to 16 feet if traffic crosses room)
	Accommodate conversation circle of 10 feet in diameter
	16 feet by 26 feet minimum if a dining area is located at one end of living room
Kitchens	Minimum: 8 feet by 10 feet
	Average: 10 feet by 10 feet
	Spacious: 12 feet by 14 feet or larger
	Sink/food preparation area, refrigerator, and cooking area should be connected by three lines forming a triangle; the cumulative length of the legs should not exceed 23 feet.
	Counters at least 18 inches deep on either side of the sink. Counters at least 15 inches deep on each side of the stove. All cabinets at least 30 inches above the range.
	Dishwasher no more than 12 feet from sink. Cooking area 4 to 6 feet from sink. Refrigerator 4 to 7 feet from sink.
	36 to 42 inches of uninterrupted counter space next to refrigerator
Dining areas	Minimum: 9 feet by 11 feet
	Ideal size: 10 feet by 12 feet
Bedrooms	With a single bed, at least 8 feet by 10 feet
	With a double bed, at least 10 feet by 11½ feet
Bathrooms	Full-size: at least 5 feet by 7 feet, ideally 6 feet by 8 feet
	Powder room: at least 4 feet by 5 feet
Family or recreation rooms	Minimum width: 10½ feet
	Typical size: 12 feet by 18 feet
Laundry areas	No standard size
Garages	One-car garage: at least 10 feet by 20 feet
	Two-car garage: at least 18½ feet by 20 feet
	Larger garages: at least 10 feet by 20 feet for each bay

8 BUILDING CONSTRUCTION

A complete building description includes detailed information about the construction of the building and the condition of its exterior, interior, and mechanical systems. There is no prescribed method for describing dwellings, but it is often useful to deal with the building components in the sequence in which they were constructed. This practice allows an appraiser to note problems that may have arisen at each stage of construction. An appraiser might use the format outlined in Figure 8.1 to describe the construction and condition of residential improvements as the individual elements are added during the construction process. Alternatively, an appraiser might concentrate on the building components listed on one of the standard form reports. For example, an appraiser might organize an examination of building improvements based on the Description of Improvements section of the Uniform Residential Appraisal Report as shown in Figure 8.2. (For more information on the descriptive data used in form reports, see Chapter 20.) Using a systematic format in the field inspection can help the appraiser avoid omitting any significant items.

> **CONCEPT**
>
> The building description notes the construction materials and techniques used, their cost, the quality of workmanship, the maintenance condition of the building, and its conformity to legal and market standards as well as physical and functional problems in the design and construction of the building or in its subsequent maintenance.

This chapter extends the discussion of building description begun in the previous chapter, focusing on the individual components of building construction (e.g., roofing materials and types of windows and doors) rather than the qualities of collections of building components (e.g., number of stories of a house or the layout of rooms). This chapter also focuses on the functional and physical problems associated with the specific building materials and construction techniques that appraisers should be aware of.

SUBSTRUCTURE

To prepare a site for construction of the substructure, the land is first cleared and staked out, test borings are drilled to examine the condition of

Figure 8.1	Components of Residential Construction

I. Exterior
    A. Substructure
        1. Clearing and stake out
        2. Test boring
        3. Excavation
        4. Footings
        5. Foundation walls
            a. Slab on ground
            b. Crawl space
            c. Basement
            d. Pier and beam
        6. Grading
    B. Superstructure
        1. Framing
        2. Exterior covering and trim
            a. Exterior walls
            b. Exterior doors
            c. Windows, storm windows, and screens
            d. Roof covering and drain system
            e. Chimneys, stacks, and vents
        3. Insulation
        4. Ventilation
II. Interior
    A. Interior covering and trim
        1. Floor covering
        2. Walls and ceiling
        3. Doors
        4. Stairs
        5. Molding and baseboards
        6. Painting, decorating, and finishing
        7. Cabinets
        8. Fireplaces
    B. Protection against decay and insect damage
III. Equipment and mechanical systems
    A. Plumbing system
        1. Piping
        2. Fixtures
    B. Hot water

Figure 8.1	Components of Residential Construction *(continued)*

   C. Heating system

      1. Warm or hot air

      2. Hot water

      3. Steam

      4. Electrical

      5. Fuels

         a. Coal

         b. Fuel oil

         c. Natural gas

         d. Electricity

         e. Solar energy

   D. Air conditioning and ventilation system

   E. Electrical system

   F. Miscellaneous systems and equipment

IV. Attachments, garages, and outbuildings

Figure 8.2	Description of Improvements Section of URAR

Description of Improvements Section of URAR

TERMS

substructure: a building's entire foundational structure, which is below grade or ground, and provides a support base or footings on which the superstructure rests.

footings: the supporting parts of a foundation that prevent excessive settlement or movement by distributing building loads directly to the soil.

mat and raft foundation: a mat, raft, or rigid foundation over the entire foundation area consisting of concrete slabs with reinforcing bars closely spaced at right angles to each other within the slab; used when the bearing power of the soil cannot support spread footings and the use of piles is not advantageous or necessary.

slab-on-ground foundation: a type of foundation in which a concrete slab is built either on the ground or on footings above it.

subflooring: plywood sheets or construction-grade lumber laid on top of the floor joists and underneath the finish floor.

the soils, and the site is excavated to accommodate footings, the foundation floor, and underground utility lines. Once the basic elements of the substructure have been installed and the site has been graded, construction of the aboveground improvements can begin. All the above-grade improvements of a building rest upon the solid base of the substructure. Typically a house will be constructed over a basement or a crawl space or on a slab directly on the ground. The characteristics of each of the three types of foundations are outlined in Table 8.1.

Footings support a house's foundation and prevent excessive settlement or movement of the structure. Generally made of concrete poured into clean trenches or wood forms, footings can be arranged in several ways depending upon their function, as shown in Table 8.2. Building codes dictate the size and depth of footings required for the intended load.

The foundation walls of a house, which are usually below grade or ground level, form an enclosure for basements and crawl spaces, and they support walls, floors, and other structural loads. The least expensive and most popular types of foundations are made of poured concrete walls or concrete-and-cinder-block walls that rest on concrete footings. Foundations in older structures may be made of cut stone or stone and brick, which are more costly materials and require more skill to install. Treated timber is sometimes used, but these foundation walls do not meet building codes in certain areas.

Columns and posts of various materials provide the central support for the building's beams and superstructure. Older buildings can have costly wood posts, masonry posts, or wood beams, while many newer structures are built with inexpensive steel Lally columns and steel I-beams. In a pier-and-beam foundation, piers resting on footings support beams or girders, which in turn support the superstructure. Many building codes prohibit the use of pier-and-beam foundations in conventional homes. Yet because of the relative inexpensiveness of this type of construction, pier-and-beam foundations are often used for

Table 8.1 Comparison of Foundation Types

Type of Foundation	Structural Characteristics	Functional Advantages	Functional Disadvantages
Slab	Slab-on-ground foundations are either permanent foundations built on footings or floating foundations used on unstable soil or in areas with poor drainage. Floating slab-on-ground foundations are also called *mat and raft foundations*. They are made of concrete slabs heavily reinforced with steel so that the entire foundation acts as a unit.	A slab-on-ground foundation is the most economical type of foundation and eliminates the need for first-floor framing. It is also suitable for mass production in tract or prefabricated housing.	Without heating coils, slab-on-ground foundations can be cold. In extremely cold regions of the country, they may be regarded as underimprovements. Furthermore, the mechanical systems in buildings with slab-on-ground foundations must be placed in the walls, the attic, or in separate rooms. Flooding can also be a problem if there are no drain tiles around the perimeter of the foundation, if the floor has an inadequate pitch, or if the finish grade of the site does not slope from the slab.
Crawl space	Footings support foundation walls, columns, and other framing members built on a crawl space. The floor of the crawl space may be sand, gravel, concrete, or undisturbed soil. **Use of space:** A crawl space can provide storage space for a home's mechanical systems and ductwork. **Access to space:** Interior or exterior hatches provide access to a crawl space.	If a crawl space foundation is used, the building's systems need not be put on the ground floor. Ductwork can be run below the floor framing, which reduces costs. In a crawl space foundation, the ground floor is elevated above the exterior ground line and foundation walls are shorter, so costs are lower.	Crawl spaces may be damp or hold standing water, and inspection of physical problems in crawl spaces can be difficult.
Basement	Basements are similar to crawl spaces, but they are usually seven to eight feet deep. The basement floor is constructed like a slab. **Use of space:** An unfinished basement provides storage space like a crawl space. A finished basement can also provide extra living area, if effectively waterproofed and ventilated. Basements can also be used for recreation and laundry rooms. **Access to space:** A basement may have an interior stairway to the living area as well as exterior access.	Basements provide extra living area at a minimum cost.	Basements are more costly than crawl spaces and are not required in many warmer climates. A basement in the Deep South and the West may well constitute an overimprovement; the cost of this feature will probably not be recaptured when the property is resold.

Table 8.2	Comparison of Types of Footings	
Type of Footing	**Construction Characteristics**	**Functional Characteristics**
Wall footing	Concrete base running around the perimeter of the site, resting on undisturbed earth below the frost line, and extending out from both sides of the foundation walls it supports. (The drain tile, a specially designed pipe laid outside the wall footings, drains ground water to a storm sewer or dry well.)	Distributes the load of the walls over the subgrade.
Column footing	Generally square slabs of concrete, though if an extra load is to be supported the concrete may be reinforced with steel rods or mesh.	Supports vertical columns and posts in the superstructure as well as fireplaces, furnaces, and chimneys.
Stepped footing	Standard concrete footings connected at different heights.	Supports structures on lots that slope.
Spread footing	Concrete slabs extending out further than normal from beneath the foundation walls they support.	Supports structures on lots where the soil has poor load-bearing capacity.

Figure 8.3	Footing and Foundation Walls (Basement/Pier-and-Beam Construction)

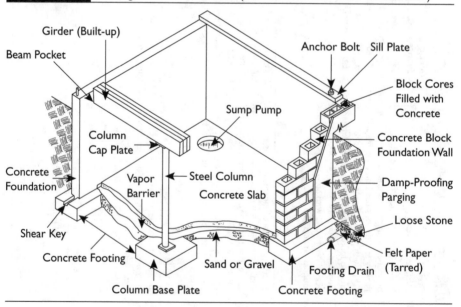

resort houses and for outbuildings and porches (see Figure 8.3).

Substructure Inspection

The substructure is the most difficult portion of a home's structure for an appraiser to inspect because most of the components are underground and not readily accessible. When possible, an appraiser should look for evidence of bulges or cracks in foundation walls, which may cause leakage, and for holes, crumbling, or poor interior surfaces, which may indicate that the concrete was not poured properly. Evidence of mineral sediment on basement walls could indicate that walls or window wells leak or that the basement has flooded in the past. Mineral powder stains on the floor may indicate cracked floors or clogged basement drains, and a musty odor or other evidence of mildew suggests leakage and inadequate ventilation.

SUPERSTRUCTURE

The term *superstructure* refers to the frame of the building and all elements of the exterior structure. The structural frame is the load-bearing skeleton of a building. Floors and ceilings, exterior and interior walls, and the roof are all attached to the frame, which can be constructed out of wood, masonry, or a combination of layers of both materials.[1]

Wood Framing

Most houses in the United States are built with wood framing, including many homes with brick veneer siding. The most common

Wood-frame construction is used for the vast majority of houses built in the U.S.

---

1. Alternative framing materials such as foam-core panels, light-gauge steel framing, and welded-wire sandwich panels may become more attractive if wood prices continue to rise. Reliable statistics are not available for the use of steel framing members in residential construction, though estimates currently place it at 3%-6% of new housing starts. The use of light steel in house frames is growing for a variety of reasons, primarily because the price of steel is less volatile than that of wood and because steel framing systems can be more efficiently assembled by properly trained contractors.

types of wooden frame construction are platform construction, balloon framing, and plank-and-beam framing.

Platform Construction

When platform construction is used, a single story of a dwelling is constructed at a time so that the ceiling of each completed level serves as the platform for the next. Studs are cut at the ceiling height of the first story, horizontal plates are laid on top of these studs, and more studs are cut for the second story (see Figure 8.4). With this method of construction, walls and partitions can be preassembled and tilted up into position. Also special framing can be used for doors and windows.

Balloon Framing

Less common today than platform construction, balloon framing was often used in the past in multistory buildings with brick, stone, or stucco veneer. The long studs running from the top of the foundation wall to the roof line, which distinguish balloon framing from platform construction, provide more stability in upper floors. In balloon frame construction, the entire wall frame acts a single unit; in contrast, one single-story unit of platform construction sits on top of another independent unit and can slide from side to side in extreme conditions. Named for its lightness, balloon framing is rarely used today because the long studs needed are expensive and the framing has poor fire resistance.

Plank-and-Beam Framing

Originally used in colonial-era houses and barns, plank-and-beam framing regained popularity in the mid-1970s when architects began to incorporate exposed-beam ceilings into house designs. The framing members used in plank-and-beam framing are much larger and heavier and are spaced farther apart than those used in other framing systems (see Figure 8.5). The wood beams can be up to eight feet apart and are supported on posts and exterior walls.

Figure 8.4 Platform Construction

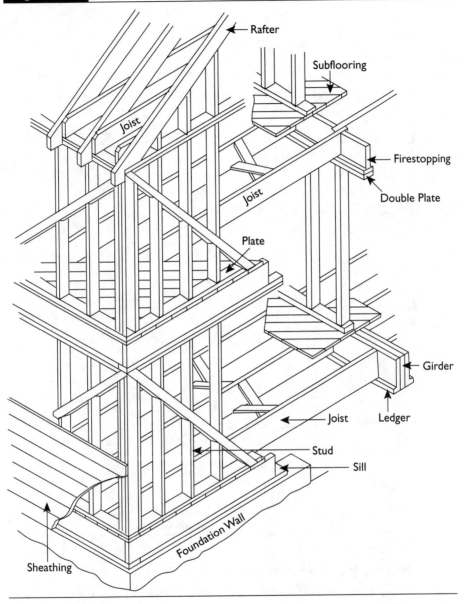

Figure 8.5 Plank-and-Beam Framing

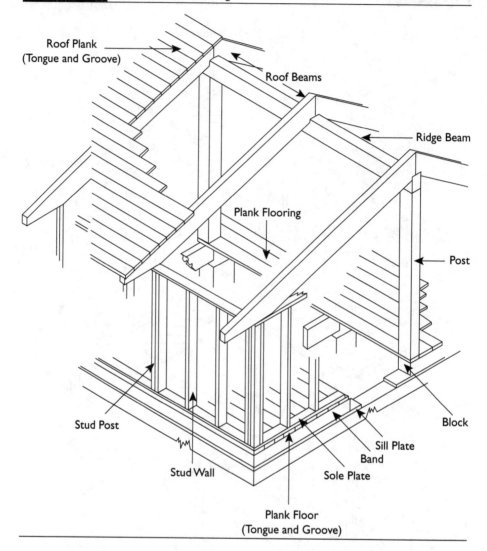

Roof Plank
(Tongue and Groove)

Roof Beams

Ridge Beam

Plank Flooring

Post

Stud Post

Block

Sill Plate
Band

Stud Wall

Sole Plate

Plank Floor
(Tongue and Groove)

Masonry Exterior Walls

Some modern buildings are constructed with solid masonry exterior walls, which act as part of the framing system. These walls are often two layers thick or have a face layer backed by masonry of another material with the two layers joined by metal wall ties or masonry headers. Other buildings are constructed with hollow masonry walls filled with insulation material and interior framing of steel beams or reinforced concrete. Because of their greater weight, masonry walls require larger footings than wood frame walls.

Roof Construction

A roof frame must be able to support its own weight as well as that of finish materials. It must also be able to withstand the pressure of snow, ice, wind, and rain, which vary by climate. Different types of roofs require different types of framing, which can usually be inspected from inside a house's attic (see Figure 8.6). Flat roofs require only horizontal joists supported by the building's exterior walls and interior load-bearing elements. Angled roofs such as gable, gambrel, and shed roofs employ rafters that slope up from the joists at the desired pitch of the roof. As an alternative to a traditional roof frame of joists and rafters, triangular trusses can be used for additional support. Because trusses do not require interior load-bearing walls, they can also be used to increase flexibility in building design.

Types of Roofs

- Flat roofs: used on industrial and commercial buildings, but less often on houses

- Lean-to shed roofs: used on sheds and saltbox houses

- Gable roofs: the common, sloped roof where the planes of the roof form a triangle with the ceiling

- Gambrel roofs: popular for barns and for Cape Ann* and Dutch colonial houses

- Hip roofs

- Mansard roofs

* Cape Ann is a variant of Cape Cod architecture and is distinguished by its roof. Whereas Cape Cod homes are gable-roofed, Cape Ann homes are gambrel-roofed.

Superstructure Inspection

An appraiser can easily identify structural problems in older homes such as:

- Exterior walls that bulge
- Girders, roof ridge lines, or rafters that sag
- Window sills that are not level
- Windows or doors that stick because of defective framing, poor carpentry, or settling
- Ponding on a flat roof

Figure 8.6 Types of Roofs

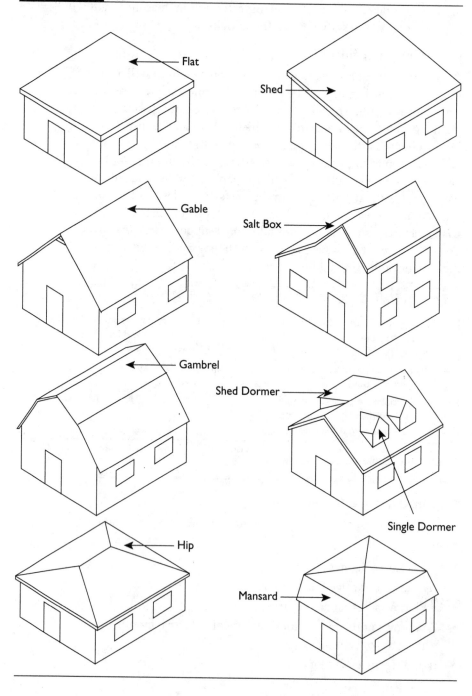

Functional Problems in Framing	
• Floor joists that are too wide and cost more than they contribute to value	• Partitions that are improperly sized or improperly placed
• Floor joists that are too narrow and may later cause the floors to buckle and sink	• Use of solid masonry, rather than wood frame or frame and veneer, except where the use of masonry conforms to the market
• Subflooring made of older materials that are costlier, noisier, and less water-resistant than newer materials	• Walls that are not wide enough to support their intended load or to accommodate sufficient insulation

Functional problems in a new house can be detected by studying blueprints. Sometimes the services of an engineer or home inspector may be needed to confirm the existence of major problems.

Visible cracks in walls do not necessarily indicate problems with framing. All houses settle unless they are built on solid rock, and most houses develop some ceiling and wall cracks. More compelling evidence of defective framing includes large cracks on the outside of the house between the chimney and the exterior wall or cracks running outward at an angle from the upper corners of window and door frames.

BUILDING MATERIALS

After the framing of a structure is complete, construction of the building's skin can begin. The structural skin includes the exterior walls, doors and windows, and roof covering. Once the exterior surfaces of the house have been covered, finish work on the interior walls, ceilings, floors, and trim can begin.

Exterior Wall Surfaces

The most visible portion of a house's skin, the exterior wall siding, is attached to a layer of wall sheathing made of wood, plywood, insulated board, or gypsum. The sheathing is nailed directly to the studs and may require additional bracing in the corners. Sheathing materials provide insulation, and sheathing paper made of felt or aluminum foil is applied over the sheathing for waterproofing. Where dissimilar materials meet, flashing (strips of tin or copper nailed to the top and bottom of the sheathing where it meets the foundation and roof) must be applied to prevent leakage.

The finish material on the exterior of the walls comes in various patterns and materials. Exterior walls of solid brick, stone, or concrete block do not require additional siding.

Exterior Wall Coverings

Horizontal Siding Materials

- Bevels or clapboards made of wood, particle board, aluminum, vinyl, masonite, steel, or other materials.
- Tongue-and-groove lap boards
- Natural wood surface of a log cabin's timber frame
- Shiplap/Dolly Varden siding

Other Types of Siding

- Wood,* asbestos, or asphalt shingles
- Stucco
- Masonry veneer
- Panels, glass block, glazed tile, plastic, or other materials

---

*Wood siding must be stained, sealed, or painted.

Roof Covering

Like exterior walls, the roof of a home comprises a layer of finish material over layers of sheathing and sheathing paper with flashing at areas prone to leakage. The exterior roof covering prevents moisture from entering the building, and the metal flashing adds further protection where roof slopes intersect and wherever projections extend through the roof.

Sheathing may be made of wood boards, plywood, or sheet material. In most parts of the United States, the sheathing is covered with asphalt shingles, which are available in various weights and styles. Other common roof coverings are shingles or shakes made of wood (usually cedar), slate, metal, or tile. Flat roofs are often covered by a final coat of hot asphalt or roofing compound applied directly to the sheathing paper for waterproofing with a layer of light-colored gravel or stone on top to reflect sunlight. Other roofs may be constructed of corrugated metal; fiberglass; or clay, plastic, or metal tile.

Most roof coverings must be replaced several times during a building's life. An appraiser must consider the overall condition of the roof to estimate its remaining useful life.

Doors

The quality of a dwelling's doors generally corresponds to the overall quality of construction. Exterior doors are typically made of solid wood, metal, or glass, while interior doors are generally hollow-core wood doors. Older houses may have solid wood interior doors. Hollow

---

Types of Doors

- Panel
- Flush
- Combination

- Batten
- Dutch
- Sliding glass

exterior doors usually indicate poor-quality construction, and may represent a deficiency in the property.

Windows

Like doors, windows give an appraiser an indication of the overall construction quality of a house. Windows have a major impact on a structure's energy efficiency, so proper installation is very important. Historically window frames have been made of wood, which is easy to work with and has good insulating properties, though aluminum and steel frames are also popular.

An appraiser must be able to identify the window type, material, and manufacturer as well as energy-saving features such as insulated glass, multiple glazing, and storm sashes (see Figure 8.7). Smaller windows and windows placed high off the floor are more energy-efficient and increase security.

Floor Coverings

The material used on floors can vary widely, depending largely on the home owner's budget and on the function of various rooms in the house. In living areas expensive hardwood floors were once standard in many areas, while soft woods are more common today in low-cost houses. Ceramic tile is popular for bathrooms and can also be found in kitchens. Less expensive floor coverings commonly found in kitchens include rolled linoleum and no-wax vinyl flooring.

Strips of wood or wood blocks are attached directly to the subflooring or to a suitable underlayer with special adhesives. Carpeting can be installed over subflooring with the necessary padding. Ceramic tile in bathrooms can be laid in a bed of plaster or attached with a special adhesive to the subflooring. The different types of kitchen flooring are all attached with adhesives.

Concrete slabs can be painted or covered with other materials. Terrazzo flooring is made of colored marble chips mixed into cement that is ground to a smooth surface after it is laid. In areas such as hearths and entry halls, a material with an irregular surface such as slate, brick, or stone can be used.

Interior Walls and Ceilings

The finishes of walls and ceilings should provide a durable, decorative cover that is waterproof in areas subject to moisture like bathrooms and basements. Today most interior walls are made of wood studs covered with drywall materials. Plaster is used less frequently than it once was

Figure 8.7 Types of Windows

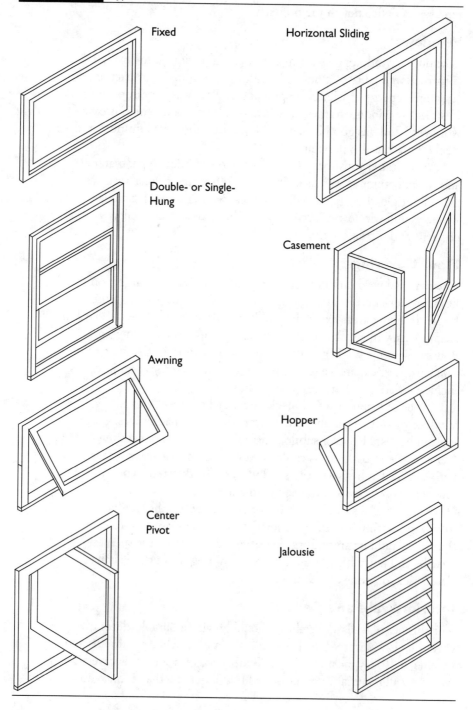

Fixed

Horizontal Sliding

Double- or Single-Hung

Casement

Awning

Hopper

Center Pivot

Jalousie

because of the material's expense and its susceptibility to cracking. Gypsum board and wood composition materials are applied directly onto studs or masonry, while ceramic wall tiles are installed in the same manner as floor tiles, using cement plaster or special adhesives.

Moldings, Baseboards, and Wainscoting

Various interior design elements can be built into a house such as moldings and trim around doors, windows, baseboards, and ceilings. Expensive moldings are made of thicker wood and have more intricate patterns.

A different finish on the lower half of a wall is known as *wainscoting*. A chair rail, designed to protect the wall from being marred by chair backs, can serve as the upper cap of the wainscot.

Materials Inspection

General construction details can be described on a room-by-room basis, but if the features do not vary significantly from room to room, they can be described for the house as a whole. Evidence of functional problems and other important, observable physical qualities of building materials should be noted (see following page).

INSULATION AND VENTILATION

Insulation helps home owners economize on fuel and provides comfort in both warm and cold climates. It also reduces noise and impedes the spread of fire. Newer homes are generally more energy-efficient than similar older buildings, though the heavy building materials used before the 1940s provided some insulation. Special insulating materials can usually be added to older homes to increase energy efficiency.

The R value of insulation materials is a quantitative measure of the ability of insulation to resist the flow of heat. The R value measures the British thermal units (Btus) that are transmitted in one hour through

Insulating Materials and Location of Use	
Loose-fill insulation	Structural cavities (e.g., attic, in hollow walls)
Flexible insulation	Where loose-fill insulation is impractical or where attached foil or paper facing is desired as a vapor barrier
Rigid insulation	Often as part of walls
Reflective insulation	Same as rigid insulation except air space is needed for foil to reflect radiated heat
Foam insulation	In wall cavities as well as around pipes, ductwork, furnaces, water heaters, etc.

Functional Problems of Building Materials

Exterior Wall Surfaces

- Sheathing that is not attached properly may bulge beneath the siding.
- An appraiser should note if flashing is loose or missing along the building walls.
- An appraiser notes whether the paint on siding is peeling, wrinkling, or buckling and discerns whether a new paint job is needed.
- Any cracks in stucco walls should be noted because they are quite expensive to repair.
- Stains on masonry veneer may indicate that the siding is not suitable for the climate.
- Concrete block is often considered unsightly.
- Brick and stone walls must be constructed by specially trained masons and are generally costly to repair.

Interior Wall Coverings

- Defective grout in tiles around a bathtub can cause problems; tiles set in plaster or held with waterproof adhesives are less susceptible to water damage.

Roof Coverings

- An appraiser notes any loose, torn, broken, or moldy shingles as well as damage to the soffit and fascia.
- Built-up roofs, often used for flat-roofed buildings, may blister and generally do not last as long as other roof coverings.

Doors

- Hanging a door is a complicated procedure and it is often done improperly. A poorly hung door will usually not close properly or will fail to make contact with the edge of its frame when closed.
- Air leakage through cracks at the bottom of doors can be stopped with door shoes, weatherproof thresholds, or sweeps.

Windows

- An appraiser may want to count all removable windows and door screens and note if any are missing. The contributory value of storm windows and doors is difficult to judge, but market expectations can be a good indicator.

Ceilings

- Bulging ceiling plaster is dangerous and should be replaced. This defect can often be detected by gently pressing a broom handle against the ceiling to see if there is any give to the plaster.

Floor Coverings

- Wood floors that have been exposed to water may warp and bulge upward. Wide cracks between the floorboards are a sign of poor workmanship or shrinkage that results from drying or storing wood improperly. Wood floors that are rough, discolored, blemished, burned, or gouged can usually be restored with refinishing.
- Carpeting over finished hardwood floors may be a superadequacy.

one thickness of the insulation. The higher the R value, the better the insulation. Local building codes establish standard R values for a region based on the climate and the type of building. Superior insulation of a house may be a superadequacy in certain markets. Appraisers should be able to judge if the combination of insulation, ventilation, and heating and air conditioning systems meets local standards.

Ventilation (usually via fans or holes) is needed to reduce heat in enclosed spaces such as attics and spaces behind walls and to prevent the condensation of water in enclosed spaces. Moisture is the great enemy of building materials, particularly wood; prolonged exposure to moisture promotes rot and decay. Ventilation holes should be covered with screens to keep out vermin (see Figure 8.8).

> **TERM**
>
> **R value:** a standard for measuring the ability of an insulation material to resist the flow of heat. R value is derived by measuring the British thermal units (Btus) transmitted in one hour through the thickness of the insulation. The higher the R value, the more effective the insulation.

Functional Problems

The means used to insulate and ventilate a house should complement the capacity of the building's heating and air-conditioning systems to maintain a comfortable living environment. A well-designed heating system will be less efficient if a house is poorly insulated, allowing heat

Figure 8.8	Ventilation

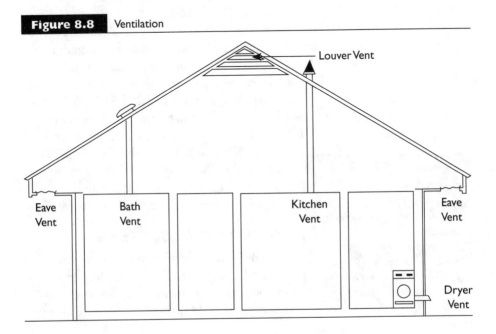

Louver Vent

Eave Vent

Bath Vent

Kitchen Vent

Eave Vent

Dryer Vent

to escape. On the other hand, superinsulation can trap harmful, naturally occurring gases such as radon within a house.

Exposure to certain insulating materials can cause health hazards for building occupants. Appraisers should be able to recognize the possible presence of asbestos and urea-formaldehyde foam insulation and know what their reporting responsibilities are in a particular assignment.

Asbestos is a nonflammable, natural mineral substance that separates into fibers. Asbestos-containing materials (ACMs) were widely used in structures built between 1945 and 1970 for insulation, fireproofing, and soundproofing. Other ACMs were used in siding and roofing shingles. Asbestos fibers pose a threat to human health when they are distributed in the air. The potential of any ACM to release fibers depends on its degree of friability—i.e., how easily it can be crumbled or pulverized. Dry, sprayed-on thermal insulation over structural steel is highly friable. Densely packed, nonfibrous ACMs such as vinyl asbestos floor covering and pipe insulation are not considered friable under normal conditions. Nevertheless, these materials will become friable if they are broken, sawed, or drilled.

In April 1982 the Consumer Product Safety Commission (CPSC) banned the use of urea-formaldehyde foam insulation in residences and schools. The ban resulted from the commission's investigation of the effects of formaldehyde gas, which can be released from the insulation at very high levels, especially immediately after installation. The ban took effect in August 1982 and was lifted in April 1983 by a federal court of appeals which held that the health risks had not been proven. The ban was not retroactive, so it did not affect the approximately 500,000 homes built between 1970 and 1982 that already had urea-formaldehyde foam insulation, but use of the material has diminished greatly in residential construction.

CONCEPT

Equipment and mechanical systems are divided into two categories: 1) those needed to provide for human comfort such as plumbing, heating, air-conditioning, and lighting and 2) process-related equipment and mechanical systems.

MECHANICAL SYSTEMS

A house's mechanical systems must be in good working order for the building to provide adequate shelter and comfort for its inhabitants and for the property to realize its

Appraisers and Hazardous Substances

The role and responsibility of the appraiser in detecting or measuring environmental substances affecting a property is addressed in Guide Note 8 to the Appraisal Institute's Standards of Professional Appraisal Practice. The guide note takes its direction from the Competency Rule of the Uniform Standards of Professional Appraisal Practice, which requires that the appraiser either

1. Have the knowledge and experience to complete a specific appraisal assignment competently or

2. Disclose his or her lack of knowledge and/or experience to the client, take all steps necessary or appropriate to complete the assignment competently, and describe the lack of knowledge and/or experience and the steps taken to complete the assignment competently in the report

Appraisers are routinely asked to complete "environmental checklists" or provide statements on environmental issues to satisfy the concerns of lenders and regulatory agencies. An Appraisal Institute Special Task Force on the Appraiser's Environmental Responsibility advises appraisers to exercise caution and to always identify the scope of the investigation and present the data upon which any conclusions are based. The task force offers the following recommendations to assist appraisers in dealing with environmental checklists:

- Any "environmental checklist" should clarify and identify the scope of services expected to be provided by the appraiser.
- In the absence of such a scope, the appraiser should identify the services to be performed by the appraiser. This identification should include the extent of the appraiser's inspection, investigation, and research, if any.
- The appraiser should determine whether he or she has sufficient expertise and/or experience to satisfy the client's checklist or scope of environmental work.
- The appraiser should reveal all environmental issues that are observed by the appraiser during the course of a normal inspection of the property in the preparation of a real estate appraisal.
- The appraisal should be prepared in compliance with the Uniform Standards of Professional Appraisal Practice (USPAP), particularly the Competency Rule, as well as Guide Note 6 and Guide Note 8 of the Standards of Professional Appraisal Practice of the Appraisal Institute.

Source: A Special Task Force Report on The Appraiser's Environmental Responsibility, presented to the Appraisal Institute Board of Directors, July 1993.

full market value. A house may contain many different types of mechanical systems and equipment, but the three essential systems in a modern residence are

1. Plumbing
2. Heating and air conditioning
3. Electrical

Plumbing

The plumbing system consists of piping, which is mostly covered or hidden, and fixtures and equipment, which are visible (see Figure 8.9).

Much of the cost of a plumbing system is spent on piping. The quality of the materials used, the way the pipes are installed, and the ease with which they can be serviced are significant factors in considering the durability of piping and the cost of maintenance. In many types of buildings, a high-quality piping system can last for the life of the building. However, many buildings have pipes that will not last. An appraiser describes the conditions of the visible pipes within the structure and notes approximately when they will need to be replaced.

Piping Materials and their Uses	
Galvanized steel, lead, or brass	Water pipes
Copper	Water pipes
Cast iron	Below-grade waste lines
Plastic	Waste, vent, and water lines

Good-quality bathroom fixtures are made of cast iron covered with acid-resistant vitreous enamel. Fiberglass and other materials are also used. Kitchen sinks may be made of Monel® metal, stainless steel, enameled steel, or cast iron covered with acid-resistant enamel. Some homes have specialized plumbing fixtures such as laundry tubs and wet bars.

Hot Water System

A typical hot water system receives its heat from a furnace or a self-standing water heater powered by electricity, gas, or oil. The size of the hot water tank needed in a residence is determined by the number of inhabitants and their water-using habits as well as the recovery rate of the unit. Newer units are smaller and heat water more quickly and efficiently.

Types of Plumbing Fixtures		
Bathrooms	**Kitchens**	**Fittings**
Washbasins	Single or double sinks	Faucets
Bathtubs	installed in countertops	Spigots
Showers	Garbage disposals	Drains
Toilets	Dishwashers	Shower heads
	Instant hot water units	Spray hoses
	Water filters	

Figure 8.9   Plumbing

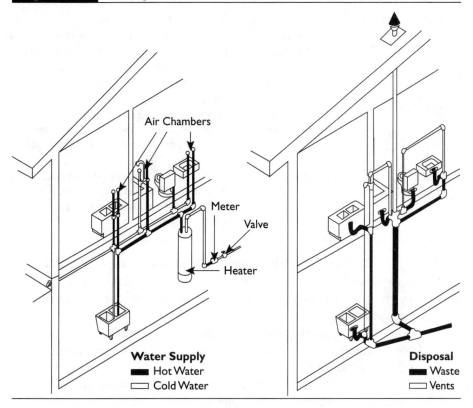

Air Chambers

Meter

Valve

Heater

Water Supply
■■■ Hot Water
☐ Cold Water

Disposal
■■■ Waste
☐ Vents

Heating Systems

Most heating systems use warm or hot air, hot water, steam, or electricity. The amount of heat a system can produce is rated in Btus. The Btu requirement for a heating plant depends on the cubic content, exposure, design, and insulation level of the structure to be heated as well as local market considerations (see Figure 8.10).

Differences Between Heating Systems

Some central air-conditioning systems use the same ducts as the warm air heating system. This is not always possible, however, because air-conditioning requires ducts of a different size. Heating registers are generally placed low on the walls, while air-conditioning registers should be placed high up or in the ceiling. Older heating systems relied on gravity and had large ducts and simple distribution patterns for circulation.

Types of Heating Systems, Fuel, and Equipment

Heating System	Fuel	Equipment
Warm or hot air	Gas, oil, coal, or electricity	Furnace, air ducts (Thermostats, filters, humidifiers, air cleaners, and air purification devices are optional.)
Hot water	Gas, oil, coal, or electricity	Cast-iron or steel boiler, pump/circulator, piping
Steam	Gas, oil, coal, or electricity	Boiler, piping, radiators (Many states require licenses for certain classes of steam boilers. Appraisers should be familiar with boiler license laws.)
Electric	Electricity	Heat pump, wall heater, baseboard units, duct heating units, heating units installed in air-conditioning ducts, extra wiring and electrical service, convectors

A distinction is made between radiant hot water heating and conventional convection heating. In a conventional system, air is warmed as it passes over the heated metal of a radiator and is then circulated in the area of colder air through convection. Radiant heating depends on heat being transferred directly from heating elements into the air, through narrow hot water pipes or electric heating elements buried in floors, walls, and ceilings.

A steam system also uses radiators to transfer heat into rooms by radiation and convection. The common, cast-iron radiator successfully accomplishes this dual process. Steam heating systems are being developed to operate more efficiently. Zone control is now widely used to meet various heating needs in different parts of a building. The amount of heat available for distribution is controlled by separate temperature controls.

An electrical heating system usually includes equipment such as a heat pump, which can also be used to cool a building. Electrical heating systems may make use of radiant floors, walls, and ceilings with panels or cables under the surface, infrared units, and electric furnaces that generate forced warm air or hot water. An electrical resistance system is the least expensive system to install because it does not require a furnace, furnace room, ducting, flue, or plumbing. However, it does need much more electrical service than would otherwise be needed and a great deal of wiring to each unit in the building.

The automatic regulation of a heating system contributes to its operating efficiency. A multiple-zone system with separate thermo-

Figure 8.10 Heating Systems

Extended Plenum System

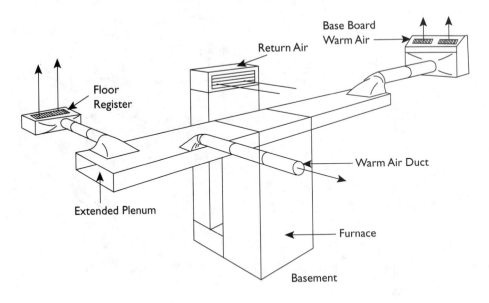

Perimeter Loop Warm Air System

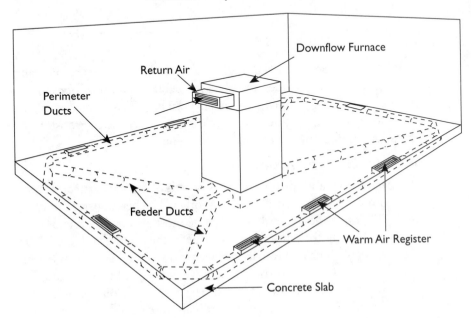

Figure 8.10 Heating Systems *(continued)*

Gravity Hot Air System

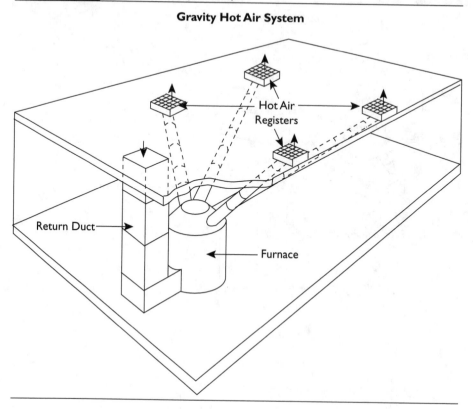

stats is more efficient than a single-zone system with one thermostat. Complex systems provide individual temperature controls for each room. The efficiency of certain systems can be increased by putting a thermostat on the outside of the building. The outside thermostat helps determine how much heat a system needs to produce.

Fuels for Heating Systems

In certain areas and for certain types of buildings, one particular type of fuel may be more desirable than another. The heating systems of many buildings, however, do not use the most economical fuel. For example, during the natural gas shortage in the middle and late 1970s, various regulations and restrictions were imposed on the use of natural gas. Many buildings constructed then were equipped with heating systems that use other fuels. Currently gas is more economical. In a given area for a specific use, different fuels have significant advantages

---

Characteristics of Various Fuel Types

- Burning certain types of **coal** creates environmental problems.
- In spite of its high cost, **fuel oil** remains popular because it is easy to transport and store. Many fuel oil tanks are found underground, which can have environmental ramifications.
- **Electric heat** is costly except in a few areas with low-cost power.

- **Natural gas** is convenient because it is continuously delivered by pipelines, eliminating the need for storage tanks. In many parts of the country, gas is the most economical fuel.
- **Solar heat** is clean and energy-efficient but may not be sufficient in all climates.

---

and disadvantages, which may occasionally change as the supply of and demand for different fuels change.

Residential appraisals reported on Fannie Mae or Freddie Mac forms must include a separate description and value estimate for solar heating systems and other alternative energy systems.

Air-Conditioning and Ventilation System

In the past ducts, fans, and windows were used to reduce heat and to provide fresh air in most buildings. Ducts and fans are still used in many buildings. In certain parts of the western United States, where humidity remains low even during periods of high heat, some buildings are cooled with a simple system that blows air across wet excelsior or another water-absorbing material. Package units that apply this procedure are still manufactured for residential and commercial use. They consume less power and are less expensive than conventional air-conditioning.

Air conditioners range from small, portable units to units that provide tons of cooling capacity. The capacity of an air-conditioning unit is rated in tons of refrigeration. One ton of refrigeration equals 12,000 Btus per hour (the amount of heat needed to melt one ton of ice in 24 hours). If an appraiser decides that a building has too much or too little air-conditioning for the climate, the appraisal report should contain data to support this conclusion.

Electrical System

A well-designed electrical system should provide sufficient electrical service to power all the electrical equipment in the building. Sometimes a single electrical service supplies power to more than one building. Wall switches and lighting fixtures are the most visible part of the electrical system.

Functional Problems of Equipment and Mechanical Systems

Plumbing

- Worn galvanized steel, lead, or brass water pipes may need to be replaced.
- The design of bathroom fixtures has undergone substantial change, so old fixtures may become obsolete during the building's economic life. An appraiser reports any modernization that the bathrooms may require. Old fixtures of good quality such as porcelain pedestal basins and legged tubs are often rehabilitated.
- The water in many areas contains minerals such as calcium, magnesium, sulfates, bicarbonates, iron, and sulfur. These minerals react unfavorably with soap to form a curdled substance that is difficult to rinse from clothing, hair, and skin. This hard water often cannot be used until it is treated. Some residences have automatic, multistage treatment systems to make hard water usable.
- Houses with inadequate hot water systems suffer functional obsolescence.

Heating and Air-Conditioning

- An appraiser cannot assume that the existing heating system contributes maximum value to a property. The heating system installed when a building was constructed is often not acceptable to current potential buyers. New technology has continued to reduce the energy consumption of large heating systems.
- Electric heat has become so expensive in some areas that buildings with electrical heating systems sell for substantially less than similar properties heated with other types of fuel.
- Buyers are sensitive to energy costs. Buildings with high ceilings, many openings, and poor insulation may be less desirable.

Electrical System

- Aluminum wiring is now prohibited by law in some sections of the United States because of its poor fire resistance compared to standard copper wiring.
- Stylized lighting fixtures often become obsolete before they wear out because styles change.

Most houses have a single-phase, three-wire system that provides at least 100 amperes of electricity. Thirty-ampere systems are now obsolete and residences with 60 amperes of service normally sell for less than similar homes with greater electrical service. Service of 150, 200, 300, or 400 amperes is needed to power electrical heating and air-conditioning. Most of these services can provide up to 220 volts by connecting three wires to the outlet.

ATTACHMENTS, GARAGES, AND OUTBUILDINGS

Certain building improvements are not included in the calculation of gross living area but they certainly add to the attractiveness and livability of a residence and increase its market value. In some parts of the country, home owners expect a two-car garage and the absence of

Types of Ancillary Improvements

Ground-Level Attachments
Porches
Patios
Decks
Breezeways

Wall Attachments
Balconies
Exterior stairwells
Window wells
Oriel windows
Bay windows
Window attachments such as awnings and shutters

Vehicle Storage
Garages
Carports

Roof Attachments
Cupolas
Skylights
Dormers
Antennas
Weather vanes
Turrets

Outbuildings
Greenhouses
Garden sheds
Carriage houses
Barns
Beach houses
Boathouses
Recreational facilities
Storage buildings

such a feature will affect the price a potential buyer would be willing to pay. An understanding of market standards is needed to judge the importance of ancillary improvements such as attachments, garages, and outbuildings.

Porches can be enclosed, screened, or open, though an open porch should not be confused with a patio. The latter need not be built onto a foundation. Decks are usually made out of wood and supported on footings; they can be located at ground level or raised above the ground. Decks are adjacent to the house and usually accessed by sliding glass doors or a service door.

Appraisers should be able to judge whether the addition of amenities such as oriel and bay windows or skylights and dormers contribute more to value than their cost. Attachments such as weather vanes and turrets can add character to a house but should not make a property incompatible with community standards. Nonessential improvements are more common in high-priced residential markets.

In addition to vehicle storage, garages can provide space for workshops, laundry rooms, and general storage. Detached garages have become less popular in certain areas of the country, although a covered breezeway between garage and house alleviates some of the inconvenience of a detached garage.

Physical and Functional Problems of Attachments, Garages, and Outbuildings

- Elaborate wall and roof attachments such as bay windows and skylights increase the chance of leakage unless flashing is installed properly.
- Like basements in certain areas, outbuildings may cost more than can be justified by the resale value of the property.

- The car storage provided should conform to market standards. A garage in an area where carports predominate is an overimprovement, while a carport in an area where garages are considered essential is an underimprovement. Oversized garages may be appealing but they are often overimprovements.

Functional Problems

Nonessential improvements and outbuildings may not have been constructed at the same time as the main structure, so appraisers should look for differences in the quality of construction of various building components. Also, amenities such as cupolas, turrets, skylights, and balconies require special construction skills, which may be scarce or expensive in certain markets.

SITE IMPROVEMENTS AND SPECIAL FEATURES

Improvements not included in the site valuation (improvements *on* a site rather than *to* a site) can be considered part of the building improvements. In form reports, some of these items are covered in the site section while others are dealt with in the description of improvements.

Landscaping modifies the natural site to achieve a functional or decorative effect. Landscaping often improves the overall appearance of a property and enhances its value, but the desirability of plants is a matter of individual taste. The more elaborate the garden, the more care it will require. The value enhancement produced by good landscaping depends on the character and standards of the neighborhood.

Some trees and shrubs are considered part of the raw land, not site improvements. An appraiser considers the maturity, health, and overall appearance of trees and notes any risk of damage that might result from dead trees or branches falling on or striking the residence in a storm. Trees and shrubs are planted for practical as well as aesthetic reasons. Deciduous trees are best placed on the west side of a property, where they will provide shade from the hot afternoon sun in the summer but allow the sun's warmth to shine through in the winter. Conifers planted on the north side of a house can act as windbreaks.

Lighting and sprinkler systems can contribute to the residents' enjoyment of an outdoor area. Special yard improvements such as

Improvements *on* a Site	
• Landscaping	• Pools and ponds
• Walls and fences	• Waterfront improvements
• Walks	• Recreational facilities
• Driveways and parking areas	

statuary, barbecues, planters, fountains, and birdbaths tend to give a residence character. However, if these improvements are in poor taste given the standards of the neighborhood, they may discourage buyers and affect property value adversely.

Walls and fences of stone, wood, or metal often form barriers around the perimeter of a lot. The cost and condition of walls and fences can vary greatly, and the structures provide varying degrees of privacy, decoration, and security. Appraisers should recognize that the walls and fences of the subject property may encroach on abutting properties and vice versa.

Walks provide access from the streets and from driveway and parking areas to the entrances of the house. Walks can be made of concrete, brick, stone, or patio blocks. They should provide convenient access and not become muddy when it rains.

Driveways and parking areas provide access from the street to the garage. They may be made of a variety of materials including gravel, stone, concrete, asphalt, or earth. The slope of a driveway should facilitate access, and both driveways and parking areas should be pitched to drain water away from the improvements. Parking areas must allow adequate space for a driver to turn around.

Pools may be heated or unheated and vary in size and quality. Pool construction, depth, equipment, and maintenance requirements will influence the value contributed by a pool. Since most above-ground pools are movable, they are usually considered personal property.

If ponds or lakes are near or on the property, their shoreline features, depth, construction, erosion, accretion, stocking, and manner of use should be described. An appraiser should also note where water enters and leaves ponds and lakes and examine the potential for flooding.

Waterfront improvements include breakwaters, seawalls, piers, boat hoists, and beaches. An appraiser notes the condition, quality, and usefulness of these improvements and considers any riparian or littoral rights.

Recreational areas such as terraces, tennis courts, bridle paths, golf courses, and whirlpool baths should always be considered in light of the probable market for the subject property.

Special Features

In addition to site improvements, appraisers must describe special interior amenities such as fireplaces, appliances, and built-in features.

Most cabinets installed before the 1940s were made of wood and custom built at the construction site, but today factory-made wood or metal cabinets are also used. Cabinets must be installed level and plumb to operate properly. They should be screwed, not nailed, to the wall studs, and the screws should go through to the framing members.

Like cabinetry, kitchen appliances such as refrigerators, dishwashers, trash compactors, and garbage disposals that are built in must be accounted for in the property description. Appraisers should note whether the appliances are compatible with the kitchen layout and whether there is any physical deterioration.

Most fireplaces do not provide a building's primary source of heat; because of their design, many fireplaces have little heating power. Some devices can be installed to make fireplaces better sources of heat. One such device is a specialized fan that returns hot air into the room.

Physical and Functional Problems of Fireplaces

- Carpeting or rugs within a few inches of the front of a fireplace may constitute a fire hazard.

- Because fireplaces are difficult to install, many are poorly built and do not function properly. One common problem is downdraft (or negative air pressure), which may blow smoke into the building when it is windy outside. This can happen if the chimney does not extend at least 2 feet above any part of the roof within 10 feet of it.

A typical fireplace has a single opening with a damper and a hearth. More complex designs feature two, three, four, or more openings. Prefabricated fireplaces or woodstoves and flues are often installed in buildings constructed without fireplaces. These fireplaces must be approved by Underwriters Laboratories, Inc., and installed according to the manufacturer's instructions or they may be a potential fire hazard. To be safe, a fireplace should be supported by noncombustible material and equipped with a noncombustible hearth that extends at least 16 inches in front of the opening and at least 8 inches on each side.

OVERALL CONDITION OF THE RESIDENCE

A complete building description includes a quality and condition survey of the main improvements. To describe their condition, an appraiser classifies building components as

1. Items requiring immediate repair
2. Items for which maintenance may be deferred
3. Items that are expected to last for the full economic life of the building

Items Requiring Immediate Repair

Some homes are exceptionally well maintained, but almost all will contain items in need of repair on the date of the appraisal. Repairing these items (commonly called *deferred maintenance items*) should add as much or more value to the property than the cost of repair. When the cost approach to value is applied, these are considered items of curable physical deterioration. The appraiser's repair list should include items that constitute a fire or safety hazard. Many clients request that these items be listed separately in the report. Sometimes the appraiser is asked to estimate the cost of each repair, which is called *cost to cure.*

Short-lived Items

The economic life of a building is the period over which the improvements contribute to property value. Items of deferred maintenance will usually have to be repaired at some time before the end of the economic life of the building. The remaining economic life of a building component is the estimated period during which the component will contribute to property value. If the remaining economic life of the component is shorter than the remaining economic life of the structure as a whole, the component is known as a *short-lived item.*

Although a building's paint, roof, and wallpaper may show signs of wear and tear, they may not be ready for replacement on the date of the appraisal. The appraiser must determine whether repairing or replacing the item will add more value to the property than it will cost. If, for example, a house has an exterior paint job that is three years old and exterior paint normally lasts five years, the paint has suffered some depreciation. Repainting the house on the date of the appraisal, however, would probably not add enough value to the property to justify its cost.

TERMS

deferred maintenance: curable, physical deterioration that should be corrected immediately, although work has not commenced; denotes the need for immediate expenditures, but does not necessarily suggest inadequate maintenance in the past.

cost to cure: the cost to restore an item of deferred maintenance to new or reasonably new condition.

short-lived item: a building component with an expected remaining economic life that is shorter than the remaining economic life of the entire structure.

Common Home Repairs Required

- Touching up exterior paint
- Doing minor carpentry on stairs, moldings, trim, floors, and porches
- Redecorating interior rooms
- Fixing leaks and noisy plumbing
- Loosening stuck doors and windows
- Repairing holes in screens and replacing broken windows or other glass
- Rehanging loose gutters and leaders

- Replacing missing roof shingles and tiles
- Fixing cracks in pavements
- Doing minor electrical repairs
- Replacing rotted floorboards
- Exterminating vermin
- Fixing cracked or loose bathroom and kitchen tiles
- Repairing septic systems
- Eliminating fire hazards

An appraiser also considers whether repairing an item is necessary to preserve other components. For example, a roof cover must be replaced because if it is not, the economic life of the other components will be reduced. Other major short-lived components probably do not require replacement unless they have a life expectancy at least equal to the remaining economic life expectancy of the overall structure.

The appraiser notes whether the condition of short-lived items is better or worse than the overall condition of the residence.

Long-lived Items

The final step in the quality and condition survey is a description of items that are not expected to require repair or replacement during the economic life of the building. A building component with an expected remaining economic life that is the same as the remaining economic life of the entire structure is a long-lived item. Repair may not be

---

Short-lived Items

- Interior paint and wallpaper
- Exterior paint
- Floor finishes
- Shades, screens, and blinds (often considered personal property)
- Waterproofing and weatherstripping
- Gutters and leaders
- Roof covering and flashing
- Water heater
- Furnace

- Air-conditioning equipment
- Carpeting
- Kitchen appliances (considered short-lived components only if built-in)
- Sump pump
- Water softener system (often this component is rented)
- Washers and dryers (often considered personal property)
- Ventilating fans

Long-lived Items

- Hot and cold water pipes
- Plumbing fixtures (may also be considered functional components)
- Electric service connection (may also be considered a functional component)
- Electric wiring
- Electric switches and outlets
- Electric fixtures
- Ducts and radiators

required because the components have been built to last and have been well maintained. However, the long-lived items in a building are rarely in exactly the same condition. The appraiser should focus on those items that are not in the same condition as the rest of the building.

TERM

long-lived item: a building component with an expected remaining economic life that is the same as the remaining economic life of the entire structure.

Sometimes defective long-lived items are not considered in need of repair because the cost of replacement or repair is greater than the amount these items contribute to the value of the property. A serious crack in a foundation wall, for example, would probably be considered incurable physical deterioration. Incurable depreciation that results from problems in the original design of a residence is considered incurable functional obsolescence.

CHAPTER 9

MARKET AND NEIGHBORHOOD ANALYSIS

The object of study in most appraisal assignments is market value, which is derived from market data and reflects the interaction of supply and demand in a particular market area. Different levels of market analysis are required depending on the purpose of the appraisal assignment.

1. To conduct a *market study,* the general market conditions that affect a specific area or a particular property type must be studied. A careful investigation of historical and potential levels of supply and demand may be needed.

2. To perform a *marketability study,* an appraiser investigates how a particular property or class of properties will be absorbed, sold, or leased under current or anticipated market conditions. Marketability studies are often requested by developers and entrepreneurs who need to know the risks associated with subdivision, condominium, or retail projects.

3. For many standard residential appraisal assignments (e.g., for mortgage underwriting purposes), a *neighborhood analysis* is required. Completing the neighborhood section of a form report is a relatively straightforward process.

Appraisers regularly update their files to include new data on the area where they usually work. Background research on the local and neighborhood market is often conducted in advance, and then

TERMS

market study: a macroeconomic analysis that examines the general market conditions of supply, demand, and pricing or the demographics of demand for a specific area or property type. A market study may also include analyses of construction and absorption trends.

marketability study: a microeconomic study that examines the marketability of a given property or class of properties, usually focusing on the market segment(s) in which the property is likely to generate demand. Marketability studies are useful in determining a specific highest and best use, testing development proposals, and projecting an appropriate tenant mix.

neighborhood analysis: the objective analysis of observable and/or quantifiable data indicating discernible patterns of urban growth, structure, and change that may detract from or enhance property values; focuses on four sets of considerations that influence value (social, economic, governmental, and environmental factors).

additional data are collected as part of the specific assignment. Typically an appraiser begins with information available in office files, makes additional inquiries to supplement and update these data, and completes the research during the field inspection by examining the characteristics of the neighborhood.

In-house research, supplemental investigation, and field inspection are undertaken to answer interrelated questions concerning:

- The basic characteristics of the residential real estate market, including price levels, price changes, supply and demand relationships, and market activity patterns
- The features, locations, and possible alternative uses of residential properties, which contribute to or detract from value in this market
- The boundaries and major characteristics of the neighborhood where the subject property is located
- The competitive advantages and disadvantages of the neighborhood in light of the amenities, facilities, and appeal of comparable neighborhoods
- The present mix of land uses and the likely pattern and direction of future changes in land use

The conclusions drawn in market analysis are likely to affect all aspects of the appraiser's subsequent analyses. An understanding of the market area, market characteristics, neighborhood land uses, and anticipated changes is essential to every appraisal. This preliminary analysis impacts the selection of appropriate market data, the determination of highest and best use, the adjustment of the sale prices of comparables, the estimation of depreciation, and the derivation of income and expense information.

Proper market analysis can ensure that the appraiser does not use inappropriate data or double-count—i.e., consider a value influence in more than one category and make two adjustments to a price for one value influence.

MARKET AREA VALUE INFLUENCES

Changes that affect real estate values can originate at the national, regional, municipal, community, and neighborhood levels. When a specific area is being studied, the influences on local property values are most relevant.

In a market study, supply and demand are investigated and the social, economic, governmental, and environmental forces that cause these conditions to change are analyzed. Trends and cycles at national and regional levels affect many types of real estate and often provide the standard against which local market fluctuations are measured. Therefore, an appraiser's analysis usually relates these broader trends to conditions in specific geographic areas. The markets studied are defined in terms of the location, type, size, age, condition, and price range of the properties considered. Table 9.1 identifies value influences and indicators at different geographic levels.

Ultimately, a specific market area is delineated for the subject property. The most useful comparable data analyzed in the appraisal are drawn from this specific market area because it is within this area that alternative, similar properties effectively compete with the subject property.

CONCEPTS

The appraiser studies social, economic, governmental, and environmental (including physical and geographic) value influences.

Important market patterns and trends are indicated by the prices of properties with different characteristics, price changes, supply and demand, and the volume of market activity.

Table 9.1	Value Influences and Indicators by Area	
Regional	**Community**	**Neighborhood**
• Regional price level indexes	• Local population	• Age
• Interest rates	• Long-term and seasonal employment	• Stage in life cycle
• Aggregate employment and unemployment statistics	• Income and wage rates	• Rates of construction and vacancy
• Housing starts, building permits issued, and dollar volume of construction	• Diversity of employment	• Market activity levels, absorption rate, turnover rate, volume of sales
• State laws governing development, environmental protection, and low- and moderate-income housing	• Net household formation	• Motivations of buyers and sellers
	• Household income	• Property use before and after sale
	• Availability of mortgage money	• Presence of desired amenities
	• Competitiveness with other communities	• Maintenance standards
	• Adequacy of utilities and transportation systems	• Economic profile and age of occupants
	• Zoning, subdivision regulations, and building codes	

VALUE INFLUENCES AT THE NEIGHBORHOOD LEVEL

In collecting data and inspecting the neighborhood, the appraiser attempts to identify major value influences, observe how they are changing, and relate these conclusions to the subject property and potentially comparable properties. As noted in Chapter 3, the forces that affect value are classified as

- Social
- Economic
- Governmental (which includes legal factors)
- Environmental (which includes physical and geographic factors)

Although these influences often overlap, it is helpful to consider each category separately.

Social Influences

Social influences on neighborhood property values include

- Population characteristics and trends
- The quality and reputation of the establishments that serve the neighborhood
- Community and neighborhood organizations
- The absence or extent of crime and litter

Population Characteristics

Area population changes as a result of natural growth or decline and movement into or out of an area. Although many factors influence an individual's decision to move, the most compelling impetus may be economic necessity.

People move to areas where they can live and work in security and comfort and where their children will have the best economic future. In the 1970s the population trend in the United States was toward the

---

Population Characteristics

- The current population
- The size and composition of households
- The population makeup
- The occupant employment profile

- Population density, which is usually important in areas dominated by high-rise residences
- The education, skill, and income levels of residents

Sunbelt states and away from the industrial states of the Midwest and Northeast. Local economic conditions altered this picture in the 1980s. The shift toward a service- and research-based economy revitalized regions such as the Boston area, but the decline in oil production and agriculture left areas such as Texas in an economic recession.

CONCEPT

Population analysis focuses on the number and rate of new household formation, the characteristics of residents, and their housing preferences.

By the 1990s the situation had changed once more. Employment levels began to decline in New England, which felt the full impact of the national economic slump. During the same period, diversification in Texas was creating a stronger employment base. Different regions of the country, and even certain areas within individual states, have very different economic characteristics. This variation is more extreme today than it has been for most of the twentieth century.

Birth and death rates, the age at which people start families, and the number of children in a typical family all affect population size over the long term. Marriage and divorce rates also influence the rate of new household formation. Furthermore, appraisers are interested not only in the numbers of units desired but also in the kinds of units desired. Specific population characteristics can explain differences in demand. Young families with children, single professionals, and older adults often have different preferences as to housing features and neighborhood amenities. These segments of the population also tend to have different levels of income, which allow them to make their preferences felt. Thus, the ages, number of children, gender, occupation, and income of residents are all likely to be relevant in a study of the market population.

Appraisers should identify and quantify the trends that population characteristics suggest. For instance, if a neighborhood is becoming increasingly attractive to households with young children, residences with extra rooms and play areas may be in great demand. If middle-

Where to Find: Population Data

- The U.S. Census Bureau
- Utility companies
- Local chambers of commerce
- County offices
- School districts
- Visitors' bureaus

Note: If census figures are not up-to-date, the population of a neighborhood can be estimated by multiplying the number of electric or water meters in the area by the ratio of population to number of meters that was calculated at the time of the last census.

and upper-income professionals prefer city neighborhoods close to restaurants and cultural facilities, low-maintenance properties in particular neighborhoods may become especially desirable. Trends can be identified by observing price changes for different types of residences and neighborhoods over several years. Understanding the social forces behind these price changes can help the appraiser forecast a neighborhood's future. Such forecasts must be based on factual evidence that is clearly stated in the appraisal report.

Quality of Services and Establishments

The appraiser should investigate how residents and potential buyers rate the quality of businesses and other establishments that serve the neighborhood, in comparison with the services provided in competitive neighborhoods.

- Are there enough restaurants in the area?
- Is parking a problem?
- Are shopping facilities, medical facilities, and recreational areas adequate?
- How good are the neighborhood schools and places of worship?
- How do potential buyers feel about area establishments and the neighborhood's future?

Community and Neighborhood Associations

The presence of neighborhood and community groups can affect the stability of a neighborhood and the value of its residential property. Some neighborhood groups are legal entities formed by the original developers or by the home owners themselves; they are concerned with maintaining common areas and providing certain services such as garbage disposal, snow removal, water supply, and police and fire protection. Voluntary associations such as crime watch groups and block clubs organize neighborhood crime protection efforts, lobby against undesirable rezoning or development, and sponsor revitalization projects, block parties, and street fairs. Community spirit can make a neighborhood more stable and may even reverse a trend toward declining property values.

Crime and Litter

When a neighborhood is reputed to have a high crime rate, some residents may move and potential residents may decide not to purchase homes there. Better street lighting, increased police protection, and effective neighborhood crime watch groups can improve a neighborhood's crime problem to some extent.

Where to Find: Crime Statistics

Local police departments usually have information on the number and types of crimes reported in an area.

The absence of litter and graffiti in public and private areas suggests that property owners care about their neighborhood. The presence of an unusual amount of litter or graffiti suggests neighborhood apathy and may indicate a change in the neighborhood's occupancy characteristics. The level of crime in the neighborhood and the presence of litter or graffiti should be stated in the neighborhood section of the appraisal report.

Economic Influences

Economic influences center around the financial ability of neighborhood occupants to rent or own property, to maintain it, and to renovate or rehabilitate it when necessary. The physical condition of individual properties indicates the relative financial strength of area occupants and how this strength is translated into neighborhood upkeep. The economic characteristics of occupants may also reflect present conditions and future trends in real estate supply and demand.

Economic Influences

- The economic profile of residents
- The types and terms of financing available
- Property price and rent levels
- The amount of development, construction, conversion, and vacant land
- The extent of owner occupancy

Economic Profile of Residents

There is a direct relationship between the income and employment profile of neighborhood residents and price and rent levels. The type, stability, and location of employment all have a strong impact on the value of residential property because employment determines the ability of individuals to purchase or rent in a particular area. Income levels tend to set a range of property values in a neighborhood.

The demand for housing can increase or decrease substantially due to a change in purchasing power, even if the size of the population remains the same.

CONCEPTS

Demand is studied primarily by analyzing the current and anticipated conditions that affect population and purchasing power.

Purchasing power is studied chiefly in terms of income and employment levels, tax levels, price levels, and housing expenditures.

TERMS

purchasing power: the ability and willingness to pay for an economic good; contingent upon disposable income.

disposable income: the personal income remaining after deducting income taxes and all other payments to federal, state, and local governments.

Overall shifts in the level of demand may occur when people have more money to spend on housing needs. The type of housing desired may also change.

Purchasing power depends on the disposable income—i.e., personal income that remains after taxes and other payments to government—that a household wants to allocate to housing expenditures. It also varies with the size of these expenditures. Employment, income, and savings levels as well as the average number of wage earners in a household should be considered. Tax levels indicate how much money is available to purchase goods and services of all kinds. The prices of other basic goods suggest how much money can be spent on housing. Housing expenditures include the price of residences, mortgage financing, property taxes, and maintenance costs.

Local business conditions must also be considered. Relevant data on local business activities include retail sales levels, real estate transfers, and new housing starts.

Where to Find: Resident Income Levels and Other Economic Indicators

Information on income levels can be found in recent census data and newspaper surveys. Other useful information can be provided by

- State employment services
- Local chambers of commerce
- Local employers
- Monthly business reviews published by academic and financial institutions

An appraiser may compile a wealth of information on local businesses, but these data are only useful if they can be used to relate recent or likely future changes in the economy to specific changes in the demand for a specific type of real estate. For example, upper-income housing in an area may respond to a factory closing differently than lower-income housing. Similarly, business fluctuations may not affect rent levels in the same way they affect the prices of single-family residences.

Types and Terms of Financing

The mortgage financing available may be the single most important factor considered in the study of demand. To assess how the income of a population affects its purchasing power, an appraiser considers the requirements

of mortgage lenders who serve the market
population in the area.

Most of the money used to buy residential properties is borrowed from thrift institutions. When these primary sources have little
credit available or the credit terms are too
restrictive, the demand for housing contracts.
High interest rates translate into high
monthly payments. If mortgage payments
exceed the portion of monthly household
income that can be spent for housing, increasing numbers of home
owners will default and others may be discouraged from entering the
real estate market. Sellers may offer creative financing arrangements,
which call for monthly payments that are lower than those required
with typical financing.

The availability and terms of mortgage financing are affected by
economic decisions and changes on many levels. Appraisers should
carefully track each influence and consider its effects. The Federal
Reserve can increase or decrease the supply of credit available to its
member banks, which will result in monetary expansion or contraction. The amount of credit that thrifts can offer home buyers also
depends on how much money other individuals have deposited with
them. The savings level, in turn, reflects national, regional, and local
business conditions. The size of the national debt is another influence
affecting credit availability. The U.S. Department of the Treasury
strongly competes with private sources to obtain a share of the
country's available credit. When the government borrows heavily to
pay its bills, the credit supply may shrink and interest rates may rise.

To provide greater liquidity for mortgages when capital is in short
supply, government and private agencies have created the secondary
mortgage market. The Federal National Mortgage Association
(Fannie Mae), the Federal Home Loan Mortgage Corporation
(Freddie Mac), and the Government National Mortgage Association
(Ginnie Mae) are the main participants in the secondary mortgage
market. When these organizations decide to purchase packages of
mortgages from primary sources, more money is available for home
buyers.

Organizations such as Fannie Mae, Freddie Mac, and Ginnie Mae
generate the greatest amount of secondary mortgage market activity,
but banks and insurance companies in the private sector also provide
substantial amounts of mortgage money. These institutions sell loan

---

Where to Find: Mortgage Information

Appraisers need broad knowledge of national and local developments to understand the full implications of specific market conditions in the immediate area.

- An appraiser may find printed data on current interest rates and the availability of financing in the survey updates of multiple listing services and title companies.
- Local Realtors® can supply information on the financing arrangements involved in their most recent transactions.

- Local lending institutions can quote the rates on conventional, VA, and FHA loans and indicate how many points are charged.
- Most local newspapers provide comprehensive listings of interest rates on everything from Treasury bills to mortgages.

---

portfolios and shares to private investors. Real estate investment trusts (REITs) purchase mortgages, providing lending institutions with greater liquidity.

Certain federal agencies either guarantee or insure home mortgages. The Department of Veterans Affairs (VA) provides a wide range of benefits, including guaranteed mortgage loans. The Federal Housing Administration (FHA), which is part of the Department of Housing and Urban Development (HUD), acts primarily as an insurer of mortgages made by private lenders. To qualify for FHA insurance, a property has to comply with FHA criteria and the mortgage must meet FHA standards regarding interest rates, lending practices, and review procedures. Because FHA mortgages call for lower down payments and interest rates, they stimulate home ownership among first-time buyers. In 1999, FHA implemented mandatory testing of appraisers involved in FHA transactions and instituted stricter approval policies on FHA appraisal work. In addition, FHA imposed more rigorous reporting requirements, in particular regarding property defects that must be repaired before an FHA loan will be made.

Property Price and Rent Levels

The price and rent levels of neighborhood properties usually fall within a narrow range. The value of a subject property is strongly affected by the prices at which similar, nearby properties have been sold. Neighborhood prices and rents constitute the primary source of market data for appraisal analysis. Price and rent levels indicate the interaction of value influences. If price levels are changing, appraisers should know what is causing this change.

Development, Construction, Conversion, and Vacant Land

Vacant land suitable for the construction of additional houses may exist within a neighborhood simply because the owners do not wish to sell or develop the land. However, the presence of vacant land may also indicate a lack of effective demand or suggest the likelihood of future construction activity.

If there are only a few vacant lots in a neighborhood, their development usually will not have a substantial impact on other neighborhood properties. However, if these lots are specifically zoned for nonresidential use or variances are granted to permit nonresidential construction, the presence of an atypical use may have an adverse effect. If a neighborhood has many vacant lots, the values of existing properties may be significantly affected by the anticipated development of these lots. Similarly, if many nonresidential properties are likely to be converted to residential use, existing residential properties may be affected.

In performing neighborhood analysis, an appraiser should obtain information about buildings under construction and proposed future development as well as the existing supply of properties. Supply increases that result from recent construction activity can be studied by analyzing new housing starts. The number, location, type of unit, and price or rent of the new units constructed should be considered. An appraiser can use data on housing starts supplemented with information on proposed construction activity and projected demand to

> **CONCEPT**
>
> Supply is studied by analyzing the inventory of various types of existing housing (i.e., vacancy and turnover rates) as well as new and proposed construction and the associated costs.

Where to Find: Housing Supply Data

- Housing stock is usually a local matter, but local situations may reflect national trends.

- Data on the number of properties available for sale and lease can be obtained from multiple listing services and realty advertisements in newspapers.

- Local and regional planning agencies and departments of development can provide data on projected expansion and authorized construction permits.

- Other good sources for housing starts are publications of local and national home builders associations.

- Appraisers can obtain data on local vacancy and occupancy levels from chambers of commerce, builders' boards, and real estate management companies.

- For information on costs, appraisers should consult local builders and developers and refer to cost estimating services, which provide multipliers that can be used to adjust national cost data to local conditions.

form a picture of the relationship between supply and demand in the market and to decide whether an oversupply is likely to be created by current construction. An analysis of trends for the past several years may be helpful. These data may show a balanced supply-demand relationship at present but project an oversupply in the future.

Extent of Owner Occupancy

Neighborhoods in which most residences are owner-occupied are often more stable and pose less investment risk to lenders than neighborhoods with many tenant-occupants. Owners generally maintain their properties better than tenants. When the ratio of owner-occupied to tenant-occupied residences in a neighborhood changes, decline or revitalization may be indicated.

Government Influences

Government and legal influences on property values include the laws, regulations, and taxes imposed on neighborhood properties and the administration and enforcement activities associated with these constraints. An appraiser gathers data on government influences in the subject neighborhood to get a picture of how the situation in this neighborhood compares with that of other, competitive neighborhoods.

Police power regulations, private restrictions, and taxes can restrict the rights of property ownership and influence property values. In neighborhood analysis an appraiser tries to ascertain the following:

1. How the benefits produced by local regulations stand in relation to the burdens they impose. The local situation is then compared with the situation in competitive neighborhoods.

2. How much government provisions and their enforcement add to or detract from the stability of the neighborhood.

3. How these provisions relate to the neighborhood or community master plan. The likelihood and effect of future changes in legislation are also assessed.

Important Factors Concerning Government

- Taxation and special assessments in relation to the services provided and in comparison with other neighborhoods in the community
- Public and private restrictions
- Schools
- The quality of fire and police protection and other public services
- Government planning and development activity

Taxation and Special Assessments

Tax burdens can vary significantly, and variations in taxes may significantly influence the decisions of potential buyers. Divergent tax rates often affect market value. Local taxes may favor or discriminate against certain types of property. Community development programs may depend on tax revenues. The appraiser should

- Examine local assessed values and tax rates
- Compare the burdens created by various taxes
- Measure their effect on the values of different types of real estate

Special assessments are directly related to the additional services or advantages provided—e.g., for private beaches or extra fire protection. Properties subject to high special assessments may or may not be penalized. A special assessment lien may reduce the price of a house by approximately the amount of the lien.

> **TERM**
>
> **special assessment:** an assessment against real estate levied by a public authority to pay for public improvements, e.g., sidewalks, street improvements, sewers.

Counties and cities may have the authority to impose optional taxes such as sales and earnings taxes on residents. When competing communities are subject to different sales and local earnings taxes, the relative desirability of the communities may be affected. These variations often have a more significant effect on the marketability of commercial and industrial real estate than ad valorem taxes do. Such variations can indirectly influence residential real estate values.

Public and Private Restrictions

Zoning regulations and building codes are important to the stability of a neighborhood. They provide legal protection against adverse influences, nuisances, and hazards. Some buyers seek out neighborhoods that have effective zoning laws, building codes, and housing and sanitary codes. The enforcement of these codes, regulations, and restrictions should be effective and equitable in comparison with enforcement in competitive neighborhoods. Figure 9.1 shows a zoning map.

Changes in zoning may have positive or negative effects on the neighborhood as a whole, and changes can have different effects on individual properties in the neighborhood. For example, rezoning a corner site from residential to commercial use might have a negative effect on the neighborhood as a whole although it increases the value of that particular property. Appraisers are concerned with both of

Figure 9.1   Zoning Map

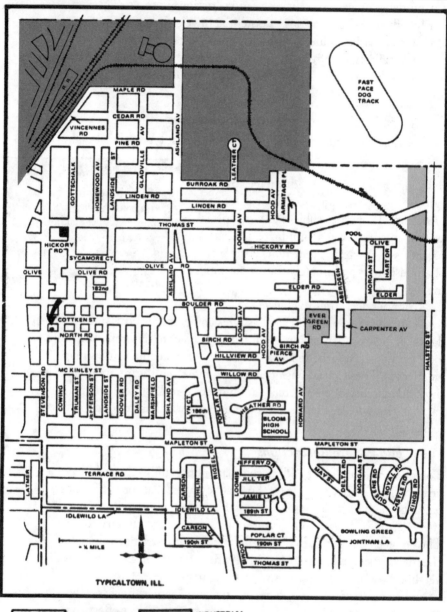

TYPICALTOWN, ILL.

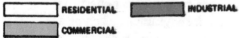

RESIDENTIAL   INDUSTRIAL   COMMERCIAL

these effects. The probability of zoning changes in transitional areas should be explored through discussions with zoning officials. Antici-pated zoning changes can affect the highest and best use, and hence the value, of the subject and potential comparable properties. *Interim uses* (i.e., temporary uses to which properties may be put until they are ready for their highest and best uses) may be considered.

When existing zoning and building regulations are not enforced, neighborhood property values may decline. When zoning variances are obtained easily and without consideration of their effect on surrounding properties, the stability of the neighborhood can be threatened and the value of neighboring properties may decrease. Zoning violations often include illegal signs, illegal business uses, and conversion of properties to a density of use that is higher than the density permitted by the zoning.

Deed restrictions often protect properties from the negative impact of an incompatible use. If these restrictions are not enforced, lower values may result. However, some deed restrictions written long ago may be obsolete or unenforceable. Generally, any deed restriction that is against the public interest cannot be upheld.

Schools

Many families choose a neighborhood for the quality of its schools because schools are of immediate concern to families with children. Because today's economy is oriented toward service and high-tech industries that require well-trained workers, communities with good educational facilities and institutions of higher learning are increas-ingly favored by business and industry. The reputation and probable future of a neighborhood's schools should be considered.

Fire and Police Protection

Government-provided services are vital to the maintenance and preservation of neighborhoods and communities. The decision of a potential home buyer may be influenced by

- The type of fire-fighting service provided
- The size of the fire district
- The distance between the residence and the nearest firehouse
- The reputation of the local police force and its effectiveness in preventing crime

Planning and Development Activity

Planning for the future development of communities is an important task of government. Good planning can maintain the integrity and

Where to Find: Information on Planned Developments

- City and county building and planning commissions, as well as real estate boards and builders' organizations, can provide detailed information on existing and proposed units.

- Building permit information, which can usually be obtained from the municipal building inspection department, indicates the types of housing most popular in the area.

- Municipal and regional planning departments have information on existing and proposed subdivisions to supplement permit information.

- If the community being investigated is too small to have a planning department, the town clerk or the public works department may have this type of information.

- The Council of Governments (COG), which is composed of representatives from several municipal and county governments, is another source of information on supply trends. These entities vary in terms of staffing and funding. Transportation plans and land use records can be obtained from COGs, and some COGs also keep detailed housing information.

character of existing neighborhoods and provide a framework for the future use of undeveloped areas. Poor planning for recreational facilities, schools, and service areas may contribute to neighborhood disintegration. The requirements imposed on developers influence the type and quality of services available to home owners and have a strong effect on the value of existing structures. By protecting open space areas, the government can ensure that developers do not modify the environment to maximize the number of units built.

Development activity may be indicated by analyzing current market sales, absorption trends, expected returns, marketing efforts, and future development plans. By comparing the number of lots being platted to the number of building permits issued, an appraiser can assess the relative oversupply or undersupply of subdivision lots.[1]

Larger communities have land-use planning facilities. Existing or proposed land-use plans can be consulted to learn about anticipated development. Many states have statutes requiring that city governments control land use according to approved plans.

Environmental Influences (Including Physical and Geographic Factors)

Natural and man-made features that affect the neighborhood and its location are considered environmental influences.

---

1. The appraisal of subdivisions and feasibility studies for proposed subdivision developments are covered more fully in Douglas D. Lovell and Robert S. Martin, *Subdivision Analysis* (Chicago: Appraisal Institute, 1993).

> **Important Environmental Considerations**
>
> - The location of the neighborhood within the community
> - The transportation system and important linkages
> - Services, amenities, and recreational facilities
> - The topography, soil, climate, and view
> - Patterns of land use and signs of change in land-use patterns
> - The age, size, style, condition, and appearance of residences and neighborhood facilities
> - The adequacy and quality of utilities

Location within the Community

The changes occurring in a neighborhood are usually affected by changes in the larger area of influence. Therefore, a neighborhood may benefit or suffer because of its location within a district. A neighborhood adjacent to a growing business district, for example, may benefit from nearby shopping and municipal services, but it may also suffer from increased congestion and other nuisances. The rapid growth of one neighborhood or district may adversely affect a competitive neighborhood or district. Areas located in the direction of growth may benefit, while other areas suffer.

Transportation Systems and Linkages

Transportation systems provide important linkages, which have a strong influence on the desirability of specific neighborhoods. An appraiser should consider the destinations to which typical occupants commute as well as the distance, time, and quality of the transportation services available. If adequate facilities are not available, the neighborhood will be at a disadvantage compared with competing neighborhoods with better linkages. In studying location and transportation, an appraiser should consider both existing and proposed transportation facilities as well as all existing and planned facilities to which residents may be expected to commute (see Figure 9.2).

For the occupants of single-family residential neighborhoods, linkages to workplaces, schools, and shopping areas are usually the most important. Access to recreational facilities, houses of worship, restaurants, and stores are somewhat less important. A nearby shopping center can enhance a neighborhood's value. Heavy, slow traffic on highways can reduce values in some areas,

> **TERM**
>
> **transportation linkage:** the movement of people, goods, services, or communications to and from the subject site, measured by the time and cost involved.

Figure 9.2 Land Use Linkages

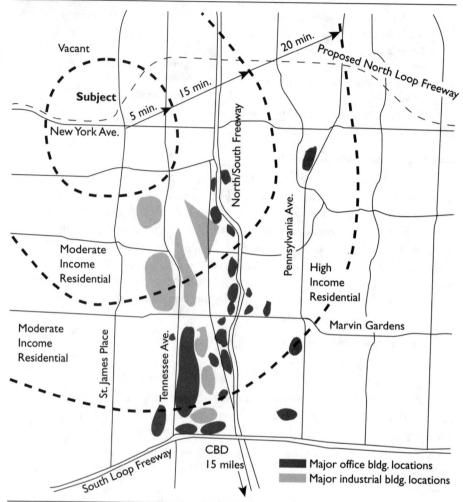

Vacant

Subject

15 min.

20 min.

Proposed North Loop Freeway

5 min.

New York Ave.

North/South Freeway

Pennsylvania Ave.

Moderate
Income
Residential

High
Income
Residential

Moderate
Income
Residential

St. James Place

Tennessee Ave.

Marvin Gardens

South Loop Freeway

CBD
15 miles

■ Major office bldg. locations
■ Major industrial bldg. locations

Note: Not to scale. Driving times are indicated by concentric circles. Reprinted with permission from *Market Analysis for Valuation Appraisals* (Chicago: Appraisal Institute, 1994).

particularly if these highways are the primary linkages between the neighborhood and major centers of employment. Some linkages have special importance to certain groups of people. Proximity to schools may be a priority for people with children, while public transportation and services are important to the elderly.

Public transportation is crucial to people who do not own automobiles or prefer not to use them for commuting. Even in areas where most families own two or more cars, unstable energy costs, high automobile maintenance and insurance costs, and the convenience of public transportation make linkages an important consideration.

The transportation characteristics of the neighborhood usually apply to most properties in the neighborhood. However, the walking distance to and from public transportation can be an important variable if residents are expected to use these facilities frequently. Urban apartment dwellers usually prefer to be within walking distance of public transportation. The territory through which commuters must pass is also important. People dislike walking through poorly lighted streets and rundown areas.

The street pattern of the neighborhood has a significant bearing on a property's location in the community and on transportation linkages. Contemporary neighborhoods are planned with curving streets, cul-de-sacs, and circular drives. These features take up valuable space and can increase land costs, but they do add privacy and reduce the traffic

Street patterns within a community and transportation linkages have a significant influence on the desirability of a property's location.

hazards often found in older neighborhoods with square-block street patterns. Streets should be laid out to make use of natural contours, wooded areas, and ponds. Traffic in residential areas should move slowly and easily. Ideally, expressways and boulevards should be outside residential neighborhoods but offer convenient access to local streets.

Appraisers should also note the quality of street lighting, pavements, sidewalks, curbs, and gutters. Well-maintained streets and shade trees contribute to the overall desirability of a neighborhood. In congested areas, the availability of street parking can also influence property values.

Services, Amenities, and Recreational Facilities

Amenities and services can have a substantial impact on the desirability of a neighborhood, particularly in more affluent areas. The businesses, schools, cultural facilities, and houses of worship that serve the neighborhood affect its desirability. More prosperous neighborhoods provide recreational facilities such as parks, beaches, pools, tennis courts, country clubs, and libraries. These facilities can help a neighborhood attract new residents. Community home owners' associations can keep a neighborhood in good condition by helping maintain recreational facilities and other amenities that increase the neighborhood's desirability. The presence, location, and accessibility of recreational facilities and services should be noted in the appraisal report.

Topography, Soil, Climate, and View

Topography and climatic conditions can have a positive or negative effect on neighborhood property values. The presence of a lake, river, bay, or hill often provides a scenic advantage. A hill may mean little in a mountainous region, but an elevated or wooded section in a predominantly flat area can enhance property values. A river, lake, or park may act as a buffer between a residential district and commercial or industrial areas and reinforce the neighborhood's identity.

Topographic and climatic features can also be disadvantageous. A river that floods penalizes the value of homes along its banks. Abrupt changes in elevation can make access difficult and construction more costly. The soil in an area may have poor bearing capacity, absorption, or drainage characteristics. Climate can also have a negative effect. Although a neighborhood usually shares the same climate as competitive neighborhoods, the subject neighborhood may suffer from special conditions such as increased wind, fog, or rain. Conversely, some neighborhoods may offer protection from such adverse conditions.

The desirability of certain types of topography depends on the kind of residential development that is present or contemplated. For expensive homes, large hillside or wooded sites are often desired. Tract developers, however, usually seek a level area or plateau, which is better suited to subdivision construction and can be developed less expensively. Generally an area slightly higher than surrounding neighborhoods is preferred.

Patterns of Land Use and Signs of Change

In a stable neighborhood the mix of land uses is balanced and conforms to market standards. Each use has a clearly defined area and these areas are well buffered from one another. The neighborhood's boundaries are usually explicit and buildings generally conform to one another and to their immediate environment. Excessive homogeneity can detract from value, but a balanced mix is typical and desirable in the market area.

Neighborhood change is often signaled by

- A poor mix of land uses
- Considerable variation in construction, maintenance standards, and ownership status
- Indistinct neighborhood boundaries

Values may be rising, falling, or about to shift. The neighborhood may be entering a stage of decline, revitalization, or conversion to another type of neighborhood.

To optimize property values, residential areas should be protected from the hazards and nuisances of nearby land uses. Excessive traffic and odors, smoke, dust, and noise from commercial and manufacturing enterprises limit a residential neighborhood's desirability, as does a location next to an airport, a nuclear power plant, or a toxic waste disposal site. Neighborhoods suffering from these conditions may have stable values, particularly if the adverse conditions have been present for some time, but property prices and values in these neighborhoods are likely to be lower than values in similar or competitive neighborhoods that do not suffer adverse influences.

Age, Size, Style, Condition, and Appearance of Residences

The character of a neighborhood is reflected by its "average" house. The structural and architectural quality, age, and condition of typical residences are physical characteristics that have a substantial effect on the desirability of a neighborhood. In stable neighborhoods the average house suggests the type of improvement that constitutes the highest and best use of the subject site. An appraiser should also note the sizes and shapes of typical sites and typical land-to-building ratios in the neighborhood.

The condition of individual homes and their architectural compatibility influence the general appearance of a neighborhood. Well-kept yards, houses, and community areas as well as good landscaping, trees, open space, and few vacant lots make a neighborhood more desirable. Public and commercial establishments should present a neat, compatible appearance. Poorly maintained public areas, vacant stores, and the presence of graffiti on buildings detract from a neighborhood's desirability and often indicate a period of change.

Adequacy and Quality of Utilities

Gas, electricity, water, telephone, cable television service, and sanitary sewers are essential in municipal areas to meet contemporary standards of living. Their absence can decrease values in a neighborhood as can unusually high costs for these services. The availability of utilities affects the direction and timing of neighborhood growth and development.

PROCEDURES FOR NEIGHBORHOOD/MARKET ANALYSIS

The subject property's neighborhood is considered the market area in most residential appraisals. The general procedures of market analysis are therefore applied to the extent appropriate for the property type and the purpose and intended use of the appraisal. Most residential appraisal assignments require a two-step analysis of value influences in the neighborhood. The appraiser

1. Plans the analysis effort and collects pertinent market information
2. Inspects the neighborhood and, when necessary, conducts additional research to resolve questions raised by the field inspection

Planning the Analysis and Collecting Data

Essential data

An appraiser begins to study the neighborhood by determining what data are needed to answer the appraisal problem, where these data can be obtained, and how they can best be collected. The data required depend on the purpose of the assignment and the use to which the appraisal will be put. The purpose of most appraisal assignments is to reach a market value conclusion, so this discussion will focus on the data needed for these appraisals. In ordinary market value appraisals such as those used by mortgage lenders, neighborhood analysis is performed to fulfill the following objectives:

- To form an understanding of market preferences and price patterns on which a market value opinion can be based. This understanding is developed by analyzing data on price and rent levels for properties of different ages with various features and by studying construction costs, supply and demand levels, anticipated changes in supply and demand, and market activity patterns.

- To reach a general conclusion concerning the highest and best use of the site as though vacant, which is required for site valuation. Many characteristics of the neighborhood—e.g., its zoning, tax assessments, accessibility, schools, and cultural facilities—contribute to the determination of the highest and best use of the site as though vacant.

- To consider which specific improvements within the general use category would constitute the highest and best use of the site as though vacant. Generally the ideal improvements for the subject property are suggested by the characteristics of other neighborhood property improvements.

> **CONCEPT**
>
> Neighborhood analysis for most residential appraisal assignments encompasses two steps:
>
> 1. Planning the analysis and collecting the data
> 2. Inspecting the neighborhood

- To determine the highest and best use of the property as improved, considering the structures already on the site as well as neighborhood and market standards.

- To identify the primary area from which comparable properties are to be selected. Several parts of the subject neighborhood or other neighborhoods may be acceptable for this purpose, but locations nearest the subject property and most similar in character are generally the best.

- To discern if and why different locations in the same neighborhood have different values. This knowledge helps the appraiser adjust sales of properties considered comparable for locational differences within the neighborhood.

- To consider the positive and negative value influence of the land uses of neighboring properties.

- To identify various value influences in the neighborhood and rate the neighborhood in comparison with other, competitive neighborhoods. This information will allow the appraiser to use comparables from competitive neighborhoods if necessary and make the necessary adjustments for neighborhood location. It may also help the appraiser understand the neighborhood's most probable future.

- To learn about recent changes in the neighborhood that may have affected values since the comparables were sold. This information provides a basis for making adjustments for market conditions (time).

- To examine the long-term prospects of the neighborhood to decide whether the subject property will qualify as security for a long-term loan. This objective is particularly important when the client is a lender or loan underwriter.

If the appraisal is to be used in a land utilization study or for site selection, a different emphasis may be required.

Once the appraiser has reviewed the objectives of the neighborhood analysis, necessary data must be collected and analyzed to identify value influences. The picture the appraiser forms from this descriptive and numerical information will be tested and refined during the field inspection of the neighborhood. The condition of the improvements and the proximity of other uses will also become evident from the field inspection.

Collection tools

In addition to a vehicle and a map of the area, the appraiser may need a form or checklist to facilitate the collection of data. Such a list can highlight important items that might otherwise be overlooked. If the appraisal is to be communicated in a form report, the appraiser should take the form along during the neighborhood inspection.

Form reports are requested by organizations, businesses, and federal agencies that wish to have the results of appraisals presented in a standardized format. The most widely used form, the Uniform Residential Appraisal Report (URAR), is required by Fannie Mae and

---

Where to Find: Essential Data for Neighborhood Analysis

- Some information can be compiled from census tables, utility line maps, and MLS listings.

- Other data will be obtained from interviewing people familiar with the neighborhood—buyers, sellers, brokers, property owners, and officials responsible for public services in the neighborhood.

- If an appraiser is unfamiliar with a given neighborhood, the field inspection is often the best place to start collecting data.

- Data on standardized or statistically defined areas such as cities, counties, tax districts, and census tracts are available from municipal and county sources. However, the areas covered rarely conform to the neighborhood boundaries that the appraiser has identified. Thus during inspection of the neighborhood, corroborative research is often necessary to ascertain whether the general data collected are appropriate for the market area being studied.

Freddie Mac for appraisals of properties with mortgages that these agencies may purchase and by the VA and HUD for appraisals of properties with mortgages these departments guarantee or insure. Appraisal report forms include space to record many variables important to neighborhood analysis (see Figure 9.3).

Figure 9.3 Neighborhood Section of the URAR

Location	☐ Urban	☐ Suburban	☐ Rural	Predominant occupancy	Single family housing PRICE $(000)	AGE (yrs)	Present land use %	Land use change
Built up	☐ Over 75%	☐ 25-75%	☐ Under 25%				One family _____	☐ Not likely ☐ Likely
Growth rate	☐ Rapid	☐ Stable	☐ Slow	☐ Owner	Low _____		2-4 family _____	☐ In process
Property values	☐ Increasing	☐ Stable	☐ Declining	☐ Tenant	High _____		Multi-family _____	To: _____
Demand/supply	☐ Shortage	☐ In balance	☐ Over supply	☐ Vacant (0-5%)	Predominant		Commercial _____	
Marketing time	☐ Under 3 mos.	☐ 3-6 mos.	☐ Over 6 mos.	☐ Vacant (over 5%)			( )	

Note: Race and the racial composition of the neighborhood are not appraisal factors.

Neighborhood boundaries and characteristics: ——————

Factors that affect the marketability of the properties in the neighborhood (proximity to employment and amenities, employment stability, appeal to market, etc.):

Market conditions in the subject neighborhood (including support for the above conclusions related to the trend of property values, demand/supply, and marketing time...such as data on competitive properties for sale in the neighborhood, description of the prevalence of sales and financing concessions, etc.):

Although the checklists provided on these forms serve an important purpose, they should not limit the appraiser's analysis. There may be important value influences in the specific neighborhood that the form does not list. However, each form does have a space for comments, and any considerations not indicated on the checklist can be addressed there. The comments require the appraiser to state conclusions pertaining to the market for the subject property. Many appraisals submitted on forms require further explanation or clarification, so the appraiser provides additional narrative material as attached sheets or addenda, which are considered part of the appraisal.

Neighborhood Inspection

The next stage in neighborhood analysis is the visual inspection, which is conducted in several steps:

• Inspect the area's physical characteristics. The appraiser drives or walks around the subject area to develop a sense of place and observe the degree of similarity among the land uses, types of structures, architectural styles, and maintenance levels in the area.

- Identify market area boundaries. On a map of the area, the appraiser notes points where the physical characteristics of the land and properties change perceptibly. A copy of this map may be included in the appraisal report. These points generally mark the limits of the market area. The appraiser also identifies any physical barriers such as major streets, hills, rivers, and railroads that coincide with or are near to the market area's boundaries. Neighborhood occupants, business people, brokers, and community representatives may be questioned to get their opinions as to how far the neighborhood extends and what features characterize its different parts.

- Observe land uses and signs of change. The appraiser looks for signs of change in the neighborhood and tries to assess the direction of change, its likely effect on the subject property, and recent changes that may have affected comparable properties. These trends are noted on the map for future reference.

- Rate the neighborhood for quality. The appraiser should rate various aspects of the neighborhood in comparison with other neighborhoods that appeal to the same market population.

A neighborhood is never rated in absolute terms. Its quality is rated only in comparison to other neighborhoods. The rating suggests the neighborhood's appeal to market participants who are shopping for houses in that neighborhood and competitive neighborhoods.

Reporting Conclusions of the Neighborhood Analysis

An appraiser specifically describes all beneficial and detrimental conditions discovered in the neighborhood analysis. A general reference to "pride of ownership" in the neighborhood is too vague and subjective. It does not indicate an actual effect on property values and it ascribes motives and attitudes to market participants. Instead, an appraiser should record precise, impartial observations made during a personal inspection of the neighborhood. Descriptive phrases such as "many broken windows," "tall weeds on site," "no litter present," or "well-kept lawns" convey meaningful information about the value-influencing factors at work in the neighborhood.

CHAPTER
10 | HIGHEST AND BEST USE

Analyses of the city and region, the neighbor-hood and the local market, and the site and improvements all contribute information that can help an appraiser determine the subject property's highest and best use. The appraiser studies the data and decides which legally permitted, physically possible, and financially feasible use of the property will be most productive.

The highest and best use of a property reflects the market's perception of its potential. As the basic principle of anticipation affirms, the potential future use of a property strongly influences its present value. Consequently, highest and best use analysis is an essential step in the valuation process.

This chapter focuses on the purpose of highest and best use analyses, the techniques employed to reach a highest and best use conclusion, and the relationship between highest and best use and the three approaches to value. Special appraisal situations that can compli-cate highest and best use analyses are also described.

DEFINITION OF HIGHEST AND BEST USE

The current definition of *highest and best use* in appraisal usage is:

> The reasonably probable and legal use of vacant land or an improved property, which is physically possible, appropriately supported, financially feasible, and that results in the highest value.

This definition indicates that there are four tests of highest and best use and that two highest and best use analyses may be undertaken in an appraisal. One analysis focuses on the *highest and best use of the site as though vacant* and available for development to its highest and best use, the other is concerned with the *highest and best use of the property as improved*. These two analyses of highest and best use are distinct and serve different functions in the valuation process.

Highest and Best Use of the Site as though Vacant

In analyzing the highest and best use of the land as though vacant, the site is considered as though it were vacant and ready for development. Even if there are improvements present, the property is considered as though it were vacant for the purposes of this analysis. The following questions must be answered:

TERM

highest and best use of land or a site as though vacant: among all reasonable, alternative uses, the use that yields the highest present land value, after payments are made for labor, capital, and coordination; the use of a property based on the assumption that the parcel of land is vacant or can be made vacant by demolishing any improvements.

- If the site is, or were, vacant, should it remain vacant or should it be improved and, if so, what type of improvement should be constructed on it?
- When should the improvement be built?

To conduct the analysis, an appraiser considers proposed uses of the land as though vacant, which may include agricultural, residential, commercial, industrial, or special-purpose uses. First each use is tested to see whether it is legally permitted, physically possible, and financially feasible. The test of financial feasibility is applied after the first two criteria are met. Uses that fail any of these tests are eliminated from further consideration. Then, of the uses that remain, the one that is maximally productive is selected as the highest and best use of the site as though vacant.

As the range of possible uses is narrowed, the uses that remain must be scrutinized. If the appraiser concludes that the site as though vacant should be improved, the client may want the appraiser to continue the analysis to determine the building characteristics that would create maximum productivity. If a residential use is the highest and best use of the site as though vacant, the appraiser should identify the specific characteristics of a residence that would be maximally productive.

- What would be the approximate size, or square foot area, and construction cost of the residence?
- How many stories would it have?
- How many bedrooms and bathrooms would it contain?
- What would the architectural design be?

To form a mental picture of the ideal improvement for the site as though vacant, the appraiser conceives of an improvement that would take maximum advantage of the site's potential and conform to the current standards of the market. Moreover, the construction cost of all building components of the ideal improvement would reflect current market rates. If this new improvement were to be the highest and best use of the land as though vacant, it presumably would have no physical deterioration or functional obsolescence. Thus, any difference in value between the existing improvement and the ideal improvement would be attributable to these forms of depreciation. The appraiser also must consider external obsolescence, which is caused by forces outside the property and would affect the existing improvement and the new improvement equally.

In market valuations, analyzing the highest and best use of the site as though vacant and preparing a cost estimate of the ideal improvement serve a variety of purposes. The appraiser's determinations provide information that can be used in all three approaches to value.

In the cost approach, the site must be valued separately from the existing improvements. This requires a separate highest and best use analysis of the site. One technique used to value the site alone is analysis of the sale prices of potentially comparable vacant sites. These vacant parcels can only be truly comparable to the subject site if they have similar highest and best uses.

Existing improvements that do not develop the land to its highest and best use are usually worth less than their cost. A new building that is poorly designed may be worth less than its cost due to functional obsolescence in its design. The improvement that constitutes the highest and best use is the one that adds the greatest value to the site.

In the sales comparison approach, highest and best use analysis serves as a test in the selection of comparables. The sites of potentially comparable properties should have the same or a similar highest and best use as though vacant as the site of the subject property. If they do not, the sale properties are not comparable.

> ### CONCEPTS
>
> Highest and best use analysis must be completed before the three valuation approaches are applied.
>
> In the cost approach, highest and best use analysis helps the appraiser estimate land value as well as improvement costs and depreciation.
>
> In the sales comparison approach, highest and best use analysis facilitates the selection of comparable properties.

A highest and best use study may be performed outside of an appraisal assignment. A client may be interested in a project's feasibility—i.e., the likelihood that the project will satisfy explicit objectives. Most feasibility studies are more detailed than highest and best use analyses conducted for market valuation purposes, but the two are closely related. If the purpose of the appraisal is to study feasibility, a more detailed analysis of alternative uses and market conditions is usually required.

Highest and Best Use of the Property as Improved

To determine the highest and best use of the property as improved, an appraiser compares the existing improvements with the ideal improvement. The appraiser attempts to answer these questions:

TERM

highest and best use of property as improved: the use that should be made of a property as it exists. An existing property should be renovated or retained as is so long as it continues to contribute to the total market value of the property, or until the return from a new improvement would more than offset the cost of demolishing the existing building and constructing a new one.

- Given the existing improvements on the site, what use should be made of the property and when should this use be implemented?
- Are any changes such as modernization, repairs, remodeling, or renovation needed?
- Would these changes contribute more value to the property than they would cost?
- How should the existing or modified structure be used and by whom?
- Should it be owner-occupied, rented, or used for commercial purposes?

In many appraisal situations, the highest and best use of the property as improved will be the same as, or similar to, the highest and best use of the site as though vacant. The potential benefits that could accrue to the site as though vacant can often be realized by the existing improvements if modest changes are made. This is particularly likely if the improvements are relatively new or suffer from only minimal deferred maintenance.

In some cases, however, the presence of improvements alters the property's potential to produce benefits. Consider, for example, a large, older residence in an area that has been rezoned for commercial use. If the site were vacant, it would probably be most likely developed for a commercial use. However, because the improvements currently on the site contribute to value, the property's highest and best use as improved could be continued use as a residence unit or conversion to a commercial use permitted by the zoning. In this case, the improvements contribute value to the property. Improvements can detract from the value of property if they contribute nothing and an expense must be incurred to demolish or remove them.

To analyze the highest and best use of the property as improved, the four tests are once again applied, with special attention paid to the features of the existing improvements that differ from those of the ideal improvement. Reasonable uses that are legally permitted, physically possible, and financially feasible are considered. Of the uses that meet these tests, the use that is maximally productive is selected as the highest and best use of the property as improved.

Alternative uses may involve minor renovations such as replacing radiators or touching up paint, or they may necessitate substantial improvements such as adding a bathroom to the residence or finishing a basement. An appraiser may conclude that the existing improvement should be completely razed and a new structure be built to take its place. In another situation, an appraiser might decide that no structural changes are necessary and determine that the most productive use would be realized by converting the building into apartments or a nonresidential use.

Analyzing the highest and best use of the property as improved helps the appraiser identify items of depreciation, which must be described in the cost approach. In the sales comparison approach, this highest and best use conclusion helps the appraiser recognize existing and potential characteristics of the subject property that contribute to value in the market area. Comparable properties should have the same or a similar highest and best use as improved.

CONCEPT OF CONSISTENT USE

It is critical that the two analyses of highest and best use not be confused in the course of an appraisal. A site value estimate, which is based on a conclusion of the land's highest and best use as though vacant, may not be added to a value estimate of an improvement based on the highest and best use of the property as improved. The concept of consistent use holds that land cannot be valued on the basis of one use while the improvements are valued on the basis of another. As long as the value of a property as improved is greater than the value of the site as unimproved, the highest and best use is the use of the property as improved.

> **TERM**
>
> **consistent use:** the concept that land cannot be valued on the basis of one use while the improvements are valued on the basis of another.

Consider the appraisal of a residential property located on a major commercial street. The site is currently occupied by a dwelling that is in fairly good condition. The site has recently been rezoned for commercial use, which is the highest and best use of the site as though vacant. Under a commercial use, the land has a market value of $30,000.

The highest and best use of the property as improved is continued residential use subject to minor repairs. Nearby residential properties that are not attractive to commercial users but are otherwise comparable to the subject property have been selling for approximately $70,000. The site value of these properties is estimated to be $10,000, and the value of the comparable improvements is estimated to be $60,000.

An appraiser would violate the concept of consistent use by adding the $60,000 improvement value to the $30,000 land value to obtain a $90,000 total value indication for the subject property. The $60,000 indication of improvement value, which was derived from an analysis of the sales of residential properties in a residential location, is based on a residential highest and best use of the property as improved, while the $30,000 indication of site value is based on a commercial highest and best use of the land as though vacant. The two indications are not compatible, so they may not be added together.

An appraiser could properly estimate the value of the subject property by analyzing sales of commercially zoned residential properties located on nearby commercial streets with similar highest and best uses of the site as though vacant.

THE FOUR TESTS

To test for the highest and best use of a site as though vacant or a property as improved, an appraiser must consider all reasonable alternative uses. The highest and best use must meet four criteria:

1. Legal permissibility
2. Physical possibility
3. Financial feasibility
4. Maximum productivity

These four criteria are often considered in the sequence described in the following pages.[1]

Each contemplated use is first tested to determine whether it is legally permissible. Next, uses that are legally permitted are examined to decide whether they are also physically possible. After the uses that pass both the legal permissibility and physical possibility tests are identified, the ap-

---

1.   The first two tests need not be considered in order at all times. Physical possibility may be considered before legal permissibility. However, the tests of financial feasibility and maximum productivity must be applied in this order.

praiser considers whether each use is financially feasible—i.e., produces a return that is at least greater than the investment. Finally, from among the legally permitted and physically possible uses that are financially feasible, the appraiser selects the one use that is maximally productive. This is the highest and best use of the land or the improved property.

Legally Permissible

Site as though Vacant

Each potential use must be tested for legal permissibility. Zoning ordinances, building codes, historic district controls, environmental regulations, and other public and private restrictions can all have an impact on the potential uses of land.

To determine whether a use is legally permissible, an appraiser must consider both present and anticipated zoning restrictions. If there is a reasonable probability that a change in zoning regulations will occur soon, an appraiser may consider a use that is not currently allowed under the existing regulations as the highest and best use. However, the appraiser is obligated to disclose all factors pertinent to this determination, including the time and expense involved in securing the

> **TERM**
>
> **legal permissibility:** the first test of highest and best use, i.e., does the property meet zoning ordinances, building codes, historic district contracts, environmental regulations, and other public and private restrictions?

zoning change and the risk that the change may not occur. Zoning changes may affect the use density and yard and bulk regulations that control the size and location of buildings.

Changes in zoning regulations can affect the highest and best use of land in another way. When regulations change, existing improvements may cease to conform to the current law. The current use will usually be permitted to continue, however, and this use may be more productive than the use allowed under the new zoning. In this case, the highest and best use of the property would be to maintain the legally nonconforming use of the existing improvements.

Building codes can prevent land from being developed to its highest and best use by imposing burdensome restrictions that increase the cost of construction. This is particularly true in metropolitan areas where different municipalities or jurisdictions have different building codes. Residential development trends in metropolitan areas are greatly influenced by offsite requirements specified in building codes. Less restrictive codes typically result in lower development costs and attract developers to an area, while more restrictive codes discourage development.

The first test of highest and best use of a site as though vacant is whether the use complies with zoning and building codes, environmental regulations, and other public and private restrictions.

Increasing concern over the effects of land use has led to environmental regulations, which also must be considered in highest and best use analysis. Appraisers must consider regulations designed to protect the air, water, wetlands, and historic areas and investigate the public's reaction to proposed projects. Opposition from local residents and community groups has stopped many real estate developments.

Property as Improved

Many legal considerations that affect the highest and best use of vacant land affect improved property as well. Major remodeling or renovation usually requires a building permit and must comply with the building codes currently in effect. Many communities use their control over permits, codes, and tax incentives to encourage renovation and discourage unwanted conversions. Legal restrictions can have a substantial effect on the highest and best use of property as improved. Commercial or income-producing uses of residences may be restricted by zoning laws or private agreements.

A trend away from demolition and toward preservation of existing structures became evident in the early 1980s. The preservationist trend has led to historic district zoning controls, which make demolition permits difficult or impossible to obtain in some areas. One effect of these controls has been to decrease significantly the number of instances in which the highest and best use of property is to demolish the existing improvements. Moreover, the special tax incentives that are sometimes available for maintaining older buildings may substantially enhance their value and thus influence their highest and best use.

Physically Possible

Site as though Vacant

Location has a substantial effect on highest and best use. Commercial and industrial uses frequently require convenient access to transportation networks and proximity to raw materials, labor pools, consumers, and distributors. Commercial enterprises must be located on thoroughfares or in other places accessible to potential customers. Residential uses generally require utility service and the amenities and environment provided by a neighborhood.

> **TERM**
>
> **physical possibility:** the second test of highest and best use, i.e., will the utilities, amenities, and environment provided by the neighborhood support the use in question?

Analysis of the community and the neighborhood can provide important clues as to how the location of a site affects its highest and best use. Current patterns and anticipated trends must both be considered. Location is studied by investigating linkages, access, and the direction of community growth. An appraiser may ask:

- How is the site situated with respect to roads and utilities?
- Will the quality of the schools, the social amenities, and the reputation or prestige of the area attract residential users of a given income level?
- How convenient would the site be for other types of uses?
- How will the pattern of community growth affect the future potential of the site?

Size, shape, and topography can also affect the highest and best use of a site as though vacant. Agricultural and industrial uses may be precluded by the small size of certain parcels, particularly if nearby land is not available for plottage. An irregular shape or uneven terrain can restrict the range of possible uses for a site and may increase the costs of constructing improvements.

> **CONCEPT**
>
> The physical possibility of a use is tested in relation to the location of the site within a community and neighborhood as well as its plot size, shape, and topography.

The highest and best use of a site may be to combine it with another parcel for a use that requires a larger area. The land would then have plottage value. An appraiser must consider the possibility that all or part of the land will be assembled with other parcels. If the highest and best use conclusion is predicated on the likelihood of an assemblage, this must be clearly stated in the appraisal report. Sometimes a site has excess land, which is land that may accommodate a separate highest and best use, or surplus land, which would not accommodate a separate highest and best use. If there is excess land, only part of the site will be used for its primary purpose. The rest may have another highest and best use or may be held for future expansion of the anticipated improvement.

When the topography, subsoil, or topsoil conditions of a site make development dangerous or costly, its value is often adversely affected. In a given area the sites available for a particular use compete with one another. If it will cost more to grade or lay foundations on one site than on more typical sites, the site may not appeal to the same users and might have a different highest and best use. Alternatively, the highest and best use might remain the same, but the site could have a lower value.

Property as Improved

Physical and environmental conditions also shape the highest and best use of the property as improved. The size, design, and condition of the improvements limit the range of productive uses to which the property can be put. For example, additions can usually be made to one-story houses more easily than to two-story houses. The property's ability to accommodate the present use is often relevant to the highest and best use conclusion. Obviously the condition of the existing improvements and the number of deferred maintenance items and short-lived items requiring repair or replacement influence the feasibility and cost-effectiveness of various remodeling projects.

Financially Feasible

After eliminating uses that do not meet the criteria of legal permissibility and physical possibility, the remaining uses must be tested for financial feasibility. If there is sufficient demand for the property, some market participant will be willing to translate that demand into value, either by buying or renting the property. A use is financially feasible if the income or value benefits that accrue from the use sufficiently exceed the expenses involved. If the benefits exceed the costs by only a marginal amount, a project may not be feasible. To estimate these benefits and costs, an appraiser must carefully examine the supply of and demand for the use in question.

Site as though Vacant

The potential highest and best uses of a site are usually long-term land uses or uses that are expected to remain on the site for the normal economic, or useful, life of the improvements. Most buildings are expected to last at least 25 years, and some may last more than 100 years. A building's value or income usually reflects a carefully considered and highly specific long-term use program. Home owners may base their decisions to buy on the anticipation of tax advantages and property appreciation, but the benefits of owning residential property are usually the benefits of occupancy and the reversion upon resale— i.e., the lump-sum benefits the investor receives when the investment is terminated.

The benefits of owner occupancy are intangible and difficult to calculate, but a developer's anticipated return from the sale of houses in a proposed residential development can be measured. After an allowance is made for the absorption period—i.e., the time it takes to market the developed units successfully—these benefits must be sufficient to justify all construction and other expenses the developer of the vacant site will incur and provide an entrepreneurial profit. In this case, financial feasibility is determined by analyzing the anticipated return rather than an income stream.

Property as Improved

The feasibility of renovation or rehabilitation projects is often more difficult to calculate than the feasibility of construction on vacant sites because costs may be harder to estimate. Renovation estimates may be based on unit-in-place costs for new work plus an allowance for the normally higher costs of repair work. Rehabilitation estimates are frequently based on recent costs for the same or equivalent work on similar properties. Home owners and property managers may keep records that include specific bids for renovation work such as exterior painting, roof repair, or exterior decorating.

The cost of repair work on existing improvements rarely equals the cost of similar work in new construction. Modernizing and remodeling work is usually more expensive for several reasons. Although the quantity of material used may be the same, more labor is involved in repair and the conditions are different. Altering a structure usually involves tearing out old work and performing smaller tasks under conditions that are not conducive to efficiency. If the contractor's estimate is a flat fee, it may be substantially higher than the cost of identical work in new construction because the contractor seeks protection against complications that may arise as the remodeling progresses. Unforeseen complications may necessitate the replacement of existing conduits, pipes, and structural load-bearing members.

The property owner must also pay the architect's fee, the cost of supervision, and the contractor's profit and lose the use of the house while the work is being done. The financial feasibility of renovation or rehabilitation is determined by analyzing whether the costs incurred will be recovered through a higher anticipated sale price or an increased income stream.

TERM

maximum productivity: the final test of highest and best use, i.e., does the use reflect the greatest return on the developer's capital expenditure?

CONCEPT

Maximum productivity is measured in terms of return, income, or cost-effectiveness.

Maximally Productive

Of the financially feasible uses, the use that produces the highest price or value consistent with market expectations for that use is the highest and best use. As mentioned previously, the primary benefits of owning many residential properties are the intangible benefit of occupancy and the anticipated reversion. Nevertheless, maximum productivity can be evaluated in the following situations:

* If the highest and best use of a vacant parcel of land is use as a single-family residence, the price derived from that use of the site must reflect the greatest return on the developer's capital expenditure.

* To apply the test of maximum productivity to projected rental units, the project's ability to generate the highest anticipated income stream and reversion are compared to the developer's investment.

* To test the maximum productivity of improved properties where the highest and best use requires renovation or rehabilitation, the most cost-effective means of modernization is investigated.

Highest and Best Use Conclusion

Upon completion of the analysis, a conclusion as to the highest and best use of the property is required. With respect to the highest and best use of the land as though vacant, the conclusion may be to leave the land vacant or to improve it. With respect to the highest and best use of the property as improved, the conclusion may be to continue the use as developed or to change it through renovation, remodeling, demolition, or conversion.

SPECIAL SITUATIONS IN HIGHEST AND BEST USE ANALYSIS

The steps described in this chapter constitute the basic procedure for testing highest and best use; they are used in many appraisal situations. However, in certain circumstances it may be difficult to determine highest and best use. Special situations in highest and best use include

- Interim uses
- Legally nonconforming uses
- Excess land

These highest and best use problems are most often encountered in appraising properties located in transitional neighborhoods.

> **CONCEPT**
>
> Special circumstances, such as interim uses, legally nonconforming uses, or excess land, can make it difficult to reach a highest and best use conclusion.

Interim Uses

The highest and best use of a site as though vacant or of property as improved may be expected to change in the foreseeable future. A tract of land may not be ready for development now, but urban growth patterns suggest that it will be suitable for development in several years. Similarly, improved urban property may not be renovated until the demand for renovated units is great enough to justify the expense. In neighborhoods that are in transition, the immediate highest and best use of the site as though vacant or the property as improved may differ from the long-term highest and best use.

A short-term highest and best use is called an *interim use*. If the appraiser determines that an interim use is warranted until the long-term highest and best use of a property can be realized, he or she must carefully estimate the duration of the interim use, the financial risks and rewards associated

> **TERM**
>
> **interim use:** the temporary use to which a site or improved property is put until it is ready to be put to its future highest and best use.

with conversion to the long-term highest and best use, and the benefits or costs that the interim use will contribute to the value of the site or the improved property. An interim use often lasts up to two or three years.

An interim use can affect the value of a site or an improved property positively or negatively. It may produce marginal benefits or income but will not contribute nearly as much as the long-term highest and best use.

Legally Nonconforming Uses

A legally nonconforming use is a use that was lawfully established and maintained but no longer conforms to the regulations of the zone in which it is located. A nonconforming use is usually created by the imposition of zoning or a change in zoning ordinances that occurs after the original construction of the improvements.

TERM
legally nonconforming use: a use that was lawfully established and maintained but no longer conforms to the use regulations of the current zoning in the zone where it is located.

A change in zoning regulations may make an improvement inadequate for the highest and best use of the site. A single-family residence in an area that has been rezoned for commercial use would no longer represent the highest and best use of the land as though vacant. In this case, the legally nonconforming residential use would probably be maintained as an interim use until the existing improvement has depreciated sufficiently to make it feasible to convert it to a commercial use or raze the existing improvements for complete commercial redevelopment of the site.

A zoning change can sometimes create a value premium for an improvement. A reduction in the permitted density or a change in development standards may make a nonconforming use more valuable. A country store, for example, might be located in an area that has been entirely rezoned for low-density residential use. Local zoning ordinances would permit the existing use to continue but prohibit any expansion or major alteration of the improvements.

Regulations concerning what may or must be done with a nonconforming use differ. Some jurisdictions require that nonconforming uses be phased out over a period of time. If a nonconforming use is discontinued or terminated because the improvements have been damaged by a storm or fire, for example, reestablishing the use may depend on the degree of damage incurred. Because laws vary in different jurisdictions, an appraiser must study the regulations that apply to the subject property and each comparable used in the appraisal and check enforcement records to determine how long the local government allows nonconforming uses to continue.

When a zoning change creates a value premium for a nonconforming improvement, continuation of the use often produces more benefits or income than would be possible if the improvement were new. In many nonconforming use situations, the property value estimate reflects the nonconforming use. Land value is estimated on the basis of the legally permissible use, assuming the land is vacant, and its value is deducted from the total property value. The remaining value reflects the contribution of the existing improvements as well as any possible premium for the nonconforming use.

Legally nonconforming uses that correspond to the highest and best use of the property as improved are often easy to recognize. In some situations, however, determining whether an existing nonconforming use is the highest and best use of the site requires careful analysis of the incomes produced or values achieved by the nonconforming property and by alternative uses to which the property could be put if it were made to conform with existing regulations.

Because few sales of properties considered comparable exist for legally nonconforming properties, application of the sales comparison approach is difficult.

Excess Land

Many large sites have more than one highest and best use. In some situations a vacant site or a site considered as though vacant may actually consist of two separate economic units. If the portion of the site allocated to one particular use is improved, complies with the zoning requirements, and is suited to the use of the improvement, the highest and best use of this part of the site would be as improved. The highest and best use of the other, unimproved portion of the site—i.e., the excess land—would be for development in conformity with zoning regulations.

In other situations, the unused portion of a site may be simply surplus land. Depending on the location of the improvement(s), the site may not be considered two economic units, each with a separate highest and best use. Instead, the highest and best use of this surplus land may be for the future expansion of the existing improvement(s). Frequently a site with surplus land is oversized compared with competitive sites. In these instances the value of the oversized site would be greater than that of competitive properties.

The application of different approaches to value may suggest different property values. For example, consider a large residential site that could be divided into two full lots for development. Under the cost approach, land value is estimated as if the land were vacant and unimproved. Accordingly, the appraiser arrives at a $10,000 value indication for each lot with a site value of $20,000. However, at present a house straddles the lot lines. Under the sales comparison approach, the land value is estimated as improved and its value is included in overall property value. In applying the sales comparison approach, the appraiser realizes that because of its impaired functional utility—as a result of the misplacement of the improvements—an adjustment to the property value is appropriate. The appraiser reconsiders the indication of property value derived from the cost approach. Here too impaired functional utility penalizes the property's value and the same adjustment must be applied. This adjustment usually takes the form of incurable functional obsolescence caused by the building's location on the lot.

Highest and Best Use in Transitional Neighborhoods

Some of the most difficult residential assignments are appraisals of properties located in areas that are undergoing transition. Transitional neighborhoods present major problems in highest and best use analysis and in the application of the three approaches to value. Many special highest and best use situations are found in transitional neighborhoods, and it is often difficult to select between alternative highest and best uses. Interim uses are common, and zoning changes and violations are more likely to occur. Multiple uses and unusual uses also increase in frequency. Appraisers using the same valuation techniques and the same market data may arrive at different opinions when valuing properties in transitional neighborhoods.

TERMS

transitional neighborhood: a market area undergoing an economic and/or demographic shift.

multiple use: a combination of compatible uses in a single building.

Neighborhood and area analyses are especially critical when the use of the subject property may be about to change. An appraiser may ask:

- What factors in the neighborhood or the larger community are causing the transition?
- Where have the most rapid changes been taking place?
- Where are changes likely to occur in the future?

The appraiser must carefully identify the different markets that may compete for use of the subject property.

- If an adjacent neighborhood is expanding, will it grow to encompass the subject property and the subject neighborhood?
- How strong is the demand for the new use and how will it be met by the anticipated supply?
- When will the effects of change be felt most acutely?
- If the subject neighborhood is declining, how and when will the subject be affected?
- Do potentially comparable properties offer the same prospects to their purchasers?
- Will the long-term highest and best use of the improvement be conversion to a more intensive use?
- If conversion is likely, when might the change occur and how will the interim use contribute to value?

These are the factors that must be investigated in appraising properties in transitional neighborhoods.

In new neighborhoods conformity to surrounding property uses is generally a reliable indication of the highest and best use of the site as though vacant. In older neighborhoods and in transitional neighborhoods in particular, conformity does not reliably indicate the probable highest and best use of the site.

For example, consider the highest and best use of a site as though vacant in a declining residential neighborhood of large, 70-year-old, two- and three-story houses that sell for $70,000 to $80,000. It would not be feasible to replace any of these houses with similar new improvements because the costs of constructing a large dwelling would probably greatly exceed its expected selling price. The highest and best use of the site might be to build a smaller house that is more compatible with the incomes of current area residents or to put the site to some alternative use.

In the past when the highest and best use of a property in a transitional neighborhood changed, the logical alternative was to raze the improvements and redevelop the site. However, in light of the current interest in preserving older structures, other alternatives should be investigated. Existing improvements can be remodeled, renovated, restored, rehabilitated, or even relocated in some cases. Tax incentives and local regulations may make one of these alternatives more probable, and more productive, than demolition.

Zoning changes frequently occur in transitional neighborhoods. When a neighborhood is declining, zoning regulations may not be enforced. As the neighborhood begins to stabilize, new ordinances are often put into effect. In growing neighborhoods there may be strong economic pressures to alter existing zoning ordinances. An appraiser investigates the probability and likely content of zoning changes and estimates their effect on the highest and best use of the site or improved property. These factors should be described in the appraisal report.

11 LAND OR SITE VALUATION

Most appraisal situations require a separate valuation of the land component of a property. Land value is the focus of assignments to derive market value opinions of vacant land. When improved residential property is being appraised, a separate land valuation is also needed to complete the cost approach. To arrive at a total property value indication using this approach, the value of the land or site must be added to the depreciated cost of the improvements.

CONCEPTS

In appraisals performed to estimate the market value of improved residential property, a land value estimate is needed to complete the cost approach. The land or site value estimate can also be used to analyze the comparability of properties in the sales comparison approach.

A separate land or site valuation can also provide information significant to the sales comparison approach. An understanding of how much value the land contributes to the total value of the subject property can help an appraiser determine the comparability of other properties. Generally a comparable property should have a land-to-property value ratio that is similar to that of the subject property. If a potential comparable and the subject property have dissimilar land-to-property value ratios, their highest and best uses may differ as well.

Land is valued as though vacant and available for development to its highest and best use. Therefore, the land component of a property must be analyzed and valued separately. A developer needs to know the value of vacant or improved land to decide if a project is feasible. Landowners may want to know the value of their land to establish a sale price. Land and improvements are sometimes taxed at different rates, so separate valuations may be needed for tax assessment purposes.

SITE AND LAND

Although the terms *site* and *land* are sometimes used synonymously, these concepts must be differentiated in an appraisal. A parcel of land is a portion of the earth's surface in its natural state, while a site is land that has been improved—e.g., cleared, graded, provided with utilities,

Raw land will usually have less value than a site that has been prepared for develop-ment with clearing, grading, and the installation of utilities and other site improvements.

drainage, and access—to prepare it for its intended use. Consequently, a site often has more value than a parcel of raw land.

It is useful to distinguish between site improvements *to* a site and site improvements *on* a site. Site improvements to a site are improvements such as clearing that *transform* a parcel of land *into* a site, and they are included in the value of the site as though vacant. In contrast, site improvements on a site are improvements such as landscaping that *contribute additional value* to the site, and they are not included in the value of the site as though vacant.

Land value and site value should never be confused in an appraisal. If sales of similar properties are used to estimate site value, the appraiser must make sure that these sales are also of sites, not raw land. If an estimate of raw land value is used in the cost approach, the depreciated value of the improvements, which is added to the value of the land, must reflect the value contribution of clearing, grading, drainage, soil compaction, installation of utilities, and other onsite and offsite improvements that were not included in the land value component. Consistency must be maintained throughout the valuation process.

LAND AS A SOURCE OF VALUE

Land is said to *have* value, while improvements *contribute* to value. Land is seen as the value base on which improvements may be built. Improvements can constitute a penalty on land value when they contribute no value as an interim use and their demolition and removal will cost money. Unlike improvements, land is not a wasting asset and therefore does not depreciate in the traditional sense. However, the value of land may change as a result of external conditions and market forces. Only improvements depreciate in value.

Commodities can be manufactured, but land is provided by nature and its supply is relatively fixed. Major changes in the earth's surface have occurred over the centuries, and the supply and quality of land may be slightly modified in one life span. Of course, these natural events rarely affect the land that appraisers are concerned with. There are, however, a few notable exceptions.

Land is affected by accretion or erosion along a shoreline, pollution with harmful wastes and other toxic materials, inundation by volcanic ash and lava flows, exhaustion by improper farming methods, and ecological imbalances that transform agricultural land into desert. Earthquakes and landslides also change the surface of the earth, and faults beneath the surface can create vast sinkholes. These occurrences are fairly rare.

Because land is generally fixed in supply and location, its value accrues entirely from its potential to serve an economically productive or beneficial use for people. A parcel of land may have utility as the site of a building, recreational facility, agricultural tract, or right-of-way for transportation routes. If land has utility for a specific use and there is demand for that use, the land has value to some category of users. Its value in the market depends on its relative attractiveness to prospective purchasers in comparison with other parcels.

> **CONCEPTS**
>
> *Land* refers to unimproved parcels, but a site is a parcel that has been improved so that it is ready to be used for a specific purpose.
>
> The value of land is determined by its potential for a beneficial or productive use. The market value of land is established by its highest and best use as though vacant.

MARKET FORCES THAT INFLUENCE LAND VALUES

The forces that affect land values are closely related to those that affect the values of improved properties. A thorough analysis of the market forces at work in the city, region, and neighborhood should yield much information that is relevant to the land value estimate. All major social, economic, governmental, and environmental value influences should be considered.

Trends in land values and the values of improved properties do differ. When the real estate market is expanding, land values may increase more slowly than the values of improved properties, and the first developers may reap unusually large profits. As competition increases and profits are cut, however, the rates of change observed in the values of land and improved property become more similar. When improvements are new, land values tend to equal the values of improved properties once all costs of construction and a normal entrepreneurial profit are deducted. When only a few lots remain in a popular location, the value of a parcel of land in that location sometimes increases beyond the level justified by its productivity. In this case prospective owners or owner-occupants may pay higher land and construction costs than the broader real estate market would seem to warrant. Nevertheless, these occurrences are comparatively rare. On the whole, the market tends toward equilibrium.

LAND VALUATION TECHNIQUES

The technique most commonly applied to value land is the sales comparison approach. If sufficient sales of comparable vacant land are not available, less direct valuation techniques can be employed. These alternative procedures include allocation and extraction, which are described later in this chapter.

Sales Comparison

Of the various techniques available for estimating land value, none is more persuasive than sales comparison. Sales of similar land parcels or sites are analyzed, compared, and adjusted to derive an indication of value for the land parcel or site being appraised. Adjustments are derived from market data using paired data set analysis or other methods, and then the adjusted prices are reconciled into an indication of land or site value.

CONCEPT

The most direct and most reliable procedure for estimating the value of land or sites is the sales comparison approach.

A full discussion of the sales comparison approach to value is provided in Chapter 15. The steps used in land valuation are summarized below.

1. Collect data on sales of similar land parcels or sites and information on listings and offers.
2. Analyze the data to determine the comparability of these land parcels or sites with the subject land parcel or site. Develop appropriate units of comparison and study each element of comparison.
3. Adjust the sale prices of the comparable land parcels or sites to reflect how they differ from the subject.
4. Reconcile these adjusted sale prices into a single value indication or range of value indications for the subject land parcel or site.

Collecting the Data

Data on land sales and ground leases are available from electronically transmitted and printed data services, newspapers, records of deeds and assessments, and other sources. Interviews with buyers, sellers, lawyers, brokers, and lenders involved in the transactions can provide more direct information. An appraiser identifies the property rights, legal encumbrances, physical characteristics, and other site features involved in each sale of a potentially comparable property. Sales with special financing or sales affected by unusual motivation must be regarded with caution. For example, parcels that are purchased for assemblage may not provide good indications of market value.

In addition to recorded sales and signed contracts, an appraiser considers offers to sell, offers to purchase, and other incomplete transactions. Offers are less reliable than signed contracts and recorded sales. A final sale price is usually lower than the initial offer to sell but higher than the initial offer to buy. Negotiations may proceed through several stages. Offers may provide an indication of the limits on value for a subject property or neighborhood, but they are not conclusive and are inadmissible in some courts.

To be comparable, a parcel of land or a site should be in the same market area as the subject or in a market area comparable to that of the subject—i.e., it should effectively compete with the subject property in the minds of potential purchasers. Comparable transactions should be recent and the parcels of land or sites should be substantially similar to the subject in terms of the elements of comparison described below. Each comparable used in the sales comparison analysis should be inspected and described.

Comparable parcels should have the same highest and best use as the subject parcel. The subject parcel is considered as though vacant in this analysis, even if improvements are located on it. The highest and best use of the subject and the comparables is determined by carefully studying the supply and demand trends in the neighborhood and the market area. All current, anticipated, and potential development activity should be investigated as part of this analysis.

Analyzing the Data for Comparability

The data collected on each property and transaction must be analyzed to ensure their comparability and consistency with other data. The units of comparison applied to the market data may include price or rent per acre, per square foot, per front foot, and per lot. Depending on the specific market, other units such as price per allowable dwelling unit may be used.

If necessary, an appraiser analyzes a sale using as many units of comparison as possible to determine whether any particular unit or units reveal a consistent pattern in the given market. It is sometimes possible to correlate the results obtained using two or more units of comparison to arrive at a land value estimate—e.g., dollars per acre and per lot or dollars per unit and per square foot. If any inconsistency is observed in the data, the cause should be investigated.

The elements of comparison used to analyze sites or vacant parcels include

- Property rights and limitations on use
- Financing terms
- Conditions of sale (motivation)
- Market conditions (time)
- Location
- Physical characteristics
- Available utilities
- Other characteristics such as zoning

As a general rule, the greater the dissimilarity between the subject and comparable, the less appropriate the comparable will be for deriving a market value indication. When a comparable requires a large adjustment for any element of comparison, the potential for distortion and error in the analysis usually increases.

Market conditions and location are often the most significant elements of comparison. If sale prices have been changing rapidly over the past several months and adequate data are available, the sale dates of the comparables should be as near as possible to the effective date of the appraisal. If an appraiser must choose between sales of properties close to the subject property that occurred several years ago and recent transactions in more distant locations, a balance must be struck. In those circumstances, the character of the market may dictate the choice of comparables. For example, in a stable market sales in more distant locations may be appropriate, while in a rapidly increasing or decreasing market more recent sales will be the most indicative.

Size is typically a less important element of comparison than sale date and location. Most types of development have an optimal site size. Additional land that may accommodate a separate highest and best use is excess land while surplus land is land that is not needed to support the existing improvements. Excess land may be sold separately in the market. Because sales of sites of different sizes may have different prices per unit, appraisers either find comparable properties that are approximately the same size as the subject property or convert the sale prices to size-related unit prices such as price per square foot or price per acre.

Zoning is often a basic criterion in the selection and analysis of comparables. Sites that are zoned the same as the subject property are more appropriate comparables. If sufficient sales of sites in the same zoning category are not available, data from sites with similar zoning can be used after adjustments are made.

Adjusting Sale Prices to Reflect Differences

After comparable data are collected and comparable properties are inspected, sales data must be assembled in an organized, logical manner. Sales data may be recorded on a market data grid that has a separate row for each important property characteristic. Adjustments for dissimilarities between the subject parcel and each comparable parcel are made to the sale price of the comparable.

Adjustments for elements of comparison can be derived from market data using various analytical techniques. The application of these techniques may produce quantitative adjustments or qualitative analyses. Quantitative adjustments are derived from

- Paired data analysis
- Statistical and graphic analysis
- Trend analysis
- Other methods, such as direct comparison, e.g., of costs of demolition or costs of environmental remediation

Qualitative differences are studied using

- Relative comparison analysis
- Ranking analysis

TERMS
paired data analysis: a quantitative technique used to identify and measure adjustments to the sale prices of comparables. To apply this technique, sales data on nearly identical properties are analyzed to isolate a single characteristic's effect on data analysis.
trend analysis: a quantitative technique used to identify and measure adjustments to the sale prices of comparable properties; useful when sales data on highly comparable properties are lacking but a broad database on properties with less similar characteristics is available. Market sensitivity is investigated by testing various factors that influence sale prices.

To perform paired data analysis, the appraiser must be able to find comparable parcels that differ significantly from the subject in only one respect. The prices of these comparables are studied to determine how that one variable affects price. Scatter diagrams and other analytical tools can be used to study the effects of location and physical property characteristics. Often an adjustment for market conditions can be derived by studying the trend

TERMS

ranking analysis: a qualitative technique for analyzing comparable sales; a variant of relative comparison analysis in which comparable sales are ranked in descending or ascending order of desirability and each is analyzed to determine its position relative to the subject.

relative comparison analysis: a qualitative technique for analyzing comparable sales; used to determine whether the characteristics of a comparable property are inferior, superior, or equal to those of the subject property. Relative comparison analysis is similar to paired data analysis, but quantitative adjustments are not derived.

in sales of comparable properties over the past several years. This technique is known as *trend analysis.* Regardless of the procedure selected, an appraiser must collect and review sufficient data to make the analysis statistically meaningful. Without a broad market sample, paired data analysis cannot provide reliable results, particularly when the data are contradictory.

Relative comparison analysis and ranking analysis are used to make qualitative judgments about the subject and comparable properties. In both, comparables are identified as inferior, superior, or equal to the subject property. These techniques are similar to paired data set analysis, but in relative comparison and ranking analyses the differences between properties are not quantified.

Once an adjustment is derived for a difference, it can be applied to the prices of all the comparables that differ from the subject in that characteristic. Quantitative adjustments may be applied in dollars or percentages and are usually made in a particular order. Adjustments for property rights, financing, conditions of sale, and market conditions are generally applied before adjustments are made for location and physical characteristics. Similarly, quantitative adjustments are typically made before sale prices are reduced to unit prices. Reducing sale prices to unit prices based on size allows the appraiser to compare parcels of different dimensions and eliminates the need to adjust for differences in size.

Qualitative differences are generally considered after quantitative adjustments have been applied. Analysis of qualitative differences provides the basis for reconciliation. If market data do not exist, quantitative adjustments are unsupportable and should not be made. All adjustments made to comparables should be set forth in the appraisal report in a logical and understandable manner. (A land value appraisal report form is shown in Figure 11.1.)

Reconciling the Results

To reconcile the value indications derived from sales comparison, each step in the analysis is reviewed. The reliability of each data source and

Figure 11.1 Land Appraisal Report

LAND APPRAISAL REPORT

File No. _____

Property Address		Census Tract		

LENDER DISCRETIONARY USE

Sale Price $ _____
Date _____
Mortgage Amount $ _____
Mortgage Type _____
Discount Points and Other Concessions
Paid by Seller $ _____
Source _____

SUBJECT

Property Address _____
City _____ County _____ State _____ Zip Code _____
Legal Description _____
Owner/Occupant _____ Map Reference _____
Sale Price $ _____ Date of Sale _____
Loan charges/concessions to be paid by seller $ _____
R.E. Taxes $ _____ Tax Year _____ HOA $/Mo. _____
Lender/Client _____

Property Rights Appraised
☐ Fee Simple
☐ Leasehold
☐ Condominium (HUD/VA)
☐ PUD

NEIGHBORHOOD

LOCATION	☐ Urban	☐ Suburban	☐ Rural
BUILT UP	☐ Over 75%	☐ 25-75%	☐ Under 25%
GROWTH RATE	☐ Rapid	☐ Stable	☐ Slow
PROPERTY VALUES	☐ Increasing	☐ Stable	☐ Declining
DEMAND/SUPPLY	☐ Shortage	☐ In Balance	☐ Over Supply
MARKETING TIME	☐ Under 3 Mos.	☐ 3-6 Mos.	☐ Over 6 Mos.

NEIGHBORHOOD ANALYSIS — Good Avg. Fair Poor

Employment Stability ☐☐☐☐
Convenience to Employment ☐☐☐☐
Convenience to Shopping ☐☐☐☐
Convenience to Schools ☐☐☐☐
Adequacy of Public Transportation ☐☐☐☐
Recreation Facilities ☐☐☐☐
Adequacy of Facilities ☐☐☐☐
Property Compatibility ☐☐☐☐
Protection from Detrimental Cond. ☐☐☐☐
Police & Fire Protection ☐☐☐☐
General Appearance of Properties ☐☐☐☐
Appeal to Market ☐☐☐☐

PRESENT LAND USE %	LAND USE CHANGE	PREDOMINANT OCCUPANCY	SINGLE FAMILY HOUSING
Single Family ___	☐ Not Likely	☐ Owner	PRICE $(000) AGE (yrs)
2-4 Family ___	☐ Likely	☐ Tenant	Low
Multi-Family ___	☐ In process	☐ Vacant (0-5%)	High
Commercial ___	To: ___	☐ Vacant (over 5%)	Predominant
Industrial ___			
Vacant ___			

Note: Race or the racial composition of the neighborhood are not considered reliable appraisal factors. COMMENTS: _____

SITE

Dimensions _____
Site Area _____
Zoning Classification _____
HIGHEST & BEST USE: Present Use _____

Corner Lot _____
Zoning Compliance _____
Other Use _____

Topography _____
Size _____
Shape _____
Drainage _____
View _____
Landscaping _____
Driveway _____
Apparent Easements _____
FEMA Flood Hazard Yes* ___ No ___
FEMA* Map/Zone _____

UTILITIES	Public	Other	SITE IMPROVEMENTS Type	Public	Private
Electricity	☐		Street	☐	☐
Gas	☐		Curb/Gutter	☐	☐
Water	☐		Sidewalk	☐	☐
Sanitary Sewer	☐		Street Lights	☐	☐
Storm Sewer	☐		Alley		

Comments (Apparent adverse easements, encroachments, special assessments, slide areas, etc.): _____

SALES COMPARISON ANALYSIS

The undersigned has recited three recent sales of properties most similar and proximate to subject and has considered these in the market analysis. The description includes a dollar adjustment, reflecting market reaction to those items of significant variation between the subject and comparable properties. If a significant item in the comparable property is superior to, or more favorable than, the subject property, a minus (-) adjustment is made, thus reducing the indicated value of subject; if a significant item in the comparable is inferior to, or less favorable than, the subject property, a plus (+) adjustment is made, thus increasing the indicated value of the subject.

ITEM	SUBJECT	COMPARABLE NO. 1		COMPARABLE NO. 2		COMPARABLE NO. 3	
Address							
Proximity to Subject							
Sales Price	$	$		$		$	
Price/	$	$		$		$	
Data Source							
VALUE ADJUSTMENTS	DESCRIPTION	DESCRIPTION	+(-)$ Adjustment	DESCRIPTION	+(-)$ Adjustment	DESCRIPTION	+(-)$ Adjustment
Sales or Financing							
Concessions							
Date of Sale/Time							
Location							
Site/View							
Net Adj. (total)		☐+ ☐- $		☐+ ☐- $		☐+ ☐- $	
Indicated Value of Subject		$		$		$	

Comments of Sales Comparison: _____

RECONCILIATION

Comments and Conditions of Appraisal: _____

Final Reconciliation: _____

I (WE) ESTIMATE THE MARKET VALUE, AS DEFINED, OF THE SUBJECT PROPERTY AS OF _____ to be $ _____
I (we) certify: that to the best of my (our) knowledge and belief, the facts and data used herein are true and correct; that I (we) personally inspected the subject property and inspected all comparable sales cited in this report; and that I (we) have no undisclosed interest, present or prospective therein.

Appraiser(s) _____
Review Appraiser _____ (if applicable)
☐ Did ☐ Did Not Inspect Property

Proprietary Land Form 04/88

This form was produced on the ACI Development RapidForms System (800) 234-8727

Appraisal Network

analytical method is considered and the reasons for any differences among the sales data for properties considered comparable are investigated. It is especially important to scrutinize the highest and best use conclusion on which the land value estimate is based:

- How current are the data that support the use conclusion?
- Do they seem to conform to the pattern of growth in the neighborhood?

Even minor differences in the zoning of neighborhoods or the regulations for subdivisions in which comparables are located may affect the factors (e.g., permissible bulk, the disposition of structures, density) on which the highest and best use conclusion is based. Variations in zoning and highest and best use are qualitative differences that should be analyzed initially in selecting comparables and again in reconciliation.

Finally, a single value indication or a range of values is selected from the adjusted sale prices of the comparable parcels. The greatest weight is usually given to the sale or sales of comparables that are most similar to the subject. The adjustment process is illustrated in the following valuation example.

Example

An appraiser is asked to estimate the value of a vacant building lot in the Pine Meadows subdivision. Several vacant lots in the subdivision have been sold recently. Analysis of these sales and others in the market area indicates that values have been increasing by 5% per year and demand for vacant lots has been sustained. The appraiser verifies that each sale of a property considered comparable occurred with market financing and without unusual motivation. The sales are similar in all characteristics except those noted. Data on the subject property and comparables are set forth below.

Subject		Sale 2	
Price	?	Price	$14,425
Size	18,000 sq. ft.	Size	19,500 sq. ft.
Date of sale	Current	Date of sale	1 month ago
Site location	Near river	Site location	Near river
Sale 1		Sale 3	
Price	$12,640	Price	$15,400
Size	16,000 sq. ft.	Size	22,000 sq. ft.
Date of sale	1 year ago	Date of sale	1 year ago
Site location	On hill	Site location	Near river

To convert each sale price into a price per square foot, the appraiser divides the sale price by the square footage. The sales information is then organized on a market data grid.

	Subject	Sale 1	Sale 2	Sale 3
Price	?	$12,640	$14,425	$15,400
Size in sq. ft.	18,000	16,000	19,500	22,000
Price per sq. ft.	?	$0.79	$0.74	$0.70
Time	Current	1 year ago	1 month ago	1 year ago
Location	River	Hill	River	River

Next the appraiser isolates the effect of different elements of comparison and makes the appropriate adjustments. Financing for all the sales is typical, so there is no need for a financing adjustment. The first adjustment will be for market conditions (time). Sales 1 and 3 occurred one year ago. An analysis of the change in market conditions indicates that they must be adjusted upward by 5%.

Sale 1:	$12,640 × 1.05	= $13,272
Sale 3:	$15,400 × 1.05	= $16,170

Then the appraiser converts the adjusted sales prices into unit prices and derives an adjustment for location. Sale 1 differs from Sales 2 and 3 in location.

	Subject	Sale 1	Sale 2	Sale 3
Price	?	$13,272	$14,425	$16,170
(adjusted for market conditions)				
Size in sq. ft.	18,000	16,000	19,500	22,000
Price per sq. ft.	?	$0.8295	$0.74	$0.735
(adjusted for market conditions)				
Location	River	Hill	River	River

The hill location is evidently superior. The difference in location is worth approximately $0.09 per square foot ($0.83 − $0.74 = $0.09). Because Sale 1 is superior to the subject, it must be adjusted downward by $0.09.

	Subject	Sale 1	Sale 2	Sale 3
Price per sq. ft.	?	$0.74	$0.74	$0.74
(adjusted for market conditions and location)				

Now the results can be reconciled. The appraiser gives special weight to Sale 2, which is similar to the subject in all elements of comparison. A value of $13,320 ($0.74 × 18,000) is concluded as the land value estimate for the subject property using the sales comparison procedure.[1]

Applicability and Limitations

Sales comparison analysis is generally the most reliable way to estimate land value. It is easy to apply and produces the most persuasive results. However, this procedure cannot be directly employed unless sufficient data on recent sales of comparable land parcels or sites are available. Furthermore, current conditions of supply and demand must be considered or the value indication produced may reflect historical, not actual, market values.

> **TERM**
>
> **allocation:** a method of estimating land value in which sales of improved properties are analyzed to establish a typical ratio of site value to total property value and this ratio is applied to the property being appraised or the comparable being analyzed.

Allocation

Allocation may be used to value land when data on recent land sales are insufficient and sales comparison analysis cannot be supported. The allocation procedure is based on the belief that a normal or typical ratio of land value to property value can be found in competitive or similar properties in comparable neighborhoods—particularly if these neighborhoods are stable. Three steps are involved in allocation:

1. Identify the typical ratio between land value and improved property value in competitive neighborhoods. An estimate of this ratio can usually be obtained only from assessor's data, although in rare cases it may be gathered from builders of new homes.
2. Find sales of improved properties in the subject neighborhood that are located on parcels of land comparable to the subject parcel.
3. Apply the allocation ratio to the sale prices of properties considered comparable to develop a value estimate for the subject parcel.

Example

For estate tax purposes, an appraiser is asked to appraise a parcel of land upon which a dilapidated house stands. Most sales in the neighborhood are of older homes, which are purchased by investors, rehabilitated, and resold to young married couples as starter homes. The subject improve-

---

1. The data in this example have been chosen for easy comparison. In a sales comparison analysis, the final adjusted sale or unit prices of all comparables seldom indicate identical values. Typically reconciliation is required.

ments are so dilapidated that they cannot be rehabilitated. They must be razed and removed. The appropriate valuation procedure in this instance is to estimate the value of the vacant land and deduct the costs of demolition and removal. These costs total $10,000.

No sales of vacant lots have occurred in the neighborhood for several years. Analysis of the assessor's records is inconclusive but does indicate that neighborhood sites represent 40% to 50% of total property assessments.

The appraiser is familiar with a major investor in the neighborhood who buys older homes to rehabilitate and resell them. This investor tells the appraiser that he usually allocates 50% of the purchase price to the land in estimating rehabilitation costs and he does not want to spend any more than twice the allocated land cost on rehabilitation.

> **CONCEPT**
>
> To value land by allocation, sales of improved properties are analyzed to establish a typical ratio of land or site value to total value, which may then be applied to the property being appraised.

During the past year, this investor has purchased and rehabilitated three properties within three blocks of the subject property. The purchase prices of these properties were $72,000, $66,000, and $80,000.

To allocate total property value between the land and building components, the appraiser applies a 50% ratio to these sale prices and arrives at indicated land values of $36,000, $33,000, and $40,000. The land value estimate established in reconciliation may fall anywhere within this range. Since the improvements on the subject site cannot be rehabilitated, reconciliation at the lower end of this range might be appropriate.

The assessor allocates site value at 40% to 50% of total property assessments. This practice probably supports the allocation indicated by the investor since neighborhood-wide averages include all kinds of properties, not just those awaiting rehabilitation. If, based on the allocation technique, a site value of $35,000 was indicated after reconciliation, the value of the subject property subject to demolition and removal of the dilapidated building would be $25,000, i.e., $35,000 minus $10,000 to cover the applicable costs.

Applicability and Limitations

Allocation is usually applied to residential projects when data on improved property sales are available but data on sales of vacant lots are not. In densely developed urban areas, vacant land sales may be so rare that values cannot be estimated by direct comparison. Similarly, vacant sites may seldom be sold in remote rural areas. Allocation usually yields less conclusive results than direct sales comparison, but in some situations it may be the only method available.

The allocation ratio can only be used in a fairly stable market, and it is generally most reliable when the improvements are relatively new. As improvements age and depreciate, the ratio between land value and total property value tends to increase. However, depreciation may occur at different rates for different properties. As the years pass, the range of land-to-property value ratios for different properties may become increasingly broad and the ratios may become less reliable indicators of total property value. When the requirements for allocation cannot be met, the extraction procedure described next may be more useful.

Allocation ratios are often cited in tax assessment rolls, which show an assessed value for the land, which is nondepreciable, and a separate assessed value for the depreciable improvements. Tax information can be used as a check on other data, but it is rarely used independently because tax valuations are conducted at infrequent intervals and may not reflect all the considerations that affect market value. Mass appraisal data and information from developers of new residential subdivisions, when available, can be used in allocation. Quantitative techniques can be applied to find patterns in these data.

Extraction

The extraction technique has similarities to the allocation procedure. To value land by allocation an appraiser applies a land-to-property value ratio to the prices of comparable improved properties. To value land with the extraction procedure, the appraiser deducts the contributory value of the improvements from the total sale price of each comparable. The extraction procedure is accomplished in three steps, as indicated below:

> **TERM**
>
> **extraction:** a method of estimating land value in which the depreciated cost of the improvements on the improved property is estimated and deducted from the total sale price to arrive at an estimated sale price for the land; most effective when the improvements contribute little to the total sale price of the property.

1. Find recent sales of comparable improved properties. If necessary, adjust the sale prices for financing, market conditions, and conditions of sale.

2. For each comparable property, estimate the cost to replace all the improvements, including an entrepreneurial profit, and deduct an estimate of depreciation from this estimate of replacement cost. The

remainder is the depreciated value of the improvements.

3. Subtract the depreciated value of the improvements from each adjusted sale price.

The resulting values are then reconciled into a land value indication.

> **CONCEPT**
>
> In the extraction technique, the contribution of the improvements is estimated and deducted from the total sale price of the property to arrive at the price of the land.

Example

An appraiser is retained to estimate the site value of a vacant lot in a fully developed, older neighborhood. There have been no recent sales of vacant lots. However, three improved properties on lots near the subject have been sold recently and these lots are identical to the subject in size.

Property 1 was sold for $97,750. The estimated replacement cost of the improvements is $100,700, and the appraiser estimates that it is 25% depreciated. Property 2 was sold for $74,000, and the appraiser estimates that the depreciated improvements contribute $54,000 to property value. Property 3 was sold for $109,250. The total cost of the recently built residence, including entrepreneurial profit, was $87,000, and the appraiser believes it has no depreciation.

The appraiser extracts the contribution of the improvements from the price of each sale as shown below.

Property 1		
Price of improved comparable		$97,750
Less contribution of improvements		
Cost of improvements	$100,700	
Less depreciation		
(25% × $100,700)	25,175	
		− 75,525
Site value		$22,225
Property 2		
Price of improved comparable		$74,000
Less contribution of		
depreciated improvements		− 54,000
Site value		$20,000
Property 3		
Price of improved comparable		$109,250
Less contribution of new		
improvements		− 87,000
Site value		$22,250

The range of indicated site values is $20,000 to $22,250. It is reasonable to conclude that the value of the subject site would fall within this range.

Applicability and Limitations

Like allocation, extraction is usually less reliable than direct sales comparison. The results are most conclusive when improvements are new and suffer little depreciation. The extraction procedure can also be used to value land in some older neighborhoods where improvements are fairly heterogeneous. Extraction is frequently used to value land in rural areas because the contributory value of improvements is often small and relatively easy to identify. The extraction procedure can be used to check the results of sales comparison analysis.

When extraction is used to estimate land value, the appraiser must remember to include an estimate of entrepreneurial profit in the replacement cost of the improvements.[2] This profit represents fair payment for the developer's expertise and assumption of risk. (The developer provides coordination, a necessary agent of production distinct from capital, labor, and land.) If an appraiser does not allow for an appropriate amount of entrepreneurial profit in the extraction procedure, the land value estimate will be unreasonably high.

To apply the extraction procedure, an appraiser must fully understand techniques for estimating costs and depreciation, which are discussed in Chapters 13 and 14.

---

2.   See Chapter 12 for an in-depth discussion of the estimation of entrepreneurial profit.

12 THE COST APPROACH

The cost approach to estimating value is based on the reasoning that a purchaser will not normally pay more for a property than it would cost to purchase comparable land and have improvements of comparable utility constructed on that land without undue delay. To apply the cost approach, an appraiser estimates the cost of reproducing or replacing the existing structure with a new building, deducts an appropriate amount for the loss in value caused by depreciation in the existing structure, and then adds the value of the depreciated improvements to an estimate of the value of the land.

The cost approach is applied in eight steps. An appraiser

1. Estimates the value of the site as though vacant and available to be developed to the highest and best use.
2. Estimates the direct (hard) and indirect (soft) costs of the improvements as of the effective appraisal date.
3. Estimates an appropriate entrepreneurial incentive or profit from analysis of the market.
4. Adds estimated direct costs, indirect costs, and the entrepreneurial incentive or profit to arrive at the total cost of the improvements.
5. Estimates the amount of depreciation in the structure and, if necessary, allocates it among the three major categories: physical deterioration, functional obsolescence, and external obsolescence.
6. Deducts the estimated depreciation from the total costs of the improvements to derive an estimate of their depreciated cost.
7. Estimates the contributory value of any site improvements that have not already been considered. (Site improvements are often appraised at their contributory value, i.e., directly on a depreciated cost basis.)
8. Adds the site value to the total depreciated cost of all improvements to arrive at the indicated value of the property.

RELATION TO APPRAISAL PRINCIPLES

The cost approach is based on fundamental appraisal principles and reflects the thinking of those buyers and sellers in the residential real estate market who relate value to cost. Market participants typically judge the value of an existing structure by considering the prices and rents of comparable, existing buildings. They may also consider the costs of creating a new building with similar physical and functional utility. Therefore, the principle of substitution, which holds that value is indicated by the prices of similar items, suggests that the appraiser should study the costs of new structures as well as the prices of existing structures.

Buyers and sellers are most likely to consider building costs when a building is relatively new and offers maximum physical and functional utility. When structures are older or possess less-than-optimal utility, market participants adjust their opinions of value accordingly. Buyers and sellers may also give considerable weight to a value estimate based on cost when the property has unique features and there are few recent sales of similar property for comparison.

> **CONCEPTS**
>
> When improvements are new, their contribution to total property value tends to approximate the cost of their construction.
>
> Supply and demand in the market affect construction costs and the prices of existing properties.

The cost of construction affects, and is affected by, the interplay of supply and demand in the marketplace. Even if the cost approach is not emphasized in an appraisal, the trend in construction costs has a significant influence on property value and should be noted. The value of existing properties may increase or decrease depending on the cost of creating competitive properties.

If total construction costs rise faster than the prices of improved properties, the prospect of lower profits will reduce the incentive to develop new properties and the supply of new units may contract. The lack of development may push existing property prices upward. Similarly, if construction costs increase more slowly than the prices of improved properties, new properties will be developed and the prices of existing properties will fall. Changes in construction costs may result from shifts in the prices of labor, materials, and land, financing charges, contractor profits, architect's fees, and many other factors. All of these costs are of concern to appraisers.

The cost of production and market value may be affected differently by externalities. Inflation may sometimes increase material and labor costs while not affecting market values; on the other hand, completion of a sewer line may increase property value but have no impact on cost. A loss in building value due to external causes is ascribed to external obsolescence, one of the three major types of depreciation.

When improvements are new, their contribution to total property value tends to approximate the cost to construct them. Developers who build overly expensive residences or are careless about costs may quickly suffer losses and be forced to abandon their projects. They leave room for other developers who are more judicious in relating the costs of building improvements to the prices sustained by market demand. Often developers who find ways to lower their costs or build where

CONCEPT

The cost approach is most applicable to new properties, properties that have little depreciation, properties proposed for construction or renovation, and properties that are not frequently exchanged in the market.

property values are comparatively high are soon joined by a host of competitors. This competition further alters the relationship between costs and property values. The process may take time, but ultimately the market moves toward balance, where the direct and indirect costs of a new building approximate the building's contribution to property value.

The cost approach is also supported by the principle of balance and the concept of highest and best use. The principle of balance indicates that in a given location, there is an optimal combination of the agents of production that creates the greatest value and utility in a property. Theoretically, the combination of land and improvements in the existing property will be the optimal combination for that location. The optimal combination is the highest and best use of the site as though vacant, so a different use will result in a loss in value.

An existing structure and the site on which it is located may be out of balance in several ways. If a dwelling is an overimprovement, it may contribute some value to the property but not nearly as much as a similar structure would have on a more appropriate site or a site in a different location. In effect, the building cannot realize its full potential to produce benefits or income on its present site. Conversely, a building that is an underimprovement will not contribute as much value as an improvement that represents the highest and best use of the site. In this situation, the full potential of the site is not being realized by the improvement that exists on it. The combination of the site and the improvement is less than optimal.

APPLICABILITY AND LIMITATIONS

Because cost and market value are often most closely related when properties are new, the cost approach is particularly useful in deriving market value indications for new or relatively new construction. The approach is especially persuasive when land value is well-supported and when the improvements are new or suffer only minor depreciation and are therefore a use that approximates the highest and best use of the land as though vacant.

The approach is widely used to estimate the market value of proposed construction and properties that are not frequently exchanged in the market. Buyers of these properties often measure the price they will pay for an existing building by the cost to build a replacement minus depreciation or by the cost to purchase an existing improvement and make any necessary modifications. Because comparable sales are not always available to analyze the market value of certain types of properties, current market indications of a building's depreciated cost or the cost to acquire and refurbish an existing building provide the best reflections of market thinking and thus of market value.

A number of factors limit the applicability of the cost approach. When improvements are older or are not the highest and best use of the land as though vacant, depreciation is more difficult to estimate. Furthermore, collecting and updating data on construction costs is a time-consuming task. As an alternative an appraiser may rely on cost service manuals, but the data in these manuals do not always produce reliable results. When land sales are few, as in built-up urban areas, the land value estimate required in the cost approach may be difficult to support. Comparable properties may not provide sufficient relevant data, or the data from comparables may be too diverse to suggest an appropriate estimate of entrepreneurial profit. It may be difficult to apply the cost approach to special-purpose residences because the unique features of these properties make it extremely difficult to estimate functional and external obsolescence. Any of these problems can seriously undermine the persuasiveness of the cost approach.

Despite these limitations, the cost approach is an essential valuation tool. It is especially significant when a lack of market activity limits the reliability of the sales comparison approach. When sales data on comparable improved properties *are* available, the cost approach can be used to test the indication produced by sales comparison. The usefulness of the cost approach as a check on the value indication derived with the sales comparison approach is particularly important because these two approaches may be the only means available to value a single-family residence. The income capitalization approach is rarely applied to single-family residences.

Not only can the cost approach be used as an independent approach to market value, but information derived in the approach can also be applied in the other valuation approaches. If a feature of the subject property or a comparable property is deficient in comparison

When comparable data for specialty properties are scarce and other approaches are hard to support, the cost approach becomes an increasingly important measure of value.

with market standards, the cost to cure the deficiency may serve as a basis for calculating an adjustment in the sales comparison approach. Adjustments for special-purpose property features, which incur extensive obsolescence, and for any new accessory buildings or site improvements, which are standard in the market and often contribute value equal to their cost, may be estimated in this way. However, because cost does not necessarily equal value, sales comparison adjustments are more reliable if supported with direct market evidence.

Depreciation estimates are extracted in the cost approach by comparing the existing structure with a newly constructed duplicate or replacement building. The subject property and the comparables used in the sales comparison approach will generally suffer from various forms of depreciation, but the extent of physical deterioration and functional obsolescence varies among different properties. The adjustments made for property condition in the sales comparison approach should be related to depreciation estimates. To reconcile the value indications derived from the cost and sales comparison approaches, an appraiser often checks the depreciation estimates in the cost approach against the adjustments for property condition derived in the sales comparison approach.

The cost approach requires separate valuations of the land and the improvements, so it may be applied whenever land or the improvements must be valued separately. The cost approach may also be used to calculate ad valorem property taxes, which require that property value be allocated to the land and the improvements.

Cost approach techniques can be especially useful when additions or renovations are being considered. The approach provides cost data that are essential to determine feasibility—i.e., whether the cost of the improvement can be recovered through an increase in the property's income stream or anticipated sale price. Cost approach data can help prevent the construction of overimprovements.

COMPONENTS OF THE COST APPROACH
Site Value

Usually the value of the site is estimated by sales comparison. Sales of vacant parcels considered comparable are analyzed, and the sale prices are adjusted to reflect differences between the sale properties considered comparable and the subject. The results are reconciled into an indication of land value. When sufficient data on recent sales of vacant land are not available, the allocation and extraction procedures can be applied to estimate site value. (These methods are described in detail in Chapter 11.)

When a land value indication is derived in the cost approach, it is essential that the principle of consistent use be observed. This principle prohibits an appraiser from valuing land on the basis of one use and the improvements on the basis of another. In many residential valuations, the use of both the land and the improvements is obvious, and the highest and best use of the land as though vacant can be the same as the highest and best use of the property as improved. Usually the existing improvements have utility but suffer depreciation.

CONCEPT
An appraiser begins the cost approach by estimating the value of the land as though vacant and available for development to its highest and best use. Next, the reproduction or replacement cost of the main improvements is estimated at current prices.

Problems can arise when the property being appraised is located in a transitional neighborhood, where it is more difficult to determine the highest and best use of a site. An appraiser must be careful not to base a land value estimate on properties that only appear similar to the subject property or properties that are similar only as improved. The comparable sites on which the value indication is based must have the same highest and best use as the subject property. A careful highest and best use analysis of the subject property and each comparable property is needed to make this determination.

Reproduction or Replacement Cost
Conceptual Differences

The terms *reproduction cost* and *replacement cost* are not synonymous. They reflect two different ways of looking at a new structure to be built in place of the existing improvements. Application of the two concepts may produce two different cost estimates. An appraiser must select one of these concepts and use it consistently throughout the cost approach. The use of reproduction or replacement cost affects how depreciation is estimated.

Reproduction cost is the estimated cost to construct, at current prices, an exact duplicate, or replica, of the building being appraised using the same materials, construction standards, design, layout, and quality of workmanship and embodying all the deficiencies, superadequacies, and obsolescence of the subject building. To estimate the reproduction cost of a structure, an appraiser must ascertain the cost to construct a replica of the existing building using the same materials at their current prices. If the improvement contains superadequate features, the cost to reproduce these features is included in the reproduction cost estimate. An appraiser might estimate reproduction cost in valuing historic properties and newly constructed improvements.

Replacement cost is the estimated cost to construct, at current prices, a building with utility equivalent to the building being appraised, using modern materials and current standards, design, and layout. To estimate replacement cost, an appraiser calculates the cost to construct an equally desirable, substitute improvement. This improvement will not necessarily be constructed with similar materials or to the same specifications. Because readily available materials would probably be substituted for the outdated or more costly materials used in the existing structure, the appraiser estimates the cost of construction with substitute materials. If the present structure contains a superadequacy such as high ceilings, the costs of producing this extra space in the existing building and all other costs resulting from the excessive ceiling height would be eliminated in the replacement cost estimate.

The use of replacement cost frequently results in a building cost estimate that is considerably lower than an estimate based on reproduction cost. However, fewer deductions are usually made for obsolescence when replacement cost is used. A replacement building has fewer items that are functionally obsolete than a reproduced building, so it suffers less depreciation. In using replacement cost, the appraiser must be careful to handle functional obsolescence appropriately.

Types of Costs

Regardless of whether reproduction or replacement cost is used, three types of costs are involved in the creation of an improvement and each must be reflected in the cost estimate. The three types of cost are

1. Direct costs
2. Indirect costs
3. Entrepreneurial profit or incentive

CONCEPT

A reproduction or replacement cost estimate includes the direct costs of the labor and materials used in construction, indirect costs for items such as administrative, professional, financing, insurance, and marketing fees, and an entrepreneurial incentive or profit.

TERMS

direct costs: expenditures for the labor and materials used in the construction of improvements; also called *hard costs*.

indirect costs: expenditures or allowances for items other than labor and materials that are necessary for construction but are not typically part of the construction contract; also called *soft costs*.

Direct costs, or *hard costs,* are expenditures for the labor and materials used in the construction of the improvement(s). The appraiser should be familiar with the types of labor and materials used in the subject property or an equivalent replacement property and with current costs in local construction markets. Direct costs can vary considerably, depending on the quality of the labor and materials involved and on current conditions in the market—i.e., the supply of and demand for contractors' services. Even when the building specifications are the same, there may be a substantial difference between the bids submitted by different contractors. A contractor who is working at full capacity is often inclined to make a high bid, while one who is not so busy may submit a lower figure.

A building contractor's overhead and profit are treated as direct costs and usually included in the construction contract. These costs should not be confused with entrepreneurial, or developer's, profit or incentive,

Direct Costs	Indirect Costs
• Labor used to construct buildings • Materials, products, and equipment • Contractor's profit and overhead, including the cost of job supervision, workers' compensation, fire and liability insurance, and unemployment insurance • Performance bonds • Use of equipment • Security • Contractor's shack, temporary fencing, and portable toilet (an OSHA requirement) • Materials storage facilities • Power line installation and utility costs	• Architectural and engineering fees for plans, plan checks, surveys to establish building lines and grades, and environmental and building permits • Appraisal, consulting, engineering, accounting, and legal fees • The cost of permanent financing as well as interest on construction loans, interest on land costs, and processing fees or service charges • Builder's, or developer's, all-risk insurance and ad valorem taxes during construction • Administrative expenses of the developer • Cost of title changes

which is neither a direct nor an indirect cost. It is classified as a separate line item. If the contractor is also the developer, both types of profit may be combined in the building contract. Nevertheless, an appraiser must carefully distinguish between the two in cost calculations and in the appraisal report.

Indirect costs, or *soft costs*, are expenditures for items other than labor and materials. Indirect costs are usually calculated separately from direct costs. Many indirect costs are calculated as a percentage of direct costs. The percentage is converted into a dollar amount and then added to the direct costs. Some indirect costs such as professional fees are not related to the size and direct cost of the improvements. These costs are expressed as lump-sum figures and added to the direct costs.

Entrepreneurial incentive is a market-derived figure of the amount an entrepreneur (i.e., the developer) expects to receive in addition to direct and indirect costs as compensation for providing coordination and expertise and assuming risk. Entrepreneurial profit is the difference between the actual total cost of development and the market value of the property. It may be considered a component of coordination, the fourth agent of production, which must be paid for along

TERMS

entrepreneurial incentive: the amount an entrepreneur expects to receive for his or her contribution to a project.

entrepreneurial profit: the difference between the actual total cost of development and the market value of the property.

with expenditures for the other three agents of production—land, labor, and capital. Normally a development will not be undertaken without the expectation of an eventual profit.

The estimation of entrepreneurial incentive or profit may present problems for an appraiser for several reasons. First, some appraisers point out that the value associated with the amenities of a residence may be such that its sale price far exceeds the sum of the development costs (land, building, and marketing). These practitioners contend that it would be a mistake to attribute the entire difference between the sale price and total development cost to entrepreneurial profit. Thus, to ensure the reasonableness of the entrepreneurial incentive or profit estimate, an appraiser should carefully examine the source of any property value that is over and above the cost of development.

Second, some practitioners observe that in owner-occupied residential properties, entrepreneurial profit is often an intangible measure. Entrepreneurial profit is realized only when the property is first sold (even if the sale takes place several years after the property was built). Over time, entrepreneurial profit becomes obscured by the appreciation in property value.

Third, the manner in which comparable properties have been developed affects the availability of data. The appraiser will usually be able to calculate entrepreneurial profit from actual cost comparables for speculatively built properties, especially residential properties such as condominium and multifamily developments. In a value estimate of a speculatively built property, entrepreneurial profit is the return to the developer for the skills employed and the risks incurred.[1] In large-scale residential developments the issue is complicated by the fact that the developer's profit may not reflect the proportional contributions of the improved site and the improvements to overall property value. Developers of tract subdivisions often realize most of their profit on the value of the finished lots rather than the value of the houses built on those lots.

For existing properties that were custom-built, data on entrepreneurial profit may not be available because the property owner, who contracted the actual builders, was acting as the developer. The prices

---

1.   The entrepreneurial profit is what was actually earned at the time of sale. This profit may differ from what the entrepreneur had anticipated (i.e., the incentive).

of upscale, custom-built properties often reflect the attractiveness of these amenity-laden properties as well as the high costs of the customized materials used. Thus, the breakdown of costs for custom-built residences may not be comparable to the breakdown for speculatively built properties, which further complicates the task of estimating a rate of entrepreneurial profit. Theoretically, however, the value of custom-built properties should also reflect an entrepreneurial incentive or profit.

Finally, the appraiser must scrutinize the cost data on which the value estimate is based to determine whether or not an allowance for entrepreneurial incentive or profit has already been made. If such research is not performed, it is possible that developer's profit could be counted among the estimated costs twice. Data derived from sales of comparable sites often include an allowance for the land developer's profit. Similarly, data extracted from sales of comparable properties may already include a profit to the developer. While cost estimating services quote direct costs (e.g., contractor's profit) and indirect costs (e.g., sales costs), they do not usually provide estimates of developer's profit.[2] Because different sources of data reflect costs in different ways, the appraiser should identify where developer's profit is considered in the estimate, i.e., whether it is an item already included in the replacement or reproduction cost plus land value or if it is a stand-alone item added to replacement or reproduction cost plus land value.

An appraiser estimates entrepreneurial incentive or profit by analyzing development activity in the local market. Entrepreneurial profit may be expressed as one of the following:

1. A percentage of direct costs
2. A percentage of direct and indirect costs
3. A percentage of direct and indirect costs plus land value
4. A percentage of the value of the completed project

An appraiser follows the practice of the local market. Entrepreneurial incentive or profit is always estimated at the rates prevailing in the market as of the date of the value estimate.

Because the amount of entrepreneurial incentive or profit varies considerably depending on economic conditions and the property type, a typical relationship between this cost and other costs may be difficult to establish. An appraiser may survey developers to establish

---

2. In actual practice, an additional estimate of entrepreneurial incentive or profit is not included in most estimates of the replacement or reproduction cost of existing residences based on cost service data.

the range of anticipated incentive and actual profit in the market. Often the appraiser will find that a developer keeps three targets in mind when estimating incentive:

1. What the developer wants to realize (maximum expectations in a best-case scenario)
2. What the developer absolutely must realize (minimum requirements in a worst-case scenario)
3. What the developer will accept and still stay motivated

To remain competitive, developers often vary their profit expectations according to the season and the condition of the market. Although it may be difficult to estimate precisely, entrepreneurial incentive or profit is an essential development cost and should therefore be recognized in the cost approach.

Methods of Estimating Cost

To estimate replacement or reproduction cost, an appraiser generally uses one of two methods:

1. The comparative-unit method
2. The unit-in-place method

To apply the comparative-unit method, an appraiser first derives an estimate of the cost per unit of area from the known costs of comparable new structures or using data from a recognized cost service. These unit costs are adjusted for the physical differences of the subject property and for time (or cost-trend) changes, and then the adjusted unit costs are applied to the dimensions of the subject building.

In the unit-in-place method, costs for specific, individual construction components (e.g., the cost per linear foot of brick wall, the cost per hour for masonry work) are derived from market research or from cost service manuals. These unit-in-place costs are applied to the corresponding components of the subject property and are added together. If the unit-in-place method is applied using extremely detailed units, it can produce very reliable results.

Although a third technique, the quantity survey method, most closely simulates the

TERMS

comparative-unit method: a method used to derive a cost estimate in terms of dollars per unit of area or volume based on known costs of similar structures that are adjusted for time and physical differences.

unit-in-place method: a cost-estimating method in which total building cost is estimated by adding together the unit costs for the various building components as installed; also called *segregated cost method.*

procedure a contractor uses to develop a construction bid, it is rarely used in residential appraisal practice because of the excessive time and expense involved in the process. In the quantity survey method, the quantity and quality of all the materials used and all the labor required are estimated, and unit cost figures are applied to these estimates to arrive at a total cost estimate for materials and labor. (The more commonly used cost-estimating methods are thoroughly discussed in Chapter 13.[3])

Depreciation

The depreciation estimate is a critical element in the cost approach and is often quite difficult to develop. The procedures used to estimate depreciation include sales comparison techniques, the age-life method, and the breakdown method. (Chapter 14 covers depreciation in great detail.)

Depreciation is the amount by which the replacement or reproduction cost of a new structure must be adjusted to reflect the value of the existing structure. There are three main types of depreciation:

1. Physical deterioration
2. Functional obsolescence
3. External obsolescence

Existing older structures usually suffer some physical deterioration. Normal wear and tear reduces the value of a building over time. Some forms of physical deterioration are economically feasible to cure, while others are incurable insofar as it would be impractical or uneconomical to correct them.

Many existing buildings suffer from design problems such as a poor floor plan, inadequate mechanical equipment, or excessively high ceilings. These forms of functional obsolescence can also reduce the

CONCEPTS

After the reproduction or replacement cost is estimated, all depreciation incurred by the main improvements is estimated and deducted from the reproduction or replacement cost.

Depreciation may be broken down into physical deterioration, functional obsolescence, and external obsolescence. Both physical deterioration and functional obsolescence may be curable or incurable. External obsolescence is always incurable by the property owner, although changing market conditions may sometimes eliminate this form of obsolescence.

TERMS

depreciation: in appraising, a loss in property value from any cause; the difference between the reproduction or replacement cost of an improvement on the effective date of the appraisal and the market value of the improvement on the same date.

physical deterioration: an element of depreciation resulting from the normal wear and tear of a structure.

---

3.   For a complete discussion of the quantity survey method refer to *The Appraisal of Real Estate*, 11th ed. (Chicago: Appraisal Institute, 1996).

value of a building. Using replacement cost instead of reproduction cost may eliminate some forms of functional obsolescence, but it usually cannot eliminate them all. Some forms of functional obsolescence are curable, while others are incurable. Curable forms of functional obsolescence may include deficiencies requiring additions, substitution, or modernization, or certain superadequacies, though superadequacies in structural components or materials are rarely curable.

If an existing structure is located on land that is inappropriate for that type of development, a further value penalty must be deducted for external obsolescence. In general, external obsolescence results from conditions outside the property such as a change in land uses, proximity to incompatible land uses, mistaken forecasts of market demand, or a downswing in regional or national economic conditions. External obsolescence is almost always considered economically incurable; however, the obsolescence may be temporary.

All three types of depreciation must be carefully estimated, added together, and deducted from the cost new of the improvements to arrive at the depreciated cost of the existing structure.

Site Improvements and Accessory Buildings

Once cost and depreciation figures for the main improvement are calculated, site improvements must be examined. The value of garages and accessory buildings as well as paving, landscaping, fences and walls, patios, swimming pools, and other site improvements are estimated either by the amount they contribute to the property or by the depreciated cost of these items. If the land value estimate is based on raw land, the appraiser must also estimate expenses for clearing and grading the site, installing utilities, and preparing the site for development.

Final Value Indication

Normally the last step in the cost approach is accomplished by adding the depreciated costs of the improvements to the value of the land. The depreciated costs of all the structures on the property are combined to obtain the value contribution of the improvements. This sum is then added to the land value estimate to obtain a total property value indication by the cost approach.

The value indication derived will be the value of the fee simple interest in the subject property. If the property rights being valued reflect a different ownership interest, the indicated fee simple value must be adjusted to reflect the interest being appraised.

13 Cost-Estimating Methods

Several methods may be used to estimate the costs of an existing or proposed building. The available techniques vary in their complexity, the time and effort required to apply them, and their relevance to the problem at hand. This chapter discusses the comparative-unit method and the unit-in-place method.

CONCEPT

Two methods are commonly used to estimate building costs: the comparative-unit method and the unit-in-place method.

COMPARATIVE-UNIT METHOD

The comparative-unit method is the simplest cost-estimating technique and usually the easiest to apply. This is the technique used in most ordinary residential appraisals.

To apply the comparative-unit method, an appraiser estimates the replacement or reproduction cost of the subject building by comparing it with recently constructed, similar buildings for which cost data are available. Unit costs are derived from these buildings and applied to the building dimensions of the subject. Adjustments are made for physical differences and for time (or cost-trend) changes, if necessary. Indirect costs and entrepreneurial incentive or profit may be included in the unit costs or they may be computed separately. Variations exist, but the comparative-unit method is typically applied in seven steps. An appraiser

1. Finds and verifies several sales of recently constructed buildings that are similar to the subject building.
2. Subtracts land value from the sale price of each comparable to obtain the replacement or reproduction cost of the improvements. Replacement or reproduction cost includes all direct and indirect costs as well as entrepreneurial incentive or profit.
3. Adjusts the replacement or reproduction cost of the improvements on the comparable properties to reflect how they differ from the subject improvements. Adjustments are made for physical differences such as size, shape, finish, and equipment. In the cost approach, adjustments are based on the cost of the item. In the

sales comparison approach, adjustments are based on the item's contributory value.

4. Divides the adjusted replacement or reproduction cost of the improvements on each comparable property by the unit area to arrive at the cost per unit of area.

5. Studies the trend in costs between the time the comparable properties were constructed and the date of the appraisal. The unit costs of the comparables are then adjusted to reflect cost differences over time.

6. Relates unit costs to property size and interpolates to arrive at the appropriate replacement or reproduction cost. Generally unit costs decline as building size increases.

7. Applies the adjusted unit cost of the comparables to measurements of the subject building to obtain the current reproduction or replacement cost of the main improvement.

Example

The subject property is a two-story residence built three years ago. The quality of construction is average for similar, mass-produced homes in the area. The house has a concrete block foundation, attractive wood siding, asphalt shingle roofing, $1/2$-in. drywall construction, and a good-to-average finish. It has 3 bedrooms, $2^1/2$ baths, a full basement, and a roof dormer. The house does not have a fireplace. The appraiser's measurements show that the structure contains 1,648 square feet of gross living area.

After inspecting comparable properties that were constructed and sold within the past three years, the appraiser decides to place the greatest emphasis on a single, similar property that has features typical of the subject neighborhood.[1] This comparable residence has 1,596 square feet of gross living area and was built and sold three years ago. It is located in the subject neighborhood and is similar to the subject, except that it has a foundation of poured concrete instead of concrete block and a brick exterior instead of wood siding. This house does not have a roof dormer but it does have a fireplace.

> **CONCEPT**
>
> In the comparative-unit method, a dollar cost per unit of area is derived from the known costs of similar structures adjusted for physical differences such as size, shape, finish, and equipment and for time (or cost-trend) changes.

---

1. This is only an illustration. Data on the other comparables and the reconciliation of cost estimates are not included.

The sale price of the comparable, including entrepreneurial incentive or profit, was $216,000. By means of sales comparison, site value on the date of construction is estimated at $28,000. The appraiser calculates the cost of the comparable dwelling as follows:

Sale price	$216,000
Less site value	− 28,000
Equals cost of comparable	$188,000

This estimate is consistent with the costs listed in the construction contract and seems reasonable for the area.

Next the appraiser derives adjustments for differences between the comparable and the subject using information obtained from local contractors and building suppliers. These adjustments are applied to the cost of the comparable, and the adjusted cost is converted into a comparative unit cost. Another adjustment is made to reflect changes in cost over the past three years. Finally, the adjusted unit cost is applied to the dimensions of the subject building. These calculations are shown below.

Cost of comparable structure three years ago	$188,000
Adjustments	
Brick siding	− 11,800
Poured concrete foundation	− 1,620
Fireplace	− 5,600
Roof dormer	+ 2,200
Equals adjusted historical cost of comparable	$171,180
Divided by gross living area of comparable (1,596 sq. ft.)	
Equals adjusted historical unit cost	$107.25
Multiplied by time adjustment for cost-trend changes (119%*)	
Equals adjusted current unit cost	$127.63
Times gross living area of subject (1,648 sq. ft.)	
Equals estimated current reproduction cost of subject	$210,341

* Based on the percentage increase indicated by the cost-estimating service used by the appraiser.

Using the comparative-unit method, the appraiser estimates the cost of the subject residence to be $210,000 (rounded).

Sales comparison was used to derive a unit cost figure in the example, but this figure can also be developed using data from a recognized cost service. Cost data sources are discussed later in this chapter, but it should be noted that cost manuals usually do not include entrepreneurial incentive or profit.

TERM

cost service: vendor of construction data, which is used in the cost approach.

Experienced appraisers recognize that the unit costs of structures typically decrease with size. Larger buildings do not necessarily cost proportionately more than smaller ones. Doors and windows can make construction more expensive, but usually the number of doors and windows in any one residence is limited. Plumbing, heating units, and kitchen equipment are major expenses, but the cost of these items is fairly stable. Equipment costs do not necessarily increase with the size of the building.[2]

Structures that are not designed in a conventional shape tend to have higher unit costs. Structures with many irregularities often incur higher costs for design, engineering, skilled labor, and additional building materials. Figure 13.1 shows how the shape of a structure can affect its costs.

Figure 13.1   Costs and Building Shapes

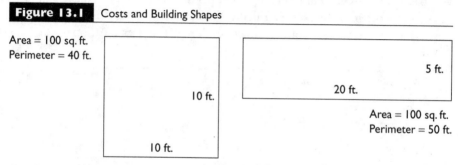

Costs are higher for the larger perimeter shown on the right.

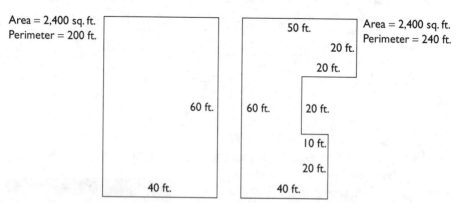

Higher costs are incurred for the larger perimeter and for the skilled labor needed to construct the irregular shape on the right.

---

2.   Appraisers should note that the ratio of equipment costs to the cost of the basic building shell has been rising steadily over the years. Additional equipment tends to increase building costs and depreciate more rapidly than the rest of the structure.

Applicability and Limitations

The apparent simplicity of the comparative-unit method can be misleading. To develop dependable unit cost figures, an appraiser must carefully compare the subject building with similar or standard structures for which actual costs are known. Inaccuracies may result if the appraiser selects a unit cost that is not appropriate to the building being appraised. Nevertheless, proper application of the comparative-unit method can provide an appraiser with a reasonably accurate estimate of reproduction or replacement cost.

To apply the method correctly, an appraiser must assemble, analyze, and catalog data on actual building costs. Construction contracts for buildings similar to the subject are primary sources of cost data. Discussions with local contractors can supplement this information. Many appraisers maintain comprehensive files on the current costs for completed structures. These costs may be classified according to types of residences. Appraisers should also follow cost trends in local and competitive markets so that they can adjust costs for market conditions and location if necessary. Unit costs can be derived from cost data services, but costs vary in different markets and a first-hand analysis of the market can often produce data that are more reliable.

UNIT-IN-PLACE METHOD

The unit-in-place, or segregated cost, method allows an appraiser to estimate costs in greater detail. The appraiser derives unit costs for individual structural components and applies them to the components found in the subject property. The unit-in-place method can be applied to all the improvements on the property or separately to the main improvements and any accessory improvements.

> **CONCEPT**
>
> The unit-in-place, or segregated cost, method establishes a total building cost by adding together the unit costs of various building components as installed.

The unit-in-place method has six steps. An appraiser

1. Collects data on current direct costs for various building components. Data can be obtained from an analysis of recent construction contracts, surveys of builders and contractors, and recognized cost services. Information on indirect costs and typical entrepreneurial incentive or profit is also collected.

2. Measures the components of the subject building, studies plans, and determines the number of units of each component that were

required to construct the building. Excavating costs are typically expressed in dollars per cubic yard. Foundation costs may be reported in dollars per linear foot of perimeter or per cubic yard of concrete. Floor construction costs are expressed in dollars per square foot. The basic unit for roofing, called a *square*, is 100 square feet. Interior partitions may be reduced to dollars per linear foot. Costs for other items such as mechanical equipment are expressed in trade units such as cost per ton of air-conditioning or other selected units.

3. Applies the unit costs for each component to the number of units of the component found in the subject.

4. Estimates contractor's overhead and profit. If these items are already included in the unit costs, which is often the case, this step is omitted.

5. Estimates any indirect costs not included in the unit costs and adds them to the direct costs.

6. Estimates entrepreneurial incentive or profit and adds this amount to the direct costs and indirect costs to arrive at a replacement or reproduction cost estimate.

Example

Table 13.1 shows unit-in-place costs for a $102,600 one-story ranch house.

> **CONCEPT**
>
> A complete unit-in-place estimate may be an adequate substitute for a comprehensive quantity survey.

Applicability and Limitations

The unit-in-place method breaks down the cost of a building into its components. Such a cost estimate is useful for recording the quality of construction components and computing the cost of their reproduction or replacement. However, assembling the basic costs of the equipment, material, and labor used in the structure and combining these costs into a final cost estimate may require specialized knowledge. When fully developed, however, the unit-in-place method substitutes for a complete quantity survey and can provide an accurate estimate of reproduction or replacement cost with considerably less effort.

Table 13.1	Unit-in-Place Costs			
Component	**Unit**	**Quantity**	**Unit Cost**	**Cost**
General expense for engineering, plans, survey, site	sq. ft.*	1,442 sq. ft	$2.38	$3,431.96
Foundation	sq. ft.	1,442 sq. ft.	3.22	4,643.24
Basement	sq. ft.	1,442 sq. ft.	4.32	6,229.44
Floors	sq. ft.	1,442 sq. ft.	4.60	6,633.20
Exterior walls and insulation, including windows and exterior doors	lin. ft./wall	1,450 lin. ft.	7.48	10,846.00
Roof	sq. ft.	1,442 sq. ft.	5.16	7,440.72
Interior walls, ceiling, doors, cabinets, trim, and accessories	sq. ft.	1,442 sq. ft.	7.52	10,846.00
Stairways	each	2 outside	500.00	1,000.00
Heating	sq. ft.	1,442 sq. ft.	3.22	4,643.24
Electrical system	sq. ft.	1,442 sq. ft.	3.78	5,450.76
Plumbing system	sq. ft.	1,442 sq. ft.	6.54	9,430.68
Fireplaces and chimneys	each	1 chimney	2,600.00	2,600.00
Built-in appliances	each	2	1,200.00	2,400.00
Patios	sq. ft./patio	144 sq. ft.	3.78	544.32
Other doors and windows	each	22	72.72	1,599.84
Site improvements not included in land value	lump sum		1,200.00	1,200.00
Garage	sq. ft./garage	460 sq. ft.	10.70	+ 4,922.00
Total direct cost				$83,859.24
Indirect cost	sq. ft.	8.28% of direct cost		+ 6,943.55
Total direct and indirect costs				$90,802.79
Plus entrepreneurial profit @ 13%†				+ 11,804.37
Total replacement cost				$102,600.00 (rounded)

* Per square foot of gross living area for all components except patio and garage
† It may not always be appropriate to consider entrepreneurial incentive or profit at this point.
Note: Other unit-in-place costs include roof dormers measured in linear feet across face, attic finish measured in square feet of finished area, cooling measured in tons of air-conditioning, and porches measured in square feet per porch. None of those costs were applicable in this example.

COST DATA SOURCES

Data for estimating the current cost of improvements are published by cost-estimating services such as Marshall & Swift, Boeckh Publications, F. W. Dodge Corporation, and R. S. Means Cost Estimating Service. Computer-assisted cost-estimating services can improve efficiency in preparing a report.

The cost manuals published by these services usually show direct unit costs, but an appraiser must conduct research to find which costs are most applicable to the appraisal problem. Depending on the source of the data, quoted construction costs may include other necessary expenses. Cost manuals almost always include indirect costs such as legal fees, and escrow fees; interest on construction loans; financing fees; the appraisal fee; carrying charges; leasing, sales, and marketing costs; and property taxes. However, discounts or bonuses paid for financing may not be included.

> **CONCEPT**
>
> Cost manuals include direct and sometimes indirect costs, but rarely are the costs of site improvements and entrepreneurial incentive or profit considered.

Often the data furnished by national cost services do not include the costs associated with site improvements. These may include the costs of demolishing existing improvements, paving roads, installing storm drains, and grading and compacting soil as well as the fees and assessments paid for utility hookup.

Estimates of entrepreneurial incentive or profit are rarely, if ever, provided by cost services. Appraisers estimate these costs separately and add them to the reproduction or replacement costs derived from published cost data, if appropriate. The appraiser will need to interview developers to estimate entrepreneurial incentive. Developers have three levels of incentive. One is the price they would like to receive for their risk. The second is what would make them continue with the project. The last is the number that they must have to do the project. The appraiser must be sure which level of incentive the developer is quoting.

Entrepreneurial profit can be extracted from developers' final costs. The appraiser should keep a file of actual final costs to estimate a percentage of profit for the entrepreneur after all other costs have been paid. This is a simple mathematical calculation.

Benchmark Buildings

The unit costs shown in cost-estimating manuals normally are given for a base, or benchmark, building of a certain size. Additions to or deductions from these unit costs are made if the actual area or volume of the subject building differs from the area or volume of the benchmark building. If the subject is larger than the benchmark building, the unit costs will generally be lower. If the subject building is smaller, the unit costs will probably be higher.

> **CONCEPT**
>
> A benchmark building provides the base from which costs are estimated, and adjustments are usually needed to apply these costs to the subject building.

Most buildings vary somewhat in size, design, and quality of construction, so the benchmark building used in the manual is rarely identical to the building being appraised. Variations in roof design, building shape, and types of mechanical equipment can substantially affect unit costs. Some published manuals indicate what adjustments should be made for such differences. Costs for materials and labor are different in different parts of the country, and they often vary considerably from one construction market to another. Many cost manuals provide specific city multipliers so that benchmark building costs can be adjusted to reflect these variations. Ultimately, however, the best way for an appraiser to derive costs and cost adjustments is to research the local market.

Cost-Index Trending

Cost services often provide cost indexes, which can be used to translate a known historical cost into a current cost estimate. Cost-index trending is useful when the comparative-unit method is applied to buildings that were constructed several years

> **TERM**
>
> **cost-index trending:** use of a multiplier to convert a known historical cost into a current cost estimate.

prior to the appraisal. Base years and regional multipliers are identified in the manuals. Base-year construction costs are based on an actual investigation of costs. Construction costs for subsequent years are calculated by multiplying these base-year costs by a multiplier, or index. To estimate the current costs of a building constructed several years earlier, an appraiser divides the current cost index by the index as of the date of construction and applies this ratio to the known historical costs. The procedure can be expressed with the following formula:

$$\frac{\text{current cost index}}{\text{index as of construction date}} \times \text{historical cost} = \text{current cost}$$

For example, consider a single-family home that cost $175,000 to build in 1995. The cost index in July 1995, when the house was completed, was 315.4. The cost index as of the date of appraisal is 342.25, which yields the following calculations for current cost:

$$(342.25 / 315.4) \times \$175,000 = \$189,897.73$$
$$= \$189,900 \text{ (rounded)}$$

Certain problems can arise when an appraiser uses cost-index trending to estimate current reproduction or replacement cost. The accuracy of the figures on which the indexes are based cannot always be ascertained, especially when the manual does not indicate which components are included—e.g., only direct costs and some indirect costs. Furthermore, historical costs may not be typical or normal for the time period, and the construction methods used in the base years may differ from those in use on the date of the appraisal. Appraisers who use cost-index trending should recognize that recent costs are more reliable than older costs adjusted with an index. Although cost-index trending may be used to confirm a cost estimate, it is not necessarily an accurate substitute for a first-hand analysis of cost trends.

BUILDING MEASUREMENT

To use cost service data or apply any cost-estimating method, the dimensions of the subject building must be measured. Building measurements are taken during the building inspection. There are many ways to take measurements, but most appraisers use the method customarily applied in their market area. When cost service data are used, the appraiser should understand the measurement technique used by the service.

14 Estimating Depreciation

In the cost approach a property value indication is derived by estimating the replacement or reproduction cost of the improvements, which comprises direct costs, indirect costs, and entrepreneurial incentive or profit. Depreciation is then subtracted from the replacement or reproduction cost estimate, and land value is added to the depreciated cost estimate. In this approach, cost is considered to be an indicator of

> **CONCEPT**
>
> Depreciation is the difference between the reproduction or replacement cost of an improvement and its market value as of the date of the appraisal.

the value of the improvements as if new. Because existing improvements usually contribute less value than their reproduction or replacement cost, an appraiser often must make an adjustment to reflect the loss in value that the existing structure has incurred since its construction. This deduction is the amount of depreciation suffered by the improvements.

Depreciation is the difference between the reproduction or replacement cost of an improvement and its market value as of the date of the appraisal. Three major factors may cause a building to lose value, or depreciate, over time:

1. Physical deterioration
2. Functional obsolescence
3. External obsolescence

These three types of depreciation can be broken down into more discrete components as illustrated in Figure 14.1. This model accounts for all the elements of the total depreciation estimate. If a particular element is not a form of physical deterioration, it must be some form of obsolescence, and elements of total depreciation that don't qualify as physical deterioration or functional obsolescence must be a form of external obsolescence.

As a building ages, it is subject to wear and tear from regular use and the impact of the elements, which reduce the value of the building over its life through physical deterioration. Careful maintenance can slow down this process, while neglect or improper maintenance can accelerate it.

Figure 14.1 Types of Depreciation

Total Depreciation

Physical Deterioration (curable or incurable; damage or vandalism is treated separately)

- Deferred maintenance (curable)
- Short-lived components (incurable)
- Long-lived components (incurable)

Functional Obsolescence (curable or incurable; caused by deficiency or superadequacy)

- Curable functional obsolescence caused by a deficiency requiring addition
- Curable functional obsolescence caused by a deficiency requiring substitution
- Curable functional obsolescence caused by a superadequacy
- Incurable functional obsolescence caused by a deficiency
- Incurable functional obsolescence caused by a superadequacy

External Obsolescence (generally incurable but not necessarily permanent)

- Economic factors
- Locational factors

All physical components of a structure fall into one of the three forms of physical deterioration:

1. Deferred maintenance
2. Deterioration of short-lived components
3. Deterioration of long-lived components

Damage or vandalism to a building (which is usually a curable and temporary influence on property value) is treated separately from physical deterioration because it is not included in the cost new of a project under development. The additional costs incurred to remediate damage on a construction site (e.g., graffiti) are not considered among the components of depreciation, nor are costs to fix damage to existing housing (e.g., a burglar rips the door off the jamb and a carpenter has to rehang it). By curing damage or vandalism, the life of the damaged building component is neither renewed nor prolonged; it is simply restored to its condition prior to the damage.

A building may also suffer from functional obsolescence due to some flaw in the site, structure, material, or design that diminishes its function, utility, and value. As the term *obsolescence* suggests, this type of value loss is often caused by the obsolete features of older properties, including buildings that are still in good repair. For example, older windows that do not provide sufficient insulation may cause functional obsolescence. Even a newly constructed building can have functional obsolescence due to a deficient feature such as a poor floor plan.

The five forms of functional obsolescence are

1. Curable functional obsolescence caused by a deficiency requiring addition of a new item
2. Curable functional obsolescence caused by a deficiency requiring substitution of an existing item
3. Curable functional obsolescence caused by a superadequacy that is economically feasible to cure
4. Incurable functional obsolescence caused by a deficiency
5. Incurable functional obsolescence caused by a superadequacy

> **TERM**
>
> **deficiency requiring substitution or modernization:** functional obsolescence resulting from the presence of something in the subject property that is substandard compared to other properties on the market or that is defective and thereby prevents some other component or system in the property from working properly.

The only ways to offset functional obsolescence are to cure it or to hope that market standards change.

To test whether or not functional obsolescence is present, an appraiser decides whether the structure or its design conforms to current market standards. The quality of construction, materials, or design of a building may be inferior to current market standards (i.e., typical improvements) for the neighborhood. In this case, any savings realized from the lower construction costs will probably result in a disproportionately greater loss in the price obtainable for the property. If the structure and its design surpass market standards (superadequacies), the additional utility provided may not justify the additional cost. In either case, functional obsolescence must be deducted from the replacement or reproduction cost of the structure to reflect its diminished utility in comparison to market standards.

In contrast to functional obsolescence, external obsolescence is caused by a factor outside the subject, most often economic factors such as oversupply in the market or expensive financing or locational factors such as proximity to a nuisance or poor access to transportation routes. Interest rates that are rising quickly, for example, may cause current construction costs to outpace building values. Similarly, overbuilding in certain markets may create a surplus of space and depress rents and values. Although external obsolescence is generally incurable, it is not always permanent; for example, market conditions such as overbuilding or high interest rates can change over time, eventually removing the influence of external obsolescence on a particular property. Unlike the other types of depreciation, which affect only the improvements, external obsolescence may affect both the site and improvements. Therefore the influence of the externality on value may have to be allocated between the site and the improvements.

A loss in value also results when a neighborhood changes and an improvement that was formerly well-suited to its location is no longer appropriate. In this situation the site may or may not lose value; it may be more valuable as the site of a more intensive use. Although the existing improvements may be well-designed and well-maintained, if they are not what the market currently demands in that location they cannot contribute value commensurate with their cost. Such a property in transition is called an *interim use*.

In some cases external or economic changes can restore the appropriateness of the location for the existing improvements. Often, however, land value or entrepreneurial incentive or profit will increase when such a change occurs, but not the value contribution of the building. The contribution of a building to property value rarely rises above its cost. One exception to this general rule might be a residence of historical significance, which contributes more value than the cost of a new structure.

All three causes of depreciation—physical deterioration, functional obsolescence, and external obsolescence—reduce the value of an existing structure in comparison with its replacement or reproduction cost. An appraiser calculates the amount of depreciation in a structure by applying one of three techniques, either independently or in conjunction with one another:

1. The market extraction method
2. The age-life method
3. The breakdown method

Depreciation and Book Depreciation

The term *depreciation* is used in both accounting and appraisal, and it is important to distinguish between the two usages.* *Book depreciation* is the amount of capital recapture written off an owner's books. This term is typically used in income tax calculations to identify the amount allowed for the retirement or replacement of an asset under the tax laws. Like depreciation in appraisal, book depreciation refers to a loss in value that accrues over time and applies only to improvements, never to land. Losses ascribed to book depreciation, however, are often measured against book value or original cost rather than current market value. Book depreciation amounts may be estimated to correspond to a depreciation schedule set by the Internal Revenue Service. Thus book depreciation is not market-derived, while depreciation is.

The estimate of depreciation in an appraisal may help a client reach a conclusion about book depreciation, but the two concepts are distinct and should not be confused.

---

* In previous editions of *Appraising Residential Properties*, the term *accrued depreciation* was used to refer to the total depreciation taken on an asset from the time of purchase to the present. (This amount would be deducted from an asset's account value to derive net book value.) While that term, *accrued depreciation*, borrowed from accounting practice, has been used in an appraisal context for a long time, the more concise and equally suitable term *depreciation* has been used throughout this edition.

Depreciation is deducted from the reproduction or replacement cost of the existing improvements to estimate their contribution to the total value of the property.

AGE AND LIFE OF RESIDENCES

The appraisal concept of depreciation is closely related to economic life, useful life, remaining economic life, remaining useful life, actual age, and effective age. Many techniques for estimating depreciation make use of these terms.

Economic Life and Useful Life

Economic life is the period of time over which improvements contribute to property value. A building's economic life begins when construction is complete and ends when the building no longer contributes any value to the property above land value. This period is usually shorter than the building's useful life, which is the total period over which a structure may reasonably be expected to perform the function for which it was designed. If buildings are adequately maintained, they may remain on the land long after they cease to contribute economically to property value. After the end of their

> **TERMS**
>
> **economic life:** the period over which improvements to real property contribute to property value.
>
> **useful life:** the period over which a structure may reasonably be expected to perform the function for which it was designed.

economic lives, buildings may be renovated, rehabilitated, or remodeled, or they may be demolished and replaced with more suitable structures.

To estimate a building's economic life, an appraiser studies the typical economic life expectancy of recently sold structures similar to the subject in the market area. (See the discussion of the market extraction technique later in this chapter.) In other words, the quality of construction and functional utility of the existing residence are considered in the estimate of economic life. The present condition of the subject property is reflected in estimates of remaining economic life and effective age.

Long-lived building components have a useful life at least as long as the building's economic life expectancy, while short-lived components will probably wear out and need to be replaced before the building has reached the end of its economic life. Structural components of a building, like the foundation, framing, and underground piping, are typical long-lived components. The roof covering, floor finishes, HVAC components, and interior decorating of a building are examples of short-lived components. The distinction between short-lived and long-lived components becomes significant in the application of the breakdown method.

CONCEPT

An improvement can suffer from three forms of depreciation:

1. Physical deterioration caused by wear and tear as the building ages
2. Functional obsolescence resulting from a structural or design flaw
3. External obsolescence brought about by external factors such as changes in the neighborhood or the economy

Although the economic life expectancy of a structure is difficult to predict, it is shaped by a number of factors, including:

- Physical considerations—i.e., the rate at which the physical components of the residence wear out, given the quality of construction, the use of the property, maintenance standards, and the climate of the region.

- Functional considerations—i.e., the rate at which building technology, tastes in architecture, and family size and composition change. These factors can make a residence obsolete or they can remove obsolescence.

- External, economic considerations, especially long-term influences such as the stage in the neighborhood's life cycle.

Many of these considerations may become significant 20, 50, or even 100 years in the future, so they are obviously difficult to forecast with any accuracy. Nevertheless, market study and analysis of historical and geographical trends may provide important information.

Remaining Economic Life and Remaining Useful Life

Remaining economic life is the estimated period over which existing improvements continue to contribute to property value. This concept refers to the economic life that remains in the existing structure. It begins on the date of the appraisal or some other specified date and extends until the end of the building's economic life. A building's remaining economic life is always less than or equal to, never more than, its total economic life.

Remaining useful life is the estimated period measured by subtracting the actual age of a component today from its total useful life expectancy. Just as useful life is usually longer than economic life, the remaining useful life of a long-lived component is equal to or, typically, greater than its remaining economic life.

Actual Age and Effective Age

Actual age, which is sometimes called *historical age* or *chronological age*, is the number of years that has elapsed since building construction was completed. The prices of newly completed buildings are compared with the prices of similar, older structures to establish a correlation between actual age and the value of residences (see Figure 14.2).

> **TERMS**
>
> **remaining economic life:** the estimated period during which improvements will continue to contribute to property value; an estimate of the number of years remaining in the economic life of the structure or structural components as of the date of the appraisal.
>
> **remaining useful life:** the estimated period from the actual age of a component to the total useful life expectancy.
>
> **actual age:** the number of years that have elapsed since construction of an improvement was completed; also called *historical* or *chronological age.*
>
> **effective age:** the age indicated by the condition and utility of a structure.

Figure 14.2 Hypothetical Correlation Between Actual Age and Property Value

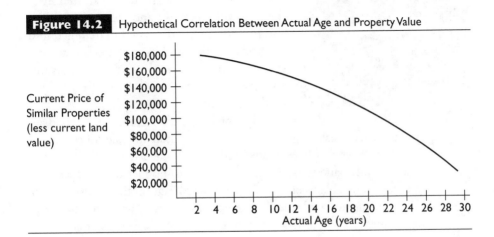

Effective age is the age indicated by the condition and utility of the structure. It is determined by an appraiser's judgment and is not market-derived. Similar buildings do not necessarily depreciate at the same rate. The maintenance standards of owners or occupants can influence the pace of building deterioration. If a building is better maintained than others in the market area, its effective age will be less than its actual age. If a building is poorly maintained, its effective age may be greater. If a building has received typical maintenance, its effective age and actual age could be the same. Effective age is related to remaining economic life. The total economic life of similar structures minus the effective age of the subject building equals the remaining economic life of the subject.

METHODS OF ESTIMATING DEPRECIATION

The three principal methods for estimating depreciation are

1. The market extraction method
2. The age-life method (and its two variations)
3. The breakdown method

The market extraction and age-life methods are used primarily to estimate the total depreciation of property, while the breakdown method can be used to allocate value loss to the individual components of depreciation.

Each of these methods is acceptable so long as it reflects the manner in which informed, prudent buyers would react to the condition of the structure being appraised, and the appraiser applies the method consistently, logically, and cautiously. The methods are summarized here and demonstrated in the following sections, and their applicability and limitations are discussed in detail. These methods may be used in combination to solve specific problems or to test the reasonableness of the estimates derived from each method.

CONCEPT

There are three principal methods for estimating depreciation:

1. The market extraction method
2. The age-life method
3. The breakdown method

To apply the market extraction method, an appraiser develops a depreciation estimate by studying sales of comparable properties that have depreciated to the same extent as the subject residence. The land value at the time of sale is subtracted from the price of each comparable to obtain the depreciated value of the improvements. When the depreciated value of the improvements is subtracted from the replacement or reproduction cost of the comparable, the result is a lump-sum, dollar estimate of depreciation reflecting all forms of depreciation.[1] This dollar amount is converted into a percentage by dividing it by the replacement or reproduction cost of the comparable. The percentage of lump-sum depreciation is then annualized by dividing it by the actual age or, if there is a significant difference between the actual age and effective age, by the effective age estimate. Once a range of annual percentages of depreciation in the comparables is established, the appraiser reconciles the range and applies the concluded rate to the age of the subject improvement. The result is a lump-sum percentage of depreciation that is then applied to the replacement or reproduction cost of the subject. This rate can also be used in developing a total economic life expectancy.

In the age-life method, an appraiser estimates the total economic life of the existing improvements as well as its effective age based on an analysis of sales of similar structures. The ratio of effective age to total economic life is considered to be the extent to which the building has depreciated. This ratio is directly applied to the replacement or reproduction cost of the structure to arrive at a lump-sum depreciation amount including all forms of depreciation, which is then deducted from the cost figure.

One variation of the age-life method distinguishes between curable and incurable items of depreciation, and another variation takes into account external obsolescence. In the first variation, the appraiser first estimates the cost to fix all curable items—i.e., items that can be repaired or replaced at a cost that is equal to or less than the amount of value that the item contributes to the total property. This amount is deducted from the replacement or reproduction cost of the structure to arrive at a figure adjusted for curable depreciation. Then the appraiser estimates the effective age and total economic life of the structure, assuming the curable items have been repaired, and

TERMS

market extraction method: a method of estimating depreciation in which the estimated percentages of depreciation in the comparables are reconciled to a rate that is applied to the age of the subject to obtain the total percentage of depreciation in the subject property.

age-life method: a method of estimating depreciation in which the ratio between the effective age of a building and its total economic life is applied to the current cost of the improvements to obtain a lump-sum depreciation estimate.

breakdown method: a method of estimating depreciation in which the total loss in the value of a property is estimated by analyzing and measuring each cause of depreciation (physical, functional, and external) separately.

---

1. An appraiser may also use this lump-sum estimate of depreciation to test the reasonableness of the depreciation estimate derived using the breakdown method.

applies the ratio of effective age to total economic life to the depreciated replacement or reproduction cost. The sum for incurable depreciation is then deducted from the depreciated cost.

In the second variation of the age-life method, the appraiser first determines if other properties in the market have incurred the same external obsolescence as the subject. If so, the appraiser can use the total economic life extracted from those sales considered comparable in the age-life ratio. If not, the appraiser must estimate depreciation exclusive of external obsolescence using a market-extracted economic life expectancy in the age-life ratio, and then estimate external obsolescence using techniques from the breakdown method. The sum of estimated depreciation from the age-life method and estimated external obsolescence using the breakdown method would yield an estimate of total depreciation.

The breakdown method is a more detailed, expanded set of techniques for estimating depreciation. Separate estimates are derived for items of

- Curable physical deterioration
- Incurable physical deterioration
- Curable functional obsolescence
- Incurable functional obsolescence
- External obsolescence

Each category of depreciation is estimated by a specific method applicable to that form of depreciation. The sum of depreciation for all items is then subtracted from the replacement or reproduction cost of the improvements. The procedures in the breakdown method can also be used to allocate a lump-sum estimate of depreciation determined by other methods into its components.

Regardless of the method applied, the appraiser must ensure that the final estimate of depreciation reflects the loss in value from all causes, and that no cause of depreciation has been considered more than once. Double charges for depreciation may produce overly low value indications in the cost approach. The first variation of the age-life method and the breakdown method provide an estimate of the cost to cure curable items of depreciation, which should be recognized in the application of the other approaches to value. This is typically done in the sales comparison approach and the income capitalization approach by deducting the cost to cure at the conclusion of each approach.

Reproduction and Replacement Cost Bases

An appraiser must estimate depreciation using the same basis from which costs were calculated—either reproduction or replacement cost.

- A reproduction is a virtual replica of the existing structure, employing the same design and similar building materials.
- A replacement is a structure of comparable utility constructed with the design and materials that are currently used in the building market.

A reproduction may contain more items of functional obsolescence than a replacement structure does. These items might include high ceilings, a lack of adequate electrical outlets and plumbing facilities, and the use of expensive, outdated building materials and techniques. Obsolete items usually cost more in the current market and do not produce a proportionate increase in utility and value. An amount must be deducted from reproduction cost for these items of functional obsolescence.

The use of replacement cost usually eliminates the need to measure some, but not all, forms of functional obsolescence. Replacement structures usually cost less than reproductions because they are constructed with materials and techniques that are more readily available and less expensive in today's market. Thus a replacement cost figure is usually lower and may provide a better indication of the existing structure's contribution to value. A replacement structure typically does not suffer functional obsolescence resulting from superadequacies, but if functional problems are found in the existing structure, an additional amount must be deducted from the replacement cost. Estimating replacement cost generally simplifies the procedure for measuring depreciation in superadequate construction components. Examples of functional obsolescence are structural defects in an existing residence or excessively thick foundations. Such obsolescence would be corrected in a replacement building.

> **CONCEPT**
>
> The use of replacement cost as the cost new instead of reproduction cost generally eliminates the need to measure certain forms of functional obsolescence.

To avoid errors in measuring depreciation, an appraiser must be consistent and clearly understand the purpose of this step in the cost approach. Depreciation is estimated and deducted to adjust the cost to create a new reproduction or replacement improvement to reflect the value contribution of the existing improvement. Even a newly constructed improvement may not contribute as much value as it costs. Although it has no physical deterioration, a reproduction or replacement structure may suffer from external obsolescence and functional obsolescence. Any feature that creates a loss in value from the cost standard must be accounted for as an item of depreciation.

Figure 14.3   Differences Between Reproduction Cost and Replacement Cost

Reproduction Cost

1. A reproduction replicates the existing structure (i.e., form).

2. A reproduction employs the same design and similar building materials as the existing structure (past).

3. A reproduction is more likely to contain items of functional obsolescence.

4. Reproduction cost is usually higher because some outdated materials and techniques may be hard to come by in the current market.

Replacement Cost

1. A replacement structure mimics the utility of the existing structure (i.e., function).

2. A replacement employs the design and materials currently used in the building market (present).

3. A replacement structure is less likely to have items of functional obsolescence, particularly superadequacies.

4. Replacement cost is usually lower and may better represent the existing structure's contribution to value.

Market Extraction Method

Market extraction is the most direct means of estimating depreciation if a sufficient amount of sales data is available to support the appraiser's conclusion. The method is used primarily to extract total depreciation, to establish total economic life expectancy, and to estimate external obsolescence. There are eight steps in the market extraction method. An appraiser

1. Finds and verifies at least two sales of similar improved properties that appear to have approximately the same amount of depreciation as the subject property.

2. Makes appropriate adjustments to the comparable sales for certain factors, including property rights conveyed, financing, and conditions of sale. If an appraiser can quantify curable depreciation for either items of deferred maintenance or functional obsolescence, this estimate should be applied to the sale price as an adjustment. (Depreciation extracted in this way will exclude curable items.)

3. Subtracts the land value at the time of sale from the sale price of each comparable property to obtain the depreciated cost of the improvements.

4. Estimates the replacement cost of the improvements on each comparable property at the time of sale.

5. Subtracts the depreciated cost of each improvement from the replacement cost of the improvements to obtain a lump-sum estimate of depreciation in dollars.

6. Converts the dollar estimates of depreciation into percentages by dividing each depreciation estimate by the replacement cost.

7. Annualizes the percentages of lump-sum depreciation by dividing each total percentage of depreciation by the actual age estimate or, if there is a significant difference between the actual age and the effective age, by the effective age estimate.

8. Reconciles the range of annual percentage rates derived and applies an approximate depreciation rate to the cost of the subject improvements.

As an optional step of this procedure, the appraiser can calculate the total economic life expectancy of the subject using the reciprocal of the average annual rate of depreciation in the comparables as indicated by the market on the date of sale.[2]

Example

The subject property is a 12-year-old frame structure with an effective age of 12 years. The subject property contains 1,496 square feet of gross living area and is situated on a site that is valued at $26,000. The replacement cost of this residence is $63.85 per square foot of gross living area.

The appraiser has found three sales of neighborhood properties similar to the subject property. Property 1 was sold recently for $92,500. The appraiser estimates that the site is worth $26,000 and the replacement cost of the improvements is $96,750. The property's actual age, 15 years, corresponds to its effective age.

Property 2 was sold recently for $103,800. The appraiser estimates that the site is worth $24,000 and the replacement cost of the improvements is $92,000. The property's actual age is 8 years, which is the same as its effective age.

Property 3 was sold recently for $94,900. The appraiser estimates the site is worth $29,000 and the replacement cost of the improve-

---

2. As explained in footnote 4, in valuing older residential properties, it may be easier for the appraiser to find support for the total economic life expectancy. Data on total economic life may be used to arrive at an average annual rate of depreciation for the property and, thereby, to establish the overall percentage the property is depreciated.

ments is $125,500. The property's actual age, which is equal to its effective age, is 20 years.

To estimate the average annual rate of depreciation in the subject property, the appraiser compares the three sales.

	Property 1	Property 2	Property 3
Sale price	$92,500	$103,800	$94,900
Less site value	− 26,000	− 24,000	− 29,000
Depreciated cost of improvements	$66,500	$79,800	$65,900
Replacement cost	$96,750	$92,000	$125,500
Less depreciated cost			
of improvements	− 66,500	− 79,800	− 65,900
Lump-sum dollar depreciation	$30,250	$12,200	$59,600
Total percentage depreciation			
(lump-sum dollar depreciation			
divided by replacement cost)	31.27%	13.26%	47.5%
Average annual depreciation rate			
(total percentage depreciation	31.27/15	13.26/8	47.5/20
divided by age)	2.08%	1.66%	2.38%
Total economic life expectancy	48 years	60 years	42 years
	(1/0.0208)	(1/0.0166)	(1/0.0238)

Because the age of the subject property (12 years) is approximately midway between the ages of Sale 1 (15 years) and Sale 2 (8 years), the average of these two annual depreciation rates (1.87% per year) becomes the reconciled rate for the subject property. The total economic life expectancy of the subject property would be approximately 53.5 years (1/0.0187).

With these figures the value of the subject property is estimated as follows:

Replacement cost	
1,496 sq. ft. @ $63.85	$95,520 (rounded)
Less depreciation	
12 years @ 1.87% × $95,520	− 21,435
Depreciated cost of improvements	$74,085
Plus site value	+ 26,000
Total property value indication	$100,085, or $100,100

Applicability and Limitations

When sales data are plentiful, market extraction usually provides a reliable, persuasive estimate of depreciation; it is the most defensible of the depreciation tools because it is measured directly from the market. If sales are truly comparable, then the land sales or site valuation method used for the subject property would apply to the comparables, the source of the estimate of replacement cost that applies to the subject would also apply to the comparables, and the use of actual age would eliminate the need to "guess" the effective age of comparables that were not actually inspected by the appraiser. Many appraisers use this method to measure depreciation in single-family homes. By using matched pairs, different types of depreciation can be measured by the extracted annual depreciation rates. Most significantly, market extraction is the only method by which meaningful data can be extracted to support the total economic life expectancy of the property as of the date of property sale. Total economic life expectancy is calculated as the reciprocal of the average annual rate of depreciation.[3]

Despite the many advantages of market extraction, the properties compared must be similar to the subject and they must suffer from similar amounts and types of depreciation. When the properties compared differ in design, quality, or construction, it is difficult to ascertain whether differences in value are attributable to differences in those components or to a difference in depreciation. The method is also difficult to apply when the type or extent of depreciation varies greatly among the properties. If the sales analyzed were affected by special financing or unusual motivation, the problem is further complicated. The accuracy of the method depends heavily on the accuracy of the land value and replacement cost estimates of the comparable properties. If the sales are located in districts or neighborhoods that are not comparable, the method may not be appropriate. In the market extraction method, all types of depreciation are considered in a lump sum; they are not broken down into various types.

> **CONCEPT**
>
> The market extraction method can only be used to estimate depreciation when data on extremely similar comparable properties are available.

The market extraction method has especially stringent market data requirements. Methods employing alternative age-life estimates allow the appraiser to rely on data from buildings with considerably more or less depreciation than the subject. Thus the age-life methods offer a broader perspective on depreciation with respect to the rate at which depreciation occurs in similar buildings and the period over which it occurs.

---

3. Using the reciprocal of the average annual rate of depreciation to calculate the total economic life expectancy of a property rests on the premise that depreciation occurs in a straight-line pattern. When the appraiser attempts to develop an estimate of total economic life expectancy on the basis of an annual rate, the straight-line assumption may have to be reconsidered in terms of its applicability to the subject and comparable properties. Because straight-line depreciation may not be the typical pattern, conclusions must be consistent with market data. Market support is more important than mathematical precision.

In spite of its limitations, market extraction provides extremely reliable and convincing results and may be used to check the results obtained by applying other methods.

Age-Life Method

Like market extraction, the age-life method assumes that depreciation occurs in a straight-line pattern. The age-life method identifies the rate at which buildings similar to the subject depreciate and then uses this rate, along with the effective age of the subject, to derive an estimate of depreciation. Although it is not always as accurate as other techniques, the age-life method is the simplest way to estimate depreciation. The method is applied in three steps. An appraiser

1. Conducts research to identify the total economic life of similar structures in the market area and estimates the effective age of the subject building. The effective age may be the same as the actual age if the building has received typical maintenance.

2. Divides the effective age of the subject by the anticipated total economic life of similar structures. The resulting ratio is then applied to the subject's reproduction or replacement cost to estimate lump-sum depreciation.[4]

3. Subtracts the estimate of depreciation from the replacement or reproduction cost to arrive at the contribution of the improvements to property value.

Example

The subject property is located in a neighborhood that was developed during a land boom 20 years ago. Most of the properties nearby are similar to the subject in size and architectural style. These buildings appear to be maintained adequately. Through use of the market extraction method, the appraiser concludes that the typical economic

---

4. The estimate of the effective age of older residential properties depends largely on the appraiser's judgment. The appraiser may find it easier to derive support for the effective age estimate by first estimating the property's total economic life expectancy. Multiplying the total economic life expectancy by the percentage amount of depreciation derived from market extraction will indicate an estimate of the effective age.

   A situation in which a property's total economic life expectancy might be estimated can be found in older residential neighborhoods where no change in highest and best use is imminent. At some point in the life of an older property, a decision must be made as to whether the existing building should be completely renovated or whether it should be razed and the site redeveloped. In either case, the building will probably have reached the end of its total economic life expectancy. (Examples of major renovation include the complete replacement of mechanical systems, the remodeling of all interior rooms, and the modernization of most building components.)

life is 75 years. The subject has been especially well-maintained, however, and the appraiser concludes that it has an effective age of only 8 years. The replacement cost is estimated at $74,000, and the land value is estimated at $12,900.

The appraiser estimates depreciation with the following calculations:

$$\text{Depreciation ratio} = \frac{8 \text{ years (effective age)}}{75 \text{ years (total economic life)}}$$

$$= 0.107, \text{ or } 10.7\%$$

10.7% × $74,000 (replacement cost)	= $7,918
Estimated depreciation =	$7,900 (rounded)

Replacement cost	$74,000
Less depreciation	− 7,900
Value contribution of the improvements	$66,100
Plus land value	+ 12,900
Total property value indication	$79,000

Applicability and Limitations

The age-life method is usually the simplest way to estimate depreciation; it works best for newer properties and is the most commonly used method. It does have certain limitations, though. First, because the percentage of depreciation is represented by the ratio of effective age to total economic life, this method assumes that every building depreciates on a straight-line basis over the course of its economic life. In other words, a house that has twice the effective age of another is presumed to suffer from twice as much depreciation. The method is flawed because depreciation does not always occur on a straight-line basis and therefore the estimate is not easy to fine tune using this method. In some markets buildings tend to depreciate more rapidly as they approach the end of their economic lives, while in other markets a different pattern may be observed. The straight-line pattern of depreciation is only an approximation, although it is usually a sufficiently accurate one.

Second, the age-life method does not divide depreciation into subcategories such as curable or incurable physical deterioration, curable or incurable functional obsolescence, and external obsolescence. Therefore, the method may not recognize differences in depreciation among residences as well as techniques that categorize different types of depreciation, and other steps may be required to divide a lump-sum estimate of depreciation into its various forms. In neighborhoods or market areas where residences suffer different types and amounts of depreciation, the age-life method may be difficult to justify.

Third, the age-life method does not recognize the difference between short-lived and long-lived items of physical deterioration. Because a single figure is used to reflect depreciation in the structure as a whole, varying amounts of depreciation in short-lived items are not directly reflected in the age-life ratio. For example, a building as a whole may be estimated to be 20% depreciated except for the roof which, unlike other roofs in the neighborhood, is estimated to be 90% depreciated. In this situation the breakdown method would allow an appraiser to make a more refined analysis.

CONCEPTS

The age-life method does not divide depreciation into subcategories or distinguish between short-lived and long-lived building components. Estimates of total economic life require expert judgment.

The market extraction and age-life methods assume depreciation occurs on a straight-line basis.

Finally, one component of the age-life ratio's denominator (the total economic life expectancy of typical, similar structures) is the remaining economic life, which refers to a future period of time. Any forecast of future events calls for judgment, so the estimates of effective age and economic life may be difficult to justify. To minimize this problem, economic life estimates should be based on objective data to the greatest extent possible. Useful information can be obtained in several ways. Historical studies may shed light on the actual lives of similar structures, or the appraiser can ask lenders, brokers, buyers, and sellers how much longer they anticipate neighborhood structures similar to the subject will be economically useful.

Because depreciation is assumed to occur on a straight-line basis, a market-derived estimate of economic life can be obtained by identifying the annual rate of depreciation for similar structures and dividing this figure into 100%. The formula is

$$\text{Economic life} = \frac{100\%}{\text{annual \% depreciation}}$$

Market-derived information can help support the depreciation estimates used in the age-life method.

Variation 1—Known Curable Items

The first variation of the age-life method provides greater accuracy by dividing depreciation into curable and incurable components. A form of depreciation is curable if, as of the date of the appraisal, the cost to cure the defect is equal to or less than the value that would be added by doing so. Otherwise, it is incurable. When an item is considered incurable it does not mean that the problem cannot physically be solved; it only means that it cannot be solved economically—i.e., the cure is simply not worth its cost.

This procedure is applied in five steps. An appraiser

1. Estimates the cost to cure all items of curable depreciation.

2. Deducts the cost to cure these items from the replacement or reproduction cost.

3. Estimates the effective age and remaining economic life of the structure *as cured.* Curing a major item can sometimes decrease the effective age of the building, prolong its remaining economic life, or both.

> **CONCEPT**
>
> The advantage of the first variation of the age-life method is that the appraiser estimates curable items of depreciation separately, which enhances the accuracy of the estimate of incurable depreciation.

4. Applies the ratio between the adjusted effective age and the total economic life of the structure to the remainder of the replacement or reproduction cost to obtain the amount of incurable depreciation found in the building.

5. Deducts the incurable depreciation from the remainder of the replacement or reproduction cost to arrive at the improvement's contribution to property value.

Example. A house with a current replacement cost of $100,000 and a land value of $26,000 was built 18 years ago. The appraiser estimates that it now has an effective age of 15 years and a 45-year remaining economic life expectancy. Total curable physical deterioration and functional obsolescence in the structure amounts to $15,000. The appraiser estimates that by curing these items effective age could be reduced to 5 years and the remaining economic life expectancy could be extended to 55 years.[5] To estimate lump-sum depreciation using this variation of the age-life method, the appraiser performs the following calculations.

---

5. It is difficult to find market support for changes in effective age and remaining economic life expectancy estimates.

Replacement cost	$100,000
Less physical and functional curable items	− 15,000
Depreciated reproduction cost	$85,000
Depreciated cost basis	
Remaining economic life	55 years
Effective age	5 years
Ratio applied to cost less physical and functional curable items (5/60)	8.33%
Less incurable items ($85,000 × 0.0833)	− 7,081
Total depreciated value of improvements	$77,919
Plus land value	+ 26,000
Total property value indication (rounded)	$103,900

Applicability. In this procedure, curable items of depreciation are cured at the outset, before estimating the incurable depreciation. This is helpful for a number of reasons. Most importantly, this procedure closely approximates the reasoning of an informed buyer contemplating a purchase.[6] A buyer frequently wants to know how much the residence will be worth after all problems that can be economically cured have been attended to. Most astute purchasers do not simply consider the property in its present, depreciated state; they are also concerned with its potential after any repairs have been made. This refinement of the age-life method addresses these concerns, which are not considered in the simpler procedure.

By curing the curable items the appraiser brings it in line with existing market standards as far as possible. If the addition or repair of an item is considered so necessary that the market is prepared to award a value increase equal to or greater than its cost, the feature to be added or repaired usually conforms to market standards. For the appraiser, this variation of the age-life method can enhance the accuracy of the depreciation estimate in three ways:

1. The amount of depreciation to be deducted for curable items can usually be established with some certainty. Typically it is simply the current cost to cure.

2. When curable items are cured, a smaller proportion of the estimate depends on the judgmental age-life technique. The age-life ratio is applied only to items of incurable depreciation, so the potential for error is decreased.

3. When a building is cured of curable defects, incurable defects can usually be assessed more accurately. A partially cured building

---

6. This statement is only partially accurate. Beyond a certain point, a buyer may not consider age and life estimates especially relevant to a purchase decision and the significance of the cost approach may be diminished.

conforms more closely to market standards, so there may be more similar structures from which to derive an appropriate estimate of effective age and remaining economic life.

Limitations. A limitation of this procedure is that, like the simpler, unmodified age-life method, it does not divide incurable depreciation into physical, functional, and external subcategories or distinguish between short-lived and long-lived items. It assumes depreciation in incurable items occurs on a straight-line basis. Moreover, the estimates of effective age and remaining economic life still require judgment on the part of the appraiser. However, because these problems influence only the incurable portion of the depreciation estimate, their adverse effects are decreased.

Variation 2—Known External Obsolescence

The second variation of the age-life method can increase the accuracy of the depreciation estimate when external obsolescence is present in the subject property, but not in comparable properties.

If sales exist of properties suffering from the same external obsolescence as the subject, then the total economic life extracted from the sales considered comparable can be used in the age-life method. If such sales do not exist, then the appraiser estimates depreciation exclusive of external obsolescence using the age-life method and adds an estimate of external obsolescence derived using techniques from the breakdown method, which is described later in this chapter.

> **CONCEPT**
>
> The second variation of the age-life method allocates a portion of the total depreciation estimate to an individual component—known external obsolescence—to enhance the accuracy of the estimate.

Example. Overbuilding in the subject market has caused sale prices of single-family homes to drop by 10% within the last year, according to the appraiser's observations of the market's history. Land value has not been affected by this market downturn. The replacement cost of the 10-year-old home being appraised is $120,000. With few sales of properties considered comparable in the market in the last year, the appraiser must consult records of older sales, from before the dip in prices. These data reveal a market-extracted total economic life expectancy of 50 years, which yields an estimate of depreciation excluding external obsolescence of 20% (10/50).

Using the age-life method, the depreciation estimate for the subject property is $24,000 ($120,000 × 0.20), and the estimate of the effect of external obsolescence is $12,000 ($120,000 × 0.10). The total depreciation then is calculated to be $36,000, with $24,000 allocated to all causes except external obsolescence and $12,000 to external obsolescence. Because the external obsolescence in this case was caused by oversupply in the market, once those additional homes are absorbed by the market, the effect of the external obsolescence will probably disappear.

Applicability. Like the first variation of the age-life method, this second variation allocates a portion of the total depreciation estimate to an individual component, in this case external obsolescence. Just as home buyers often want to know the value of a property after curable items have been repaired, those buyers are also concerned with the influence of external market forces on a potential purchase.

Limitations. The limitations of this procedure are similar to those of the less-complicated market extraction and age-life methods. The technique assumes depreciation in incurable items occurs on a straight-line basis. Also, the estimates of effective age and remaining economic life still require judgment on the part of the appraiser. Because these problems affect only the depreciation estimate exclusive of external obsolescence, though, their adverse influence on the total depreciation estimate is decreased.

Breakdown Method

The breakdown method is the most comprehensive and detailed way to measure depreciation, though in actual practice the complete, formal breakdown method is rarely used because of the time and expense involved in collecting and analyzing the necessary data. The market extraction and age-life methods both yield a lump-sum estimate of total depreciation, whereas the breakdown method is used to allocate, or "break down," the lump-sum estimates into the individual depreciation components. The process of allocating depreciation is particularly important in the appraisal of residential properties because most form reports require that depreciation be allocated to its physical, functional, and external components.

Applying the Breakdown Method

The appraiser uses five basic techniques to estimate different types of depreciation in the various stages of the breakdown method:

1. Estimation of cost to cure, which measures curable physical deterioration and curable functional obsolescence

2. Application of an age-life ratio, which measures curable and incurable physical deterioration for both long- and short-lived components

3. Application of the functional obsolescence procedure, which measures all types of functional obsolescence

4. Paired data analysis, which can measure incurable functional obsolescence caused by a deficiency and also external obsolescence

5. Capitalization of rent loss, which can measure the same forms of depreciation as paired data analysis

Using the breakdown method, the appraiser can approach the estimation of individual components of total depreciation from opposite ends of the sequence of calculations:

• Given an estimate of total depreciation from the market extraction or age-life methods, the appraiser can work from the top down, allocating the total amount among the various components of depreciation.

• If an estimate of total depreciation cannot be derived from the market extraction or age-life methods, the appraiser can generate that figure from the bottom up, estimating each individual component of value. Adding these estimates together yield the total depreciation estimate.

Examples of these types of calculations are illustrated in Figure 14.4.

Because the complete breakdown method is rarely used in residential appraisal practice, detailed discussion of the various techniques for estimating each component of depreciation has been omitted here; instead, common applications of those techniques are presented. (*The Appraisal of Real Estate* covers the breakdown method in great detail, and readers interested in further study of the subject should refer to that text.)

Example: Curable Physical Deterioration

The first step in the breakdown method is to estimate items of curable physical deterioration, also known as *deferred maintenance.* Cosmetic repairs, touch-up painting, carpentry, plumbing, and electrical repairs fall into this category. Real estate agents have long recognized that most minor repairs add value that equals or exceeds their cost, so they encourage home owners to make these repairs before a house is offered for sale.

Items of curable physical deterioration are items in need of repair on the date of the appraisal whether they are going to be repaired or

Figure 14.4 Breakdown Method Calculations

Top Down

Total Depreciation Estimate (from market extraction or age-life method)		$10,000
− Damage (vandalism)		− 500
= **Depreciation** (exclusive of damage)		$9,500
Curable Physical Deterioration		
Deferred Maintenance	1,500	
Incurable Physical Deterioration		
Short-lived Components	2,000	
+ Long-lived Components	+ 500	
− **Physical Deterioration**		− $4,000
= **Total Obsolescence** (functional and external)		$5,500
Curable Functional Obsolescence		
Curable Functional Obsolescence Caused by Deficiency Requiring Addition	2,500	
Curable Functional Obsolescence Caused by Deficiency Requiring Substitution	0	
Curable Functional Obsolescence Caused by Superadequacy	0	
Incurable Functional Obsolescence		
Incurable Functional Obsolescence Caused by Deficiency	1,000	
+ Incurable Functional Obsolescence Caused by Superadequacy	+ 0	
− **Functional Obsolescence**		− $3,500
= **External Obsolescence**		$2,000

Bottom Up

Curable Physical Deterioration		
Deferred Maintenance	$1,500	
Incurable Physical Deterioration		
Short-lived Components	2,000	
+ Long-lived Components	+ 500	
= **Physical Deterioration**		$4,000
Curable Functional Obsolescence		
Curable Functional Obsolescence Caused by Deficiency Requiring Addition	2,500	
Curable Functional Obsolescence Caused by Deficiency Requiring Substitution	0	
Curable Functional Obsolescence Caused by Superadequacy	0	
Incurable Functional Obsolescence		
Incurable Functional Obsolescence Caused by Deficiency	1,000	
+ Incurable Functional Obsolescence Caused by Superadequacy	+ 0	
+ **Functional Obsolescence**		+ $3,500
= Depreciation (exclusive of external obsolescence)		$7,500
+ **External Obsolescence** (from paired data analysis or income capitalization)		+ $2,000
= **Total Depreciation Estimate**		$9,500
+ Damage (vandalism)		+ 500
= **Total Deduction from Reproduction or Replacement Cost**		$10,000

not. The amount of depreciation to be allocated for these items is simply the cost to cure them. Often an appraisal client will request that these curable items be listed in the appraisal report along with an estimate of the cost to cure, which is the cost to restore an item of deferred maintenance to new or reasonably new condition.[7]

> **CONCEPT**
>
> Specific procedures are applied to estimate each of the items in the breakdown method. When this method is used, the appraiser must be very careful not to count any item of depreciation more than once.

Cost-to-cure estimates should be based on actual contractors' bids or on the amounts indicated in contracts for similar work in recently completed properties. National cost services cannot be used to provide reliable estimates of the cost of repair and maintenance work because the cost for such work usually depends on the specific problems found in the house and the cost of repair services in the local market.

As an example, during a house inspection an appraiser notes the need to repaint the interior at a cost of $900 and refinish the interior floor at a cost of $800. Curable physical deterioration is estimated as the total cost to cure these items:

Interior painting	$900
Plus interior floor finish	+ 800
Total curable physical deterioration	$1,700

Example: Functional Obsolescence (Excess Cost to Cure)

Functional obsolescence may be evident in the original design of the residence, or changes in market standards may have made some aspect of the structure, its design, or its components obsolete.

There are two major tests of curability for an item of functional obsolescence:

- If spending the money to cure the item will result in a value increment equal to or greater than the expenditure, then the item is normally considered curable.

- Also, if spending the money to cure the item will not result in a value increment equal to or greater than the expenditure but will allow existing items to maintain their value, then the item is still considered curable.

When it is possible and reasonable to cure an item but there is no economic advantage to curing it, then the item is considered incurable.

---

7. If damage or vandalism is severe enough, it becomes curable physical deterioration and is treated accordingly. The measure of damage is the cost to cure.

TERM

functional obsolescence procedure: a sequence of calculations that can be used to estimate all forms of functional obsolescence caused by a deficiency or a superadequacy, whether the obsolescence is curable or incurable.

All forms of functional obsolescence, whether curable or incurable or caused by a deficiency or a superadequacy, can be estimated using the procedure illustrated in Figure 14.5. The use of the functional obsolescence procedure ensures that none of the components of this type of depreciation will be treated more than once and no charges will be incurred for an item already dealt with, e.g., elements already depreciated under physical deterioration.

The functional obsolescence procedure involves five steps:

1. *The cost of the existing item is identified.* This cost is derived from the replacement or reproduction cost estimate. Of course, for items of curable functional obsolescence caused by a deficiency requiring an addition, there will be no cost to enter on this line.

2. *Any depreciation that has already been charged for the item is deducted.* In nearly all instances, any depreciation already charged for the item will be physical deterioration. As in Step 1, there will be no depreciation charged for items that do not currently exist such as a deficiency requiring an addition.

3. *If curable, all costs associated with curing the item are added, e.g., the cost of installing a new item, the cost of removing the old item, and net salvage value.* The appraiser will have to calculate the cost to cure when testing an item for curability.

   or

   If incurable, the value of the loss attributable to the obsolescence is added. The value of the loss can be obtained either through capitalization of rent loss or through paired data analysis. Again, this value will have to be calculated when testing for curability.

4. *A deduction is made for the cost of the item as though installed new on the date of the value estimate, if appropriate.*

5. *The total of all previous entries yields the depreciation estimate for functional obsolescence.*

When functional obsolescence takes the form of a deficiency requiring an addition, a component that is currently desired in the market such as an additional powder room (i.e., a half bath) is not present in the existing structure. Expenditures for the addition would not be included in the reproduction or replacement cost. The defi-

Figure 14.5	The Functional Obsolescence Procedure	
Step 1.	Cost of existing item	$xxx,xxx
Step 2.	Less depreciation previously charged	– $xxx,xxx
Step 3.	Plus cost to cure (all curable costs) or	+ $xxx,xxx
	Plus value of the loss (incurable items)	+ $xxx,xxx
Step 4.	Less cost if installed new	– $xxx,xxx
Step 5.	Equals depreciation for functional obsolescence	$xxx,xxx

ciency might be curable, but an additional cost is required to bring the building up to market standards. The cost to install an item in an existing building is almost always greater than the cost to install the same item in new construction. Depreciation must be allocated for the extra expense the owner of the subject building must now incur, reflecting a cost that will not be realized as value. Curable functional obsolescence is measured as the difference between the cost of adding the component now, when the structure is complete, and the cost if the component were included in the structure as if built new on the date of the value opinion. This is commonly referred to as the *excess cost to cure*.

TERMS

deficiency requiring additions: functional obsolescence resulting from the lack of something that other properties in the market have.

excess cost to cure: the difference between the cost of adding the component when the structure is complete and the cost if the component were included in the structure as if built on the date of the value opinion.

For example, consider a residence that has no powder room on the first floor, a feature that is standard in the market for this type of property. A powder room can be installed for $1,800, but it would have cost only $1,200 if it had been installed on the date of the value opinion as part of new construction. The curable functional obsolescence due to this deficiency is measured as the amount by which the cost of creating the addition exceeds the normal cost of the item installed new during construction, calculated as follows:

Cost of existing item	$0
Less depreciation previously charged	– 0
Plus cost to cure (all curable costs) or	+ 1,800
Plus value of the loss (incurable items)	+ 0
Less cost if installed new	– 1,200
Equals depreciation for functional obsolescence	$600

In other words, it will take $1,800 spent after construction is complete to accomplish the same amount of utility as $1,200 spent during construction, both measured as of the date of appraisal.

Example: External Obsolescence

External obsolescence is a loss in value due to influences outside the property. It is usually incurable, but it is not always permanent. A home owner or landlord cannot cure an environmental problem such as a deteriorating neighborhood or an economic recession that creates a sluggish market. Forces outside of the control of the owner, though, may change the detrimental factor.

External obsolescence generally results in a loss in the value contribution of the improvements, but it may also lessen the value of the land. It may be caused by neighborhood decline, changes in market conditions, or the property's proximity to a detrimental influence such as an airport, railroad, landfill, commercial district, or other sort of nuisance. When market data are studied to estimate external obsolescence, it is important to isolate the effects of changes in land value from the effects of changes in the value of the improvements. In some situations, external obsolescence may be attributed entirely to the land; in other situations, it may be attributed entirely to the improvements.[8] Often external obsolescence can be allocated between land and improvements. This is an important step if the external obsolescence is already reflected in the land value estimate. A building-to-property-value ratio derived through market analysis may be used to allocate the value loss attributable to the building.

The two primary methods of measuring external obsolescence are paired data analysis and capitalization of rent loss. In appraisals of single-family residences, external obsolescence is usually estimated by paired data analysis. Sales of properties that are subject to the negative external influence are compared with sales of properties that are not. Not only must the effects of land value differences be isolated, but the effects of differences in the physical deterioration and functional obsolescence of the comparable structures must also be studied. Many of the problems that limit the usefulness of the paired data method in estimating total depreciation create difficulties in this portion of the breakdown method as well.

---

8.   External obsolescence would be attributable entirely to the land in a situation in which the cost to construct a particular home is identical on two subdivision lots, but one adjoins an expressway and sells for less than the other located away from the expressway. External obsolescence would be attributable entirely to the improvement in the case of a home in a transitional neighborhood where land use is changing from residential to commercial.

As an example, a single-family residence located on a noisy street is being appraised. The appraiser finds two very similar comparable properties that were recently sold. One is adjacent to the subject and the other is farther away from the noisy street. The adjacent property was sold for $189,000, while the other property was sold for $192,000. Using paired data analysis, the appraiser estimates external obsolescence as follows:

$$\$192,000 - \$189,000 = \$3,000$$

The land-to-improvement ratio is 1:4. Therefore 20% (1/5) of the external obsolescence would be applicable to the land and the remaining 80% (4/5) would apply to the improvements. The amount applicable to the improvements is $2,400 ($3,000 × 0.80).

Applicability and Limitations

As the most detailed method of estimating depreciation, the breakdown method requires large amounts of data—often available only to appraisers who have accumulated files over long periods of time. In addition, identifying and quantifying each item of depreciation may not be an efficient use of an appraiser's time.

> **CONCEPT**
>
> When neither the market extraction method nor the age-life method can be used to reach an estimate of total depreciation, the appraiser can employ the breakdown method to estimate the contribution of all the various types of depreciation.

Depreciation is estimated differently according to the type and cause of loss in value, and those types and causes often overlap, complicating the application of the breakdown method. For example, older structures may be affected by a number of different forms of deterioration and obsolescence. Also, distinguishing between deficiencies and superadequacies and between functional and external obsolescence can be difficult.

When the market allocation and age-life methods of estimating depreciation cannot be applied, the breakdown method can be used to estimate all the various items of depreciation, with the sum of the individual components yielding a total depreciation estimate.

Combined Methods

Different methods of estimating depreciation can be combined to solve specific problems, or the results of one method can be used to test the results of another. For example, if external obsolescence cannot be accurately estimated through paired data analysis or capitalization of an income loss, a lump-sum indication of total depreciation can be derived through market extraction. Then an indication of depreciation from all causes other than external obsolescence can be derived with the breakdown method, and this figure can be subtracted from the estimate of total depreciation to derive an estimate of external obsolescence.

Market extraction can also be used to derive or verify an estimate of the annual overall rate of depreciation, which is the basis of the economic life estimate (economic life = 1/annual rate of depreciation). The overall percentage of depreciation in each comparable is obtained by dividing its sale price minus the current land value and value contribution of the site improvements by its replacement or reproduction cost. This overall percentage is divided by the actual age of the comparable or, if there is a significant difference between the actual age and the effective age, by the effective age to estimate the annual percentage of depreciation. Conversely, the total economic life expectancy is derived from data obtained in market extraction. The amount of depreciation in a comparable is divided by the replacement or reproduction cost of the comparable. The resulting percentage is divided by the age of the comparable to obtain the average annual rate of depreciation, the inverse of which is the total economic life expectancy.

Example

The subject is a 25-year-old home that has a replacement cost of $175,000. The total useful life expectancy is 100 years. There is no external obsolescence in this market and a site value of $40,000 is well supported. The estimated contribution of the site improvements is $10,000. Data on three sales of similar properties are shown below.

	Sale A	Sale B	Sale C
Sale price	$210,000	$150,000	$125,000
Land value	$51,000	$37,500	$45,000
Replacement cost	$204,500	$216,350	$121,000
Age	20 years	30 years	25 years

The subject residence has a broken door, which must be replaced at a cost of $500. Data on the short-lived building components of the subject property follow:

Short-Lived Item	Age	Life	Cost to Replace
Roof cover	10 years	15 years	$9,000
Paint	New	5 years	$4,000
HVAC	5 years	20 years	$8,000
Floor finish	5 years	10 years	$6,000

The first step is to extract the average annual depreciation rate from the sales data provided.

	Sale A	**Sale B**	**Sale C**
Sale price	$210,000	$150,000	$125,000
Less land value	− 51,000	− 37,500	− 45,000
Depreciated cost of improvements	$159,000	$112,500	$80,000
Replacement cost	$204,500	$216,350	$121,000
Less depreciated cost of improvements	− 159,000	− 112,500	− 80,000
Depreciation	$45,500	$103,850	$41,000
% of replacement cost	22.25%	48.00%	33.88%
Average annual rate of depreciation	1.11%	1.60%	1.36%
Total economic life expectancy	90 years	62 years	74 years

The second step is to reconcile the range of total economic life expectancy estimates into an appropriate estimate for the subject property. Then the age-life method can be applied to estimate total depreciation for the subject property. Since Sale C is the same age as the subject, a total economic life expectancy estimate of 74 years is considered appropriate.

Using the age-life method, the depreciation percentage is estimated by dividing the age of the subject property (25 years) by its estimated total economic life expectancy (74 years). The resulting depreciation percentage of 33.78% (25/74) is applied to the replacement cost ($175,000) to produce a lump-sum depreciation estimate of $59,115.

$$\frac{\text{age of subject property}}{\text{total economic life estimate}} = \text{total depreciation estimate (percentage)}$$

$$\frac{25 \text{ years}}{74 \text{ years}} = 33.78\%$$

total depreciation estimate × replacement cost = lump-sum depreciation

$$33.78\% \times \$175,000 = \$59,115$$

The estimate of curable physical deterioration is $500, the amount to cure the broken door. The incurable physical deterioration of short-lived items is estimated in the following table.

Short-Lived Item	Age	Life	Percentage Deteriorated	Cost to Replace	Deterioration Charged
Roof cover	10	15	66.67%	$9,000	$6,000
Paint	New	5	0.00%	$4,000	$0
HVAC	5	20	25.00%	$8,000	$2,000
Floor finish	5	10	50.00%	$6,000	$3,000
Incurable physical deterioration of short-lived items					$11,000

The total amount of incurable physical deterioration is the sum of the four depreciation estimates, or $11,000. Since the painting is new, it does not suffer from any physical deterioration.

The physical deterioration of long-lived items is estimated by applying the age-life ratio of 25% (the 25-year age of the long-lived items divided by their total useful life expectancy of 100 years) to the replacement cost less the cost to cure curable items (the broken door) and the sum of the costs to replace the items of short-lived physical deterioration.

Replacement cost	$175,000
Less cost to cure the broken door	− 500
Less total costs to replace all short-lived items	
($9,000 + $4,000 + $8,000 + $6,000)	− 27,000
	$147,500
Times age-life ratio	× 0.25
Incurable physical deterioration for long-lived items	$36,875

Thus the estimate of incurable physical deterioration for long-lived items is $36,875.

Total physical deterioration is calculated by adding together curable deterioration ($500), incurable physical deterioration in short-lived items ($11,000), and incurable physical deterioration in long-lived items ($36,875).

Curable physical deterioration	$500
Incurable physical deterioration in short-lived items	11,000
Incurable physical deterioration in long-lived items	+ 36,875
Total physical deterioration	$48,375

The lump-sum estimate of depreciation derived using the age-life method was $59,121. There was no external obsolescence. Therefore an estimate of functional obsolescence can be obtained by deducting the estimate of total physical deterioration ($48,375) from the lump-sum estimate of depreciation ($59,121). The residual sum is the functional obsolescence incurred.

Lump-sum estimate of depreciation	$59,121
Less total physical deterioration	− 48,375
Less total external obsolescence	− 0
Total functional obsolescence	$10,746

CHAPTER 15

THE SALES COMPARISON APPROACH

The sales comparison approach is the most direct and reliable valuation approach in many appraisal situations. Five basic steps are involved in the sales comparison approach. An appraiser

1. Finds recent sales, listings, and offers for properties that are comparable to the subject property.
2. Verifies that the data obtained are accurate.
3. Selects relevant units of comparison to analyze each sale.
4. Compares comparables to the the subject in terms of various elements of comparison and adjusts the sale prices of the comparables to reflect how they differ from the subject.
5. Reconciles the various value indications derived into a single value indication or a range of values.

This chapter examines the strengths and limitations of the sales comparison approach, the importance of comparability, and the techniques employed to identify and select comparable properties. The elements of comparison used to isolate property differences are also discussed. Chapter 16 covers mortgages and financing adjustments, and Chapter 17 focuses on how the sales comparison approach is applied and how the various value indications derived in the approach are reconciled.

STRENGTHS OF THE APPROACH

The sales comparison approach is a tool appraisers apply in many situations with a variety of quantitative techniques. The approach derives its usefulness and analytic power from several factors:

- The sales comparison approach is a direct application of the principle of substitution.
- It is simple.
- It makes use of observable market data.
- It has wide applicability.

The principle of substitution holds that when similar or commensurate objects or commodities are available for sale, the one with the lowest price will attract the greatest demand and the widest distribution. The price at which an item will most likely sell in a market is closely related to the prices at which similar items in the same market are selling. The sales comparison approach is firmly based on this principle. Properties similar to the subject are found and the sale prices of these properties are adjusted to account for differences between the comparables and the subject. These adjusted sale prices serve as the basis for a value opinion.

The sales comparison approach is generally easy to apply. Furthermore, clients find the approach persuasive because the reasoning is easy to follow. A simple method based on reliable data and sound reasoning often results in extremely reliable conclusions.

In the sales comparison approach, an appraiser focuses on the property characteristics that make a difference in the market. From the market the appraiser obtains quantifiable data that indicate the differences in price caused by differences in building features, site size, location, and other property characteristics. Adjustments for differences are based directly on the observed preferences of market participants.

> **CONCEPT**
>
> The sales comparison approach is a direct application of the principle of substitution, which relies on objective market data and can be used in a broad range of appraisal situations.

The market data on which sales comparisons are based lend themselves to various types of quantitative analysis. Paired data analysis, scatter diagrams, and other analytical tools can be used to isolate the effect of specific variables on market prices. Statistical sampling can be used in the selection of comparables. By selecting some comparables that may be slightly superior to the subject and others that may be slightly inferior, an appraiser can develop a good sense of the value range for the subject property. Tabulated or graphed historical data on sales of similar property can be used to identify trends and discern changes in the market.

All three valuation approaches make use of sales comparison to some degree. The cost approach requires that land or site value be estimated separately, and this is often accomplished by analyzing the prices of comparable vacant land or land considered as though vacant. The cost of buildings and depreciation may also be estimated by sales comparison. In the income capitalization approach, the rent that the subject property is likely to produce is estimated by analyzing the rents of comparable properties, and capitalization rates and gross income multipliers are also derived from sales. Thus sales comparison techniques have broad application in the valuation process.

LIMITATIONS OF THE APPROACH

The sales comparison approach has some important limitations. A conclusion derived from sales considered comparable is only as reliable as the data that support it. If the only recent sales are of properties that differ substantially from the subject, the prices of these properties will be subject to major adjustments and the reliability of the conclusion may be questionable. Properties with unique or special features often cannot be valued with sales comparison analysis. When the approach is applied in markets with few recent sales, the appraiser must proceed with extreme caution and pay careful attention to all factors that could affect current market conditions. The results of sales comparison reflect historical, rather than current, market conditions because market changes that have occurred since the sale dates of the comparables are not always readily discernible.

> **CONCEPT**
>
> The sales comparison approach cannot be applied when sales data are too limited to produce reliable conclusions and when the data available pertain to properties that are not comparable to the subject property.

COMPARABLES AS COMPETITIVE PROPERTIES

For valuation purposes a property used as a comparable should be competitive with the subject property. Each potential comparable property should be similar to the subject in important features and be located in the same area or in a similar market area, i.e., both comparable and competitive. Properties that do not appeal to the same market population should not be considered competitive, even if they are comparable to the subject in other ways. In ideal circumstances, comparable properties used in the sales comparison approach would compete directly with the subject property in the same market area, but sometimes data on sales of local comparables are unavailable; in that case transactions involving properties in other comparable, but not directly competitive, neighborhoods or locations may be used in the analysis.

What features must be similar for properties and neighborhoods to be considered comparable? Individual property features are important if the market population regards them as significant. Property characteristics established during the neighborhood analysis are used as a basis for the elements of comparison. An appraiser learns about the significance of property characteristics by observing variations and correlations in the sale prices of properties with different locations, sizes, designs, taxes, and other characteristics. Further insights into the comparability of neighborhoods can be gained by identifying the income levels, ages, and family sizes of prospective buyers. A careful highest and best use study can help identify which elements of comparison are important in the market.

There is no set rule as to how far a property may be from the subject property and still remain competitive with it. The size of market areas can vary considerably depending on the size of the city, the distances that residents commute, the transportation available, and the property type. If there are many similar houses or neighborhoods that purchasers regard as more or less equal, the market area can be quite extensive. In other situations a market area may be quite small. Again, it is best to select comparable properties from the immediate neighborhood of the subject, but if sales data are not available, sales from the broader neighborhood or an altogether different, yet still comparable neighborhood, may be acceptable.

RESEARCH AND SELECTION OF SALES OF COMPARABLE PROPERTIES

Investigating and selecting comparable properties is accomplished in five steps. An appraiser

1. Researches and identifies potentially comparable properties.
2. Inspects the subject property, the neighborhood, and each potential comparable (to the extent possible).
3. Analyzes the highest and best use of each potential comparable to test its comparability with the subject.
4. Verifies data and eliminates sales that are not arm's-length transactions if an accurate adjustment for atypical conditions of sale cannot be calculated.
5. Analyzes differences between the subject property and each potential comparable and selects only true comparables for use in the sales comparison approach.

The process begins with the identification of potential comparables and concludes with the selection of the actual comparables to be used in the appraisal. Although the steps are not always followed in the order indicated, each task must be performed at some point in the valuation process. If the appraiser concludes that the differences between the subject property and a given comparable are not too great, the transaction may be used in sales comparison analysis.

Identification of Comparable Properties

Procedures for identifying comparable properties were discussed at length in Chapter 5. In brief, an appraiser first collects general information on the subject property, which can be used to help identify comparables. Usually data on the property location, house type, building size, number of stories, number of bedrooms and bathrooms, and site size are sufficient, but additional detail can be helpful. Next, the appraiser tries to generate a list of properties in the subject neighborhood and competitive neighborhoods that meet this general description. Information may be obtained from office files, multiple listing services (MLS), public records, news publications, title companies, and knowledgeable individuals such as other appraisers, brokers, and bankers. An appraiser is primarily interested in comparable properties that have been sold recently. Contracts, offers, refusals, and listing prices of competitive properties may provide additional insights into the character of the local market.

How many comparables should be identified? An appraiser must have an adequate number of sales to establish a firm basis for the value conclusion. If the quality of the data collected is questionable, a larger pool of comparable properties should be considered. Increasing the number of comparables used adds time and expense, but a larger sample can produce more reliable results.

The appraiser collects important data on each comparable transaction and records the legal, physical, and locational characteristics of the property as of the date of sale. Table 15.1 lists the items of information that are generally needed.

Field Inspection

After the neighborhood and the subject property have been inspected, the appraiser can usually eliminate several potentially comparable properties from consideration. Some of these properties may be located outside the boundaries of the subject neighborhood or com-

Table 15.1	Useful Comparable Data

Transactional Characteristics	**Legal, Physical, and Locational Characteristics**
Sale price	Legal description of the real estate
Financing terms	Real property rights conveyed
Date of sale	Location and neighborhood
Names of parties (or others who can verify data)	Site size, shape, and location
Motivations of parties	Assessments
Personalty included in sale	Public and private restrictions
	Building type and size
	Total number of rooms and number of bedrooms and bathrooms
	Age of building
	Physical condition
	Functional utility
	Size and type of garage
	Non-realty components of value
	Expenditures made immediately after purchase
	Market conditions

petitive neighborhoods, which have now been more precisely identified. Other properties may no longer qualify as comparables because inspection of the subject has revealed that they are dissimilar.

Each remaining potential comparable must then be inspected. Generally comparable properties are inspected from the outside because many property owners are reluctant to allow strangers into their homes. Moreover, a complete inspection of each comparable might be too time-consuming and costly. Information on construction features may be obtained from MLS data and tax assessment records and from building permits and blueprints kept on file at county and municipal offices. Photographs should be taken of each comparable for inclusion in the appraisal report.

Highest and Best Use Analysis

Each potential comparable should be analyzed to determine the highest and best use of the land as though vacant and the property as improved. When the sales comparison approach is used to value a residence, a detailed analysis of the highest and best use of the comparables is often unnecessary. However, the appraiser's analysis must be sufficient to establish that the properties are indeed comparable. Highest and best use analysis is particularly important in transitional neighborhoods.

The appraiser must also consider the markets to which the potentially comparable properties appeal. Does the land considered as though vacant have any special appeal for commercial users? Is the location of the improved site suitable for a nonresidential use? In some areas a residence located on a corner site or a busy street could accommodate an office. If this property is a potential comparable and the subject property is located on an interior site or secondary street, the highest and best use of the improved subject and the potential comparable may well differ. The highest and best use of the subject property and a potential comparable must be the same or similar for *both* the site as though vacant and the property as improved. Otherwise the comparable should be eliminated from further consideration.

Verification of Data

Data on sales of properties considered comparable can be obtained by interviewing one of the parties to the transaction. Although buyers and sellers are actively and directly involved in transactions, appraisers must recognize that these market participants are not disinterested parties. If necessary, information provided by interested parties can be corroborated through other sources. Statements of fact can be verified by real estate agents, closing agencies, lending institutions, property managers, and lawyers involved in the sale. Owners and tenants of neighboring properties can sometimes provide important clues about the reasons for the sale. In verifying data, an appraiser must recognize that some sources of information may be more reliable than others. An appraiser should always ensure the confidentiality of the parties consulted.

An appraiser seeks answers to the following questions:

- What was the sale price and what were the terms of the financing?
- Were any concessions or incentives other than financing involved in the sale?
- Were items of personal property included?
- Exactly when was the closing price established?
- Are the parties to the transaction related?

Sales used as comparables should be arm's-length transactions made in the open market by unrelated parties under no duress.

Analysis of Comparables: Elements of Comparison

Individual properties and the transactions in which they are exchanged may differ in many ways. From an appraiser's point of view, the important differences are those that affect the value of the property and the price obtained for it. These differences, which are called *elements of comparison,* include

CONCEPT
Elements of comparison are property characteristics that cause prices to vary. They include
• Legal characteristics such as the property rights conveyed
• Transactional characteristics such as financing terms, conditions of sale (motivation), and market conditions (time)
• Physical characteristics such as size and condition
• Locational features such as the neighborhood and siting
• Other pertinent information such as expenditures made immediately after purchase, economic characteristics, personalty, and use

1. Real property rights conveyed
2. Financing terms
3. Conditions of sale
4. Expenditures made immediately after purchase
5. Market conditions
6. Location
7. Physical characteristics
8. Economic characteristics
9. Use/zoning
10. Non-realty components of value

Other differences may be relevant in certain markets.

By studying transactions in the market area, an appraiser learns how much effect on value each different element of comparison produces. The comparables are analyzed in light of these differences and their sale prices are adjusted to reflect the value of the subject. When the differences are minor, the adjusted sale prices of comparable properties provide a persuasive indication of value. When differences are more substantial, greater adjustments are required and the results are less reliable.

Differences between a sale and the subject property can be addressed either by the application of quantitative adjustments, expressed as dollar or percentage amounts, or by the use of qualitative analysis, in which differences are assessed using relative comparisons, not specific adjustments. (Examples of the application of quantitative adjustments and qualitative analysis are provided in Chapter 17.) Quantitative adjustments are applied to the sale price of the comparable. These adjustments are usually made in a particular order. Adjustments for property rights, financing, conditions of sale, expenditures made immediately after purchase, and market conditions are applied before adjustments for location, physical characteristics, and other differences.[1] The first five quantitative adjustments are typically made before the sale prices are reduced to unit prices. Reducing sale prices to unit prices based on size allows the appraiser to compare houses with different dimensions and may eliminate the need to make an adjustment for differences in size.

Analysis of qualitative differences provides the basis for reconciliation. Qualitative differences are generally taken into consideration after the application of quantitative adjustments. If market data do not exist, quantitative adjustments are insupportable and should not be made. Qualitative differences may be analyzed by means of an array in which the appraiser ranks the comparables as more or less similar to the subject. This ranking is used to determine which comparable or comparables are the most reliable indicators of the subject's value.

> **CONCEPT**
>
> Reducing sale prices to unit prices based on size allows the appraiser to compare houses with different dimensions and may eliminate the need to make an adjustment for differences in size.

Real Property Rights Conveyed

At the outset an appraiser identifies the real property interest to be valued. For single-family residential properties, this is generally the fee simple estate. If the valuation assignment involves an unencumbered fee simple property, the appraiser should ascertain that the legal estate of each comparable is identical to that of the subject. Income-producing real estate may be subject to existing leases, which may create a leased fee or leasehold interest.

Financing Terms

Financing terms can affect the price at which a property is sold. Sellers sometimes offer buyers a special inducement to purchase their property in the form of creative financing instruments; buyers sometimes pay above-market interest rates to lower the purchase price. In these cases the final sale price reflects the value of both the financing inducement and the property. The value of financing reflects personal property, not real property, so the sale price of the comparable must be adjusted before it can be used as an indication of market value.

---

1.   The sequence in which adjustments are applied is determined by the market data and the appraiser's analysis of those data. The sequence presented in this chapter and in Chapter 17 is provided for purposes of illustration. While this is a typical sequence for applying quantitative adjustments, it is not the only sequence in which such adjustments can be made.

Financing plans can vary significantly. Special financing terms include seller-paid points, FHA insurance, VA guarantees, second mortgages, and buydown plans. These financing plans appear in the market when interest rates are high; they become less popular when rates fall. Sellers, lenders, and others use financing instruments to sustain the demand for real estate at current price levels.

Various techniques can be used to measure how financing considerations affect price. Two such techniques are paired data analysis and the calculation of cash equivalency with discounting procedures. Because of the importance of financing considerations, Chapter 16 is devoted to this topic. Note that a financing adjustment is only required when the sale of a comparable was transacted with unusual financing terms.

CONCEPTS

Financing may be conventional, or creative instruments may affect the price of a property considered comparable.

A conditions of sale adjustment may be needed if the parties to a transaction were subject to pressures uncharacteristic of those operating on typical market participants.

Conditions of Sale

Unusual conditions of sale can also cause a comparable property to sell at a price that does not reflect its value. The motivations of the buyer and the seller are important conditions of sale. For example, a buyer who owns an adjoining site may be prepared to pay a price for the property that is higher than its market value. If a financial, business, or family relationship exists between the parties, the sale may not be an arm's-length transaction. One family member may sell property to another at a reduced price, or an individual might pay a higher-than-market price to acquire a property built or owned by an ancestor.

Any special pressure, duress, or undue stimulus on a buyer or seller that does not affect typical market participants may produce an atypical price. For example, the price paid for a property in a liquidation sale will probably not reflect its market value.

Market exposure is another important condition of sale. To qualify as an open-market transaction, the property should have received adequate exposure in the market. In many markets this means that a sign was posted in front of the house or an advertisement was placed in a local publication, and that the comparable property was exposed for sale for the normal marketing time for similar properties. Bids and acceptable prices usually stabilize around market value within the normal marketing period. Some appraisal assignments may call for an indication of value based on a quick sale, a liquidation sale, or a transaction consummated within a specific number of days.

When a property sells much more quickly than expected, this may suggest that the buyer was unusually motivated or that the seller was poorly informed. When a property is on the market for an unusually long time, it may be because the seller was holding out for a certain price or a certain buyer or because the property has problems that the market recognizes. Whatever the reason, the transaction is probably less reliable as a comparable and should be investigated further or eliminated from consideration.

> **CONCEPT**
>
> Any sales considered comparable that are not arm's-length transactions should be eliminated if an accurate adjustment for atypical conditions of sale cannot be calculated.

No transaction is perfect. Appraisers must occasionally use sales data that do not precisely reflect open-market, arm's-length transactions. An appraiser should carefully judge each situation to determine how much the variance affects the price of the comparable. If the transaction is substantially different from the norm, the sales data should not be used regardless of how similar the subject and comparable may be in other ways. Only modest differences can be accounted for with an adjustment for conditions of sale.

Expenditures Made Immediately After Purchase

A knowledgeable home buyer would only agree to purchase a property if any expenditures that will have to be made upon the purchase of the property are reflected in the final sale price. The listing price of a property requiring environmental remediation, demolition of unwanted improvements, or repairs would have to be discounted to reflect the costs to the buyer.

Market Conditions

Market conditions generally change over time. The date of the appraisal is a specific point in time, so sales transacted before this point must be examined and adjusted to reflect any changes that may have occurred in the interim. Otherwise the sale prices of the comparables will reflect the market conditions as of the date when they were sold, not the current value of similar real estate. Changes in market conditions are usually measured as a percentage relative to previous price levels.

Market conditions can change for various reasons, but two of the most important considerations are inflation or deflation and changes in supply and demand. Inflation and deflation generally can be observed throughout the regional economy. The rate of change in price levels is often easy to estimate. Tracking changes in supply and demand requires more research. Overbuilding is one common cause of an increase in

> **CONCEPT**
>
> The effects of market changes may be investigated by studying the prices of unchanged properties that have been resold several times.

supply, and the unexpected departure of a major employer can cause demand to fall suddenly. (Changes in supply and demand are discussed in Chapters 4 and 9.)

The best indications of changes in market conditions are provided by the prices of properties that have been sold and resold several times. Because different types of properties are affected differently by changing market conditions, these properties should be similar to the subject property. If several property resales can be collected, they will provide an adequate database.

The market conditions adjustment is sometimes referred to as a *time* adjustment. It should be emphasized, however, that it is not time that necessitates this adjustment but shifts in the market. If considerable time has elapsed but market conditions have not changed, no adjustment is required.

Location

Adjustments for location are often difficult to make. The adjustment and the reasoning behind it should be carefully supported in the appraisal report. Generally the largest adjustments for location are required when the comparable properties are not located in the subject neighborhood. Adjustments might also be required for properties in the same neighborhood that are subject to different influences. The character of the immediate neighborhood, traffic density, view, and siting are all significant factors in making location adjustments.

Every location has its advantages and disadvantages. The desirability of a location is judged in comparison to alternative locations. An appraiser investigates the effects of location by considering how the prices of physically similar properties in various locations differ. Location adjustments are generally calculated as percentage adjustments. If some difference related to location has already been considered in the estimate of site value, the appraiser should be careful not to overstate the size of the location adjustment.

Physical Characteristics

A comparable may differ from the subject property in many physical characteristics, including building size, architectural style, functional utility, building materials, construction quality, age and condition of improvements, and site size. Overall attractiveness and special amenities can introduce other variables. Sometimes separate adjustments are required to reflect each major difference in physical characteristics.

Adjustments for the physical differences between the subject and other improved properties usually cannot be made simply by adding or subtracting the difference in the reproduction or replacement cost of the varying components. Unless the subject and comparable improvements are both new, the cost of a component does not usually reflect its contribution to value accurately. The effect on value produced by a physical difference must be estimated through careful analysis of the market. To perform this analysis, an appraiser collects information on how variables such as age, size, and condition affect the prices of similar real estate in the local market.

Economic Characteristics

This element of comparison is usually applied to income-producing properties. For residential properties with a demonstrable rental market, income-producing characteristics such as tenant mix, the length of lease terms, lease conditions, operating expenses, the management history of the property, and similar factors are significant in the valuation process.

An adjustment for an economic characteristic should not be made if the property attribute that affects income is already reflected in another element of comparison. If a comparable home is in a neighborhood with a lower property tax rate, the comparable's lower expenses could be considered an economic characteristic warranting an adjustment, but the lower tax rate probably translates into higher property values and will already be reflected in the adjustment for location. Also, the economic characteristics of a property that affect value must be distinguished from differences in real property rights conveyed and from changes in market conditions.

Use/Zoning

In general, a potential comparable will be discarded if its highest and best use is not the same as that of the subject property. When sales transactions considered comparable are scarce, though, the use of comparable properties with a different current use or highest and best use may be warranted; in these situations an adjustment for differences in use is necessary.

Zoning is one of the primary determinants of the highest and best use of vacant land because it serves as the test of legal permissibility. When comparable properties with similar zoning are scarce, parcels with slightly different zoning but the same highest and best use as the subject property may be used as comparables; an adjustment may not be necessary if the highest and best use is the same. An adjustment may be made to take into account differences in utility.

Non-Realty Components of Value

Personalty, business value, and other non-realty items that influence either the sale prices of comparables or the ownership interest in the subject property should be analyzed separately from the real property. The economic characteristics of non-realty components of value—e.g., economic life, associated investment risks, rate of return criteria, and collateral security—differ from those of the realty in most cases.

Properties such as timeshare condominiums, which have high expense ratios attributable to the business operation, typically include a significant business value component. If the business operation is essential to the use of the real property, the value of the non-realty component must be analyzed and reported.

MARKET DATA GRIDS

One important analytical tool used in the sales comparison approach is the market data grid. An appraiser may sketch a grid during the field inspection to record data quickly or fill in the spaces on a preprinted table. Market data grids can take many forms, but usually each comparable is identified at the top of the grid. The sale prices of the comparables are entered in the next row, and the gross living area and unit price of each comparable are shown in the following rows. The elements of comparison are listed on the left side of the grid.

The blank spaces across from each element of comparison are filled in with information that indicates the difference or similarity between the subject and each comparable property. The differences in value resulting from these variances are also noted once the amounts have been established by market analysis. Amounts of differences, or adjustments, may be expressed in dollars or percentages. Whenever adjustments are made, they should be applied in a particular sequence, which is discussed in Chapter 17. The market data grid shown in Figure 15.1 calls for dollar adjustments to reflect value differences.

Market data grids are extremely useful in the analysis of comparables. They show at a glance which comparables are most similar to the subject and should therefore be accorded the most weight in reconciling the results. With a market data grid an appraiser can quickly locate pairs of comparables that are similar in all but one

Figure 15.1 Sales Comparison Analysis Section of the URAR Form (Revised 6/93)

ITEM	SUBJECT	COMPARABLE NO. 1		COMPARABLE NO. 2		COMPARABLE NO. 3	
Address							
Proximity to Subject							
Sales Price	$		$		$		$
Price/Gross Liv. Area	$	$		$		$	
Data and/or Verification Sources							
VALUE ADJUSTMENTS	DESCRIPTION	DESCRIPTION	+(−)$Adjustment	DESCRIPTION	+(−)$Adjustment	DESCRIPTION	+(−)$Adjustment
Sales or Financing Concessions							
Date of Sale/Time							
Location							
Leasehold/Fee Simple							
Site							
View							
Design and Appeal							
Quality of Construction							
Age							
Condition							
Above Grade Room Count	Total Bdrms Baths	Total Bdrms Baths		Total Bdrms Baths		Total Bdrms Baths	
Gross Living Area	Sq. Ft.	Sq. Ft.		Sq. Ft.		Sq. Ft.	
Basement & Finished Rooms Below Grade							
Functional Utility							
Heating/Cooling							
Energy Efficient Items							
Garage/Carport							
Porch, Patio, Deck, Fireplace(s), etc.							
Fence, Pool, etc.							
Net Adj. (total)		□+ □− $		□+ □− $		□+ □− $	
Adjusted Sales Price of Comparable		$		$		$	

Comments on Sales Comparison (including the subject property's compatibility to the neighborhood, etc.): _____

ITEM	SUBJECT	COMPARABLE NO. 1	COMPARABLE NO. 2	COMPARABLE NO. 3
Date, Price and Data Source for prior sales within year of appraisal				

Analysis of any current agreement of sale, option, or listing of the subject property and analysis of any prior sales of subject and comparables within one year of the date of appraisal:

INDICATED VALUE BY SALES COMPARISON APPROACH .... $

SALES COMPARISON ANALYSIS

element of comparison. These paired data can be analyzed to pinpoint how much value the market ascribes to a particular property characteristic.

The total difference in value between the subject property and each comparable can also be calculated from the market data grid. The price of each comparable is adjusted for value differences ascribed to the elements of comparison. The resulting figures indicate a range of values for the subject property derived by the sales comparison approach.

Mortgage financing is very important to residential appraisers, who are concerned with the topic for two reasons. First, appraisers observe market activity patterns to ascertain how changes in these patterns affect the availability of mortgage funds and the terms on which funds can be obtained. The market for residential property is strongly influenced by trends in mortgage financing and their effects on supply and demand. The types of financing currently available must be thoroughly researched and historical trends must be analyzed to make a reasonable forecast. Mortgage analysis is normally conducted as part of the market analysis of the subject property's neighborhood.

> **CONCEPT**
>
> The availability of money influences the supply of and demand for residential housing, and special financing plans affect property sale prices.

Second, appraisers must understand the different types of market and nonmarket financing plans available to apply the sales comparison approach. Whenever a comparable property is sold with nonmarket financing, the special financing may be considered an inducement to either the buyer or the seller. As an inducement, its value must be separated from the value of the property. Special financing arrangements include

- Mortgage assumptions
- Seller financing at below-market rates
- Installment sale contracts
- Buydowns
- Reverse mortgages

When a property that was sold with special financing is used as a comparable in a market valuation, the appraiser must calculate the value of the financing inducement and adjust the property's sale price accordingly. Financing inducements may also be tied to unusual conditions of sale—i.e., special motivations that encourage either the buyer or the seller to conclude the transaction. In these cases, adjustments must be made for the effects of both the financing and the conditions of sale.

This chapter focuses on the typical and atypical financing plans found in the market, sources of mortgage money, and factors that influence the mortgage market. In appraisals undertaken to estimate market value, a financing adjustment is required if special financing has influenced the sale price of a comparable property. The various techniques used to estimate adjustments for special financing include analysis of market-derived paired data, simple arithmetic for estimating the value of seller-paid points and considerations other than cash, and cash equivalency calculations that involve discounting. Before those specific applications are demonstrated, however, the nature of residential mortgage financing must be examined.

FINANCING PLANS
Traditional Loans

Many kinds of financing are available to home buyers. The most common is the fully amortizing, fixed-rate, first mortgage loan. A fully amortizing loan is repaid with equal, periodic payments, usually on a monthly basis, which provide the lending institution with both a return *of* the investment through the recovery of principal over the term of the loan and a return *on* the investment in the form of interest. The interest rate of a fixed-rate loan does not vary; it remains at the same percentage over the life of the loan. The mortgage payments are structured so that the payments in the first years are mostly interest and the payments made in later years reduce the principal. This repayment schedule allows for level periodic payments and gradual equity buildup over the term of the loan. By the end of the term, the loan is fully amortized—i.e., the principal and the interest are entirely paid.

Variable-rate mortgages have become quite common in many parts of the country. A variable-rate mortgage has an interest rate that rises or falls according to a specified schedule or, more commonly, follows the movements of a standard or index to which the interest rate is tied. Variable-rate mortgages protect the lender because their interest rates rise when interest rates in the general money market rise. When rates are rising, the yield, or rate of return, from a fixed-rate mortgage investment may not be competitive with the yields available from other real estate investments or securities.

CONCEPTS

Conventional fixed-rate, fully amortizing first mortgage loans are repaid with equal, periodic payments, which provide the lending institution with both a return on the investment, in the form of interest, and a return of the investment, through recovery of principal over the term of the loan.

A variable-rate mortgage has an interest rate that may move up or down following a specified schedule or the movements of a standard or index.

A balloon mortgage is a financial obligation in which the monthly installment mainly repays the interest on the loan, usually set at a fixed rate for a short term. The balance on the principal of a balloon mortgage becomes due when the obligation matures and is paid with the final installment as a lump sum, or "balloon." Balloon mortgages are often used for second mortgages in which the monthly payments only partially amortize the principal balance over the duration of the loan.

> **TERM**
>
> **balloon mortgage:** a mortgage that is not fully amortized at maturity and thus requires a lump-sum, or balloon, payment of the outstanding balance.

Normally, traditional mortgages cannot be obtained for the full purchase price of a property. Most institutional lenders are subject to state laws and federal regulations that prescribe maximum loan-to-value ratios between the amount of the mortgage loan and the value of the security pledged. Many lending institutions require a buyer to make a cash down payment of at least 10% of the sale price. Most loans are for a specified term, usually 15 to 30 years. If the mortgagor, or borrower, defaults on the loan, the mortgagee, or lender, can foreclose—i.e., take legal action to force a sale and recover all or part of the loan amount.

Mortgages are either conventional, guaranteed, or insured. The typical first mortgage is a conventional mortgage that is not guaranteed or insured by any institution. Nonconventional mortgages are guaranteed or insured by a governmental agency such as the Federal Housing Administration (FHA) or the Department of Veterans Affairs (VA) or by a private company. Since the 1930s the FHA has been insuring loans, principally but not solely to people with limited financial means. The VA, which is the largest source of guaranteed mortgages, provides a similar service to veterans. FHA and VA mortgages tend to have lower interest rates, longer terms, and higher loan-to-value ratios than conventional loans.

> **CONCEPT**
>
> Most traditional mortgages conform to established loan-to-value ratios and are not insured or guaranteed. Nonconventional mortgages are insured or guaranteed and may be offered by a government agency such as the FHA or VA or by a private insuring company.

A type of insured loan is offered by private mortgage insurance companies that cover conventional mortgages. These companies insure the risk to lenders who advance 10% or 15% more than the amount traditionally loaned on a conventional mortgage. If an 80% loan-to-value mortgage is standard, a private mortgage company can provide insurance for an additional 10% or 15%, which increases the loan-to-value ratio to 90% or 95%.

The legal restrictions and requirements that apply to mortgages vary from state to state. These requirements provide home owners with protection and encouragement and also address the lender's risk. The interests of both parties must be balanced, as can be clearly seen by examining the foreclosure laws of various states. A state with foreclosure legislation that is extremely favorable to the borrower may attract few funds from outside the state. States that provide more protection for the lender by requiring short periods for foreclosure tend to attract more funds from around the country.

Other Types of Financing

In addition to a first mortgage, second or additional mortgages, which are commonly called home equity loans, can be used to facilitate the purchase of a home. Such junior mortgages are subordinate to the rights of the first mortgagee, the primary lender. A junior mortgage is required when the buyer is unable to arrange for adequate financing through a single mortgage. Because the first mortgagee has lien priority, a secondary lender can incur a substantial loss if the borrower defaults. To prevent the first lender from foreclosing, which would cut off or wipe out the junior position, the secondary lender is obliged to meet all first mortgage payments to keep that loan current. Interest rates on junior mortgages reflect this increased risk to the lender. They can, however, provide additional funds to the borrower and facilitate a purchase that might not be possible otherwise.

A mortgage is the traditional means of financing the purchase of a house, but in some states the same result is accomplished with different legal arrangements. In some western states, deeds of trust are used instead of mortgages. Money is borrowed in the same manner as it is with a mortgage loan, but a third party, the trustee, holds title to the property. When the borrower has met all of the financial obligations, the title is conveyed to the borrower.

Occasionally a buyer will purchase a residence with all cash, obtained from the sale of other property or from savings. A lump-sum cash payment can expedite a purchase and enhance the negotiating ability of the

CONCEPT

Junior mortgages, which are obtained to acquire additional funds and are subordinate to the rights of the primary lender, usually have higher interest rates to reflect the greater risks to the lender.

TERMS

home equity loan: a second or additional junior mortgage on a residence.

deed of trust: a legal instrument similar to a mortgage that, when executed and delivered, conveys or transfers property title to a trustee.

buyer. Often, however, a lump-sum cash payment may not represent the best financial strategy for a home owner. Mortgage interest payments can be deducted from taxable income and the rate of interest paid on a mortgage may be considerably lower than the home owner's tax bracket. By paying all cash, home owners forfeit a mortgage interest deduction that could reduce their taxes. Furthermore, the appreciation realized upon the sale of a home may not match the capital gains that could be realized on other investments.

Creative Financing

When interest rates are high, the monthly payments on typical loans can be higher than many consumers can afford to pay. Faced with a shrinking market for their properties, sellers may entice buyers by adjusting prices. Sellers who are reluctant to lower their prices can sometimes appeal to buyers by offering alternative or creative financing. These plans may call for monthly payments that are lower than those required with typical financing. In some of these arrangements, the seller provides the financing rather than a lending institution. In others, both the seller and a lending institution play a role.

Besides high interest rates, there are other reasons for using alternative financing arrangements such as mortgage assumptions and installment sale contracts. When mortgages do not prohibit assumptions or require lender approval, easier credit requirements may make creative financing attractive to buyers. Sellers who provide financing may have less stringent credit requirements than lending institutions. Furthermore, loan assumptions and contract sales generally close faster and are less costly.

Described below are some common creative financing instruments that came into existence in the early 1980s.[1] Appraisers should be familiar with all creative financing plans available and be aware of those that were typical of market practices at the time of sale and those that were not.

Mortgage Assumption

In a mortgage assumption, a buyer takes over the remaining payments on a loan originally made to the seller. Because the original loan usually carries a rate of interest that is lower

> **TERM**
>
> **mortgage assumption:** a purchase of mortgaged property in which the buyer accepts liability for existing debt. The seller remains liable to the lender unless the lender agrees to release the seller.

---

1. See Terrence M. Clauretie and James R. Webb, *The Theory and Practice of Real Estate Finance* (Fort Worth, Texas: Dryden Press, 1993).

than current rates, the buyer may be willing to pay a higher price for the property to obtain the favorable financing terms. The interest rate, monthly payment, and maturity of the mortgage remain the same when the loan is assumed. Mortgages guaranteed by the VA may be taken over by a third party without the approval of the lender, but mortgages insured by the FHA are assumable only with lender approval.

Not all mortgages can be assumed. Some contain due-on-sale clauses stipulating that the outstanding loan balance will become due when the mortgaged property is sold or transferred.

Seller Loan

A seller may be willing to finance all or part of the purchase price of a property at a below-market interest rate. Such loans are typically called *purchase-money mortgages.* If the seller finances the entire amount, the loan would usually then serve as a first mortgage, often in the form of a balloon mortgage. More commonly, only a portion of the price is financed by the seller. In this case the loan functions as a second mortgage that is subordinate to the first mortgage obtained from a financial institution. A buyer may be willing to pay a higher price for a property to obtain favorable, below-market financing terms from the seller.

Installment Sale Contract

Under an installment sale contract, a seller allows a buyer to purchase property by making periodic payments. The title does not pass from the seller to the buyer until the buyer has satisfied the contract by paying all or a specified portion of the purchase price. If the buyer defaults, all payments made are normally forfeited. Quite often the terms of a sale contract are different from those available for a first mortgage. An installment sale contract may have a shorter term, specify a balloon payment, or provide for a higher loan-to-value ratio. Interest rates may be higher or lower than those available through conventional means. If the terms are favorable, a buyer may be willing to pay a higher price for a property purchased in this manner.

> **TERMS**
>
> **seller loan:** a mortgage in which the seller finances all or part of the purchase price of the property at a below-market interest rate; also called *purchase-money mortgage.*
>
> **installment sale:** a sale in which the proceeds are to be received in more than one payment.

Buydown Plan

In a buydown plan, a home seller advances a lump-sum payment to the lender to reduce, or buy down, the interest payments of the borrower. The buydown period may range from one year to the entire term of the mortgage. Builders sometimes buy down interest rates on loans to increase sales activity in new subdivisions.

Reverse Mortgage

Home owners at least 62 years old may tap into their home equity during their retirement years through a reverse mortgage, a financing tool created in the 1980s to provide seniors who are "cash-poor" but "house-rich" with a source of income allowing them to stay in the home they own free and clear for the rest of their lives. This arrangement reverses the normal lending process, with the home owner receiving payments from the lender for the length of the loan, which can last as long as the borrowers live in the property.

The total amount of the loan and any fees and interest that have accrued are not repaid until the property is sold after the borrowers have left the house. The lender relies on the anticipated value of the home as the eventual source for repayment. Factors beyond the market value of the property influence the value of a reverse mortgage. Such factors include the age (but not the income or credit rating) of the occupant of the house, current interest rates, the specific characteristics of the reverse mortgage program, and forecasts of the anticipated sale price of the home.

SOURCES OF MORTGAGE MONEY

Funds for financing the purchase of a single-family residence can come from either primary or secondary sources. Primary sources are institutions that assemble money deposited by savers and lend it directly to borrowers. Individuals who make mortgage loans are also included in this category. Institutions that are secondary financing sources do not raise money or make mortgage loans directly. These institutions facilitate financing opportunities by buying and selling existing mortgages, which increases the effectiveness of the lending market.

Primary Sources

Mortgage pools and trusts, banks, and mortgage companies provide funds for most home purchases. Life insurance companies invest some money, but they tend to be interested in multifamily residences and other types of income-producing property. Table 16.1 shows the percentage of mortgage funds loaned by various primary sources in 1997.

Table 16.1 Distribution of Mortgage Funds for One- to Four-Family Homes	
Loan Source	**% of Loans**
Savings institutions	12.9%
Mortgage pools or trusts	52.4
(Ginnie Mae, Fannie Mae, Freddie Mac, private mortgage conduits)	
Commercial banks	19.0
Federal and other agencies	5.5
Mortgage companies, REITs, pension funds, finance companies, and others	10.0
Life insurance companies	0.2
Total	100.0%

Based on statistics compiled by the Federal Reserve, Table No. 816 in the Statistical Abstract of the United States, U.S. Department of Commerce, Bureau of the Census, U.S. Government Printing Office, 1998, p. 521.

TERMS

disintermediation: the transfer of money from low interest-bearing accounts to higher interest-bearing accounts.

secondary mortgage market: a market created by government and private agencies for the purchase and sale of existing mortgages; provides greater liquidity for mortgages. Fannie Mae, Freddie Mac, and Ginnie Mae are the principal operators in the secondary mortgage market.

Banks and other savings institutions act as financial intermediaries. When other investments offer better interest rates, depositors withdraw their money and invest elsewhere. This is called *disintermediation,* and it affects the availability of mortgage funds. During the past 15 years, disintermediation has reduced the funds available for home financing more than once. The operations of the secondary mortgage market can help offset these shortages.

Secondary Mortgage Market

The development of the secondary mortgage market has greatly facilitated the financing of real estate over the past few decades. Formerly many lending institutions made home loans and held them until maturity. Now they can sell packages of mortgage loans in the secondary mortgage market and free additional funds for further home financing. Private investors and institutions purchase home mortgages as do governmental and quasi-governmental agencies. The Federal National Mortgage Association (Fannie Mae) is an independent government agency with lines of credit to the Federal

Reserve System. The Federal Home Loan Mortgage Corporation (Freddie Mac) is a federal agency regulated by the VA and the FHA. The Government National Mortgage Association (Ginnie Mae) is a federally owned and financed corporation under the Department of Housing and Urban Development. Because governmental and monetary authorities believe that home buying and home building can improve a depressed economy, the secondary mortgage market is often used to stimulate home sales.

Fannie Mae

Fannie Mae has a major influence on the secondary mortgage market. Its principal purpose is to purchase mortgages from the primary mortgage market, which increases the liquidity of primary lenders. Fannie Mae then resells packages of these pooled mortgages to investors at a discount. Two important activities of the association are the over-the-counter program, in which Fannie Mae posts the prices it will pay for the immediate delivery of mortgages, and the free market system commitment auction, in which FHA, VA, and conventional mortgages are sold in separate, simultaneous auctions.

Freddie Mac

Freddie Mac was created in 1970 to increase the availability of mortgage funds and generate greater flexibility for mortgage investors. Since the Federal Home Loan Bank Board became defunct in 1989, the Office of Thrift Supervision (OTS) has overseen the operation of this organization, which is related to the system of federally chartered savings and loan associations. Freddie Mac helps expand and distribute capital for mortgage purposes by conducting both purchase and sales programs.

CONCEPTS

The secondary mortgage market includes governmental and quasi-governmental agencies as well as private investors and institutions such as banks, insurance companies, and real estate investment trusts. By purchasing packages of mortgage loans, these secondary sources increase the liquidity of the primary sources of residential financing.

The Federal National Mortgage Association (Fannie Mae) conducts two important activities:

1. An over-the-counter program
2. A free market system commitment auction

TERMS

Fannie Mae: Federal National Mortgage Association; an independent government agency that purchases mortgages from banks, trust companies, mortgage companies, savings and loan associations, and insurance companies to help distribute funds for home mortgages.

Freddie Mac: Federal Home Loan Mortgage Corporation; an agency that facilitates secondary residential mortgages sponsored by the Veterans Administration and the Federal Housing Administration as well as residential mortgages that are not government-protected.

CONCEPTS

The Federal Home Loan Mortgage Corporation (Freddie Mac) purchases and sells mortgage packages.

The Government National Mortgage Association (Ginnie Mae) provides housing assistance by sponsoring mortgage loans that require special support.

In its purchase programs, Freddie Mac buys single-family and condominium mortgages from approved financial institutions. This gives the institutions greater liquidity in times of credit stringency so they can continue making mortgage funds available for housing. While Fannie Mae programs include insured and guaranteed mortgages, most Freddie Mac activity is in the conventional mortgage field. In its sales programs, Freddie Mac sells its mortgage inventories, thus acquiring funds from organizations that have excess capital. These funds are used to purchase mortgages from organizations with shortages. Because Freddie Mac operations are conducted nationally, they help make mortgage capital available in all regions of the country.

Ginnie Mae

Ginnie Mae is a third major player in the secondary mortgage market. Its operations also make mortgage capital available for housing. Fannie Mae is an independent agency, but Ginnie Mae is a government organization that gets financial support from the U.S. Department of the Treasury. Ginnie Mae has special assistance programs that facilitate mortgage loans that could not be handled otherwise. The organization also manages and liquidates certain mortgages acquired by the government, but its most important role in the secondary mortgage market is in the mortgage-backed securities program.

TERMS

Ginnie Mae: Government National Mortgage Association; a federally owned and financed corporation under the Department of Housing and Urban Development that subsidizes mortgages through its secondary mortgage market operations and issues mortgage-backed, federally insured securities.

pass-through certificate: a form of mortgage-backed security in which mortgage payments are passed on to the holder of the security.

Ginnie Mae is authorized to guarantee the timely payment of principal and interest on long-term securities that are backed by pools of insured or guaranteed mortgages. The most popular security is called a *pass-through certificate* because it is based on mortgage payments that are passed on to the holder of the security. In the mortgage-backed securities program, mortgage originators pool loans in groups of $1 million or more, issue covering securities, and obtain a Ginnie Mae guarantee. Through this program, investors who do not have the capacity to make mortgages can still be involved in home financing markets. Ginnie Mae securities make excellent investments and are traded extensively.

The development of collateralized mortgage obligations (CMOs) as a major investment banking activity is due in part to Ginnie Mae guarantee arrangements. These investment instruments are attractive because the debt is usually secured by Ginnie Mae certificates covering pools of residential mortgages. Due to Ginnie Mae's participation, these bonds receive a AAA rating, the highest-quality risk rating. Ginnie Mae

> **TERM**
>
> **collateralized mortgage obligations (CMOs):** bonds issued and sold in capital markets on debt collateralized by pools of Ginnie Mae, Fannie Mae, Freddie Mac, and conventional institutional mortgages. CMOs are an important source of liquidity for the mortgage industry.

guarantees also allow these bonds to be sold at low interest rates. As CMOs have proliferated, some have been secured using Fannie Mae, Freddie Mac, and even conventional institutional mortgages as collateral. The CMO vehicle has provided great liquidity for the mortgage industry and has helped monetize the mortgage element in real estate investment.

Private Sector Transactions

Although most secondary mortgage market activity is generated by Fannie Mae, Freddie Mac, and Ginnie Mae, many private sector transactions also take place. Banks and insurance companies that make mortgages often sell loan portfolios, or participations, to private or institutional investors. Real estate investment trusts (REITs) also purchase mortgages from institutions, which gives the sellers the liquidity they need to continue their lending programs.

The development and growth of private mortgage insurance programs has facilitated private activity in the secondary mortgage market. In the residential market, private programs have been successful in insuring mortgage loan increments that exceed legal ratios. This has encouraged private secondary mortgage market operations, which could not occur without insurance.

INFLUENCES ON THE MORTGAGE MARKET

The availability of mortgage financing in the United States is influenced by many organizations and by developments at various levels. The decisions of the Federal Reserve are of great importance because they affect the amount of credit available throughout the nation. The activities of the Treasury Department, which reflect the economic policy of the federal government, also influence mortgage rates.

Competition in international financial markets and fluctuations in the business cycle can also have pronounced effects. These forces combine to create the economic climate within which the secondary mortgage market operates. In turn the secondary mortgage market influences the availability of funds in the primary mortgage market.

Primary lenders are subject to other constraints in addition to those imposed by secondary mortgage market conditions. To measure the risk associated with a mortgage loan, primary lenders must also consider the economic health of the region, the community, and the neighborhood as well as the location of the specific property, the property type, and the income level and credit rating of the potential buyers. Lenders adjust the terms of financing by raising interest rates, charging "points," or using other devices to reflect the risks they associate with the loan.

Mortgage loan underwriters frequently call on appraisers for the unbiased value estimates they need to assess loan risk. An underwriter analyzes a property based on the appraisal and judges the property's acceptability as security for the loan being sought. Neighborhood analysis is critical to the underwriter's determinations. Properties in neighborhoods characterized by instability or declining values usually are not eligible for maximum financing.

The Federal Reserve System

The policies of the Federal Reserve System have the most significant influence on the terms and availability of mortgage financing. Through its actions, the Federal Reserve regulates the supply of credit available throughout the national economy. To a limited extent, the Federal Reserve can even influence the timing and severity of the major economic shifts that create business and real estate cycles.

The Federal Reserve System is composed of 12 regional banks, which serve the 12 Federal Reserve regional districts, and numerous member banks, which include all nationally chartered commercial banks and many state-chartered banks. The Federal Reserve can act independently to further national economic goals. "The function of the Federal Reserve System is to foster a flow of credit and money that will facilitate orderly economic growth, a stable dollar, and long-run balance in our

> **TERM**
>
> **Federal Reserve System:** the central banking system of the United States, which was created in 1913 to manage money and credit and to promote orderly growth of the economy. The Federal Reserve regulates the money supply, determines the legal reserve of member banks, oversees the mint, effects transfers of funds, promotes and facilitates the clearance and collection of checks, examines member banks, and serves other functions.

international payments. Its original purposes, as expressed by the founders, were to give the country a lasting currency, to provide facilities for discounting commercial paper, and to improve the supervision of banking."[2] As the economy has changed, broader objectives have been outlined, namely "to help counteract inflationary and deflationary movements, and to share in creating conditions favorable to a high level of employment, a stable dollar, growth of the country, and a rising level of consumption."

Credit Regulation Devices

The Federal Reserve uses three devices to regulate the supply of money and credit:

1. The reserve requirement
2. The federal discount rate
3. The Federal Open Market Committee (FOMC)

The reserve requirement establishes the amount of deposit liabilities that member banks must keep in reserve accounts. These funds cannot be made available for business loans. The Federal Reserve can expand or contract the supply of available credit by changing its reserve requirement, which alters the amount of money banks can lend.

The federal discount rate is the rate of interest at which member banks can borrow funds from the Federal Reserve. This borrowing privilege gives member banks an important advantage over other banks in times of great demand. The Federal Reserve can encourage or discourage borrowing by raising or lowering the interest rate charged. When borrowing is discouraged by the Federal Reserve, banks have fewer funds available for loan programs.

The third credit regulation device, the Federal Open Market Committee, is the most potent of the Federal Reserve's tools and the most commonly used. To increase the supply of credit, the FOMC writes Federal Reserve checks and buys U.S. government securities from securities dealers who deposit the checks with their banks. This increases balances in

TERMS

reserve requirement: a requirement of the Federal Reserve System that member banks keep part of their deposit liabilities frozen in reserve accounts.

federal discount rate: the interest rate charged by the Federal Reserve for funds borrowed by member banks.

Federal Open Market Committee (FOMC): a committee composed of the Federal Reserve's Board of Governors, the president of the New York Federal Reserve Bank, and four district reserve bank presidents, which buys and sells government securities in the open market to regulate the money supply and interest rates.

2.   The Federal Reserve Board, *The Federal Reserve System: Purposes and Functions* (Washington, D.C., 1985).

the reserve accounts of these banks and permits them to make more loans. To restrict credit, the FOMC sells securities to dealers who pay with their checks, which reduces their banks' reserve account balances. Thus business loans and economic growth are discouraged.

U.S. Department of the Treasury

The U.S. Department of the Treasury implements the fiscal policies of the United States government and exerts a substantial influence on credit and mortgage markets. The Treasury Department helps manage the government's finances by raising funds and paying bills. To raise funds, the Treasury Department prints currency, collects taxes, and borrows money. Bills are paid when Congress appropriates funds for various national projects. The treasury department does not have a day-to-day regulative influence on money markets like the Federal Reserve, but it does have a sizable impact. When the government borrows heavily to meet its deficit payments, less money is usually available to the private sector. When the government prints money to meet its obligations, it weakens the buying power of the dollar and contributes to inflation.

> **CONCEPT**
>
> The U.S. Department of the Treasury prints currency, collects taxes, and borrows money to meet budget deficits.

Impact on Real Estate Activities

Restricted credit can have a severe impact on activities that require borrowed funds, including property purchases and home construction. When the Federal Reserve pursues a tight monetary policy and interest rates rise, the market for real estate can go into a steep decline. In 1981 and 1982 the prime rate, which is the interest rate that banks charge their best customers, rose to 21.5%. Mortgage loans are usually about two percentage points higher than the prime. Consequently, during these years very few home loans were made. Mortgage funds were scarce because lenders were reluctant to lend for long terms without knowing how high money costs might run. As a result, variable-rate mortgages were introduced and for a time they dominated the market. Rollover mortgages, periodic adjustable-rate mortgages, and other renewable mortgages were common. Still many buyers kept away from the market entirely due to high rates and unfamiliar financing arrangements.

To bring people back into the real estate market, many sellers offered nonmarket financing terms geared to the buyers' ability to pay. Builders arranged to buy down institutional mortgage charges by making initial lump-sum payments for buyers, thereby selling off existing housing stock and increasing the pace of development.

The experience of the market in the early 1980s demonstrates how sensitive the mortgage market is to conditions in the money market. In the mid 1980s, a less restrictive climate returned to the money market. With inflation tamed, the Federal Reserve was able to relax its credit policy. Interest rates fell and more funds became available. The mortgage market was quick to respond. Variable-rate mortgages became less popular, and long-term, fixed-rate, fully amortizing first mortgages once again became the dominant form of financing for most single-family residences. The precipitous decline in interest rates during the early 1990s helped stabilize financing for real estate and increase the volume and velocity of real estate market activity.

> **CONCEPT**
>
> The mortgage market is very sensitive to conditions in money markets.

Loan Risk and Points

Institutions and individuals who lend money analyze the risks associated with a residential loan in the same way they would consider any other investment. The security of real estate provides an added incentive for many institutions and individuals to make mortgage loans. Real estate is typically considered excellent collateral because it is fixed in location and likely to remain useful for a long period. Its utility and therefore its value are protected by a wide range of public services and governmental organizations. However, certain risks are involved in making mortgage loans. Delinquencies and foreclosures can be costly, and at some point the loan may be greater than the price the real estate would bring in a forced sale. These risks could result in losses for the financial institution.

To analyze the relationship between financing and real estate values, an appraiser must consider the mortgage lending system and the specific risks involved. The interest rate that is quoted for a mortgage loan represents the cost of the money. This annual rate of return reflects the risks of the specific investment given the property type, the neighborhood and region where the property is located, and the credit rating of the borrower. The rates for residential real estate mortgages, however, also depend on the cost of money in money markets. Home buyers must compete with other groups for funds. When the supply of money available in money markets is substantially reduced, the housing market is one of the first areas to suffer.

To compete in the market, lenders often find it necessary to charge points or use a discount rate. For example, a lender making a $100,000 loan at the going rate of 9% may feel that conditions in financial markets warrant some adjustment of the loan. The lender may ask the borrower to pay points for the right to borrow the money. One point equals 1% of the loan amount. If four points are required on a $100,000 loan, the buyer would pay $4,000. Alternatively, the lender might adjust the loan by applying a discount rate. If the loan is discounted at 3%, the amount of money actually advanced at the time of closing is 3% less than the original $100,000. Thus the borrower pays 9% interest on $100,000, even though only $97,000 was loaned. The discount increases the yield to the lender; it can compensate for higher risk or make the mortgage yield meet the yields obtainable on other investments.

CASH EQUIVALENCY

Whenever a property sells with atypical financing, the financing plan may have influenced the sale price. Most creative financing plans are inducements offered by the seller that allow the buyer to make periodic payments that are lower than those required with market financing. The value of financing represents personal property, not real property. If comparables with unusual financing are to be used in sales comparison, the value of the financing incentive must be distinguished from the value of the real property. The price of the comparable must be adjusted to reflect the amount of cash the seller would have received if no special financing agreement had been made.

An understanding of typical market financing is critical in determining whether the financing arranged for a sale considered comparable involves any special advantages or disadvantages. Market financing is conventional, readily available financing as opposed to financing obtained from the VA or FHA. Whether financing is conventional or nonconventional may be established by analyzing six factors. (These six significant factors are shown in Figure 16.1.) Financing terms are continually subject to change, so the appraiser is advised to check the local market.

CONCEPTS

The cash equivalency of a special financing plan may be calculated with paired data analysis.

Discounting procedures are sometimes used to find the cash equivalent value of mortgage assumptions, seller loans, and balloon mortgages.

TERM

cash equivalency analysis: the procedure in which the sale prices of comparable properties sold with atypical financing are adjusted to reflect typical market terms.

Figure 16.1	Significant Factors in Residential Financing
1. Loan-to-value ratio	Typically loan-to-value ratios range from 70% to 80%, but they may run as high as 95%.
2. Interest rate	In recent years interest rates have ranged between 7.5% and 10%, although in the late 1990s residential mortgage rates were at 30-year lows of 6% to 8%.*
3. Amortization period	Periods of 25 to 30 years are typical. Amortization periods in excess of 30 years should be investigated.
4. Term of the balloon	Most mortgages that provide for a balloon payment have terms of three to five years, but some may extend up to 10 years.
5. Number of points	Typically one to three points are charged on a 70% to 80% loan-to-value mortgage. The lower the loan-to-value ratio, the lower the points charged.
6. Frequency of payments	Conventionally payments are made on a monthly basis, but a mortgage may be paid quarterly, semiannually, or annually.

* Although interest rates have remained near historically low levels in recent years, the Mortgage Bankers Association of America expects rates to edge up over the next 10 years, reaching 8.7% by the year 2007, according to *Bank Rate Monitor* on March 13, 1998. When mortgage rates are low, home owners take out traditional fixed-rate mortgage loans and cash equivalency considerations are less important.

Nonmarket financing plans can be translated into terms that represent the cash paid to the seller as of the date of sale. This is called "rendering the terms cash equivalent."[3] Cash equivalency is estimated in several ways. The effect of special financing can be measured by analyzing market-derived paired data, or the amount can be calculated with simple arithmetic or the use of discounting techniques. Calculated adjustments for special financing are often somewhat higher than market-derived adjustments. Appraisers should only use a calculated adjustment when they are confident that the adjustment accurately reflects market thinking.

Comparison of Sales Transactions

Adjustments for cash equivalency derived by comparing recent sales transactions are generally the most reliable. These adjustments can be estimated from paired data analysis. To apply this technique an appraiser finds pairs of sales considered comparable that are essentially similar except for the form of financing used. The effect of financing is indicated by the difference between the prices of the paired sales. Similarly, if a newspaper advertisement quotes a sale price for a new home and indicates that the developer is offering a $5,000 or 5% discount for an all-cash purchase, the appraiser has a solid basis for estimating the effect

3. See Guide Note 2 to the Appraisal Institute's Standards of Professional Appraisal Practice, "Cash Equivalency in Value Estimates in Accordance with Standards Rule 1-2 (b)."

CONCEPT

Paired data analysis is extremely reliable for deriving cash equivalency, but appraisers often have difficulty finding a sufficient number of comparables.

of the financing arrangement on the price of the house.

Deriving cash equivalency directly from sales transaction data may be problematic because sales with financing terms that require adjustment are, by definition, atypical for the market. Therefore, it is unlikely that an appraiser will find sufficient comparables to conduct a reliable paired data analysis. One or two sets of matched data may not constitute an adequate sample. However, even a limited sample can be useful if the reasonableness of the adjustment derived from paired data analysis is tested against the results of other cash equivalency techniques.

In purchases transacted with atypical financing, one of the parties involved often has a special motivation to complete the sale. When paired data analysis is used to derive an adjustment, the price difference between comparables usually reflects both a financing inducement and special motivation. Consequently, financing and conditions of sale may be combined into a single adjustment. Sales considered comparable that do not reflect arm's-length transactions should only be used with extreme caution.

Adjusting for Seller-Paid Points

An adjustment for seller-paid points is one cash equivalency adjustment that is relatively easy to calculate. The points are applied to the mortgage amount and the result is deducted from the total price.[4] For example, consider a comparable property that was sold for $130,000. The buyer made a $30,000 cash down payment and financed the balance of the sale price with a $100,000 FHA-insured mortgage. The seller paid the lender three points, which is 3% of the mortgage amount of $100,000, or $3,000. The cash equivalent price of the comparable is therefore $127,000 ($100,000 − $3,000 + $30,000). This cash equivalent price is then used as the basis for further sales comparison adjustments. It is imperative that the calculated adjustment be checked against the market.

In other instances, the buyer pays some or all of the points. Research conducted in 1983 indicated that approximately one-third of the cost of points was actually recovered in the pricing. Some clients may not require that the payment of points be converted into cash

---

4. At one time, the VA and FHA required the seller to pay the points that apply to mortgages underwritten by these agencies. This requirement has been discontinued.

equivalent terms. However, to satisfy the cash equivalent assumptions in the definition of market value, an appraiser must calculate the adjustment. Although adjustments for points are easy to calculate, the VA and FHA issue their own guidelines on points. Appraisers who work for these agencies must use procedures that are consistent with agency regulations.

Adjusting for Considerations Other Than Cash

In a property sale, the seller and buyer may agree on a price that includes items of real or personal property. To determine the cash equivalency of the sale price in this situation, the appraiser focuses on the cash amount that the seller received for the items traded.

For example, an appraiser is analyzing a complicated sale in which the seller reportedly sold the property for $86,000. The sale was financed with a 10% cash down payment, and the buyer assumed the existing mortgage balance of $50,000 at current market rates. The seller also received a property in trade from the buyer. The seller believed that this property was worth $15,000 but was only able to sell it for $10,000. The seller also received a new car with a sticker price of $7,500. The seller sold the car for $9,400.

To estimate the cash equivalent value of the sale, the appraiser totals the following figures:

Cash down payment	$8,600
Mortgage balance	50,000
Trade property	10,000
Car	+ 9,400
Cash equivalent sale price	$78,000

Some might argue that cash equivalent sale prices should reflect what the sellers thought they were getting at the time of the sales. This is incorrect, however, because financing adjustments must reflect values that are ultimately determined in the market.

Discounting Cash Flows

Many techniques for deriving cash equivalency adjustments involve discounting cash flows. Lenders and investors commonly discount cash flows to estimate what a future stream of payments is worth today. They use discounting procedures and financial function tables to make these calculations. Appraisers can apply the same principles to convert future payments into the present value of a financing plan when the pattern of the anticipated payments is known. Such cash equivalent adjustments should only be used with extreme caution; they

TERM

discount factor: an adjustment made to a future income stream to obtain its present value.

should be checked against more reliable adjustments derived directly from sales data, if such data are available.

A stream of income expected in the future is not currently worth the sum of all the anticipated payments to be received. Normally, money that is invested today is expected to earn interest and produce more money in the future. This is why a future income stream must be *discounted*. A discount factor is applied to the income stream to obtain its present value.

Several terms used in cash equivalency analysis are defined below.

- **Present value** is the value of a future payment or series of future payments discounted to the current date. The present value of a series of payments depends on the size of the payments, the schedule of payments, and the interest rate that applies to each portion of the schedule. When these variables are known, present value can be estimated using an appropriate financial function table, a financial function calculator, or a computer program.

- **Present value of $1** is a compound interest factor that indicates how much $1 due in the future is worth today. A future amount due, such as a balloon payment, is multiplied by this factor to obtain its present value. When the payment amount and the interest rate are known, the present value factor can be found with an appropriate financial function table, a financial function calculator, or a computer program.

- **Present value of $1 per period** is a compound interest factor that indicates how much $1 paid periodically is worth today. An amount payable periodically, such as a monthly mortgage payment, is multiplied by this factor to obtain its present value. When the payment amount and the interest rate are known, the present value factor can be found with a financial function table, a financial function calculator, or a computer program.

- **Mortgage constant (R_M)** is a rate that reflects the relationship between annual debt service and the principal of the mortgage loan. It is used to convert annual debt service into mortgage loan value. The mortgage constant equals the annual debt service divided by the mortgage loan value. Using the debt service payment or the mortgage loan principal and the interest rate and term, the mortgage constant can be obtained with a direct-reduction loan factor table, a financial function calculator, or a computer.

Discounting Mortgages Made at a Below-Market Rate

Procedures for estimating the present value of a financing instrument vary, depending on what information is known about the financing plan and how future repayment is scheduled. When a mortgage at a below-market rate is assumed or the seller makes a mortgage loan at a below-market rate, the cash flow for the entire stated term of the mortgage can be discounted in three steps:

1. Determine the monthly payment. When the mortgage amount, the contract interest rate, and the term are known, the mortgage constant can be obtained from the appropriate table and the monthly payment can be calculated.
2. Determine the present value of the monthly payments over the stated term at the market interest rate by applying a present value of $1 per period factor. The result is the market value of the mortgage.
3. Add the down payment to the value of the mortgage. This sum is the cash equivalent sale price.

Example. A comparable single-family residence was sold for $110,000 with a down payment of $25,000 and an $85,000 mortgage from the seller for a 20-year term. The seller charged 10% interest when market rates were 13%. The cash equivalent sale price can be calculated as follows:

> Monthly payment on $85,000 for 20 years @ 10%
>
> $85,000 × 0.00965 (direct-reduction loan factor or mortgage constant, R_M) = $820.25
>
> Present value of $820.25 for 20 years @ market rate of 13%
> (monthly conversion frequency) = $820.25 × 85.3551
> (PV of $1 per period) = $70,012.52

Cash equivalent value of mortgage (rounded)	$70,000
Plus down payment	+ 25,000
Sale price adjusted for financing	$95,000

Discounting Mortgage Assumptions, Seller Loans, and Balloon Mortgages

A slightly more complicated calculation can be used to estimate the cash equivalency of mortgage assumptions and seller loans. Many mortgage loans are not held for the entire mortgage term but are repaid early. A more elaborate calculation is used to reflect this fact. Financing plans that involve balloon payments may also be adjusted using this technique. A balloon mortgage is not fully amortized at maturity, so a lump-sum, or balloon, payment of the outstanding balance is required.

To estimate cash equivalency when a balloon mortgage is used, present value is determined separately for two distinct phases of the loan repayment schedule:

- The period during which scheduled payments are being made
- The point at which the balance is recovered in a balloon, or lump-sum, payment

The following five-step procedure is recommended.

1. Determine the monthly payment.
2. Estimate the probable life expectancy of the loan. This can be either the actual term of the mortgage stated in the loan document or the average mortgage life of loans for the type of property in question.
3. Discount the monthly payments over the probable life expectancy of the loan by applying a present value of $1 per period factor at the market interest rate.
4. Discount the projected loan balance at the due date of the balloon or at the end of the average mortgage life by applying a present value of $1 factor at the market interest rate.
5. Add together the present value of the monthly payments (from Step 3), the present value of the projected balance (from Step 4), and the down payment amount. The resulting sum is the cash equivalent sale price of the property.

Example. The procedure for balloon mortgages is demonstrated using the same data presented in the previous example:

Monthly payment: $820.25
Average mortgage life for similar property (from lenders): 7 years
Present value of $820.25 per month for 7 years at market rate of 13% (monthly conversion frequency):

  $820.25 × 54.9693 (*PV of $1 per period*) = $45,090 (rounded)

Present value of future mortgage balance
Number of years remaining: 20 − 7 = 13
PV of $820.25 per month @ 10% contract rate for 13 years (monthly conversion frequency):

  $820.25 × 87.1195 (*PV of $1 per period*) = $71,460 (rounded)

Future balance payment converted to present value
PV of $1 factor for 7 years @ 13% market rate (monthly conversion frequency):
  $71,460 × 0.4045 (*PV of $1*) = $28,906 (rounded)
$45,090 (*PV of mortgage paid in 7 years*) + $28,906 (*PV of balance*)

Cash equivalent value of the mortgage	$73,996
Plus down payment	+ 25,000
Adjusted sale price of comparable	$98,996
	or $99,000, (rounded)

This second procedure requires more calculations, but it more accurately reflects the accounting method used by lending institutions.

Limitations of Discounting Procedures

Discounting procedures for estimating cash equivalency can provide mathematical solutions to a wide range of financing problems. However, appraisers should only use these calculations when they are confident that they reflect market behavior accurately. Calculated adjustments are often somewhat larger than market-derived adjustments. Adjustments derived by comparing recent sales transactions are more reliable than adjustments based on discounting procedures alone.

17 APPLICATION OF THE SALES COMPARISON APPROACH

After all potentially comparable properties have been identified and inspected and the transaction data have been verified, the appraiser selects the comparables that will actually be used in the appraisal. The comparable properties may be quite similar to the subject property, but they can never be exactly identical to it. Therefore, the prices of the comparables must be adjusted to reflect their differences from the subject.

The appraiser first identifies the effect on value produced by each difference. This is accomplished through analysis of market data. Paired data analysis may facilitate this task. Next the appraiser applies dollar or percentage adjustments to the price of each comparable. Adjustments are usually made in a particular sequence. As the sequence of adjustments proceeds, the price of each comparable is reshaped until it ultimately approximates a current, open-market sale price that corresponds to the value of the subject property. Qualitative analysis is then applied to consider the influence of the elements of comparison that resist precise mathematical adjustment. (Quantitative adjustments and qualitative analysis complement each other and are often used in combination.) The adjusted prices of the comparables are reconciled to provide a final indication of the value of the subject property by the sales comparison approach.

PURPOSE OF ADJUSTMENT

Each sales comparison adjustment is made to account for a specific difference between the subject property and a comparable property. As the comparable is made more like the subject, its price is brought closer to the subject's unknown value.

- If the comparable is *superior* to the subject, a *downward* adjustment must be applied to the price of the comparable.
- If the comparable is *inferior* to the subject, the price of the comparable must be adjusted *upward* to reflect the difference.

Because only the price of the comparable is known, only it can be adjusted. The unknown value of the subject is suggested by the price of the comparable once it has been adjusted for all differences from the subject.

UNITS OF COMPARISON

Units of comparison are the components into which a property may be divided for purposes of comparison. Because only like units can be compared, each sale price is stated in the same units of comparison. All units must be appropriate to the appraisal problem. When unit prices related to size are used, adjustments for differences in size may be unnecessary. Single-family residential properties are usually compared on the basis of gross living area or above-grade living area. Apartment properties are often analyzed on the basis of price per apartment and price per room. Price per square foot of gross building area or leasable building area may also be used.

Many properties can be analyzed with several different units of comparison, so an appraiser should determine which unit or units are the most appropriate and reliable. The units of comparison selected can have a significant bearing on the reconciliation of value indications in the sales comparison approach. Adjustments can be made either to the total sale price of the comparable property or to a unit price such as price per square foot of gross living area.

Units of comparison can help an appraiser decide whether a potentially comparable property is in fact comparable to the subject property. For example, if an appraiser finds that one potentially comparable property sold for $150 per square foot of gross living area while most other properties similar to the subject sold for about $80 per square foot of gross living area, the discrepancy would suggest that there is something different about the more expensive property. The reasons for the discrepancy should be investigated, and if the potential comparable is not truly comparable, it must be eliminated from further consideration. In this example, the unit of com-

---

CONCEPTS

The purpose of the adjustment procedure is to bring the known price of each comparable property as close as possible to the unknown value of the subject property.

If the comparable is superior to the subject, a negative adjustment is applied to the price of the comparable; if the comparable is inferior to the subject, a positive adjustment is applied to the price of the comparable.

Using units of comparison, the sale prices of the comparables may be converted into unit prices such as price per square foot. Adjustments are then applied to the unit sale price of each comparable.

TERM

units of comparison: the components into which a property may be divided for purposes of comparison, e.g., price per square foot, front foot, cubic foot, room, bed, seat, apartment unit.

parison applied was price per square foot of gross living area.

SCATTER DIAGRAMS

A scatter diagram is an analytical instrument that can be used to help organize data and set up a market data grid. Scatter diagrams used in sales comparison typically list a unit of comparison along one coordinate axis and the unit price on the other. The coordinates of each comparable are plotted on the graph. Table 17.1 lists the sale prices, gross living areas, and price per gross living area of nine comparable properties. These data are plotted on the scatter diagram in Figure 17.1.

Table 17.1	Tabular Representation of Data								
Sale	A	B	C	D	E	F	G	H	I
Price	$84,000	$72,000	$96,000	$92,000	$89,000	$83,000	$79,000	$81,000	$85,000
Gross living area in sq. ft.	2,150	1,800	2,700	2,500	2,400	2,100	1,900	2,060	2,300
Price per sq. ft.	$39.00	$40.00	$35.60	$36.80	$37.10	$39.50	$41.60	$39.30	$37.00

Note: Figures are rounded

Figure 17.1   Scatter Diagram

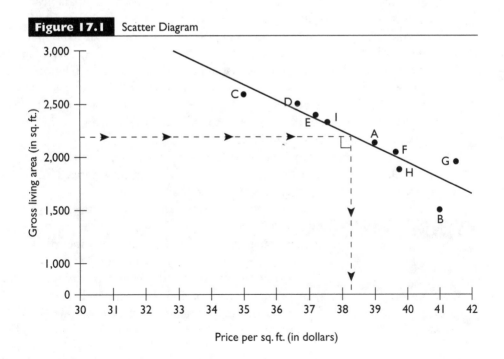

Price per sq. ft. (in dollars)

An appraiser could analyze this scatter diagram to derive an estimate of the unit price of the subject property. A line or curve that corresponds to the central tendency of the scatter pattern is plotted. Then the position of the subject property along this line or curve is located by drawing a perpendicular line from the gross living area of the subject on the vertical axis of the graph to the point where it intersects the curve. A perpendicular line drawn from this point to the horizontal axis will indicate the unit price of the subject property.

The sale properties' comparability in relation to the subject is also depicted in the diagram. This analytical tool allows an appraiser to distinguish readily between closely comparable properties and those that are less comparable. However, the points in a scatter diagram do not always fall into a roughly linear pattern. When no line approximating a central tendency is suggested by the graph, the scatter diagram technique is unreliable.

DOLLAR AND PERCENTAGE ADJUSTMENTS

Quantitative adjustments may be applied to the prices of comparables in two ways. The dollar amount of the difference can be calculated and added to or subtracted from the total price or unit price of the comparable. Adjustments derived from paired data analysis are often entered on a market data grid as dollar adjustments. Alternatively, the relationship between the subject and a comparable property can be expressed in terms of a percentage of value. When percentage adjustments are employed, the price of the comparable is adjusted to reflect a percentage of increase or decrease in value.

The adjustments required for certain elements of comparison, in particular for market conditions and location, are frequently derived in percentages. Sales data may indicate that market conditions have resulted in a 5% increase in overall prices during the past year or that prices for a particular category of property have recently increased 0.5% per month. Similarly, an appraiser may analyze market data and conclude that properties in one location command prices that are approximately 10% higher than similar properties in another location.

Whether they are expressed in dollars or percentages, all adjustments are derived from the sale price of the comparable property.

SEQUENCE OF ADJUSTMENTS

Once quantitative adjustments are derived, they must be applied to the price of the comparable. In applying both percentage and dollar adjustments, the sequence of adjustments is important. Percentage adjustments are not transitive—i.e., their order is not interchangeable. Consequently, whenever percentage adjustments are added to or subtracted from an intermediate price in the adjustment process, the sequence should be carefully considered. This sequence is determined by the market data and the appraiser's analysis of those data. For purposes of illustration, the following sequence of dollar adjustments is provided:

1. Property rights conveyed
2. Financing (cash equivalency)
3. Conditions of sale (motivation)
4. Expenditures made immediately after purchase
5. Market conditions (time)

After applying these five adjustments, additional adjustments may be made for

6. Location
7. Physical characteristics
8. Economic characteristics
9. Use/zoning
10. Non-realty components of value[1]

The sequence of adjustments is illustrated in Table 17.2.

MARKET DATA GRID

Data on the subject property and comparable properties may be organized and analyzed on a market data grid. Each important

> **TERM**
>
> **sequence of adjustments:** the order in which quantitative adjustments are applied to the sale prices of comparable properties. The sequence of adjustments is determined by the market and through analysis of the data.

> **CONCEPT**
>
> When percentage and dollar adjustments are applied to the sale prices of comparables, the sequence must be carefully considered.

---

1. The sequence illustrated in this chapter is based on a sequence first presented by Halbert C. Smith in *Real Estate Appraisal* (Columbus, Ohio: Grid, Inc., 1976). While it is a typical sequence for applying quantitative adjustments, it is not the only sequence in which such adjustments may be made.

Table 17.2 Market Adjustments Applied on a Gross Dollar Basis

Element	Subject	Sale 1	Sale 2	Sale 3	Sale 4	Sale 5
Sale price	?	$201,000	$200,500	$205,000	$195,000	$205,500
Real property rights conveyed	Fee simple	Fee simple	Fee simple	Fee simple	Fee simple	Fee simple
Comparison		Same	Same	Same	Same	Same
Adjustment		0	0	0	0	0
Financing	Conventional	Seller	Conventional	Seller	Seller	Conventional
Comparison		Superior	Similar	Superior	Superior	Similar
Adjustment		– 3,500	0	– 3,500	– 3,500	0
Conditions of sale	Arm's-length	Arm's-length	Arm's-length	Arm's-length	Arm's-length	Arm's-length
Comparison		Same	Same	Same	Same	Same
Adjustment		0	0	0	0	0
Adjusted price*		$197,500	$200,500	$201,500	$191,500	$205,500
Expenditures made immediately after purchase	None	None	None	None	None	None
Comparison		Same	Same	Same	Same	Same
Adjustment		0	0	0	0	0
Date of sale	Current	One year ago	Current	Current	One year ago	Current
Comparison		Inferior	Similar	Similar	Inferior	Similar
Adjustment		+ 5,000	0	0	+ 5,000	0
Adjusted price†		$202,500	$200,500	$201,500	$196,500	$205,500
Location	Average	Good	Average	Average	Average	Average
Comparison		Superior	Similar	Similar	Similar	Similar
Adjustment		– 6,000	0	0	0	0

Table 17.2 Market Adjustments Applied on a Gross Dollar Basis *(continued)*

Element	Subject	Sale 1	Sale 2	Sale 3	Sale 4	Sale 5
Garage	2-car	1-car	2-car	1-car	1-car	2-car
Comparison		Inferior	Similar	Inferior	Inferior	Similar
Adjustment		+4,000	0	+4,000	+4,000	0
Pool	No	No	No	Yes	No	Yes
Comparison		Similar	Similar	Superior	Similar	Superior
Adjustment		0	0	−5,000	0	−5,000
Use/Zoning	Single-family residence	Same	Same	Same	Same	Same
Comparison		Similar	Similar	Similar	Similar	Similar
Adjustment		0	0	0	0	0
Economic characteristics	None	None	None	None	None	None
Comparison		Similar	Similar	Similar	Similar	Similar
Adjustment		0	0	0	0	0
Non-realty components	None	None	None	None	None	None
Comparison		Similar	Similar	Similar	Similar	Similar
Adjustment		0	0	0	0	0
Net adjustment‡		−2,000	0	−1,000	+4,000	−5,000
Final adjusted sale price		$200,500	$200,500	$200,500	$200,500	$200,500
For reconciliation purposes:						
Gross adjustment§		$18,500	0	$12,500	$12,500	$5,000
Total adjustment as percentage of sale price		9.20%	0.00%	6.10%	6.41%	2.43%

* Sale price adjusted for financing
† Sale price further adjusted for market conditions
‡ Difference between positive and negative adjustments made for location, garage, and the absence or presence of a pool
§ Total positive and negative adjustments applied to each comparable

difference between the subject and the comparable properties that can affect value is considered an element of comparison. Each element is assigned a row on the grid and the total prices or unit prices of the comparables are adjusted to reflect the value of these differences.

Market data grids can be extremely useful. They identify which comparables have the fewest differences from the subject and should be accorded the most weight in reconciliation. Market data grids also facilitate the totaling of adjustments to calculate the value differences between the subject property and each comparable.

Table 17.2 is a sample market data grid that reflects typical elements of comparison and the proper sequence of adjustments. The sample grid has a separate line for each applicable element of comparison. When the subject and a comparable are similar in regard to a given element of comparison, no adjustment is required for that element. This grid includes separate lines for comparison and adjustment to ensure that adjustments are made in a consistent manner. In this market data grid, adjustments are applied on a gross dollar basis.

QUANTITATIVE ADJUSTMENTS

Sales of comparable properties are analyzed so an appraiser can judge how property differences affect price and identify whether individual elements of comparison must be adjusted and by how much. Any recent sale of the subject property should also be analyzed to see whether it falls within the range reflected by the sales considered comparable. Several methods can be used to study market data to determine quantitative adjustments, including analysis of paired data and units of comparison.

Paired Data Analysis

Through paired data analysis an appraiser can derive the amount of value attributable to a difference in an element of comparison directly from the market data. When two sales considered comparable are very similar in all but one characteristic, the appraiser may be able to conclude that the difference in this single characteristic accounts for the difference in their prices.

For example, assume that a property has been sold twice within a short period of time and no changes have occurred in the property or the neighborhood during this period. An adjustment for market conditions may be derived from the prices of the two transactions. Similarly, if two very similar properties located in different neighborhoods are sold within a limited period, an adjustment for location can be calculated from their sale prices. After adjustments are made for market conditions and location, the effects of other variables on price should be isolated, if possible. In practice, it is often difficult for an appraiser to identify several matched pairs from among the sales of comparable or similar properties. Listings and offers to buy can also be used for this analysis, but they provide less reliable results.

Usually the number of available comparables is limited and an appraiser rarely finds pairs that directly indicate the effect of each element of comparison. Many pairs of comparables on the market data grid differ from one another in more than one element, so it can be difficult to isolate the effects of each individual variation. Often a more complicated procedure must be applied to obtain the necessary information. To apply this procedure the appraiser makes a series of paired data identifications and repeated adjustments directly on the market data grid. Each step in this procedure is demonstrated in the following example.

CONCEPT

Paired data analysis can be applied when two comparable properties are identical or very similar in all but one characteristic. The difference in their sale prices is attributed to the dissimilar characteristic.

Paired data analysis might be used to estimate the influence of an in-ground pool on the value of a comparable property.

Step 1

On a market data grid, the appraiser notes the significant differences between each comparable property and the subject property in the appropriate spaces. If a comparable is identical to the subject in a given respect, "same" is indicated on the grid (see Table 17.3).

Step 2

The appraiser finds a pair of comparables that differ from one another in only one respect. In this case, Sales 4 and 6 are paired because they differ only in the condition of the improvements (see Table 17.4).

Table 17.3 Step 1

	Subject	Sale 1	Sale 2	Sale 3	Sale 4	Sale 5	Sale 6
Price*	?	$105,000	$101,000	$96,000	$109,800	$103,000	$103,800
Condition of improvements	Good	Good (same)	Poor	Poor	Good (same)	Good (same)	Poor
Site shape	Irreg.	Reg.	Reg.	Irreg. (same)	Irreg. (same)	Reg.	Irreg. (same)
Garage	1-car	2-car	1-car (same)	1-car (same)	2-car	1-car (same)	2-car
View	Yes	No	Yes (same)	No	Yes (same)	No	Yes (same)
Access	Poor	Poor (same)	Poor (same)	Poor (same)	Good	Poor (same)	Good

* Throughout this example it will be assumed that the sale prices of the comparables have already been adjusted for property rights, financing, expenditures made immediately after purchase, market conditions, conditions of sale, and location.

Table 17.4 Step 2

	Subject	Sale 1	Sale 2	Sale 3	Sale 4	Sale 5	Sale 6
Price	?	$105,000	$101,000	$96,000	**$109,800**	$103,000	**$103,800**
Condition of improvements	Good	Good (same)	Poor	Poor	**Good (same)**	Good (same)	**Poor**
Site shape	Irreg.	Reg.	Reg.	Irreg. (same)	**Irreg. (same)**	Reg.	**Irreg. (same)**
Garage	1-car	2-car	1-car (same)	1-car (same)	**2-car**	1-car (same)	**2-car**
View	Yes	No	Yes (same)	No	**Yes (same)**	No	**Yes (same)**
Access	Poor	Poor (same)	Poor (same)	Poor (same)	**Good**	Poor (same)	**Good**

Step 3

Using paired data analysis, the appraiser determines whether the presence of the feature in question is an advantage or a disadvantage, and how much value the market ascribes to it.

Next the direction of the adjustment must be determined. If the comparable is inferior to the subject, an upward adjustment is called for. If the comparable is superior to the subject, a downward adjustment is needed. If the comparable is equal to the subject in this respect, no adjustment is made. The goal of the analysis is to find what the price of the comparable would be if the comparable were more like the subject.

Table 17.5 Step 3

	Subject	Sale 1	Sale 2	Sale 3	Sale 4	Sale 5	Sale 6
Price	?	$105,000	$101,000	$96,000	$109,800	$103,000	$103,800
Condition of improvements	Good	Good (same)	Poor + **$6,000**	Poor + **$6,000**	Good (same)	Good (same)	Poor + **$6,000**
Site shape	Irreg.	Reg.	Reg.	Irreg. (same)	Irreg. (same)	Reg.	Irreg. (same)
Garage	1-car	2-car	1-car (same)	1-car (same)	2-car	1-car (same)	2-car
View	Yes	No	Yes (same)	No	Yes (same)	No	Yes (same)
Access	Poor	Poor (same)	Poor (same)	Poor (same)	Good	Poor (same)	Good

An adjustment amount is entered on the grid *only* when the comparable differs from the subject. In this example, the good condition of the improvements in Sale 4 is an advantage valued at $6,000 (see Table 17.5).

Step 4

The price of each comparable that differs from the subject is adjusted by the amount indicated. After all necessary adjustments are made, the impact of a single difference will have been identified in the market data grid (see Table 17.6). Once one variable has been eliminated, other pairs of comparables that are identical in all but one characteristic can be identified by repeating Steps 2, 3, and 4.

Table 17.6 Step 4

	Subject	Sale 1	Sale 2	Sale 3	Sale 4	Sale 5	Sale 6
Price	?	$105,000	$101,000	$96,000	$109,800	$103,000	$103,800
Cond. of improv.			+ 6,000	+ 6,000			+ 6,000
Adjusted price			**$107,000**	**$102,000**			**$109,800**
Site shape	Irreg.	Reg.	Reg.	Irreg. (same)	Irreg. (same)	Reg.	Irreg. (same)
Garage	1-car	2-car	1-car (same)	1-car (same)	2-car	1-car (same)	2-car
View	Yes	No	Yes (same)	No	Yes (same)	No	Yes (same)
Access	Poor	Poor (same)	Poor (same)	Poor (same)	Good	Poor (same)	Good

Step 5

Steps 2, 3, and 4 are repeated until the values of all differences in the elements of comparison have been found (see Table 17.7). The adjusted figures are the prices the comparable properties would have sold for if they had resembled the subject property more closely. These figures provide the basis for deriving a value indication for the subject property using paired data analysis.

Table 17.7 Step 5	Subject	Sale 1	Sale 2	Sale 3	Sale 4	Sale 5	Sale 6
Price	?	$105,000	$101,000	$96,000	$109,800	$103,000	$103,800
Cond. of improv.			+ 6,000	+ 6,000			+ 6,000
Adjusted price			$107,000	$102,000			$109,800
Site shape		− 1,000	− 1,000			− 1,000	
Adjusted price		$104,000	$106,000			$102,000	
Garage		− 2,000			− 2,000		− 2,000
Adjusted price		$102,000			$107,800		$107,800
View		+ 4,000		+ 4,000		+ 4,000	
Adjusted price		$106,000		$106,000		$106,000	
Access					− 1,800		− 1,800
Adjusted price					$106,000		$106,000
Comparable prices after adjustment		$106,000	$106,000	$106,000	$106,000	$106,000	$106,000

In this example the adjusted prices of the comparables are identical. The adjusted prices will not coincide when two sets of paired data yield different adjustments for the same element of comparison, or when other techniques are applied to produce different adjustments. In practice, the adjusted prices of comparable properties are almost never identical. (Note: For educational purposes, data for this example have been chosen to produce a result that would not require reconciliation, which is covered later in the chapter.)

Limitations of Paired Data Analyses

This brief discussion of paired data analysis may seem to suggest that identifying the effects of property differences from market data is a straightforward procedure that can produce accurate, complete mathematical results in all appraisals. Such an impression would be misleading. Appraisal is an art in which appraisers apply their judgment to the analysis and interpretation of data. Paired data analysis is a tool that an appraiser can apply to market data in some circumstances. When used in conjunction with other tools, this type of analysis supports and guides the appraiser's judgment, but it does not take its place.[2]

Perfect sets of comparables that vary in a single, identifiable respect are rarely found. Because properties that are sufficiently similar to the subject are usually limited in number, the decision to apply paired data analysis in a given situation is a matter of judgment. Often the sampling size may not be large enough to provide a solid statistical foundation for the appraiser's conclusions.

Nevertheless, paired data procedures are important valuation tools that appraisers should use whenever possible. Identifying matched pairs and isolating the effects of variables is a practical methodology for studying market data, even if a comprehensive paired data analysis cannot be performed. When only a narrow sample of market data is available, which would not lend itself to statistical analysis, paired data analysis can be used to test the results of other analytical procedures.

> **CONCEPT**
>
> The use of paired data analysis is limited because perfect sets of comparables that differ in only one respect are rarely found.

Units of Comparison

Units of comparison can also be used to identify the effects of variations in property characteristics. Units of comparison play various roles in different parts of the valuation process, but they are especially significant in the analysis of comparables, where they can be applied to derive adjustments on a per-unit basis.

Although properties can be divided into many different component parts, only a few units of comparison are commonly used in residential valuations. One property is generally compared with another in terms of the total property price, the price per square foot

---

2. For example, an appraiser may find three properties that are alike in all characteristics except that House A has a garage and Houses B and C do not. The difference in price between House A and House B is $2,000. Yet House C, which has no garage, is sold for the same price as House A, which has a garage.

   Another appraiser may find two comparable houses, priced at $50,000 and $52,000, which differ in four features. House Y does not have a garage. House Z does not have a backyard fence. House Y is painted white. House Z is painted blue. House Y is 17 years old. House Z is 15 years old. It may be virtually impossible to determine how much each of the four variables has contributed to the $2,000 price differential.

of gross living area, the price per room, or the price per living unit. Parcels of land may be compared in terms of total price, price per acre, price per lot, price per square foot, or price per front foot.

By applying units of comparison, an appraiser can make adjustments for size differences between the subject and comparable properties. After adjustments are made for financing, conditions of sale, market conditions, and location, an appraiser may need to isolate the amount of value difference attributable to size. The appraiser can use a scatter diagram, plotting the square footage of gross living area on one axis and the price per square foot on the other. The results may then be reconciled to derive the amount of the size adjustment.

Adjustments may be applied on a unit sale price basis as the market data grid in Table 17.8 illustrates. Units of comparison may also facilitate paired data analysis. Their use can help isolate the effects of differences and resolve problems. Units of comparison are applied to paired data analysis in four steps:

1. Select a relevant unit of comparison such as price per square foot of gross living area.
2. Divide the sale price of each comparable by the number of units in that comparable. If, for example, the price of the comparable is $104,000 and its gross living area is 1,600 square feet, the calculation would be

$$\$104,000/1,600 \text{ sq. ft.} = \$65 \text{ per sq. ft.}$$

   The derivation of a unit price helps reveal relationships and facilitates analysis of paired data and scatter diagrams.
3. Analyze paired data making adjustments to the unit sale price of the comparable rather than the total sale price.
4. After all adjustments have been made, multiply the adjusted unit sale price of each comparable by the number of units of comparison in the subject to obtain a value indication for the subject property.

Other Quantitative Adjustment Techniques

In addition to paired data analysis, an appraiser may use several other techniques to arrive at quantitative adjustments in the sales comparison approach—e.g., judgment, cost and depreciated cost data, rental

Table 17.8	Market Data Grid Adjustments Applied on a Unit Price Basis						

Element	Subject	Sale 1	Sale 2	Sale 3	Sale 4	Sale 5	Sale 6
Sale price	?	$99,000	$100,050	$96,100	$104,000	$99,200	$105,000
Gross living area in sq. ft.	1,425	1,650	1,450	1,550	1,600	1,600	1,500
Unit price		$60	$69	$62	$65	$62	$70
Real property rights conveyed							
Comparison	Fee simple	Same	Same	Same	Same	Same	Same
Adjustment		0	0	0	0	0	0
Financing	Conv.	Conv.	Special	Conv.	Conv.	Conv.	Conv.
Comparison		Similar	Superior	Similar	Similar	Similar	Similar
Adjustment		0	– $2	0	0	0	0
Conditions of sale							
Comparison	Arm's-length	Same	Same	Same	Same	Same	Same
Adjustment		0	0	0	0	0	0
Adjusted price*		$60	$67	$62	$65	$62	$70
Expenditures made immediately after purchase							
Comparison	None	Same	Same	Same	Same	Same	Same
Adjustment		0	0	0	0	0	0
Date of sale	Current	Current	6 mos.	Current	Current	6 mos.	Current
Comparison		Similar	Inferior	Similar	Similar	Inferior	Similar
Adjustment		0	+ $3	0	0	+ $3	0
Adjusted price†		$60	$70	$62	$65	$65	$70
Location	Average	Fair	Average	Fair	Fair	Average	Average
Comparison		Inferior	Similar	Inferior	Inferior	Similar	Similar
Adjustment		+ $5	0	+ $5	+ $5	0	0
Garage	2-car	1-car	2-car	2-car	2-car	1-car	2-car
Comparison		Inferior	Similar	Similar	Similar	Inferior	Similar
Adjustment		+ $2	0	0	0	+ $2	0
Quality of construction	Average	Fair	Average	Fair	Average	Fair	Average
Comparison		Inferior	Similar	Inferior	Similar	Inferior	Similar
Adjustment		+ $3	0	+ $3	0	+ $3	0
Net adjustment‡		+ $10	0	+ $8	+ $5	+ $5	0
Final adjusted sale price		$70	$70	$70	$70	$70	$70
For reconciliation purposes:							
Gross adjustment§		$10	$5	$8	$5	$8	0
Total adjustment as percentage of sale price		16.67%	7.25%	12.90%	7.69%	12.90%	0.00%

* Unit sale price adjusted for financing

† Unit sale price further adjusted for market conditions

‡ Adjustments for location, garage size, and quality of construction

§ Total positive and negative adjustments applied to each comparable

and land value data, depreciation rates, regression analysis, ranking analysis.

In some situations in which paired data analysis is not conclusive, the appraiser may apply judgment to resolve the problem. For example, assume one house has a two-car garage, brick siding, and a fenced yard and sold for $120,000. Another house has a one-car garage, vinyl siding, and an unfenced yard and sold for $116,000. Based on an understanding of buyers' preferences in the market, the appraiser knows that the two-car garage is the most appealing feature of the first house and accounts for the entire $4,000 price differential.

Cost and depreciated cost data may be used in making adjustments. Especially useful are data on the costs of upgrading existing homes and installing amenity features in subdivision houses under construction. Buyers of new homes usually purchase a basic model and select various upgrade features to be installed during construction. Such features include garages, decks, basements, and air-conditioning systems. Interviews with contractors, construction experts, buyers, sellers, and brokers can provide an appraiser with information on the costs of such features. In appraising older houses, the appraiser may arrive at the value contribution of an amenity feature by adjusting its current cost downward, i.e., depreciating the current cost for the age of the house.

> **CONCEPT**
>
> Other adjustment techniques make use of cost and depreciated cost data, especially data on the costs of upgrading existing housing and outfitting new residences with additional amenities. Interviews with contractors, construction experts, buyers, sellers, and brokers can provide useful information. Rental and land value data may help to determine adjustments for changes in market conditions and differences in location or physical condition.

The difference in rent attributable to a difference between otherwise similar income-producing properties can be capitalized to derive an indication of the difference in the values of the properties. For example, the difference in the rent charged for two duplexes, one with a garage and the other without, can be multiplied by the appropriate gross rent multiplier to derive the amount of the adjustment for a garage. (See the discussion of the income capitalization approach in Chapter 18.)

Rental data can also be used in another way. In markets where current sales data are not available because few sales have been transacted recently, an appraiser may calculate an adjustment for market conditions by analyzing changes in rents since the last sales occurred. For example, if rents have increased from $750 to $770 since the last sales were transacted, the appraiser may conclude that a market adjustment of 2.6% (20/750) is warranted.

Data on the rate of depreciation may also be used to derive an adjustment for the age of the property and condition of the improvement (physical characteristics). For example, using market-extracted depreciation (as discussed in Chapter 14), the appraiser is able to establish a 2% average annual rate of depreciation for properties in the subject market. Thus a 12-year-old subject property is assumed to be 24% depreciated, while a 15-year-old comparable is 30% depreciated. In this situation an upward adjustment of 6% to the sale price of the comparable, less land value, would seem to be appropriate.

Differences in land values may also reflect the size of an adjustment for locational differences (i.e., immediate neighborhood, traffic density, view, frontage, and siting). After the appraiser estimates the land value of each comparable at the time of its sale, direct comparison of these values should shed light on the amount of a location adjustment.

Regression analysis can be used to isolate and test the significance of specific value determinants. Regression analysis reveals apparent relationships between the values of different variables and their tendency to vary regularly with one another. Due to the ever-increasing power and affordability of personal computers, as well as the greater acceptance of statistical methods among practioners, more real estate professionals are using regression analysis as an analytical tool in both appraisal practice and related real estate research. Data of sufficient quantity and quality are now available, as are the hardware and software needed to apply statistical methods to a relatively wide range of valuation assignments.

TERM

regression analysis: a statistical method that examines the relationship between one or more independent variables and a dependent variable by plotting points on a graph; used to identify and weight analytical factors and to make forecasts.

QUALITATIVE ANALYSIS

Qualitative analysis can be undertaken after quantitative adjustments have been made. The analysis of qualitative differences generally forms the basis for reconciliation by revealing which comparables are the more reliable indicators of the value of the subject. The process of qualitative analysis takes into account the inefficiencies of real estate markets and the difficulty of precisely mea-

CONCEPT

Qualitative analysis is often used in conjunction with quantitative adjustments. This analysis takes into account value influences that cannot be determined with mathematical precision from available market data.

suring the differences between comparable properties and the subject. Techniques for studying qualitative differences among properties include relative comparison analysis and ranking analysis.

Relative Comparison Analysis

Relative comparison analysis is the study of the relationships indicated by market data without recourse to quantification. Appraisers often use this technique because it allows for the imprecisions and imperfections that are characteristic of real estate markets. In relative comparison analysis, adjustments for differences among various elements of comparison are expressed in qualitative terms. The appraiser determines whether, on an overall basis, the comparable is inferior, superior, or equal to the subject property.

CONCEPT

Relative comparison analysis makes allowances for the imprecisions and imperfections of real estate markets.

As an example, consider a 1,500-sq.-ft. single-family home in good condition with 3 bedrooms, 2 bathrooms, and a 2-car garage. The location and view of the subject property are considered average for the market. The fee simple interest is being appraised for an arm's-length sale of the property with conventional financing terms.

All the comparable properties have 3 bedrooms, 2 bathrooms, and 2-car garages, and all were sold in arm's-length transactions with conventional market financing. Furthermore, no adjustments are needed for real property rights conveyed or expenditures made immediately after purchase. In addition, the market for single-family homes had been stable for the past 18 months, with negligible price fluctuations. The data used in the relative comparison analysis process are summarized in Table 17.9.

The first comparable property, a 1,600-sq.-ft. home in good condition and of average quality construction, was sold recently for $174,800. The property is considered to have better access to transportation routes and a better view than the subject. The price per square foot of Sale 1 is $109.25.

The second comparable, a 1,550-sq.-ft. home in fair condition and of poor quality construction, was sold six months previously for $157,500. Sale 2, which has a view and location similar in quality to the subject, has a price per square foot of $101.61.

Sale 3, a 1,450-sq.-ft. single-family property in fair condition and of poor quality construction, sold three months previously for $150,000, which indicates a price per square foot of $103.45. The location of the

Table 17.9 Market Data Grid for Relative Comparison Analysis

	Subject	Sale 1	Sale 2	Sale 3	Sale 4	Sale 5
Sale price	?	$174,800	$157,500	$150,000	$147,000	$161,550
Size in square feet	1,500	1,600	1,550	1,450	1,400	1,550
Price per square foot	?	$109.25	$101.61	$103.45	$105	$104.23
Real property rights conveyed	Fee simple	Fee simple	Fee simple	Fee simple	Fee simple	Fee simple
Financing	Conventional	Conventional	Conventional	Conventional	Conventional	Conventional
Conditions of sale	Arm's-length	Arm's-length	Arm's-length	Arm's-length	Arm's-length	Arm's-length
Expenditures made immediately after purchase	None	None	None	None	None	None
Date of sale	Current	Current	6 months ago	3 months ago	9 months ago	Current
Location (access)	Average	Good (Superior)	Average (Similar)	Poor (Inferior)	Average (Similar)	Average (Similar)
Quality of construction	Average	Average (Similar)	Poor (Inferior)	Poor (Inferior)	Average (Similar)	Average (Similar)
View	Average	Good (Superior)	Average (Similar)	Good (Superior)	Average (Similar)	Poor (Inferior)
Condition of improvements	Good	Good (Similar)	Fair (Inferior)	Fair (Inferior)	Excellent (Superior)	Good (Similar)
Overall comparability		**Superior**	**Inferior**	**Inferior**	**Superior**	**Inferior**

comparable property is considered inferior to the subject, but the view afforded by the less accessible site is considered superior.

The fourth comparable property is a 1,400-sq.-ft. home in excellent condition and of average quality construction. Nine months previously, the property sold for $147,000, indicating a price per square foot of $105. The location and view elements of comparison of Sale 4 are considered similar in quality to those of the subject.

The final comparable, a 1,550-sq.-ft. property in good condition and of average quality construction, sold for $161,550 recently. The location of Sale 5 is considered similar to that of the subject, but the view is considered inferior. Sale 5 had a price per square foot of $104.23.

Of the five comparable properties, Sales 1 and 4 are superior to the subject property, and Sales 2, 3, and 5 are inferior. To determine a bracket for the value of the subject property, the comparables are arranged in order relative to their comparability:

Superior	Sale 1	$109.25
Superior	Sale 4	$105.00
	Subject	
Inferior	Sale 5	$104.23
Inferior	Sale 3	$103.45
Inferior	Sale 2	$101.61

The unit price of the subject property should be greater than that of the highest comparable of inferior quality and less than that of the lowest comparable of superior quality. In this example, the value of the subject property should fall within the range of $104.23 to $105.00.

If the comparables are all superior or all inferior, only a lower or upper bound can be set and no range of possible values for the subject can be defined. If the available comparable market data do not bracket the subject property, other analytical techniques, such as the use of quantitative adjustments, should be considered.

Ranking analysis can deepen the appraiser's understanding of the influence on value of the various qualitative property characteristics.

CONCEPT

Ranking analysis arrays properties according to their degree of similarity or dissimilarity to the subject.

Ranking Analysis

Ranking analysis is generally used in conjunction with relative comparison analysis. Comparable properties are arrayed either in descending or ascending order according to their degree of similarity or dissimilarity to the subject property.

Ranking the comparables in the previous example generates the following data:

	Sale 1	Sale 2	Sale 3	Sale 4	Sale 5
Location (Access)	Superior	Similar	Inferior	Similar	Similar
Quality of construction	Similar	Inferior	Inferior	Similar	Similar
View	Superior	Similar	Superior	Similar	Inferior
Condition of improvements	Similar	Inferior	Inferior	Superior	Similar
Overall comparability	**Superior**	**Inferior**	**Inferior**	**Superior**	**Inferior**

Arrayed in this format the number of qualitative differences can be counted easily, and the appraiser can see that Sales 4 and 5, with only one qualitative difference each, are the most similar to the subject property.

When combined with the application of quantitative adjustments, relative comparison and ranking analysis form the basis for reconciliation in the sales comparison approach.

RECONCILIATION

The final step in the sales comparison approach is the reconciliation of data. In this phase of the valuation process, the appraiser reviews the quality of the data and analyzes the appropriateness of the methodology applied, asking questions like:

- How reliable were the sources that supplied data on each sale considered comparable?
- Did the field inspection corroborate the factual data obtained from secondary sources?
- Was all information obtained from the parties to the sale verified?

To begin the process of reconciliation, an appraiser asks, "What could possibly be wrong with the data I have collected?"

After the legal, transactional, physical, and locational data on each sale considered comparable have been reviewed, the appraiser analyzes the data sources and the procedures used to derive adjustments, asking the following questions:

- What sales information was used?
- Was the sample large enough?

> **CONCEPT**
>
> In the reconciliation step of the sales comparison approach, an appraiser reviews the reliability, type, and scope of the data and evaluates the analytical procedures used. The value penalty or reward attributed to a specific characteristic should not be considered more than once; the relative advantages and disadvantages of property features with mixed benefits must be weighed.

- If listings and offers were used as well as sales, how reliable are these data?
- How similar to the subject are the properties used in the database?
- How old are the data and do they conform to current market patterns?
- If they do not, why not?

The analytical procedures used to derive adjustments are also investigated by asking the following questions:

- Was paired data analysis used?
- If so, how well matched were the paired sales?
- Were scatter diagrams drawn?
- Which of the procedures applied is most reliable given the constraints of the data?

All relevant analytical procedures should be applied to the data so the results of each analysis can be tested against the results of others. If these results vary widely, the appraiser should find out why; if the results are similar, they must be reconciled. The greatest weight is given to the most reliable procedure.

Each adjustment must be fully understood before it is applied. Often appraisers erroneously reward or penalize a comparable twice for the same difference. If both quantitative adjustments and qualitative analysis are employed, adjustments must be applied consistently for each element of comparison—i.e., qualitative analysis of a particular element of comparison should not be performed on some comparables while quantitative adjustments are made to other comparables for the same element of comparison. Certain differences between properties may represent mixed blessings. For example, a property may suffer from special tax assessments but benefit from the additional services that these taxes support. It is inconsistent to penalize a property for an obvious disadvantage without considering a compensating advantage, which may be less obvious.

Once all the prices of the comparables have been adjusted, a range of prices is indicated for the value of the subject property. These different prices must be reconciled. Greater reliance is generally placed on comparables that were sold most recently and those that are most similar to the subject property. Comparables that require few adjustments are also highly reliable. Near the bottom of the market data grid there is a line labeled "For reconciliation purposes." Here the appraiser indicates the total adjustment to the sale price of each comparable and the total adjustment as a percentage of the price. This figure can help the appraiser assess each sale's comparability and aid in reconciliation.

Because the market is not perfect, many appraisers arrive at a range of values for the subject property in the reconciliation phase of the sales comparison approach. Often a single value opinion can be obtained only after all three approaches are completed. An appraisal is more credible if the indications of value derived in the other approaches fall into the range suggested by the sales comparison approach.

In the example used in the discussion of qualitative analysis, the unit price of the subject was estimated to be within the range generated in the relative comparison analysis—i.e., $104.23 to $105.00. Ranking analysis showed that Sales 4 and 5 had the least number of qualitative differences from the subject property, but Sale 5 could reasonably be considered the most comparable because a deficiency in the view amenity would probably have less of an impact on value than the superior quality of the improvements in Sale 4. Considering the results of the qualitative analysis, the final unit price of the subject property should be weighted toward the price of Sale 5 within the range, yielding an estimate of $104.50 per sq. ft. This figure produces a total value indication of $156,750 for the 1,500-sq.-ft. subject property.

SAMPLE APPLICATION

The following appraisal problem illustrates the application of quantitative adjustment techniques, qualitative analysis, and an appropriate sequence of adjustments in the sales comparison approach. The problem solution is presented as it might appear in an appraisal report.

The subject property is a 10-year-old single-family residence on a single lot. It has the original kitchen, a one-car garage, and no air-conditioning. It contains 1,100 square feet of gross living area. The construction quality of the structure is good, and the site enjoys a lake view considered an amenity by the market.

Comparable A is a current cash sale of a property that was sold for $91,500. The house is on a double lot and has a modern kitchen, a one-car garage, and no air-conditioning. The 10-year-old property contains 1,100 square feet of gross living area. The structure is of good construction quality, but the site does not have the view amenity of the subject.

Comparable B was sold a year ago for $73,800 with market financing. The 10-year-old house is on a single lot and has an old kitchen, a one-car garage, and no air-conditioning. It contains 1,150 square feet of gross living area. The house features a similar view of the lake as the subject, and the construction quality of the structure is excellent.

Comparable C is a current cash sale of a property that was sold for $82,000. The house is on a single lot and has an old kitchen, a two-car garage, and central air-conditioning. It contains 1,300 square feet of gross living area. The structure is only of average construction quality, and the site does not enjoy the same view of the lake as the subject. The 12-year-old property was also sold two years ago for $74,550.

Comparable D is a current sale of a 14-year-old property that was sold for $80,000 with a 90% FHA loan requiring the seller to pay three points. The house is on a single lot with a view of the lake and has an old kitchen, a one-car garage, and central air-conditioning. It contains 1,200 square feet of gross living area. The construction quality of the structure is good.

Additional market data include these facts:

- Sites in this area are worth $10,000. The extra lot in Sale A could easily be sold for this amount.

- The cost to modernize a kitchen in the subject neighborhood averages $7,500. However, the appraiser's study of subsequent sales of homes with modern kitchens indicates that the market is willing to pay $10,000 more for a home with a modern kitchen.

- Central air-conditioning is currently available in a new development of similar homes, at a cost of $1,500. Many purchasers elect to have central air-conditioning installed as an upgrade feature. Although some homes in the subject neighborhood have central air-conditioning, an insufficiency of data rules out the use of paired data analysis to derive an adjustment for this feature.

- The average depreciation rate for homes in the subject's neighborhood is approximately 33.33%.

The first step toward solving the appraisal problem is to array the data by identifying both typical elements of comparison and those that are apparent from the problem statement. An array like Table 17.10 will help the appraiser determine which adjustments will not have to be made.

Analysis of the array indicates that three characteristics—property rights conveyed, conditions of sale, and expenditures made immediately after purchase—are similar for all the sales and for the subject property. Since these features are the same for all properties, they cannot account for differences in value and therefore may be elimi-

Table 17.10	Elements of Comparison				
	Subject	**Sale A**	**Sale B**	**Sale C**	**Sale D**
Property rights	Fee simple	Fee simple	Fee simple	Fee simple	Fee simple
Financing	Market	Cash	Market	Cash	3 points
Conditions of sale	Arm's-length	Arm's-length	Arm's-length	Arm's-length	Arm's-length
Expenditures made immediately after purchase	None	None	None	None	None
Date of sale	Current	Current	I year ago	Current	Current
Property age	10 years	10 years	10 years	12 years	14 years
Lot	Single	Double	Single	Single	Single
Kitchen	Old	Modern	Old	Old	Old
Garage	I-car	I-car	I-car	2-car	I-car
Air-conditioning	No	No	No	Yes	Yes
View amenity	Yes	No	Yes	No	Yes
Construction quality	Good	Good	Excellent	Average	Good
Size (*GLA*)	1,100 sq. ft.	1,100 sq. ft.	1,150 sq. ft.	1,300 sq. ft.	1,200 sq. ft.

nated from the adjustment grid. Many of the required adjustments can be derived from information given in the problem statement.

The financing adjustment for Sale D is calculated by multiplying the amount of the mortgage, $72,000 (90% of a sale price of $80,000), by 0.03 (i.e., the three points). Thus the price of Sale D is adjusted downward by $2,160 and the cash-equivalent price becomes $77,840.

The adjustment to Sale B for market conditions is derived by analyzing the sale price and resale price of Sale C, which sold two years prior to the current sale for $74,550. The total change over the two-year period was approximately 5% per year. Since Sale B sold one year ago, it is adjusted upward by 5%, or $3,690. After the adjustment for market conditions, the sale price of Sale B becomes $77,490.

The adjustment for the double lot in Sale A is $10,000, derived from the market data provided.

The adjustment for the modern kitchen in Sale A is $10,000, also derived from the market data. In this instance the adjustment is based on the contributory value of the modern kitchen, not the cost of modernization.

The contributory value of the central air-conditioning in Sales C and D is estimated to be $1,000. The cost of this feature in new construction is $1,500. Properties in the subject neighborhood are depreciated by approximately 33.33%. Since property components suffer similar depreciation, an air-conditioning system installed in a home in the subject neighborhood would reflect the overall depreciation of the property. Thus the basis of the adjustment is the depreciated cost of the air-conditioning.

After all these adjustments have been estimated, a market data grid (Table 17.11) can be used to help derive the remaining adjustment for the difference in garage size.

Table 17.11 Market Data Grid: Quantitative Adjustments

	Subject	Sale A	Sale B	Sale C	Sale D
Sale price	?	$91,500	$73,800	$82,000	$80,000
Financing	Market	Cash	Market	Cash	3 points
Adjustment		0	0	0	− 2,160
Cash equivalent price		$91,500	$73,800	$82,000	$77,840
Date of sale	Current	Current	I year ago	Current	Current
Adjustment		0	+ 3,690	0	0
Current cash equivalent price		$91,500	$77,490	$82,000	$77,840
Lot	Single	Double	Single	Single	Single
Adjustment		− 10,000	0	0	0
Kitchen	Old	Modern	Old	Old	Old
Adjustment		− 10,000	0	0	0
Air-conditioning	No	No	No	Yes	Yes
Adjustment		0	0	− 1,000	− 1,000
Property age	10 years	10 years	10 years	12 years	14 years
Adjustment		0	0	?	?
Garage	I-car	I-car	I-car	2-car	I-car
Adjustment		0	0	?	0
View amenity	Yes	No	Yes	No	Yes
Adjustment		?	0	?	0
Construction quality	Good	Good	Excellent	Average	Good
Adjustment		0	?	?	0

Adjustments for the last four elements of comparison listed in the Table 17.11 cannot be determined from the available market data, though they should contribute to differences in value. The value influence of these elements of comparison will be addressed later in qualitative analysis. The quantitative adjustments are applied to generate the adjusted sale prices shown in Table 17.12.

Table 17.12 Market Data Grid

	Subject	Sale A	Sale B	Sale C	Sale D
Sale price	?	$91,500	$73,800	$82,000	$80,000
Financing	Market	Cash	Market	Cash	3 points
Adjustment		0	0	0	− 2,160
Cash equivalent price		$91,500	$73,800	$82,000	$77,840
Date of sale	Current	Current	I year ago	Current	Current
Adjustment		0	+ 3,690	0	0
Current cash equivalent price		$91,500	$77,490	$82,000	$77,840
Lot	Single	Double	Single	Single	Single
Adjustment		− 10,000	0	0	0
Kitchen	Old	Modern	Old	Old	Old
Adjustment		− 10,000	0	0	0
Air conditioning	No	No	No	Yes	Yes
Adjustment		0	0	− 1,000	− 1,000
Net adjustments (for kitchen, air-conditioning, and garage)		− 20,000	0	− 1,000	− 1,000
Adjusted sale price		$71,500	$77,490	$81,000	$76,840

In this example, the range of value opinions is still somewhat broad. Qualitative analysis can be based on unit prices, which are derived by dividing the adjusted sale price of each comparable by the amount of gross living area. Reducing sale prices to a size-related unit price usually eliminates the need to make a size adjustment.

Newer homes generally sell for more than older homes. Comparables C and D, which are older than the subject, are probably inferior to the subject, while Comparables A and B are similar.

An adjustment for a larger garage cannot be isolated from an analysis of the available market data, but the extra space of the garage of Comparable C should add to the value of that property in comparison to the subject.

The view of the lake is desirable in this market and should increase property value. Comparables B and D have a view similar to the subject, but Comparables A and C do not and therefore they are probably slightly inferior to the subject.

The construction quality of the subject property is good, which is similar to the quality of the structures of Comparables A and D. The construction quality of Comparable B is excellent, though, which is superior to the subject, and the quality of construction of Comparable C is only average, which is inferior to the subject.

A qualitative analysis of all the attributes of the comparable properties that cannot be quantified is shown in Table 17.13. The data are arrayed in descending order in Table 17.14, bracketing the subject property according to the indicated prices per square foot of the comparables. The ranking analysis also shows the overall comparability of the subject property to the individual comparables.

Table 17.13 Market Data Grid for Qualitative Analysis

	Subject	Sale A	Sale B	Sale C	Sale D
Adjusted sale price	?	$71,500	$77,490	$81,000	$76,840
Gross living area	1,100 sq. ft.	1,100 sq. ft.	1,150 sq. ft.	1,300 sq. ft.	1,200 sq. ft.
Unit price	?	$65.00	$67.38	$62.31	$64.03
Property age	10 years	10 years	10 years	12 years	14 years
		Similar	Similar	Inferior	Inferior
Garage	1-car	1-car	1-car	2-car	1-car
		Similar	Similar	Superior	Similar
View amenity	Yes	No	Yes	No	Yes
		Inferior	Similar	Inferior	Similar
Construction quality	Good	Good	Excellent	Average	Good
		Similar	Superior	Inferior	Similar
Overall comparability		**Inferior**	**Superior**	**Inferior**	**Inferior**

Table 17.14 Ranking Analysis

Comparable	Price per Square Foot	Overall Comparability
B	$67.38	Superior
Subject		
A	$65.00	Inferior
D	$64.03	Inferior
C	$62.31	Inferior

Comparable A is most similar to the subject property with respect to gross living area, while Comparable D had the fewest number of qualitative differences. The unit price of Comparable A serves as the bottom of the bracket derived from qualitative analysis. The range can be reconciled at $65.00 per square foot and this unit price can be used to derive a value indication for the subject. The value of the subject property can therefore be estimated at $71,500 (1,100 sq. ft. x $65 per sqare foot).

CHAPTER

18 | THE INCOME CAPITALIZATION APPROACH

In the valuation of residential property, the income capitalization approach is only applicable to properties for which an active rental market exists. To apply the approach, an appraiser estimates the gross monthly income a property is expected to generate and capitalizes this income into a value indication using a gross rent multiplier (*GRM*).

The income capitalization approach is based on the assumption that the value of a rental property is directly related to its ability to produce income. The approach reflects the appraisal concept of anticipation, which affirms that value is created by the expectation of benefits to be derived in the future. Capitalization is the process of converting income into value. In one common capitalization procedure, a multiplier is applied to the anticipated income of a property to derive an indication of its value.

Different property types are valued with different income capitalization methods. The method and procedure selected should correspond closely to the market's perception of the relationship between income and value for the property being appraised. Only income capitalization with a gross rent multiplier is discussed here. This is usually the most appropriate procedure for valuing single-family residences. A similar procedure can be applied to two- to four-unit buildings. Generally the rental income of these properties is analyzed by applying additional units of comparison such as monthly rent per square foot of gross living area, per room, and per unit.[1] Appraisals of larger income-producing residential properties

CONCEPTS

The income capitalization approach is applicable to properties for which an active rental market exists.

To value an income-producing, single-family residential property, an appraiser estimates the rental income the property is expected to generate and converts this income into an indication of value by applying a gross rent multiplier.

TERM

capitalization: the conversion of income into value.

---

1. A refinement of this simple capitalization procedure is applied to two- to four-unit buildings. The procedure employs an effective gross rent multiplier, which is the ratio between the value or sale price of a property and its effective gross rent—i.e., gross monthly rental income minus vacancy and collection loss.

usually call for more advanced capitalization techniques and procedures, which are beyond the scope of this text.[2]

OUTLINE OF THE APPROACH

Income capitalization with a *GRM* is applied in three steps. To obtain a value indication for the subject property, an appraiser

1. Derives a *GRM* from market data. To do this, the appraiser finds recent sales of similar properties that were rented at the time of sale, divides the sale price of each property by its monthly rental income, and reconciles the results. Alternatively, an appraiser may derive a *GRM* from data on two very similar properties, one of which is owner-occupied and the other rented out, when the sale price of the former and the monthly rent of the latter are known.

2. Estimates the monthly market rent the subject property should command. This estimate is based on the actual rents of competitive properties that have been adjusted for the advantageous or disadvantageous features of the subject.

3. Multiplies the estimated monthly market rent for the subject by the estimated *GRM* to obtain a value indication for the subject property.

The income capitalization approach is often appropriate for the valuation of two- to four-unit residential properties.

APPLICABILITY

The income capitalization approach is only applicable to properties for which reliable sales and rental data exist. Residential properties that can produce income but are more typically owner-occupied may be valued with this approach if data are available. Assume, for example, that due to unfavorable economic conditions home purchases have declined. As a result, 20 units in a 200-site residential subdivision intended for owner-occupants have to be rented out instead. Some of these rental units are eventually sold to owners or investors. In this case, meaningful comparative data can be derived for application of the income capitalization approach.

2. For a complete discussion of the appraisal techniques used in the valuation of all types of multifamily properties, see *The Valuation of Apartment Properties* (Chicago: Appraisal Institute, 1999) by Arlen C. Mills, MAI, SRA, and Anthony Reynolds, MAI.

An active rental market for the subject property must exist to ensure a sufficient quantity of sales and rental data. The quality of the data is also important. The properties from which the gross rent multiplier is derived should be competitive with the subject property and similar to it in terms of market appeal, size, occupancy levels, lease characteristics, and expense ratios. The market rent estimated for the subject property should also be based on data from properties that are sufficiently comparable.

> **CONCEPT**
>
> Gross rent multipliers can be used when reliable sales and rental data are available. If a property cannot be put to an income-producing use due to legal or economic restrictions or if sufficient, appropriate data are not available, the income capitalization approach is inapplicable.

LIMITATIONS

The applicability of the income capitalization approach may be limited by legal and economic restrictions on property use. If, for example, the owner-occupant of a property is considering converting it to a rental use, zoning regulations must be investigated to determine if the contemplated use is legally permissible. Assuming the use is permitted, the costs and benefits of conversion must also be weighed.

The prevalence of rent control programs in some metropolitan areas affects the reliability of market rent data and the *GRM*s derived. Rent controls make future rental income less certain, but most rent control ordinances allow for some growth in rents and increased operating expenses can often be passed on to tenants. If rents are prevented from keeping pace with operating expenses, property owners may try to further reduce operating expenses or to divest themselves of the property through sale or condominium conversion. Therefore, rent controls can represent a value penalty. To determine the impact of rent controls on property values in a given area, an appraiser might compare income-producing properties subject to rent controls with similar properties that are not.[3]

GROSS RENT MULTIPLIER
Derivation of a *GRM* from Market Data

The first step in the income capitalization approach is the derivation of a gross rent multiplier (*GRM*) from market data. An appraiser

---

3. Harold A. Davidson, "The Impact of Rent Control on Apartment Investment," *The Appraisal Journal* (October 1978), Robert J. Strachota and Howard E. Shenehon, "Market Rent vs. Replacement Rent: Is Rent Control the Solution?" *The Appraisal Journal* (January 1983), and G. Donald Jud, John D. Benjamin, and G. Stacy Sirmans, "What Do We Know about Apartments and Their Markets?" *Journal of Real Estate Research*, Vol. 11, No. 3 (1996).

begins by gathering recent sales of properties that are competitive with the subject and similar to it in terms of lease, expense, and income characteristics. The price of each property is divided by the monthly rent from all units in the property as of the date of sale. (For two- to four-unit residential properties, the resulting *GRM* indications are reconciled into a single figure.) Differences in the properties are usually reflected in their rents, so *GRM*s are not adjusted.

A *GRM* reflects a typical ratio between the value or sale price of a property and its gross rent, which is the gross monthly rental income at the time of sale before expenses or vacancy and collection losses are deducted. When this ratio is applied to the subject property's market rent it will provide a reliable value indication if the properties from which it was derived are truly comparable. The division of utility expenses between tenants and the landlord must be similar. The properties analyzed must also have similar expense-to-income ratios and lease terms.

CONCEPTS

The comparable properties from which the *GRM* is derived must be similar to and competitive with the subject in terms of lease provisions, expenses, and income characteristics.

The reliability of the *GRM* depends on the comparability of the properties from which it is derived.

The rental properties from which the *GRM* is derived need not be identical to the subject, but they should be competitive with it. They should be located in the same market area as the subject property or a similar market area and appeal to tenants of approximately the same income levels and household sizes. Four-bedroom houses are usually not in direct competition with two-bedroom houses. Sales should be fairly recent, especially if the market appears to be changing. In some areas a *GRM* derived from data that are more than six months old may prove unreliable; in others a *GRM* derived from two-year-old data may still be valid.

At this point in the income capitalization approach, the appraiser is concerned with the relationship between property value and rent. Thus a competitive property that has a slightly higher rent than the subject because of its larger size or additional amenities can still be used to derive a *GRM* provided the competitive property has a correspondingly higher value. The ratio between property value and income usually changes more slowly than either value or income. The comparability of market data becomes even more critical in the second step of the income capitalization approach, when the appraiser analyzes the current rents of the most similar properties to estimate the rent that the subject property can command.

Expense Characteristics

The ratio between the operating expenses that the landlord incurs and the rent the building can command must be similar for the subject and all sale properties used in the analysis. Two houses that are equally desirable dwellings in the eyes of tenants may have different expense-to-income ratios. From a landlord's point of view, these properties will be regarded quite differently. It may be less economically productive to own and operate one building than to own and operate the other. A building that requires extraordinary maintenance or has higher taxes without higher rental income is obviously worth less. When such variations are found in the market data, the reliability of the *GRM* is diminished.

The typical operating expenses of rental properties can be divided into two categories:

1. *Fixed expenses* such as taxes and insurance charges that must be paid regardless of the level of occupancy.
2. *Variable expenses* that are determined by the level of occupancy. These include charges for routine cleaning, repair, and maintenance, for interior and exterior painting, garbage removal, and pest control, for electricity and other utilities paid by the landlord, and for other expense items.

An appraiser studies fixed and variable expenses by analyzing operating statements for the subject property and similar properties or by reviewing published statistics. This investigation is part of the rent survey and data collection effort.

Lease Provisions

The lease provisions applicable to the sale properties should be similar to those of the subject property. Because leases specify the obligations of the landlord and the tenant, differences in leases can influence the expenses the landlord must pay or the rent the property can command. Thus unusual lease provisions may distort the relationship between income and value in a property. A lease that is especially favorable to the tenant, for example, may command a higher-than-normal rent, although the value of the property is not proportionately higher.

> **TERM**
>
> **lease provisions:** language in a lease that specifies the obligations of the landlord and the tenant, e.g., lease period, amount of security deposit, division of expenses, penalties for breaking the lease or for late payment of rent, restrictions on tenant activities, etc.

Important Lease Provisions That Often Vary in Residential Properties	
• Lease period • Amount of security deposit (Some landlords may not require a security deposit, while others may insist on one-half the monthly rent, a full month's rent, or more.) • Division of expenses between tenant and landlord • Penalty for breaking lease • Penalty for late payment of rent • Restrictions on tenant activities	• Conditions that constitute violation of the lease by the tenant • Provisions for termination of the lease by the tenant or landlord • Landlord's maintenance obligations • Landlord's landscaping obligations • Furniture included in the lease agreement • Options to renew the lease • Conditions under which the tenant may sublet

Reconciling GRMs

After the market data are assembled and several indicated *GRM*s are derived, the appraiser reconciles the results and selects a *GRM* that is appropriate for the subject property. The greatest emphasis is placed on *GRM*s derived from properties that are most similar to the subject. Rent and property value generally move in tandem, so *GRM* ratios should remain fairly stable. The indicated *GRM*s are not adjusted because property differences are already reflected in the *GRM*s. By adjusting *GRM*s an appraiser would consider these differences twice. Adjustments are only made in the second step of the income capitalization approach when the market rent of the subject property is estimated.

> **CONCEPT**
>
> No adjustments are made to GRMs because differences between the comparable properties are already reflected in their rents.

Example

After gathering sales of similar properties and verifying their prices and rents, the appraiser arranges the market data shown in Table 18.1. The appraiser selects a gross rent multiplier of 110 because this is the multiplier derived from the properties that are most similar to the subject in terms of location, size, property features, and expense characteristics.

MONTHLY MARKET RENT ESTIMATE

To derive a value indication, the *GRM* is multiplied by the subject property's market rent. Appraisers must distinguish between market rent and contract rent. Market rent is the rental income a property would most probably command in the open market as of the date of

Table 18.1 Calculating GRMs

Sale	Verified Sale Price	Verified Monthly Rent	Indicated Gross Rent Multiplier
1	$199,500	$1,865	107
2	$290,000	$2,636	110
3	$206,000	$1,900	108
4	$212,500	$1,900	112
5	$214,750	$1,925	112
6	$270,000	$2,432	111
7	$160,000	$1,467	109
8	$265,000	$2,410	110
9	$222,500	$2,025	110
10	$224,500	$2,025	111
11	$220,000	$2,000	110

the appraisal. Contract rent is the actual rent specified in a lease or actually received on a month-to-month basis.

The rent that the subject property currently generates may differ from market rent for a number of reasons. At the time of the lease agreement, the landlord or tenant may have been poorly informed or acting under duress. Market conditions may have changed since the lease was signed, or for some reason the lease terms may be unusually favorable to the tenant or the landlord. Contract rent is often lower than market rent if the parties are related or if the tenant has agreed to work for the landlord in exchange for lower monthly payments. To maintain full occupancy, the landlord may keep rents slightly below market levels.

An appraiser estimates the market rent the subject property should command by studying the rents of the most comparable rental properties and adjusting these rents for differences in lease terms and provisions, if applicable.[4] The appraiser also examines the

TERMS

contract rent: the actual rental income specified in a lease.

market rent: the rental income that a property would most probably command in the open market; indicated by the current rents paid and asked for comparable space as of the date of the appraisal.

CONCEPT

The actual rent of a comparable property can be adjusted to reflect the market rent the subject is capable of generating.

---

4. The data used to estimate the market rent that the subject should command may come from the same sale properties used to derive the *GRM* or from different sale properties.

rent the subject is currently generating, studies the existing lease, and asks the tenant and the landlord whether they believe the lease terms and rent are fair. This investigation is supported by the appraiser's analysis of the rents of competitive rental properties in the subject neighborhood.

Adjusting Market Data

When differences among properties influence the amount of income that the properties can generate, adjustments must be made. The size of these adjustments can be derived with paired data analysis or other techniques. Data are arranged on a market data grid, differences for properties that vary in only one feature are isolated, and adjustments are made. The example that follows illustrates this process. The market data grid that accompanies the example is presented for purposes of illustration; all the adjustments shown will not be required in every application. Percentage adjustments for differences are provided.

Rental income for single-family residences is typically stated as a dollar amount per month. For two- to four-unit apartment properties, rental income is typically broken down into monthly rent per square foot of gross living area or monthly rent per unit. Monthly rent per square foot of gross living area is used in the example, so a separate adjustment for differences in size is not needed. Note that the lot sizes of the comparable properties also vary slightly. No adjustment is made for lot size because the differences are negligible.

Example

In analyzing the market for a subject property, an appraiser finds a number of closely comparable rental properties. These properties vary in terms of gross living area, leasing dates, lease provisions (the payment of utilities), expense ratios, location, construction quality, room count, and lot size. The rent data are displayed in Table 18.2 and adjusted in the market data grid that follows (Table 18.3).

The market rent of the subject is estimated to be $0.60 per square foot of gross living area per month.

Elements of Comparison

In estimating the monthly market rent the subject should command, adjustments are made to the actual rents of comparable properties for

- Transactional variations, chiefly market conditions and lease provisions

Table 18.2	Adjusting Market Data				
	Subject	**Rental 1**	**Rental 2**	**Rental 3**	**Rental 4**
Monthly rent	?	$915	$1,100	$950	$1,100
Gross living area in sq. ft.	1,450	1,450	1,475	1,500	1,475
Date of lease	—	6 mos.	Current	Current	Current
Lease provisions:					
Payment of utilities	Tenant	Tenant	Owner	Tenant	Owner
Expense ratio*	—	25%	30%	30%	30%
Location	—	Inferior	Similar	Superior	Similar
Construction	—	Similar	Similar	Similar	Superior
Room count	6/3/2	6/3/2	7/3/2	6/3/2	6/3/2
Basement	Finished	Finished	Finished	Finished	Finished
Garage	2-car	2-car	2-car	2-car	2-car
Lot size in sq. ft.	9,450	9,450	9,475	9,450	9,475

* Expense ratios are derived by dividing total operating expenses by rental income.

- Characteristics that influence the amount of income the property can generate such as location, size, quality, condition, and amenities
- Variations in operating expenses

Market Conditions and Lease Provisions

Changing market conditions can alter property income over time. When this is the case, the rental data of the comparable properties must be adjusted to reflect changes in market conditions. A percentage adjustment for market conditions is derived by analyzing the trend in rentals of income-producing property over several years. If all the rent data are current, a separate adjustment for market conditions is not needed unless market conditions have changed appreciably.

At times a market conditions adjustment may be needed when the data are only a few months old. If the rental data analyzed reflect a seasonal peak or trough, the estimate of rent derived from these data may be distorted. Many markets experience seasonal fluctuations in supply and demand that may affect property rents, particularly in areas where most leases turn over once a year. An appraiser should adjust comparable rents for these seasonal fluctuations when estimating the typical monthly rental for the subject property over the course of an entire year.

Rents can only be truly comparable if lease provisions are similar. An adjustment must be made for any significant lease difference that

Table 18.3 Market Data Grid for Market Rent Analysis

Element	Subject	Rental 1	Rental 2	Rental 3	Rental 4
Monthly rent	?	$915	$1,100	$950	$1,100
Gross living area in sq. ft.	1,450	1,450	1,475	1,500	1,475
Rent per sq. ft. of gross living area	—	$0.63	$0.75	$0.63	$0.75
Market conditions and lease provisions					
Date of lease					
Comparison	—	6 mos.	Current	Current	Current
Adjustment (5%)		– 0.03			
Lease provisions:					
Payment of utilities					
Comparison	Tenant	Tenant	Owner	Tenant	Owner
Adjustment ($0.75 – $0.63 = $0.12)			– 0.12		– 0.12
Operating expenses					
Expense ratio					
Comparison	—	25%	30%	30%	30%
Adjustment (5%)		– 0.03			
Characteristics influencing income					
Location					
Comparison	—	Inferior	Similar	Superior	Similar
Adjustment (5%)		+ 0.03		– 0.03	
Construction					
Comparison	—	Similar	Similar	Similar	Superior
Adjustment (10%)					– 0.08
Room count	6	6	7	6	6
Comparison		Similar	Superior	Similar	Similar
Adjustment (5%)			– 0.03		
Net adjustment*		– 0.03	– 0.15	– 0.03	– 0.20
Adjusted rent per sq. ft. of gross living area		$0.60	$0.60	$0.60	$0.55

* Difference between the positive and negative adjustments applied to each comparable or total adjustments if only negative or positive adjustments have been applied to the comparable.

affects the rent a property can command or the obligations and expenses of the landlord. Adjustments for lease provisions are common when a property owner pays for utilities and when off-street parking is provided as part of the lease agreement. A downward adjustment is made when the comparable's lease terms are more favorable to the tenant than those contemplated for the subject property; upward adjustments are made for leases that are favorable to the owner. An appraiser would also consider the effect of a long-term lease at below-market levels.

A landlord's reputation for honoring lease terms and performing maintenance and repairs punctually may also influence the actual rent of a property. If the appraiser finds that a comparable property is generating a lower rent because the landlord has an unusually poor maintenance record, an upward adjustment of the comparable rent may be justified.

The amount of rent charged is an important provision of the lease. An overly high rent can discourage prospective tenants and reduce the property's occupancy rate.

Property Characteristics That Influence Income

Many features influence the rent a property is able to command. Location is a primary consideration. Tenants usually prefer a secure, central location with a pleasant view, adequate light, and available parking. Access to public transportation, proximity to schools, places of worship, and entertainment, and good linkages with workplaces and commercial centers are advantages in most rental markets.

Size is another important factor. Size needs vary with typical household sizes, the income of tenants, and the sizes of competitive properties in the area. Adjustments for size differences are based on an analysis of the trend in rents per square foot of gross living area in the market region.

The quality and condition of the rental property and the amenities it provides have a substantial impact on its rent. Residences with sunny, eat-in kitchens and an extra half-bathroom are popular in many areas. Compact designs are usually preferred over linear layouts, and high ceilings, large windows, and cross ventilation are advantageous in hot climates. Closet space is generally more critical in rental properties than owner-occupied dwellings because tenants usually have less room in which to store their possessions.

Private access to the units in a rental property is desirable, particularly if the owner lives on the first floor. Building entrances should be secure. Intercoms and buzzers are standard in some locations. Built-in appliances such as microwave ovens and dishwashers and any furniture included in the lease can influence the rent. Fireplaces, fine woodwork, clean carpeting, freshly painted or papered walls, soundproofing, adequate climate control, well-placed light fixtures and electrical outlets, sufficient hot water, and good water pressure are all appreciated by tenants. The value of any personal property included under the lease terms should be identified and its effect on income should be measured.

Operating Expenses

Adjustments for variations in leases and the characteristics that influence property income must be made before the market rent of the subject property can be estimated. Some further adjustment may be necessary if the subject property has an expense-to-income ratio that is especially high or low. Variations in this ratio can affect the value of properties even when the income they produce remains constant. Because the *GRM* is never adjusted in the income capitalization approach, if an adjustment for the subject's atypical expense ratio is required, it is made in deriving the estimated market rent of the subject property.

DATA COLLECTION AND RENT SURVEY

An appraiser may have difficulty compiling all the rental data needed to complete the first two steps of the income capitalization approach. Experienced appraisers collect relevant information continuously and keep it on file for use in specific appraisal assignments. Newspaper advertisements are a good source of data for analyzing trends in rents. Asking rents and actual rents do not vary as much as asking prices and sale prices for similar property. Interviews with landlords, tenants, real estate brokers, property managers, and neighbors can also provide useful information. In addition to rents and sales, data on typical expenses for a variety of residential properties should be collected. The appraiser can file these data by date and property type in a database for future use.[5]

In performing an appraisal the appraiser may collect required market data by conducting a rent survey. The focus of a rent survey is the subject property. The appraiser notes the size and characteristics of the subject property and interviews the current tenant or tenants. The appraiser asks about the rent being paid, anticipated rent increases or decreases, the benefits and drawbacks of the property, whether the rent and lease provisions are fair, and whether the tenant plans to leave when the lease expires. The actual rent and lease provisions may not be supported in the current market, but these data provide a good starting point for the appraiser's investigation.

---

5.   All the quantitative data an appraiser collects can be stored electronically in a database, which allows the information to be accessed and disseminated quickly using EDI.

The appraiser then researches the properties from which the *GRM* and comparable rents are to be derived. A separate form can be completed for each rental property to help organize the data and ensure that the appraiser has collected all the necessary information. The location of the property, the names of the tenant and the landlord, and a brief rental history can be recorded on the form along with the property size, condition, special features, and other pertinent data. These data can be stored in a computerized database for future use.

> **CONCEPT**
>
> To estimate the market rents of properties, appraisers maintain a database on rental trends and typical operating expenses. Rent surveys are conducted to determine current rents, anticipated rent changes, lease provisions, and the advantages and disadvantages associated with specific rental properties.

Neighbors and tenants can frequently supply valuable information on the desirability of a property. Rental data should be verified, if possible, by interviewing both the tenant and the landlord. The appraiser determines the amount of rent that is actually being paid, not how much the landlord would like to obtain for the property.

Data are collected for each rental property separately and additional information is often needed. A brief sales history of the property and a schedule of expenses can be useful. Sometimes expenses are detailed in a published operating statement compiled by the property owner for tax purposes. Accounting methods vary, so figures obtained from operating statements should be examined critically.

APPLICATION OF *GRM* TO MONTHLY MARKET RENT

To arrive at the market value of a residence using the income capitalization approach, the monthly market rent of the residence is estimated and then multiplied by the *GRM* selected. If, for example, a *GRM* of 140 is selected based on market analysis and the monthly market rent of the subject property is estimated to be $1,200, the property's market value would be estimated as follows:

Estimated monthly market rent of property being appraised	$1,200
Times gross rent multiplier	× 140
Indicated market value	$168,000

In some situations it may be necessary to calculate market rent on an annual basis. Assume a property rents for $1,400 per month during the nine-month school year and $900 per month during the remaining three months. The annual property rent is $15,300 ([9 × $1,400] + [3 × $900]) and the average monthly rent is $15,300/12, or $1,275. When this rent is multiplied by the *GRM* of 140, the indicated value of this property can be calculated as follows:

Average monthly rent of property being appraised	$1,275
Times gross rent multiplier	× 140
Indicated market value	$178,500

19 FINAL RECONCILIATION

The last analytical step in the valuation process is the final reconciliation of value estimates. The different valuation approaches that an appraiser applies typically yield a number of different opinions, which must be reconciled.

In fact, reconciliation occurs throughout the valuation process. Sometimes different results are obtained from a single approach. In the cost approach, for example, estimates of depreciation may vary, depending on the method employed. In the sales comparison approach the adjusted sale prices of comparable properties can indicate different values; qualitative analysis may also have to be considered. In the income capitalization approach, rents and *GRMs* are reconciled. Some appraisers choose to reconcile these variations within the individual approaches only after the data associated with the other valuation approaches have been considered. In any case, all remaining differences in the value opinions derived must be reconciled at this stage in the valuation process.

Final reconciliation begins with a review of the entire appraisal. The purpose and intended use of the appraisal, the methods of data collection, and the analytical tools employed are reexamined in reconciliation. Each step of the valuation process is tested for logic, consistency, and appropriateness. Mathematical errors are corrected and gaps in the data are filled in with further research. If the data are inadequate and additional data are not available, the effect of the incomplete data on the valuation conclusion is explained.

The results produced by each of the approaches to value are weighed. The greatest emphasis is placed on the approach or approaches that are most applicable to the problem and make use of the most reliable and representative data. Finally, a single value indication or a range of value is selected. The figures are rounded to reflect the appraiser's confidence in their accuracy, and the value conclusion is

CONCEPT

There is no prescribed formula for selecting the final indication; rather, the appraiser applies reasoning, judgment, and experience in this process.

presented to the client with the reasoning and documentation in the appraisal report.

The measures of central tendency (mean, median, and mode) may serve as useful tools in final reconciliation,[1] but the final value opinion does not simply represent the average of different value opinions. In final reconciliation the different value estimates are *not* averaged. No mechanical formula is used to select one indication over the others; rather, the appraiser relies on the application of appraisal judgment and experience. The appraiser's judgment, experience, and proper application of appraisal techniques are critical in final reconciliation.

REVIEW

To provide a basis for final reconciliation, an appraiser reviews the entire valuation process. The nature of this review and the need for it depend on the complexity of the assignment and the appraiser's confidence in the data and the analytical techniques applied. Even experienced appraisers review their valuations before submitting the conclusions to their clients to reduce the chances of error.

To perform a comprehensive review, the appraiser proceeds methodically through each step of the valuation process. Typically an appraiser considers whether

1. The appraisal is logical and the stated conclusion is appropriate to the purpose and intended use of the appraisal.
2. The data are accurate, adequate, and properly analyzed.
3. The data have been used in a consistent manner within each approach and are correlated from one approach to another.
4. The calculations are correct.

Logical Answer to the Client's Question

An appraisal is performed to provide an answer to a client's specific question, which the client will use to make some decision concerning the real estate in question. The appraiser must make sure that the

---

1. The mean is the arithmetic average of the sum of the items in an array of data. The median represents the middle value in an array containing an uneven number of items or the average of the two middle values in an array of an even number of items. The mode is the value appearing with the greatest frequency in an array. The average of the highest value and the lowest value in a range of values is also a useful gauge. The utility of these measures increases with the quantity of data analyzed. It is useful to apply measures of central tendency even when other reconciliation criteria are available.

solution provided is appropriate and is presented in a way that is meaningful and useful to the client.

Thus, the first question to ask is: Do the approaches and methods applied lead to meaningful conclusions that relate to the purpose, use, and scope of the appraisal? In most residential appraisals the purpose of the valuation will be to estimate market value, and the intended use of the appraisal will be to serve as a basis for a mortgage loan decision or a relocation purchase offer. The definition of value employed should be reviewed along with the assumptions and limiting conditions applicable to the appraisal to ensure that the value opinion derived satisfies all of the client's requirements as well as those of the appraisal profession. The extent of work carried out in collecting, confirming, and reporting data should correspond to the scope of the appraisal as described in the definition of the appraisal problem.

> **CONCEPT**
>
> The appraiser must ascertain that the methods employed lead to a meaningful conclusion that relates to the purpose and intended use of the appraisal.

If a valuation is to be used in court, the value definition should be closely scrutinized. The definition used in a particular jurisdiction may contain subtleties that merit special attention. The value conclusion must be consistent with the property interests being appraised. The court may seek specific evidence regarding the amount a seller could obtain for a property in the open market or the amount a buyer would be willing to pay in the same market. A value indication reflecting the current highest and best use of the property may be sought, rather than one that considers other uses for which the property might be legally, physically, and economically suited. Various legal considerations may affect the character of the assignment and the appraiser's conclusions.

Accuracy and Adequacy of Data and Analysis

The data an appraiser collects must be factual. They must support the conclusions drawn and provide a convincing representation of market patterns. Accuracy is enhanced if the appraiser is knowledgeable about the sources of the data and their relative reliability. Certain information cannot be taken too seriously. For example, market projections issued by local chambers of commerce can be inaccurate. Nevertheless, this type of information should be considered because it may supply important leads. Suspect information can be checked against data from independent sources. As a general rule, firsthand research is more persuasive than outdated, generalized information obtained from reference manuals.

Critical details pertaining to the subject and comparable properties and aspects of transactions that may have influenced sale prices must always be verified personally. The appraiser should interview one of the parties to the transaction, preferably the buyer or the seller, although attorneys, real estate agents, brokers, and lenders can also be contacted. Often documented evidence that is verified by one of these individuals is the most reliable and compelling form of data for appraisal purposes.

Appraisers should avoid using suspicious or questionable data. A property sale between related parties may not qualify as an arm's-length transaction and therefore the property should not be used as a comparable. The comparable sales selected must be truly representative of the market.

Using a reliable data source may not be enough. The appraiser must also be satisfied that the data accurately represent the thinking and behavior of market participants. To ensure that the data are representative, an appraiser attempts to locate and study a broad sample of comparable properties located in the same neighborhood as the subject property. A large base of general market data can also provide support for the valuation conclusion, even if these data are not derived from perfectly comparable properties. General information on market trends can be almost as revealing as specific sales of very similar properties. Therefore, it is very important that appraisers maintain good records on all kinds of real estate transactions.

To review the data collection effort, the appraiser first reexamines the purpose of the appraisal, the property interests being valued, and the assumptions and limiting conditions. Next the appraiser scrutinizes the neighborhood analysis. The comparables selected should all be located within the boundaries of the subject neighborhood or in similar, competitive neighborhoods.

By the reconciliation stage of the valuation, the appraiser has a broader picture of the market and can better judge whether the comparables are truly comparable. The observations made during the field inspection are also examined. Any changes in property boundaries, additions to the improvements since their original construction, and subsequent encroachments or easements should be carefully noted. Such changes can alter the appraiser's market value conclusion.

The accuracy and reliability of transactional data should be ascertained. Cost data are reviewed. Income and expense data must also be reexamined.

The appraiser should ask the following questions concerning:

Purpose of appraisal, property interest being valued, and assumptions and limiting conditions
- Given these parameters, was the data collection effort complete?
- Were city and regional data collected to provide a background for neighborhood analysis?
- If these data were collected, how reliable and current are they?
- Do market trends in real estate values support the adjustments for market conditions applied to the comparable properties?

Neighborhood analysis
- How were the neighborhood boundaries drawn?
- In light of what the appraiser has learned from the field inspection, should these boundaries be redrawn?
- If so, does this change affect the selection or reliability of the data used?

Comparability of comparables
- Do they provide the best indications of the value of the subject property in the market area?
- If they do not, what other evidence would be more persuasive?
- Would it be worthwhile to replace a comparable or include additional comparables?
- Have all available data on the subject property been used?
- If the subject property has been sold recently, has all information about that transaction been considered?
- How confident is the appraiser of the reasonableness of the adjustments made for property differences?

Observations during field inspection
- Does this information correspond to published information about the subject and comparable properties?
- Are the sketches and maps that were used accurate and up-to-date?

Accuracy and reliability of transactional data
- What sources were contacted for this information?
- How were the data verified—by the buyer, the seller, an attorney, or a lender?
- Is the information complete?
- Are sale prices, sales concessions, and special financing arrangements specified?
- Are any items of personal property included in the transactions listed?
- How were adjustments for special financing derived?
- Were the methods applied appropriate?

Cost data
- If a cost service was used, is the appraiser satisfied with the reliability of the cost estimates?
- Should these costs be confirmed by local contractors?
- Were costs for all the components of the subject property taken into account?
- Was a reasonable amount added for entrepreneurial profit?
- How reliable is the appraiser's estimate of land value?
- Are the estimates of various types of depreciation well supported?

Income and expense data
- Do the comparables have similar expense ratios and lease terms?
- Do the monthly rents of the comparables accurately reflect the rent the subject property can be expected to command?
- Are these rent levels supported by the current market?
- Is the reconciliation of *GRMs* appropriate?

Consistency

An appraiser checks the consistency of the data and the reasoning applied in each valuation approach as well as the correlation between the approaches. Although the valuation approaches reflect different appraisal strategies, the data considered in the different approaches should be consistent.

To ensure consistency, the same highest and best use conclusion must be used throughout the appraisal. In the cost approach the appraiser values the land or site as though vacant and the property as improved based on the same use.

In reconciliation an appraiser checks to see that no item has been mistakenly counted twice in the appraisal. In the sales comparison approach, for example, adjustments should not be made twice for the same difference under two separate headings. Sometimes an adjustment for a difference in age is partially duplicated in an adjustment for physical condition. If these adjustments reflect the same difference, only one should be used.

In the cost approach an appraiser could mistakenly penalize a property twice by considering the same item of depreciation under two separate categories. If, for example, the functional obsolescence of a kitchen appliance is measured in terms of the cost to remove and replace it, additional depreciation cannot be charged for the deteriorated physical condition of the same appliance.

Review of Calculations

All mathematical calculations should be checked, preferably by someone other than the person who originally performed them. Errors in arithmetic can lead to erroneous value indications and undermine the credibility of the entire appraisal. It is easy for people to overlook their own errors, so an independent check of numerical calculations is an important part of the appraiser's review.

RECONCILIATION CRITERIA

After the appraisal has been reviewed and the appropriateness of the value opinions derived in the various approaches has been determined, differences in the value opinions must be reconciled. There is no simple arithmetical or statistical procedure for reconciling value opinions. Rather, appraisers reach a final value indication or a range of conclusions by assessing their confidence in each estimate. The degree of confidence associated with a given opinion usually depends on the appropriateness of the valuation approach to the problem at hand and the quality and quantity of the data used.

Appropriateness

The criterion of appropriateness helps an appraiser decide how much weight to accord the value opinion derived from a particular approach. The appropriateness of a given approach is usually related to the type of property being appraised and the viability of the market. Market value reflects how the market perceives value, so the approach that most closely mirrors market perceptions usually yields the most credible results.

In most residential appraisals the sales comparison approach is accorded the greatest weight. Sales comparison reflects the thinking of most buyers and sellers, who study and compare the prices of similar property to find a reasonable price at which to buy or sell. However, this approach may not be applicable in areas where sales are few or when the property being appraised has unique features.

In these situations, market participants may base their value decisions on cost factors. The cost approach is more appropriate when an improvement is newer and when it represents the highest and best use. In these instances, depreciation is minimal. Cost analysis might also be important if typical purchasers interested in the property would plan on making substantial repairs or renovations.

In valuing older properties with a great deal of incurable depreciation, the cost approach tends to be less appropriate. Market participants, like real estate appraisers, have difficulty deciding how much depreciation the property has incurred.

When an active rental market exists and potential purchasers are interested in the property's ability to generate an income, income capitalization may be the most reliable approach. The income capitalization approach is applicable when sufficient rental and sales data can

TERM

final value indication: the range of values or single dollar figure derived from the reconciliation of value indications and stated in the appraisal report.

CONCEPTS

Once the review is completed and the appropriateness of the value indications derived in the various approaches is determined, the appraiser must reconcile the differing estimates.

Three criteria are used to weigh the reliability of the preliminary value indications:

1. The appropriateness of the approach to the specific problem
2. The quality of the data collected
3. The quantity of the data analyzed

The sales comparison approach is appropriate when sales data are abundant and the property is fairly typical for its market. If data are insufficient or the property is unique, greater reliance may be placed on the cost approach to value.

CONCEPT

When a residence produces an income and sufficient rental and sales data are available, use of the income capitalization approach is appropriate.

be obtained; if such data for residential properties are unavailable, the income capitalization approach is not appropriate.

Quality of Data

The specific items of data used in an appraisal may reflect different degrees of accuracy. Therefore, an appraiser should consider the relative quality of the data used in each approach to weigh the reliability of the estimates derived. For example, are the cost data and depreciation estimates used in the cost approach as accurate as the adjustments made in the sales comparison approach or the market rent data and gross rent multipliers used in the income capitalization approach? An appraiser may have more confidence in the accuracy of the data used in one approach than those used in another.

There are several ways to measure the quality of the data used in the sales comparison approach. If the adjustments made to the sale prices of properties considered comparable are too large or too numerous, then the margin of error is broad and accuracy is diminished. The need for many adjustments suggests that the comparable properties are not truly comparable. To judge the quality of the data, an appraiser may look at the number of adjustments made to each comparable. As the number of adjustments increases, the reliability of the value indication derived from that comparable decreases.

Another important measure is the size of the net adjustment as a percentage of the comparable's unadjusted sale price. The net adjustment to a comparable is calculated by adding the dollar amounts of all positive adjustments and deducting the sum of all negative adjustments. One problem with this test of comparability is that the appraiser cannot assume that positive and negative adjustments cancel each other out. A comparable with a net adjustment similar to those of other comparables may seem reasonable when actually either the positive or the negative adjustments have been incorrectly weighted. For this reason appraisers also consider gross adjustments. The gross adjustment to a comparable is the sum of the amounts of all the adjustments made to the comparable's sale price, regardless of whether

TERMS

gross adjustment: the total adjustment to each comparable sale price calculated in absolute terms. All the adjustments, both positive and negative, are added together to determine the gross adjustment to a comparable sale price.

net adjustment: the difference between the total positive and negative adjustments made to a comparable sale price.

these adjustments are positive or negative. This sum is expressed as a percentage of the unadjusted sale price.

At times, however, the gross size of dollar adjustments may not be a good indicator of the quality of the comparable data either, particularly if few adjustments are needed. A single large adjustment may be more accurate and defensible than many smaller adjustments. For example, an appraiser may find abundant market evidence in a community to indicate the value added by a swimming pool, a garage, or an extra bedroom. An adjustment for the presence or absence of such a large item in a comparable might result in a gross adjustment that is larger than the gross adjustments made to other comparables. However, greater accuracy may be attributed to this adjustment because there is reliable market evidence to support it.

The tests described above are applied to check the reliability of each sale considered comparable as a basis for deriving a value indication for the subject property. These tests may also be used to reconcile different value opinions in the sales comparison approach and to determine the relative applicability of the approach.

The overall persuasiveness of the sales comparison approach is often enhanced by using a large number of sales considered comparable, but using a certain number of sales cannot guarantee a reasonable conclusion. The number of sales examined depends on the reliability of the sales and the client's requirements. Some clients insist on a minimum number of sales. The appropriateness of the valuation approach applied and the quality of the data employed determine the relevance of the value opinion derived from a given approach or sale considered comparable.

Quantity of Data

Although the data used in a given approach meet the criteria of appropriateness and quality, they may still be insufficient. When few reliable, recent sales are available but cost and depreciation data are abundant, increased emphasis may be given to the cost approach. Similarly, abundant data on one comparable may increase the appraiser's confidence in the value indication derived from this sale.

Of course, an appraiser will not be persuaded by the quantity of data alone. The data considered must be both relevant and accurate. When these data are interpreted by an experienced appraiser in a manner consistent with the purpose of the appraisal, a reliable value opinion will result. Sound appraisal conclusions rest on the application of reasoning and judgment to market data, not on the mere manipulation of data.

FINAL VALUE INDICATIONS

After the various value opinions are weighed, the appraiser must reconcile them. The final value indication may be expressed as a point estimate, as a range of value, or as a value within a designated range.

A point estimate is the traditional way of expressing a value conclusion. The estimate of the subject property's value is stated as a single dollar amount—e.g., $92,000, $187,000, or $365,000. A point estimate that reflects the appraiser's best opinion as to the approximate value of a property is required for many types of appraisal assignments. Point estimates are requested for real estate tax purposes, just compensation estimates, and certain property transfer decisions. They are also used to calculate federal income tax depreciation deductions and to determine lease terms based on value. Clients may expect a point estimate even when they have not specifically requested one because this type of opinion is customary.

One problem associated with point estimates is that the presentation of a single dollar figure may suggest greater precision than is warranted. Properly understood, a point estimate implies a range of value in which the property value most probably falls. The estimate on which a value indication is based is impartial, well-reasoned, and the very best a professional appraiser can provide in view of the evidence gathered and analyzed. Nevertheless, a point estimate is an opinion of the most likely dollar value of the interest being appraised subject to certain qualifying conditions. This opinion may, in fact, be too high or too low.

> **CONCEPT**
>
> The final value indication may be expressed
>
> - As a point estimate
> - As a range of value
> - As a value within a designated range

Occasionally an appraiser may have reason to avoid offering a "best" opinion and instead specify a range of value between two dollar figures. By reporting a range, the appraiser is indicating that the actual value is probably no lower than the low end of the range and no higher than the high end.

Stating a range of value can present serious problems, however. A wide range is of no use to a client, and a narrow range can be incorrectly interpreted as a guarantee that the price will fall between the extreme values. A client who is provided with a value range is likely to hold fast to whichever extreme suits his or her purposes.

Rounding

It is customary to round appraisal conclusions to reflect the lack of precision associated with them. Rounding may be based on rules of significant digits, but often the degree to which a value conclusion is rounded reflects the appraiser's confidence in the accuracy of the value estimates.

Rounding also reflects how prices are expressed in the market. If market study reveals a pattern in pricing, the appraiser should round accordingly.[2]

2. The Appraisal Institute adopted a rounding policy for its courses and exams, which states that solutions to numerical problems or sequences of related problems should generally be rounded at the end of the (final) problem only. Using the HP-12C calculator, all intermediate numerical results are stored internally but are displayed on solution sheets to a convenient and consistent number of digits, using the HP-12C's rounding function. This rounding policy is not appropriate for use outside the classroom.

CHAPTER 20
THE APPRAISAL REPORT

Like a well-crafted argument, an appraisal report leads its reader from the definition of the appraisal problem through the appraiser's reasoning and relevant descriptive data to a specific value conclusion. The appraiser must present all facts, analysis, and conclusions clearly and succinctly. The length, type, and content of appraisal reports are based on the client's needs, regulatory requirements, the courts, the type of property being appraised, and the nature of the valuation problem.

> **CONCEPT**
>
> An appraisal report should lead the reader from the definition of the appraisal problem through the reasoning and analysis of relevant data to a specific conclusion.

Every appraisal report is prepared to answer a particular question and provide information needed by a client. Some common appraisal questions are

- What is the market value of the property?
- What is the highest and best use of the land as though vacant and the property as improved?
- What is the value of the part taken in condemnation and what is the damage or benefit to the remainder of the property as a result of the taking?

USPAP REPORTING REQUIREMENTS

To ensure the quality of appraisal reports, The Appraisal Foundation has set minimum standards for the factual content, descriptive material, and statements of work and purpose included in all types of appraisal reports. These standards have been adapted by professional appraisal organizations and by the individual states. To comply with the reporting requirements of the Uniform Standards of Professional Appraisal Practice (USPAP), as promulgated by the Appraisal Standards Board of The Appraisal Foundation, an appraiser must communicate each analysis, opinion, and conclusion in a manner that is not misleading. Each written or oral real property appraisal report must

(a) clearly and accurately set forth the appraisal in a manner that will not be misleading;

(b) contain sufficient information to enable the intended users of the appraisal to understand the report properly;

(c) clearly and accurately disclose any extraordinary assumption, hypothetical condition, or limiting condition that directly affects the appraisal and indicate its impact on value.

Specific reporting requirements for written real property appraisal reports are set forth in Standards Rule 2-2. Standards Rule 2-3 indicates the required certification to be included with all written reports. Reporting requirements for oral reports are presented in Standards Rule 2-4.

Various types of reports can be identified by the reporting requirements applicable to them.[1]

TYPES OF REPORTS

An appraisal report may be oral or written. There are three types of written reports:

1. Self-contained
2. Summary
3. Restricted use

Usually a report is presented in the format dictated by the needs of the client.

Oral Reports

An appraiser may prepare an oral report if the circumstances or the needs of the client do not permit or warrant a written report. Sometimes a client asks for the appraiser's opinion without detailed documentation. In this case, the appraiser must perform the analysis required and keep all the material, data, and working papers used to prepare the report in a file.[2]

---

1. See Standard 2 and Standards Rule 2-2 of the Uniform Standards of Professional Appraisal Practice, effective March 31, 1999.

2. See the Ethics Rule of the Uniform Standards of Professional Appraisal Practice for regulations governing recordkeeping, including the length of time an appraiser must retain a workfile.

Expert testimony is considered an oral report, whether it is presented in a deposition or in court. However, most oral reports are not made under oath; they are communicated to the client in person or by telephone. Today some appraisers transmit their reports to clients electronically, taking advantage of the capabilities of e-mail and EDI technology.

Each oral report should identify the property and present the facts, assumptions, conditions, and reasoning on which the value conclusion is based. Before communicating an oral report, the appraiser should file all notes and data relating to the assignment and prepare a complete memorandum of the appraisal analysis, conclusion, and opinion.

The Uniform Standards of Professional Appraisal Practice have specific reporting requirements for oral reports. Standards Rule 2-4 requires that oral reports address the substantive matters set forth for self-contained or summary written reports.

> **TERM**
>
> **workfile:** documentation necessary to support an appraiser's analysis, opinions, and conclusions. (USPAP, 1999 edition)

> **CONCEPTS**
>
> An oral report must include a property description and all the facts, assumptions, conditions, and reasoning on which the conclusion is based.
>
> Expert testimony is considered an oral report, as are other presentations made in person or by telephone.

Written Reports

According to Standards Rule 2-2, "Each written appraisal report must be prepared under one of the following three options and prominently state which option is used: Self-Contained Appraisal Report, Summary Appraisal Report, or Restricted Use Appraisal Report."

Self-Contained Report

A self-contained report usually requires the most thorough and time-consuming preparation. Within such reports appraisers have the opportunity to support and explain their opinions and conclusions and convince report readers of the soundness of the final value indication. This type of report answers the client's questions in writing and substantiates these answers with facts and reasoning. To be most useful to the client, the appraisal report must present adequate, pertinent supporting data and logical analysis that lead to the appraiser's conclusions.

A self-contained report describes all the facts and appraisal methods and techniques that have been applied in the valuation process to arrive at the value opinion or another conclusion. The report demonstrates the appraiser's ability to interpret relevant data, select appropriate valuation methods and techniques, and ultimately estimate a specifically defined value.

In preparing an appraisal report, descriptive material should be separated from analysis and interpretation. Typically factual and descriptive data are presented in the early sections of the report so that subsequent sections on data analysis and interpretation can refer to these facts and discuss how they contribute to the final value opinion. Unnecessary repetition is undesirable, but the presentation of data may depend on the nature and length of the report. Appraisal reports are usually organized to follow the steps in the valuation process.

The appraiser may not be present when the report is reviewed or examined, so the report is the appraiser's representative. A good report will give the client a favorable impression of the appraiser's professional competence.

Summary Report

As its name implies, a summary report summarizes the information reported and is therefore usually a shorter report. The basic difference between a self-contained report and a summary report is the level of detail provided. The information presented on two pages in a self-contained report might take up only two paragraphs in a summary report. Similarly, material presented in narrative form in a self-contained report might be presented in tabular form in a summary report.

The specific reporting requirements for a summary report do not differ greatly from the requirements for a self-contained report. Note, however, that the term *describe,* as used in the requirements for a self-contained report, is replaced with the term *summarize* in the requirements for a summary report, indicating that less detail is required in the latter type of report.

Restricted Use Report

The third type of written report is the restricted use report. This document is less detailed and must include a use restriction that limits the client's or user's reliance on the report. The reporting requirements for this type of report are substantially different.

The reporting requirements for the three types of written reports can be compared in Table 20.1.

CONCEPTS

A self-contained appraisal report is the most descriptive type of appraisal report.

A summary report provides a more concise presentation of information.

A restricted use report contains minimal information and must include a prominent use restriction that limits reliance on the report and warns that it cannot be properly understood without additional information.

Table 20.1	Comparison of Report Types

Self-Contained	Summary	Restricted Use
i. State the identity of the client and any intended users, by name or type.	i. State the identity of the client and any intended users, by name or type.	i. State the identity of the client, by name or type.
ii. State the intended use of the appraisal.	ii. State the intended use of the appraisal.	ii. State the intended use of the appraisal.
iii. Describe information sufficient to identify the real estate involved in the appraisal, including the physical and economic property characteristics relevant to the assignment.	iii. Summarize information sufficient to identify the real estate involved in the appraisal, including the physical and economic property characteristics relevant to the assignment.	iii. State information sufficient to identify the real estate involved in the appraisal.
iv. State the real property interest appraised.	iv. State the real property interest appraised.	iv. State the real property interest appraised.
v. State the purpose of the appraisal, including the type and definition of value and its source.	v. State the purpose of the appraisal, including the type and definition of value and its source.	v. State the purpose of the appraisal, including the type of value, and refer to the definition of the value pertinent to the purpose of the assignment.
vi. State the effective date of the appraisal and the date of the report.	vi. State the effective date of the appraisal and the date of the report.	vi. State the effective date of the appraisal and the date of the report.
vii. Describe sufficient information to disclose to the client and any intended users of the appraisal the scope of work used to develop the appraisal.	vii. Summarize sufficient information to disclose to the client and any intended users of the appraisal the scope of work used to develop the appraisal.	vii. State the extent of the process of collecting, confirming, and reporting data or refer to an assignment agreement retained in the appraiser's workfile, which describes the scope of the work to be performed.
viii. State all assumptions, hypothetical conditions, and limiting conditions that affected the analyses, opinions, and conclusions.	viii. State all assumptions, hypothetical conditions, and limiting conditions that affected the analyses, opinions, and conclusions.	viii. State all assumptions, hypothetical conditions, and limiting conditions that affected the analyses, opinions, and conclusions.
ix. Describe the information analyzed, the appraisal procedures followed, and the reasoning that supports the analyses, opinions, and conclusions.	ix. Summarize the information analyzed, the appraisal procedures followed, and the reasoning that supports the analyses, opinions, and conclusions.	ix. State the appraisal procedures followed, and the value opinion(s) and conclusion(s), and reference the workfile.

Table 20.1   Comparison of Report Types *(continued)*

Self-Contained	Summary	Restricted Use
x. State the use of the real estate existing as of the date of value, and the use of the real estate reflected in the appraisal; and, when the purpose of the assignment is market value, describe the support and rationale for the appraiser's opinion of the highest and best use of the real estate.	x. State the use of the real estate existing as of the date of value, and the use of the real estate reflected in the appraisal; and, when the purpose of the assignment is market value, summarize the support and rationale for the appraiser's opinion of the highest and best use of the real estate.	x. State the use of the real estate existing as of the date of value, and the use of the real estate reflected in the appraisal; and, when the purpose of the assignment is market value, state the appraiser's opinion of the highest and best use of the real estate.
xi. State and explain any permitted departures from specific requirements of Standard 1, and the reason for excluding any of the usual valuation approaches.	xi. State and explain any permitted departures from specific requirements of Standard 1, and the reason for excluding any of the usual valuation approaches.	xi. State and explain any permitted departures from applicable specific requirements of Standard 1; state the exclusion of any of the usual valuation approaches; and state a prominent use restriction that limits use of the report to the client and warns that the appraiser's opinions and conclusions set forth in the report cannot be understood properly without additional information in the appraiser's workfile.
xii. Include a signed certification in accordance with Standards Rule 2-3.	xii. Include a signed certification in accordance with Standards Rule 2-3.	xii. Include a signed certification in accordance with Standards Rule 2-3.

Note: No comment sections are included in this chart; the chart has been prepared for discussion purposes only.
Source: Uniform Standards of Appraisal Practice, 1999 edition.

HIGHEST AND BEST USE STATEMENTS IN THE APPRAISAL REPORT

All appraisal reports should contain a summary statement that describes the appraiser's highest and best use conclusions. When the appraisal is performed as part of an analysis assignment to determine highest and best use, the analysis and conclusion of highest and best use are described in considerable detail and probable future incomes or returns are calculated. If the purpose of the appraisal is to reach a market value opinion, the highest and best use section is usually briefer.

All narrative appraisal reports must explicitly state the reasoning and supporting evidence that led to the highest and best use conclusion. Extensive discussion may be required in appraisal reports concerned with properties in transitional neighborhoods, sites that show the effect of substantial external obsolescence, or properties that indicate an interim use, a use dependent on assemblage, a use contingent on a zoning change, or other unusual uses. *i.e. plotage, putting lots together*

The cost approach to value requires a separate land valuation, so a report on an appraisal in which the cost approach is applied must include statements of the highest and best use of the site as though vacant and of the property as improved. In a narrative report communicating a cost approach appraisal, the highest and best use of the site should be reported along with a statement that the opinion was made under the theoretical presumption that the land was vacant and available for development. Then the highest and best use of the property as improved should be reported along with a statement that the opinion was made in consideration of the future potential of the existing improvements and site. If the site is already improved to its highest and best use, the appraiser's report should state this explicitly.

CERTIFICATION

In accordance with Standards Rule 2-3, all written reports must contain a certification similar in content to the following:

> I certify that, to the best of my knowledge and belief:
>
> - The statements of fact contained in this report are true and correct.
> - The reported analyses, opinions, and conclusions are limited only by the reported assumptions and limiting conditions, and are my personal, impartial, and unbiased professional analyses, opinions, and conclusions.

CONCEPT

Each written appraisal report must state which of the three options is used and must include an appropriate certification.

- I have no (or the specified) present or prospective interest in the property that is the subject of this report, and no (or the specified) personal interest with respect to the parties involved.

- I have no bias with respect to the property that is the subject of this report or to the parties involved with this assignment.

- My engagement in this assignment was not contingent upon developing or reporting predetermined results.

- My compensation for completing this assignment is not contingent upon the development or reporting of a predetermined value or direction in value that favors the cause of the client, the amount of the value opinion, the attainment of a stipulated result, or the occurrence of a subsequent event directly related to the intended use of this appraisal.

- My analyses, opinions, and conclusions were developed, and this report has been prepared, in conformity with the Uniform Standards of Professional Appraisal Practice.

- I have (or have not) made a personal inspection of the property that is the subject of this report. (If more than one person signs the report, this certification must clearly specify which individuals did and which individuals did not make a personal inspection of the appraisal property.)

- No one provided significant professional assistance to the person signing this report. (If there are exceptions, the name of each individual providing significant professional assistance must be stated.)

FORM REPORTS

In many appraisal situations, form reports meet the needs of financial institutions, insurance companies, and government agencies. In the secondary mortgage market created by government agencies and private organizations, form reports are required for the purchase and sale of most existing mortgages on residential properties. Because these clients review many appraisals, using a standard report form is more efficient and convenient. When a form is used, those responsible for reviewing the appraisal know exactly where to find each category or item of data in the report. By completing the form, an appraiser ensures that no item required by the reviewer has been overlooked. The Appraisal Institute's Guide Note 3 addresses the use of form reports for residential property. Each form report must comply with all reporting and certification requirements.

> **CONCEPT**
>
> Form reports are often used by financial institutions, insurance companies, and government agencies. They provide a standard, comprehensive format for recording data and may be supplemented with attachments.

The method of valuation employed in an appraisal is determined by the nature of the specific appraisal problem. If a report form seems too rigid and does not provide for the inclusion of all the data that the appraiser believes to be pertinent, the relevant information and the appraiser's comments should be added as a supplement.

The appraiser should make sure that the completed report is consistent in its description of the property and provides all the data indicated by the categories listed. If the appraiser's determination of the highest and best use of the property does not conform to the use for which the form is appropriate, the form cannot be used. All data must be presented in a clear and comprehensible manner, and all form reports should include a proper certification and statement of limiting conditions.

A form appraisal report is unacceptable if the appraiser fails to

1. Consider the purpose of the report, the value definition, and the assumptions, limitations, and conditions inherent in the report

2. Question the client about any underwriting criteria that might conflict with proper appraisal practice and explain how such criteria affect the value opinion, given the value definition on the form

3. Conduct an appropriate review before signing the report as a review appraiser

4. Consider, analyze, and discuss any prior sales, offers, or listings of the property within one year of the date of the appraisal[3]

The most widely used form report for residential appraisals is the Uniform Residential Appraisal Report (URAR) form, which is required by the Department of Housing and Urban Development (HUD), the Federal Housing Administration (FHA), the Department of Veterans Affairs (VA), the Farmers Home Administration (FmHA), Fannie Mae,[4] and Freddie Mac. The last two entities have developed the following additional appraisal forms as their automated underwriting programs have grown:

- Loan Prospector® Quantitative Analysis Appraisal Report (Freddie Mac Form 2055)
- Loan Prospector® Condition and Marketability Report (Freddie Mac Form 2070)
- Desktop Underwriter™ Quantitative Analysis Appraisal Report (Fannie Mae Form 2055)

---

3. Guide Note 3 to the Appraisal Institute's Standards of Professional Appraisal Practice, "The Use of Form Appraisal Reports for Residential Property."

4. The reader is advised that, for lending purposes, Fannie Mae will not accept appraisals of prospective value that include adjustments for anticipated market conditions.

- Desktop Underwriter™ Qualitative Analysis Appraisal Report (Fannie Mae Form 2065)
- Desktop Underwriter™ Property Inspection Report (Fannie Mae Form 2075)

Other forms used by government agencies include

- Individual Condominium Unit Appraisal Report (Fannie Mae Form 1073/Freddie Mac Form 465)
- Small Residential Income Property Appraisal Report (Fannie Mae Form 1025/Freddie Mac 72)

The Employee Relocation Council (ERC) Residential Appraisal Report form was developed for use by members of the ERC, which is an independent organization that assists in the transfer of corporate employees.

Uniform Residential Appraisal Report

Fannie Mae and Freddie Mac introduced the Uniform Residential Appraisal Report (URAR) form in 1986. This was the first instance of all the major government agencies involved in mortgage activities agreeing to use a common appraisal report form. The revised URAR form released in June 1993 reflected changes in industry standards and requirements over the intervening years and refinements of reporting standards.

All appraisals for mortgages issued by Fannie Mae, Freddie Mac, HUD, VA, and FHA that may be sold in the secondary mortgage market must be reported on the URAR form.

Individual Condominium Unit Appraisal Report

Freddie Mac Form 465/Fannie Mae Form 1073 was revised in 1994 to be more consistent with the URAR form. This form, the Individual Condominium Unit Appraisal Report, is used for appraisals of residential properties held in condominium ownership.

Although most condominium valuations are reported using this form, the Departments of Housing and Urban Development and Veterans Affairs accept condominium appraisals using the URAR form. Fannie Mae will accept appraisals of individual condominium units reported on the URAR form as long as the property improvements are

> **TERM**
>
> **Individual Condominium Unit Appraisal Report:** a two-page form report used by Fannie Mae and Freddie Mac in the appraisal of an individual condominium unit.

adequately described and sufficient information is included about the home owners association fees, management practices, and maintenance requirements.

A planned unit development (PUD) is not a type of housing but rather a zoning alternative. PUD units may appear physically similar to condominium units, but the valuation of an individual PUD unit is usually reported on the URAR form.

Small Residential Income Property Appraisal Report

The Small Residential Income Property Appraisal Report was most recently revised in 1994 to ensure conformity with the requirements of the Uniform Standards of Professional Appraisal Practice and also to make the form consistent with the format of the URAR.

A small residential income property can be defined as a group of rental housing units, usually two to six, combined to create a multiple living space complex. This type of residential property shares many characteristics with apartment buildings, but the owner of a small residential income property often occupies a unit within the complex whereas apartment properties are often professionally managed on behalf of an owner who may live elsewhere. When small residential income properties have few units, they often take on the investment characteristics of a single-family home.

Employee Relocation Council Residential Appraisal Report

The Employee Relocation Council Residential Appraisal Report form is published by the ERC, a nonprofit membership organization founded in 1964. Its members include corporations, relocation service companies, brokers, and appraisers involved in the transfer of corporate employees.

The purpose of a relocation appraisal is to estimate the anticipated sale price of a relocating employee's primary residence; the intended use of the appraisal is to assist an employer in facilitating the employee relocation process.

> **TERMS**
>
> **Small Residential Income Property Appraisal Report:** a four-page form report used by Fannie Mae and Freddie Mac in the appraisal of small residential income-producing properties.
>
> **Employee Relocation Council (ERC) Residential Appraisal Report:** a six-page appraisal form used in relocation by the ERC, a nonprofit organization that provides relocation assistance to transferred employees who wish to sell their homes and acquire new ones.

Figure 20.1 URAR Form

Property Description	UNIFORM RESIDENTIAL APPRAISAL REPORT	File No.

SUBJECT

Property Address		City		State	Zip Code
Legal Description				County	
Assessor's Parcel No.		Tax Year	R.E. Taxes $	Special Assessments $	
Borrower	Current Owner		Occupant	☐ Owner ☐ Tenant ☐ Vacant	
Property rights appraised ☐ Fee Simple ☐ Leasehold	Project Type ☐ PUD ☐ Condominium (HUD/VA only)	HOA$	/Mo.		
Neighborhood or Project Name		Map Reference	Census Tract		
Sales Price $	Date of Sale	Description and $ amount of loan charges/concessions to be paid by seller			
Lender/Client		Address			
Appraiser		Address			

NEIGHBORHOOD

Location	☐ Urban	☐ Suburban	☐ Rural	Predominant occupancy	Single family housing	Present land use %	Land use change
Built up	☐ Over 75%	☐ 25-75%	☐ Under 25%		PRICE $(000) / AGE (yrs)	One family	☐ Not likely ☐ Likely
Growth rate	☐ Rapid	☐ Stable	☐ Slow	☐ Owner		2-4 family	☐ In process
Property values	☐ Increasing	☐ Stable	☐ Declining	☐ Tenant	Low	Multi-family	To:
Demand/supply	☐ Shortage	☐ In balance	☐ Over supply	☐ Vacant (0-5%)	High	Commercial	
Marketing time	☐ Under 3 mos.	☐ 3-6 mos.	☐ Over 6 mos.	☐ Vacant (over 5%)	Predominant	( )	

Note: Race and the racial composition of the neighborhood are not appraisal factors.

Neighborhood boundaries and characteristics: _____

Factors that affect the marketability of the properties in the neighborhood (proximity to employment and amenities, employment stability, appeal to market, etc.):

Market conditions in the subject neighborhood (including support for the above conclusions related to the trend of property values, demand/supply, and marketing time...such as data on competitive properties for sale in the neighborhood, description of the prevalence of sales and financing concessions, etc.): _____

PUD

Project information for PUDs (If applicable) — Is the developer/builder in control of the Home Owners' Association (HOA)? ☐ Yes ☐ No
Approximate total number of units in the subject project _____. Approximate total number of units for sale in the subject project _____.
Describe common elements and recreational facilities:

SITE

Dimensions _____	Topography _____
Site area _____ Corner Lot ☐ Yes ☐ No	Size _____
Specific zoning classification and description _____	Shape _____
Zoning compliance ☐ Legal ☐ Legal nonconforming (Grandfathered use) ☐ Illegal ☐ No zoning	Drainage _____
Highest & best use as improved: ☐ Present use ☐ Other use (explain)	View _____

Utilities	Public	Other	Off-site improvements	Driveway	Public	Private	Landscaping _____
Electricity	☐		Street		☐	☐	Driveway Surface _____
Gas	☐		Curb/gutter		☐	☐	Apparent easements _____
Water	☐		Sidewalk		☐	☐	FEMA Special Flood Hazard Area ☐ Yes ☐ No
Sanitary sewer	☐		Street lights		☐	☐	FEMA Zone _____ Map Date _____
Storm sewer	☐		Alley		☐	☐	FEMA Map No. _____

Comments (apparent adverse easements, encroachments, special assessments, slide areas, illegal or nonconforming zoning use, etc.): _____

DESCRIPTION OF IMPROVEMENTS

GENERAL DESCRIPTION	EXTERIOR DESCRIPTION	FOUNDATION	BASEMENT	INSULATION
No. of Units _____	Foundation _____	Slab _____	Area Sq. Ft. _____	Roof _____ ☐
No. of Stories _____	Exterior Walls _____	Crawl Space _____	% Finished _____	Ceiling _____ ☐
Type (Det./Att.) _____	Roof Surface _____	Basement _____	Ceiling _____	Walls _____ ☐
Design (Style) _____	Gutters & Dwnspts. _____	Sump Pump _____	Walls _____	Floor _____ ☐
Existing/Proposed _____	Window Type _____	Dampness _____	Floor _____	None _____ ☐
Age (Yrs.) _____	Storm/Screens _____	Settlement _____	Outside Entry _____	Unknown _____ ☐
Effective Age (Yrs.) _____	Manufactured House _____	Infestation _____		

ROOMS	Foyer	Living	Dining	Kitchen	Den	Family Rm.	Rec. Rm.	Bedrooms	# Baths	Laundry	Other	Area Sq. Ft.
Basement												
Level 1												
Level 2												

Finished area **above** grade contains: _____ Rooms; _____ Bedroom(s); _____ Bath(s); _____ Square Feet of Gross Living Area

INTERIOR	Materials/Condition	HEATING	KITCHEN EQUIP.	ATTIC	AMENITIES	CAR STORAGE
Floors	_____	Type _____	Refrigerator ☐	None ☐	Fireplace(s)# ____ ☐	None ☐
Walls	_____	Fuel _____	Range/Oven ☐	Stairs ☐	Patio _____ ☐	Garage ____ # of cars
Trim/Finish	_____	Condition _____	Disposal ☐	Drop Stair ☐	Deck _____ ☐	Attached _____
Bath Floor	_____	COOLING	Dishwasher ☐	Scuttle ☐	Porch _____ ☐	Detached _____
Bath Wainscot	_____	Central _____	Fan/Hood ☐	Floor ☐	Fence _____ ☐	Built-In _____
Doors	_____	Other _____	Microwave ☐	Heated ☐	Pool _____ ☐	Carport _____
		Condition _____	Washer/Dryer ☐	Finished ☐		

Additional features (special energy efficient items, etc.): _____

COMMENTS

Condition of the improvements, depreciation (physical, functional, and external), repairs needed, quality of construction, remodeling/additions, etc.: _____

Adverse environmental conditions (such as, but not limited to, hazardous wastes, toxic substances, etc.) present in the improvements, on the site, or in the immediate vicinity of the subject property: _____

Figure 20.1   URAR Form *(continued)*

Valuation Section

UNIFORM RESIDENTIAL APPRAISAL REPORT   File No. _____

COST APPROACH

ESTIMATED SITE VALUE .... = $ _____

ESTIMATED REPRODUCTION COST-NEW OF IMPROVEMENTS:

Dwelling _____ Sq. Ft. @ $ _____ = $ _____

_____ Sq. Ft. @ $ _____ = _____

= _____

Garage/Carport _____ Sq. Ft. @ $ _____ = _____

Total Estimated Cost New .... = $ _____

Less   Physical | Functional | External

Depreciation _____ = $ _____

Depreciated Value of Improvements .... = $ _____

"As-is" Value of Site Improvements .... = $ _____

INDICATED VALUE BY COST APPROACH .... = $ _____

Comments on Cost Approach (such as, source of cost estimate, site value, square foot calculation and, for HUD, VA, and FmHA, the estimated remaining economic life of the property): _____

SALES COMPARISON ANALYSIS

ITEM	SUBJECT	COMPARABLE NO. 1		COMPARABLE NO. 2		COMPARABLE NO. 3	
Address							
Proximity to Subject							
Sales Price	$		$		$		$
Price/Gross Liv. Area	$ ☒	$ ☒		$ ☒		$ ☒	
Data and/or Verification Sources							
VALUE ADJUSTMENTS	DESCRIPTION	DESCRIPTION	+ (−) $Adjustment	DESCRIPTION	+ (−) $Adjustment	DESCRIPTION	
Sales or Financing Concessions							
Date of Sale/Time							
Location							
Leasehold/Fee Simple							
Site							
View							
Design and Appeal							
Quality of Construction							
Age							
Condition							
Above Grade Room Count	Total Bdrms Baths	Total Bdrms Baths		Total Bdrms Baths		Total Bdrms Baths	
Gross Living Area	Sq. Ft.	Sq. Ft.		Sq. Ft.		Sq. Ft.	
Basement & Finished Rooms Below Grade							
Functional Utility							
Heating/Cooling							
Energy Efficient Items			+ (−) $Adjustment				
Garage/Carport							
Porch, Patio, Deck, Fireplace(s), etc.							
Fence, Pool, etc.							
Net Adj. (total)		☐ + ☐ −	$	☐ + ☐ −	$	☐ + ☐ −	$
Adjusted Sales Price of Comparable			$		$		$

Comments on Sales Comparison (including the subject property's compatibility to the neighborhood, etc.): _____

ITEM	SUBJECT	COMPARABLE NO. 1	COMPARABLE NO. 2	COMPARABLE NO. 3
Date, Price and Data Source for prior sales within year of appraisal				

Analysis of any current agreement of sale, option, or listing of the subject property and analysis of any prior sales of subject and comparables within one year of the date of appraisal:

_____

RECONCILIATION

INDICATED VALUE BY SALES COMPARISON APPROACH .... $ _____

INDICATED VALUE BY INCOME APPROACH (If Applicable) Estimated Market Rent $ _____ /Mo. x Gross Rent Multiplier _____ = $ _____

This appraisal is made   ☐ "as is"   ☐ subject to the repairs, alterations, inspections, or conditions listed below   ☐ subject to completion per plans and specifications.

Conditions of Appraisal: _____

Final Reconciliation: _____

The purpose of this appraisal is to estimate the market value of the real property that is the subject of this report, based on the above conditions and the certification, contingent and limiting conditions, and market value definition that are stated in the attached Freddie Mac Form 439/Fannie Mae Form 1004B (Revised _____).

I (WE) ESTIMATE THE MARKET VALUE, AS DEFINED, OF THE REAL PROPERTY THAT IS THE SUBJECT OF THIS REPORT, AS OF _____

(WHICH IS THE DATE OF INSPECTION AND THE EFFECTIVE DATE OF THIS REPORT) TO BE $ _____ .

APPRAISER: SUPERVISORY APPRAISER (ONLY IF REQUIRED):

Signature _____   Signature _____   ☐ Did   ☐ Did Not

Name _____   Name _____   Inspect Property

Date Report Signed _____   Date Report Signed _____

State Certification # _____ State   State Certification # _____ State

Or State License # _____ State   Or State License # _____ State

Freddie Mac Form 70   6-93   PAGE 2 OF 2   Fannie Mae Form 1004   6-93

Filling Out Form Reports

The use of form reports requires special considerations, which are detailed in the Appraisal Institute's *Communicating the Appraisal* series of publications:

- *Communicating the Appraisal: Fannie Mae Desktop Underwriter™ Quantitative Analysis Appraisal Report Form 2055 and Qualitative Analysis Appraisal Report Form 2065*
- *Communicating the Appraisal: The Individual Condominium Unit Appraisal Report,* second edition
- *Communicating the Appraisal: The Small Residential Income Property Appraisal Report,* second edition
- *Communicating the Appraisal: The Uniform Residential Appraisal Report,* second edition

These publications are updated more frequently than this textbook and therefore contain more timely information on the various forms, which change regularly.

A PROFESSIONAL PRACTICE

The body of knowledge that comprises the discipline of appraisal is the foundation of professional practice. In solving most appraisal problems, however, the final conclusions depend to a great extent on the ability, judgment, and integrity of individual appraisers. To form a sound conclusion, relevant data must be available and the appraiser must be committed to finding and analyzing the data. A valid analysis also depends on the skillful application of appraisal techniques. Because appraisal is an inexact science, appraisers must reach their conclusions in an impartial, objective manner, without bias or any desire to accommodate their own interests or the interests of their clients. Professional appraisers have the requisite knowledge and the ability to apply valuation techniques capably and objectively.

A profession is distinguished from a trade or service industry by a combination of the following factors:

- High standards of competence in a specialized field
- A distinct body of knowledge that is continually augmented by the contributions of members and can be imparted to future generations
- A code of ethics or standards of practice and members who are willing to be regulated by peer review

The Appraisal Institute was formed for three purposes:

1. To establish criteria for selecting and recognizing individuals with real estate valuation skills who are committed to competent and ethical practice
2. To develop a system of education to train new appraisers and sharpen the skills of practicing appraisers
3. To formulate a code of professional ethics and standards of professional conduct to guide real estate appraisers and serve as a model for other practitioners

The heart of the Appraisal Institute's commitment to professionalism is contained in the five canons of the Code of Professional Ethics and the Standards of Professional Appraisal Practice, which include the Uniform Standards of Professional Appraisal Practice.[1]

CODE OF PROFESSIONAL ETHICS
Canon 1
A Member must refrain from conduct that is detrimental to the Appraisal Institute, the appraisal profession and the public

Canon 2
A Member must assist the Appraisal Institute in carrying out its responsibilities to the users of appraisal services and the public.

Canon 3
In the performance of an assignment, a Member must develop and communicate each analysis and opinion without being misleading, without bias for the client's interest and without accommodation of his or her own interests.

Canon 4
A Member must not violate the confidential nature of the appraiser-client relationship.

Canon 5
A Member must use care to avoid advertising or solicitations that are misleading or otherwise contrary to the public interest.

UNIFORM STANDARDS OF PROFESSIONAL APPRAISAL PRACTICE
In January 1989, the Appraisal Standards Board of The Appraisal Foundation adopted the Uniform Standards of Professional Appraisal Practice. These standards reflect the current standards of the appraisal profession.

---

1. The language in the five canons of the Appraisal Institute's Code of Professional Ethics and the Standards of Professional Appraisal Practice is periodically updated. In this appendix the following editions of these documents are cited:

    •   Code of Professional Ethics (Chicago: Appraisal Institute, 1999)
    •   Supplemental Standards of Professional Appraisal Practice (Chicago: Appraisal Institute, 1999)
    •   Uniform Standards of Professional Appraisal Practice (Washington, D.C.: Appraisal Standards Board, 1999)

    Readers should consult the most recent editions of these documents for the current wording of the regulations.

Standard I   Real Property Appraisal, Development

In developing a real property appraisal, an appraiser must identify the problem to be solved and the scope of work necessary to solve the problem, and correctly complete research and analysis necessary to produce a credible appraisal.

Standard 2   Real Property Appraisal, Reporting

In reporting the results of a real property appraisal, an appraiser must communicate each analysis, opinion, and conclusion in a manner that is not misleading.

Standard 3   Real Property Appraisal Review, Development, and Reporting

In reviewing a real property appraisal and reporting the results of that review, an appraiser must form an opinion as to the adequacy and appropriateness of the report being reviewed and must clearly disclose the nature of the review process undertaken.

Standard 4   Real Property/Real Estate Consulting, Development

In performing real estate or real property consulting services, an appraiser must be aware of, understand, and correctly employ those recognized methods and techniques that are necessary to produce a credible result.

Standard 5   Real Property/Real Estate Consulting, Reporting

In reporting the results of a real estate or real property consulting service, an appraiser must communicate each analysis, opinion, and conclusion in a manner that is not misleading.

Standard 6   Mass Appraisal, Development, and Reporting

In developing a mass appraisal, an appraiser must be aware of, understand, and correctly employ those generally accepted methods and techniques necessary to produce and communicate credible appraisals.

Standard 7   Personal Property Appraisal, Development

In developing a personal property appraisal, an appraiser must be aware of, understand, and correctly employ those recognized methods and techniques that are necessary to produce a credible appraisal.

Standard 8   Personal Property Appraisal, Reporting

In reporting the results of a personal property appraisal, an appraiser must communicate each analysis, opinion, and conclusion in a manner that is not misleading.

Standard 9   Business Appraisal, Development

In developing a business or intangible asset appraisal, an appraiser must be aware of, understand, and correctly employ those recognized methods and procedures that are necessary to produce a credible appraisal.

Standard 10 Business Appraisal, Reporting

In reporting the results of a business or intangible asset appraisal, an appraiser must communicate each analysis, opinion, and conclusion in a manner that is not misleading.

Standards 7 through 10 are not enforced by the Appraisal Institute. Additional explanatory comments and guide notes have been developed to help appraisers understand the standards and illustrate their application to specific appraisal problems.

SUPPLEMENTAL STANDARDS

Two supplemental standards follow. These standards apply only to members of the Appraisal Institute.

Supplemental Standard 1

The form of certification used by a Member in a written report must include:

1. A statement indicating compliance with the Code of Professional Ethics and Standards of Professional Appraisal Practice; and
2. A statement advising the client and third parties of the Appraisal Institute's right to review the report; and
3. A statement indicating the current status of the Designated Member under the Appraisal Institute's continuing education program.

Supplemental Standard 2

The Uniform Standards of Professional Appraisal Practice contain an Ethics Rule. The language in this Ethics Rule is very broad and the Appraisal Institute has interpreted this Ethics Rule to apply to appraisal conduct only. The Appraisal Institute has an existing Code of Professional Ethics that is adequate to carry out the intent of the Ethics Rule. Therefore, the Appraisal Institute will enforce its own Code of Professional Ethics under its existing enforcement procedures as the proper means of enforcing the Ethics Rule of the Uniform Standards of Professional Appraisal Practice.

Professional appraisers must know residential construction details and local building codes. The following pages provide descriptive data on the construction components of a sample residence as well as floor plans and diagrams of the building's dimensions.

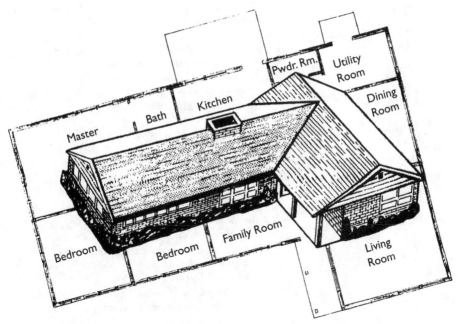

Residential construction details vary greatly in different sections of the country. In Louisiana, basements are not built because of a high water table. In Florida, it is unnecessary to build a deep foundation wall since there is no long period of freezing weather. In the Midwest, wide overhangs are used to get added protection from the hot sun.

Building codes often are different in adjoining municipalities within the same county. Therefore, what might be considered good construction in one area, could be below acceptable standards just five miles away.

The following is offered to show construction details generally accepted as quality workmanship in southeastern Pennsylvania. It must be pointed out, however, that certain differences may exist when compared to a local building code. Obviously, the local building code takes precedence.

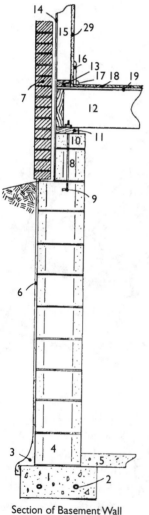

Foundation

1. *Concrete Footing*—Usually 8" high and 4" wider (on each side) than the foundation wall.

2. *Reinforcing rods*—⅜" or ½" in diameter and used to strengthen the concrete footing, especially where the soil is porous or not firm.

3. *Cement Cove*—Part of the cement parging on the exterior of the basement wall.

4. *Foundation Wall*—Good construction requires 12" concrete block—sometimes 10" poured concrete is used. In small basements, 8" block is used to reduce cost. Cinderblock should not be used below grade because it will deteriorate in certain soils.

5. *Concrete Basement Floor*—Usually 3" thick. Sometimes a plastic vapor barrier is installed under the slab.

6. *Cement Parging and Waterproofing*—Applied to the exterior to keep the basement dry.

7. *Brick Veneer*—Standard size brick, used on the exterior to give the effect of a masonry dwelling. Often only part of the front wall is done this way.

8. When brick veneer is used, the tenth course of basement block is an 8" block to allow the 4" brick to bear on the outer edge of the 12" block.

9. *Anchor Bolt*—½" in. diameter—16" or 18" long—Used to secure frame construction to masonry foundation.

Section of Basement Wall
With Brick Veneer

Scale: ¾" = 1'

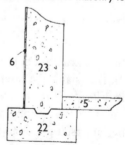

Poured Concrete
Foundation

10. The top course of block is a solid block which provides better bearing for the frame section of the building and also acts as a termite repellent since there are no openings through which termites could travel. Note the grading is held at least 12" below the nearest frame member.

11. *Sill Plate*—A 2 x 6 or a 2 x 8 which is the first wood member installed in a building.

12. *Floor Joists*—Depending on the span, 2 x 8, 2 x 10, or larger joists are used to support the floor load. Variances in type of lumber, grade of lumber, and size all have a bearing on the maximum permissible span.

13. *Sole Plate*—The bottom member of frame wall section, 2 x 4 in a bearing wall and 2 x 3 in a nonbearing wall. Bearing walls support joists and rafters.

14. *Wall Sheathing*—Usually asphalt impregnated celotex or gypsum. Sometimes 3/8" sheathing plywood or 1 x 8 sheathing boards are used.

15. *Wall Stud*—2 x 4 in bearing walls and 2 x 3 in non-bearing walls. They are placed directly over floor joists for strength and are spaced 16" on centers since most building materials come in four-foot increments.

16. *Baseboard*—Usually 1 x 4 white pine trim lumber.

17. *Quarter Round*—Usually ¾ x ¾—used to finish joint of baseboard and flooring. It is not installed when wall-to-wall carpeting is used.

18. *Finish Flooring*—⁵⁄₁₆" strip hardwood, top-nailed. ²⁵⁄₃₂" tongue and groove hardwood in better floors and nails are concealed.

19. *Subflooring*—Usually ½" sheathing plywood. Better floors use 1 x 5 tongue-and-groove subfloors for extra strength and rigidity.

20. A masonry exterior wall above the basement level is about 9" thick. It consists of 4" face brick, a 1" air space, and a 4" back-up cinderblock. Wood stripping is nailed to the blockwood on the inside so that lath can be installed.

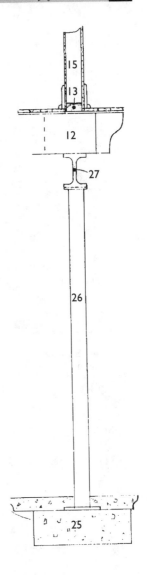

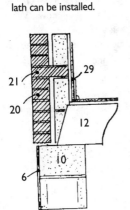

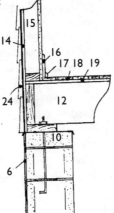

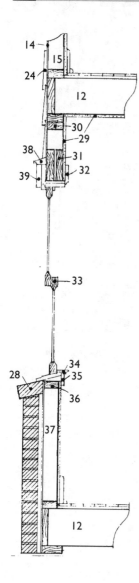

21. Every seventh course of brick is installed so as to bond the brickwork and blockwork together. Sometimes corrugated metal strips called *wall ties* are used in the mortar instead of bonding with brick.

22. Poured concrete foundations are usually 4" wider (on each side) than the foundation wall. Note the keyway built into the footing so that the wall will lock into the footing.

23. A poured concrete foundation is usually 10" wide in residential construction. Plywood forms are erected to joist level. The forms are removed after the concrete has hardened and used again on another job.

24. Wood siding is applied over sheathing on frame exterior walls. Asbestos and aluminum siding are installed the same way.

Center Wall

25. The concrete footing under a Lally column is usually 24" x 24" x 10" high. The extra size is used to distribute the weight over a greater area and to prevent settling of the column.

26. A Lally column is a steel post, usually 4" in diameter and filled with concrete. It supports the steel center beam above it. Flanges are used as end caps to distribute the load.

27. Steel center beams vary in size according to the weight above. Typically, this beam is an 8" wide flange weighing 17 lbs. per linear foot of length.

28. A rowlock of brick, laid on edge beneath window sills.

29. *Drywall or Plaster*—Drywall is usually ½" on walls and ⅜" on ceilings. Plaster is ⅜" rocklath plus two coats of wet plaster or a total thickness of ¾". A good plaster wall is three coats and ⅞" thick.

First Floor Wall

30. *Double Top Plate*—Two 2 x 4 members used to tie framing together at the ceiling line of all frame construction.

31. *Window Header*—Double 2 x 6 over standard window rough opening to support load above windows. Wide windows require heavier headers.

32. White pine trim lumber around window on the inside.

33. Lower sash of double hung window.

34. *Stool*—Part of window assembly.

35. *Apron*—Part of window assembly.

36. *Rough Header*—Part of opening prepared to receive window assembly.

37. Short stud called *cripple stud*.

38. Wood drip cap which sheds rainwater.

39. *Wood Casing*—Part of exterior window frame.

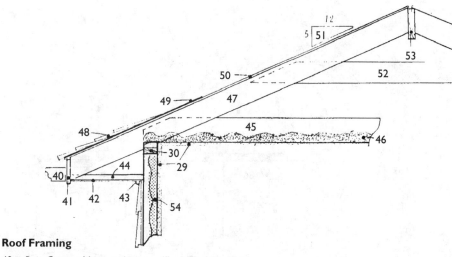

Roof Framing

40. *Rain Gutter*—Various shapes—4" or 5". Attached to fascia.

41. *Fascia Board*—1 x 8 white pine trim lumber.

42. *Soffit*—1/4" plywood with vents inserted to relieve summer heat in attic space.

43. *Quarter Round*—Used to seal joint between shingles and soffit.

44. *Outlooker*—2 x 3 or 2 x 2 on 16" centers to support soffit.

45. *Ceiling Joist*—2 x 6 or heavier. Size depends on attic floor load above it.

46. *Insulation*—Loose spun glass or batts of glass wool.

47. *Roof Rafter*—2 x 6 on 16" centers placed over studs which are directly over joists for maximum support.

48. *Roof Shingles*—Wood, asbestos, or asphalt. Usually asphalt weighing 235# per square (10' x 10' or 100 sq. ft.).

49. *Felt Paper*—15# roofing paper.

50. *Roof Sheathing*—½" sheathing plywood or 1 x 8 roofing boards.

51. Diagram which indicates pitch of roof. This roof rises 5" for every 12" of run (horizontal).

52. *Collar Beam*—2 x 8 used on alternate roof rafters to strengthen roof framing in order to support snow loads.

53. *Ridge Rafter*—2 x 8 center beam—ties roof rafters together.

54. *Sidewall Insulation*—Usually 2" batts.

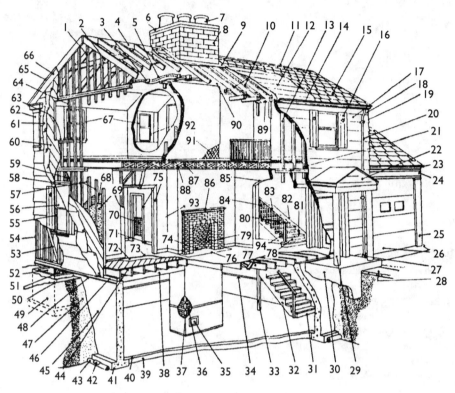

1. Gable stud	21. Double plate
2. Collar beam	22. Entrance canopy
3. Ceiling joist	23. Garage cornice
4. Ridge board	24. Frieze
5. Insulation	25. Door jamb
6. Chimney cap	26. Garage door
7. Chimney pots	27. Downspout shoe
8. Chimney	28. Sidewalk
9. Chimney flashing	29. Entrance post
10. Rafters	30. Entrance platform
11. Ridge	31. Stair riser
12. Roof boards	32. Stair stringer
13. Stud	33. Girder post
14. Eave gutter	*34. Chair rail
15. Roofing	35. Cleanout door
16. Blind or shutter	36. Furring strips
17. Bevel siding	37. Corner stud
18. Downspout gooseneck	38. Girder
19. Downspout strap	39. Gravel fill
20. Downspout leader	40. Concrete floor

41. Foundation footing
42. Paper strip
43. Drain tile
*44. Diagonal subfloor
45. Foundation wall
46. Sill
47. Backfill
48. Termite shield
49. Areaway wall
50. Grade line
51. Basement sash
52. Areaway
53. Corner brace
54. Corner stud
55. Window frame
56. Window light
57. Wall studs
58. Header
59. Window cripple
*60. Wall sheathing

* These items are found only in older homes

61. Building paper
62. Pilaster
63. Rough header
64. Window stud
65. Cornice moulding
66. Frieze board
67. Window casing
68. Lath
69. Insulation
70. Wainscoting
71. Baseboard
72. Building paper

73. Finish floor
74. Ash dump
75. Door trim
76. Fireplace hearth
77. Floor joists
78. Stair riser
79. Fire brick
80. Newel cap
81. Stair tread
82. Finish stringer
83. Stair rail

84. Balusters
85. Plaster arch
86. Mantel
87. Floor joists
88. Bridging
89. Lookout
90. Attic space
91. Metal lath
92. Window sash
93. Chimney breast
94. Newel

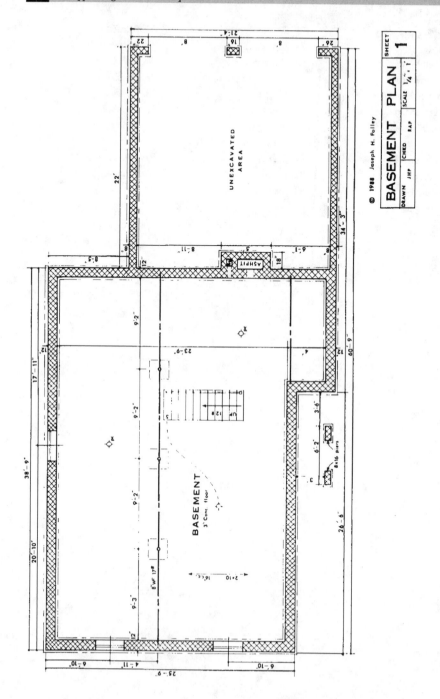

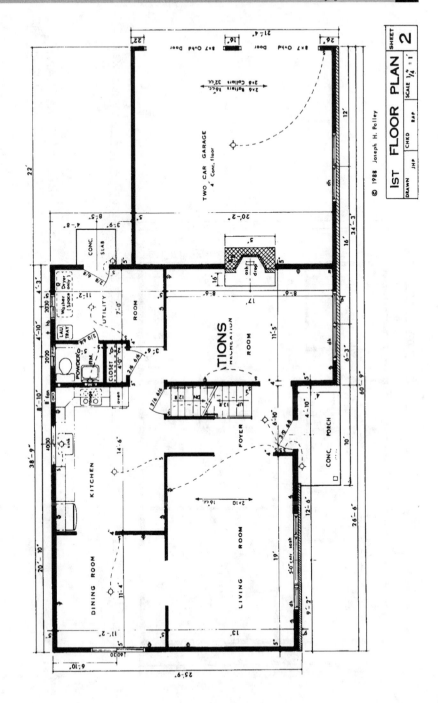

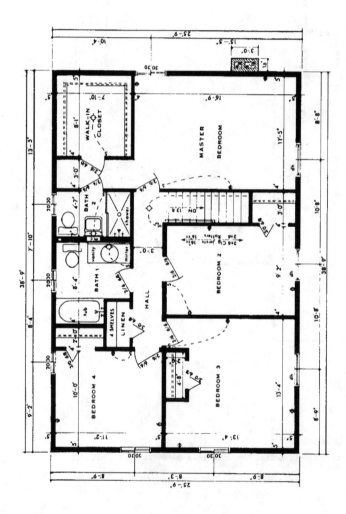

2ND FLOOR PLAN | SHEET 3

DRAWN	CHKD	SCALE ¼'=1'
JHP	RAP	

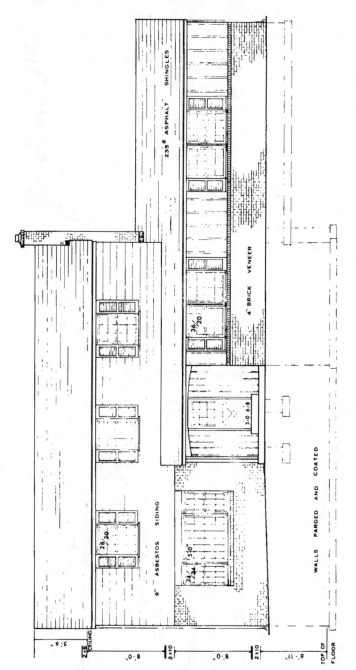

FRONT ELEVATION

DRAWN	CHKD		SCALE	SHEET
RAP	JHP		1/4"=1'	4

235# ASPHALT SHINGLES

4" BRICK VENEER

9" ASBESTOS SIDING

WALLS PARGED AND COATED

36/20

28/20

24/24 5'10"

3/0 6/8

CEILING

TOP OF FLOOR

8'-0"

8'-0"

6'-11"

5'-6"

2x6

2x10

2x10

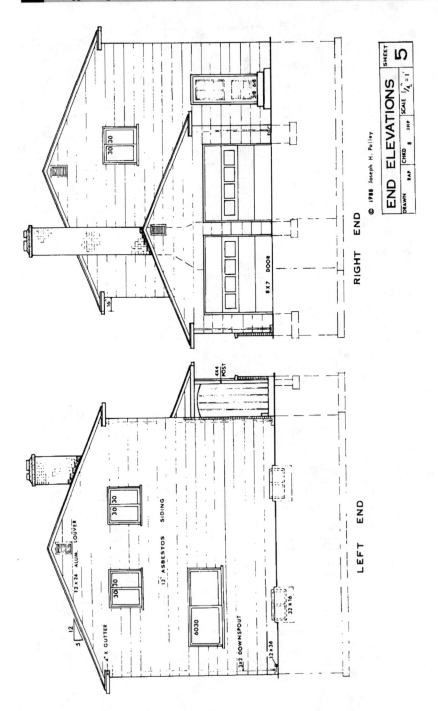

RIGHT END

LEFT END

© 1988 Joseph H. Polley

END ELEVATIONS			SHEET
DRAWN	CHKD		5
RAP	B JHP	SCALE 1/4" = 1'	

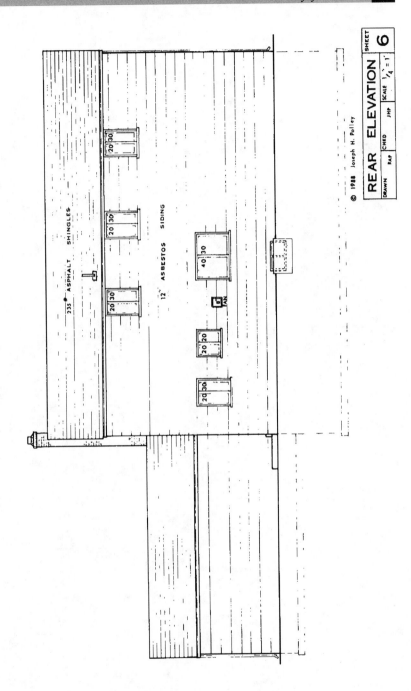

235# ASPHALT SHINGLES

12" ASBESTOS SIDING

© 1988 Joseph H. Polley

REAR ELEVATION SHEET 6

SCALE 1/4" = 1'

DRAWN RAP | CHKD JHP

Bibliography

BOOKS AND EDUCATIONAL MATERIALS

American Institute of Real Estate Appraisers. *The Appraisal of Rural Property*. Chicago: American Institute of Real Estate Appraisers, 1983.

Appraisal Institute. Advanced Residential Form and Narrative Report Writing course handbook (Course 500). Chicago: Appraisal Institute, 1999.

___. Advanced Sales Comparison and Cost Approaches course handbook (Course 530). Chicago: Appraisal Institute, 1999.

___. *The Appraisal of Real Estate*, 11th ed. Chicago: Appraisal Institute, 1996.

___. *The Dictionary of Real Estate Appraisal*, 3d ed. Chicago: Appraisal Institute, 1993.

___. Case Studies in Residential Highest and Best Use seminar handbook. Chicago: Appraisal Institute, 1999.

___. Internet Search Strategies for the Real Estate Appraiser online seminar. Chicago: Appraisal Institute, 1998. [Online] http://www.appraisalinstitute.org/onlineed.

___. Regression Analysis in Appraisal Practice: Concepts and Applications seminar handbook. Chicago: Appraisal Institute, 1999.

___. Residential Case Study course handbook (Course 210). Chicago: Appraisal Institute, 1999.

Betts, Richard M., and Silas J. Ely. *Basic Real Estate Appraisal*. 4th ed. Englewood Cliffs, N.J.: Prentice-Hall, Inc., 1997.

Blankenship, Alan. *The Appraisal Writing Handbook*. Chicago: Appraisal Institute, 1998.

Bloom, George F., and Henry S. Harrison. *Appraising the Single Family Residence*. Chicago: American Institute of Real Estate Appraisers, 1980.

Boyce, Byrl N., and William N. Kinnard, Jr. *Appraising Real Property*. Lexington, Mass.: D.C. Heath and Company, 1986.

Castle, Gilbert H., III, et al. *GIS in Real Estate: Integrating, Analyzing, and Presenting Locational Information*. Chicago: Appraisal Institute, 1998.

Conroy, Kathleen. *Valuing the Timeshare Property*. Chicago: American Institute of Real Estate Appraisers, 1981.

Davis, Andrew N., and Paul E. Schaffman. *The Home Environmental Sourcebook: 50 Environmental Hazards to Avoid When Buying, Selling, or Maintaining a Home.* New York: Henry Holt and Company/Owl Books, 1996.

Dombal, Robert W. *Appraising Condominiums: Suggested Data Analysis Techniques.* Chicago: American Institute of Real Estate Appraisers, 1981.

___. *Residential Condominiums: A Guide to Analysis and Appraisal.* Chicago: American Institute of Real Estate Appraisers, 1976.

Fanning, Stephen F., Terry V. Grissom, and Thomas D. Pearson. *Market Analysis for Valuation Appraisals.* Chicago: Appraisal Institute, 1994.

Fisher, Clifford E., Jr. *Mathematics for Real Estate Appraisers.* Chicago: Appraisal Institute, 1996.

___. *Rates and Ratios Used in the Income Capitalization Approach.* Chicago: Appraisal Institute, 1995.

Friedman, Edith J., ed. *Encyclopedia of Real Estate Appraising.* Englewood Cliffs, N.J.: Prentice-Hall, Inc., 1978.

Gimmy, Arthur E., with Susan B. Brecht and Clifford J. Dowd. *Senior Housing: Looking Toward the Third Millennium.* Chicago: Appraisal Institute, 1998.

Harrison, Frank E. *Appraising the Tough Ones: Creative Ways to Value Complex Residential Properties.* Chicago: Appraisal Institute, 1996.

Harrison, Henry S. *Houses: The Illustrated Guide to Construction, Design, and Systems,* 3d ed. Chicago: Residential Sales Council of the Realtors National Marketing Institute, an affiliate of the National Association of Realtors.® Published by Real Estate Education Company, a division of Dearborn Financial Publishing Inc., 1998.

Himstreet, William C. *Communicating the Appraisal: The Narrative Report.* Chicago: Appraisal Institute, 1991.

Hines, Mary Alice. *Real Estate Appraisal.* New York: Macmillan Publishing Co., Inc., 1981.

Jackson, Kenneth T. *Crabgrass Frontier: The Suburbanization of the United States.* New York: Oxford University Press, 1985.

Jacobs, Jane. *The Death and Life of Great American Cities.* New York: Random House, 1961.

Kostof, Spiro. *America by Design.* New York: Oxford University Press, 1987.

Lovell, Douglas D., and Robert S. Martin. *Subdivision Analysis.* Chicago: Appraisal Institute, 1993.

Miller, George H., and Kenneth W. Gilbeau. *Residential Real Estate Appraisal, An Introduction to Real Estate Appraising,* 3d ed. Englewood Cliffs, N.J.: Prentice-Hall, Inc., 1997.

Mills, Arlen C., and Dorothy Z. Mills. *Communicating the Appraisal: The Individual Condominium Unit Appraisal Report,* 2d. ed. Chicago: Appraisal Institute, 1995.

___. *Communicating the Appraisal: The Small Residential Income Property Appraisal Report,* 2d. ed. Chicago: Appraisal Institute, 1995.

___. *Communicating the Appraisal: The Uniform Residential Appraisal Report,* 2d ed. Chicago: Appraisal Institute, 1994.

Mills, Arlen C., and Anthony Reynolds. *The Valuation of Apartment Properties.* Chicago: Appraisal Institute, 1999.

Minnerly, W. Lee. *Electronic Data Interchange (EDI) and the Appraisal Office.* Chicago: Appraisal Institute, 1996.

Minnich, Joseph L., III. *Communicating the Appraisal: Fannie Mae Desktop Underwriter™ Quantitative Analysis Appraisal Report Form 2055 and Qualitative Analysis Appraisal Report Form 2065.* Chicago: Appraisal Institute, 1997.

Rayburn, William B. *Exam Preparation for Residential Appraiser Certification.* Chicago: Dearborn Financial Publishing, Inc. and the Appraisal Institute, 1992.

Rayburn, William B., and Dennis S. Tosh. *Fair Lending and the Appraiser.* Chicago: Appraisal Institute and Robert Morris Associates, 1996.

Reynolds, Judith. *Historic Properties: Preservation and the Valuation Process,* 2d. ed. Chicago: Appraisal Institute, 1996.

Rybczynski, Witold. *Home: The History of an Idea.* New York: Viking Penguin, 1987.

___. *The Most Beautiful House in the World.* New York: Viking Penguin, 1989.

Shenkel, William M. *Modern Real Estate Appraisal.* New York: McGraw-Hill, 1978.

Simpson, John A. *Property Inspection: An Appraiser's Guide.* Chicago: Appraisal Institute, 1997.

Stern, Robert. *Pride of Place: Building the American Dream.* Boston: Houghton Mifflin, 1986.

Werner, Raymond J., and Robert Kratovil. *Real Estate Law.* 10th ed. Englewood Cliffs, N.J.: Prentice-Hall, Inc., 1993.

BUILDING COST MANUALS

Boeckh Building Cost Guides: Residential; Commercial, Institutional, Light Industrial Building; Agricultural; High-Valued; Mobile-Manufactured Housing; Apartment and Condominium Personal Property. Milwaukee: American Appraisal Co.

Includes wide variety of building models. Built up from unit-in-place costs converted to cost per square foot of floor or ground area.

Building Construction Cost Data. Duxbury, Mass.: Robert Snow Means Co.
(annual).

> Lists average unit prices on many building construction items for use
> in engineering estimates. Components arranged according to
> uniform system adopted by the American Institute of Architects,
> Associated General Contractors, and Construction Specifications
> Institute.

Marshall Valuation Service. Los Angeles: Marshall and Swift Publication Co.
(looseleaf service, monthly supplements).

> Cost data for determining replacement costs of buildings and other
> improvements in the United States and Canada. Includes current
> cost multipliers and local modifiers.

Residential Cost Handbook. Los Angeles: Marshall and Swift Publication Co.
(looseleaf service, quarterly supplements).

> Presents square-foot method and segregated-cost method. Local
> modifiers and cost-trend modifiers included.

PERIODICALS

American Right of Way Proceedings. American Right of Way Association, Los
Angeles.

> Annual. Papers presented at national seminars.

The Appraisal Journal. Appraisal Institute, Chicago.

> Quarterly. Oldest periodical in the appraisal field. Includes technical
> articles on all phases of real property appraisal and regular feature on
> legal decisions.

Appraiser News in Brief. Appraisal Institute, Chicago.

> Quarterly. News bulletin covering current events and trends in
> appraisal practice.

Assessment Journal. International Association of Assessing Officers, Chicago.

> Bimonthly. Includes articles on property taxation and assessment
> administration. *Property Tax Journal* ceased publication in 1993 and
> was absorbed into *Assessment Journal.*

Buildings. Stamats Communications, Inc., Cedar Rapids, Iowa.

> Monthly. Journal of building construction and management.

The Canadian Appraiser. Appraisal Institute of Canada, Winnipeg, Manitoba.

> Quarterly. General and technical articles on appraisal and expropria-
> tion in Canada. Includes information on institute programs, news,
> etc.

Editor and Publisher Market Guide. Editor and Publisher, New York.

> Annual. Standardized market data for more than 1,500 areas in the
> United States and Canada, including population estimates for
> trading areas. List of principal industries, transportation, climate,
> chain store outlets, etc.

Journal of the American Society of Farm Managers and Rural Appraisers. Denver. Annual. Includes appraisal articles.

Journal of Property Management. Institute of Real Estate Management, Chicago.
Bimonthly. Covers a broad range of property investment and management issues.

Journal of Real Estate Research. American Real Estate Society, Cleveland, Ohio.
Quarterly. Publishes the results of applied research on real estate development, finance, investment, management, market analysis, marketing, and valuation.

Just Compensation. Sherman Oaks, California.
Monthly. Reports on condemnation cases.

Land Economics. University of Wisconsin, Madison.
Quarterly. Devoted to the study of economics and social institutions. Includes reports on university research and trends in land utilization. Frequently publishes articles on developments in other countries.

MarketSource. Appraisal Institute, Chicago.
Quarterly. Published since 1991. Statistical bulletin providing data on key rates, the CPI, employment, housing permits, housing starts and completions, vacancies, and mortgage rates and terms.

Real Estate Economics. Bloomington, Indiana.
Quarterly. Focuses on research and scholarly studies of current and emerging real estate issues. Formerly *Journal of the American Real Estate and Urban Economics Association.*

Real Estate Issues. American Society of Real Estate Counselors, Chicago.
Quarterly.

Real Estate Law Journal. Warren, Gorham and Lamont, Inc., Boston.
Quarterly. Publishes articles on legal issues and reviews current litigation of concern to real estate professionals.

Right of Way. American Right of Way Association, Los Angeles.
Bimonthly. Publishes articles on all phases of right-of-way activity— e.g., condemnation, negotiation, pipelines, electric power transmission lines, highways. Includes association news.

Survey of Buying Power. Sales Management, New York.
Annual supplement to *Sales and Marketing Management.* Includes population totals and characteristics and income and consumption data presented in national, regional, metropolitan area, county, and city categories. Separate section for Canadian information. Population estimates between decennial censuses.

Survey of Current Business. U.S. Bureau of Economic Analysis, U.S. Department of Commerce, Washington, D.C.

> Monthly. Includes statistical and price data. Biennial supplement, *Business Statistics.*

Valuation. American Society of Appraisers, Washington, D.C.

> Annual. Articles on real property valuation and the appraisal of personal and intangible property. Includes society news. Previously published as *Technical Valuation.*

Valuation Insights & Perspectives. Appraisal Institute, Chicago.

> Published quarterly. Provides timely, practical information and ideas to assist real estate appraisers in conducting their businesses effectively.

INDEX